THE
DECLINE
OF SOCIALISM
IN AMERICA
1912-1925

THE DECLINE

OF SOCIALISM IN AMERICA 1912–1925

BY JAMES WEINSTEIN

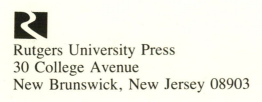

Rutgers University Press
30 College Avenue
New Brunswick, New Jersey 08903

This edition published in 1984 by Rutgers University Press.

First published in cloth by Monthly Review Press, 1967. First published in paperback by Vintage Books, a Division of Random House, 1969.

Library of Congress Cataloging in Publication Data

Weinstein, James, 1926–
    The decline of socialism in America, 1912–1925.

    Bibliography: p.
    Includes index.
    1. Socialism—United States—History. 2. Socialist
party (U.S.)—History. 3. Socialist parties—United
States—History. I. Title.
HX83.W4 1984   335'.00973   84-11490
ISBN 0-8135-1068-6
ISBN 0-8135-1069-4 (pbk.)

To Lisa and Josh

ACKNOWLEDGEMENTS

The Author wishes to thank the following for permission to reprint:

The Journal of American History—"Radicalism in the Midst of Normalcy," by James Weinstein, Volume LII, No. 4, March 1966.

The Political Science Quarterly—"Anti-war Sentiment and the Socialist Party, 1917-1918," by James Weinstein, Volume LXXIV, No. 2, June 1959.

Studies on the Left—"The American Socialist Party, Its Roots and Strength," by James Weinstein, Volume I, No. 2, 1960.

The Author also wishes to thank the Louis M. Rabinowitz Foundation for a grant that made possible the completion of this work.

CONTENTS

LIST OF TABLES

INTRODUCTION TO THE RUTGERS EDITION

When the manuscript for this book was completed in 1962, the American left was a shambles, the victim of its own internal weaknesses and of Cold War McCarthyism. Written in the aftermath of the collapse of the Communist-led left of the New Deal and post-World War II years, the book was an attempt to find out what had gone wrong.

Five years later, when the first edition of the book appeared in print, the New Left was in the ascendancy, having reached one peak of popularity with the Mississippi summer of 1964, and a second with the launching of large-scale opposition to the war in Vietnam marked by the April 1965 March on Washington. But within another five years—by 1970—the New Left had blown itself apart in a fit of frustration and despair. Now, in 1984 when the second edition of the book is published, the American left is once again a shambles.

Explosive growth and subsequent collapse have been the fate of the American Socialist left throughout this century. The old Socialist Party, organized in 1901, expanded rapidly, reached a plateau by 1912, and then broke up in the late teens and early twenties, for reasons I hope will be made clear in the pages that follow. The Communist-led left also enjoyed a period of rapid growth and influence—in the Depression and New Deal years. But it could never sustain a popular movement, because not only its policies but also its concept of socialism and democracy was based on the profoundly undemocratic system of the Soviet Union. Though the Cold War and McCarthyism finally did it in in the 1950's, the Communist Party's inherent weaknesses had prepared the ground and made it an easy victim.

The New Left of the 1960's was in many ways an entirely new phenomenon. A movement of young people who were the beneficiaries of the post-war boom in college and university

education, the New Left was based neither in the labor movement nor among working class immigrants, as both the Old Socialist Party and the Communist Party had been. Both older
movements were built in large part around the struggles of industrial workers to build and legitimize trade unions and to win
basic social protections, while the New Left was a movement
that saw itself as part of the middle class. But like the older
movements, the New Left focused on inequality in American
society and was motivated by a growing awareness of the disparity
between the professions of American democracy and the underlying reality, both at home and abroad.

Being a movement for the realization of the promise of liberty
and equality, the New Left initially dismissed any connection
with the Communist movement of the 1930's and 1940's, even
while it sympathized with the victims of McCarthyism. The New
Left distanced itself from both the Communists and the Socialist
anti-Communists, because it saw the former as not supporting
its position on civil rights and the Vietnam War and the latter
as repugnant advocates of Cold War McCarthyism. Being cut
adrift from these forebears, while being the largest movement
on the left within their memories, gave most New Leftists feelings
ranging from indifference to contempt for Communists and
Socialists—and led to a belief that as leftists they had no history.
That, in turn, condemned them to re-create in rapid and often
ludicrous succession the history they didn't consider worth
knowing.

That, of course, was what this book had been written to help
prevent. My purpose in exploring the history of American socialism was both to rediscover a lost and useful past and to come
to grips with the reasons for socialism's successes and failures.
When I began working on the book, Daniel Bell, Ira Kipnis,
and David A. Shannon had already explored the history of the
Socialist Party, and Theodore Draper had written his two volumes on the first ten years of American communism (Irving Howe
and Lewis Coser completed their history of the Communist Party

from 1919 to 1957 before I finished my work). But none of these monographs and essays explored the decline of the old Socialist Party and the rise of the Communist Party after 1919 as one process. Nor did they look at other popular leftist movements during and after the First World War was intimately related.

Yet the old Socialist Party, the Communist-led movement, and the New Left were all part of one broad historic tendency in American life in that their members and followers shared a commitment to the fulfillment of the promises of American democracy and a belief that this dream is frustrated in a society dominated by corporate capitalism and subordinate to its imperatives. That perspective informed the writing of this book.

Everybody recognizes the United States as the only industrialized nation in the world with no significant movement for socialism. Since World War II, most Americans have come to assume that this has always been so, for not only in the affluent post-war years but even during the Great Depression (when American capitalism had collapsed and could revive itself only with the start of arms production for another world war), the idea of socialism remained the property of small and isolated groups. The reasons for this are also well known. They include the high American standard of living, the impact of free land and unique class mobility in a society with no feudal past, and the speed and ease with which sophisticated liberals, starting with Theodore Roosevelt, have been able to appropriate enough of the left's demands to capture a good part of a potential Socialist following. Then, too, the United States, being an immigrant nation, has been as sharply divided along lines of race and national origin as along those of class. Suppression of leftists and of their right to speak, removal of Socialist publications from the mails, harassment of Socialist organizations and prosecution of their leaders by federal, state and local governments have also weakened the left.

Unquestionably, the success of American capitalism has been outstanding. Yet the reasons for the absense of a coherent

Socialist movement in the United States for the past sixty-five years cannot be wholly understood by the celebration of entrepreneurial vigor and nature's largesse, much less by the success of the repressive state apparatus. In large part, the failure of the American left has been internal.

But the failure should not be understood as the Socialists' inability to win a majority to their cause or as their inability to take power. Given the strength of American capitalism, that was never a possibility. Rather, the failure of American socialism has been in its episodic character, in the inability of Socialists to create and sustain a political movement that is a part of the mainstream of American political life—something the old Socialist Party briefly became—and that is able to survive defeats, learn from its mistakes, and retain organizational and intellectual continuity and growth. In short, the left has failed in not being able to create a community that is based on a set of clearly articulated principles and sustained by its application of those principles to the major political problems of the day.

In tracing the development of the old Socialist Party during the years of its greatest strength and through the period of its break-up and decline, I have tried to set the record straight on what was actually achieved and what was inadequately understood or acted upon. For me, writing this book was a process of discovery, of attempting to answer my own questions about the failure of socialism in America. Today, with the American left once again in a period of decline, these questions still seem worth exploring.

James Weinstein, Chicago, 1984

THE
DECLINE
OF SOCIALISM
IN AMERICA
1912-1925

1 THE SCOPE OF AMERICAN SOCIALISM
1900-1912

Unlike the "movement" today, when radicals cluster around ever-changing combinations and permutations of committees, societies, sects, and parties, radicalism in the years before 1920 focused in one organization: the Socialist Party of America. Some anticapitalist radicals remained outside the Party and organized separately or as rivals, but these groups were marginal. The Socialist Labor Party, which has maintained its identity from its founding in 1877 to the present, was the Socialist Party's major competitor; after the split in 1899 that led to the formation of the Socialist Party, the SLP remained static and isolated. The Industrial Workers of the World likewise rejected the Socialist Party, although at its founding in 1905 it had close ties with such leading Socialists as Eugene V. Debs and Algie M. Simons. As time passed, the IWW moved further from political action and became more intolerant of Socialist attitudes toward the trade union movement. In the course of this development, it also attracted many radical intellectuals—Max Eastman, John Reed, Floyd Dell, Arturo Giovanetti—as sympathizers; the result of this association has been a mythology that places the IWW at the center of early twentieth-century American radicalism. But while the romantic appeal of the Wobblies has triumphed in literature and history, as a social force the IWW did not approach the Socialist Party in its impact on contemporary American life.

The organization of the Socialist Party of America in 1901 was the result of a confluence of the major socialist and radical tendencies in the United States and marked the coming of age of the movement. The Party was far from homogeneous or orthodox in the present sense of that word, but it grew rapidly in the years from 1901 to 1912, and retained its basic character and strength until 1919. Spreading its roots widely, American socialism reached into many parts of the country and into areas of American life never since affected by openly socialist ideas. This was possible in large part because of the Party's internal diversity and its democratic and open structure. Unlike radical movements of the last four decades, the old Socialist Party permitted and benefited from a wide range of doctrinal and ideological views and tendencies within its ranks. Since the early 1920's, debates between socialists of different tendencies have increasingly become disputes between parties; before 1920 such differences were generally accepted as normal and desirable aspects of the process of developing a viable mass party.

The character of American radicalism since 1925 has obscured the nature of pre-World War I socialism in the United States. Historians of American socialism have been led by the obsession of New Deal and post-New Deal radicals with the ideological disputes between Stalinist and Trotskyist (in which many of them were enmeshed) to assume that the old movement was equally narrow and isolated—that it never succeeded in introducing the ideas of socialism into the consciousness of large numbers of Americans. The prevailing tendency is to assume that socialism was, as it now seems to be, alien to the United States. Daniel Bell, for example, points to the failure of Marxian socialism during the Great Depression and the New Deal and, correctly in my opinion, goes on to seek the reason for this failure in the nature of the movement, rather than in general social or political conditions in the 1930's. But, in common with most other historians of American socialism, Bell views the pre-

1920 movement as politically and ideologically consistent with that of the Depression decade, and so misses much about the nature of the earlier movement.[1]

Bell's treatment conforms well with the myths and traditions of post-1920 radicalism, as well as with the predispositions of other historians. This projection of the characteristics of the Socialist and Communist Parties of the 1930's back into the prewar period leaves us with a view of the old Party as narrow and marginal, and also as divided into hostile sects whose spectrum from right to left was analogous to the divisions in European socialism during the First World War.

Such a view serves better to obscure than to clarify the American socialist past; yet a tradition has grown up that treats "Left" versus "Right" in the old Socialist Party as a conflict of worker against petty bourgeois, industrial unionist against craft unionist, fighter for equality against racist, antiwar versus pro-war. In short, "Left" is equated with fidelity, or at least adherence, to "Marxist" principles, and "Right" with opportunism. However, few such polarities existed in the Socialist Party before 1920—though of course the problem of determining when an innovation is principled and when opportunist is always present in politics.

It is true that factionalism existed in the early movement and that there was a superficial, or rhetorical, continuity. In the Socialist Party of America the categories of Left, Right, and Center were more useful in defining attitudes toward others than as guides to how a group would line up on any given issue; yet there were four clearly discernible groupings within the Party, each relating to these categories. Party members were conscious of divisions between Left and Right. They thought in these terms; and the Left, Center, and Right groupings had their own publications and often competed for leadership in city, state,

[1] Daniel Bell, *The End of Ideology* (Glencoe, Illinois, 1960), pp. 268 ff.; see also "The Background and Development of Marxian Socialism in the United States," *Socialism and American Life*, eds. Donald D. Egbert and Stow Persons (Princeton, 1952), pp. 216-217.

and national structures of the Party. Hulet Wells, a left winger
in Seattle, Washington, believed that the "real line of demarcation" was always acceptance or rejection of the "class philosophy
of Marx." In Washington, the right-wing neo-populists in the
Party hoped to "appeal to all classes," Wells explains, whereas
the trade unionists and the IWW's based their policies on the
working class.[2] But another contemporary Socialist, Jesse Wallace Hughan, believed that the Socialist Party was "divided
neither into two opposing camps nor into a number of warring
factions." This was demonstrated, she wrote, by the "unanimity
with which all groups cooperate in such enterprises as the party
press, a contest for free speech, or a labor conflict." Still, she
recognized "a gradual shading" from "revolutionists on the left
to constructivists on the right," with groups in between whose
characteristics were "seldom exact and always changing," and
"whose members indulge in mutual criticism."[3]

Hughan's view comes nearer the mark. There were differences
in tactical approaches among the several tendencies. Some
looked to a coalition of workers with farmers or other middle-
class radicals, while some frowned on such an alliance. Defining
the working class was also a source of difficulty. The IWW-
oriented Left tended to regard only the unskilled and migratory
workers as genuine proletarians, while the Right and Center
emphasized the importance of the organized industrial workers
in such unions as the United Mine Workers, The International
Association of Machinists, The United Brewery Workers, the
Western Federation of Miners, and the Railroad Brotherhoods.
These differences within Socialist ranks, along with others, led
some contemporary observers and later historians to describe
the right-wing Socialists as merely the left wing of progressivism.[4] But this approach underestimates the unifying strength of

[2] Hulet Wells to the author, Seattle, Washington, May 1, 1962.
[3] Jesse Wallace Hughan, *The Present Status of Socialism in America* (New
York, 1911), p. 221.
[4] See, for example, R. F. Hoxie, *National Municipal Review*, I (1912), p.
500, who wrote that the Socialist electoral successes in 1911 were but
"one phase of the progressive, democratic movement which is sweeping

the Socialists' anticapitalist perspective. In terms of their ultimate commitment to thoroughgoing social transformation, both wings of the Party, or, rather, all groups, were "revolutionary." In terms of their ability to adjust their tactics to the needs of their constituencies, all groups were "constructivists." How principled each group was, was rarely tested; when it was, as on the question of racism and opposition to American participation in the First World War, the divisions did not follow Left-Right lines, as we shall see.

II

Each of the four discernible tendencies within the Party had a leader of nation-wide renown whose ideas and attitudes roughly characterized the grouping he led. On the Right was Victor Berger, German-born schoolteacher, printer, editor, and professional politician, who represented the "constructive" wing of the movement. Berger was the most successful of American Socialists in building a stable political organization based upon the trade unions. In Milwaukee, the great majority of union locals were Socialist, and the Socialist organs spoke for the unions. Berger's newspaper, *The Milwaukee Leader,* proclaimed its status as the official paper of both the Federated Trades Council of Milwaukee and the Wisconsin State Federation of Labor, and the unions served as the hard core of Berger's political base.[5]

From the day in 1893 that he became editor of the *Wisconsin Vorwaerts,* daily organ of the Socialist Labor Party, Berger was the undisputed leader of Milwaukee socialism. Like most early Socialists, his initial experience was in the Socialist Labor Party, but his devotion to the adaptation of "scientific socialism" to the American environment quickly led to a break with the doctri-

---

the country." Also, Ira B. Cross, "Socialism in California Municipalities," *ibid.,* pp. 611-619. Arthur S. Link, *American Epoch* (New York, 1958), pp. 63-64, takes the same position.
[5] Shannon, *The Socialist Party of America* (New York, 1955), pp. 21-25; see also Marvin Wachman, *The History of the Social Democratic Party of Milwaukee, 1897-1910* (Champaign, Illinois, 1945).

naire organization. Soon after he began editing the *Vorwaerts,* Berger broke with the Socialist Labor Party, founded the Social Democratic Society, and forged a three-way alliance with the local People's Party and the Federated Trades Council. In 1896, however, he lost hope in populism; and soon after Eugene V. Debs announced his conversion to socialism in January 1897 (Berger had brought Debs a copy of *Das Kapital* to his cell in the Woodstock jail), he and Debs helped form the Social Democracy of America. It was this organization that joined a dissident group of Socialist Laborites to form the Socialist Party of America in 1901.

In the Socialist Party, Berger constantly asserted the need to make socialism relevant to the existing problems of American workers. He saw no immediate prospects for the transition to socialism in the United States, or in any other part of the world. In this respect, as in many others, Berger shared the orthodox Marxist view that the revolution would come first in the most advanced capitalist countries. "In the trust system," he believed, "capitalism has just stepped into a new phase," the duration of which was "unlimited according to our present light." At the same time, Berger observed, capitalism was no longer a civilizing force, but had "already become a menace to civilization"— and this created the possibility of achieving socialism in the foreseeable future, "if the working class understands its mission."[6] Meanwhile, it was the task of the Socialists to educate workers and to struggle to improve their lot "economically, morally, and physically."

Some people viewed this concern for social reform as an identification of socialism and progressivism, but Berger insisted that "every success in this direction will naturally compel us to make new demands and attain new benefits for the proletariat which will weaken the capitalist system."[7] Only through such a process

---

[6] Victor Berger, "How Will Socialism Come?" *Broadsides* (Milwaukee, 1913), pp. 23-24.
[7] "Moving By the Light of Reason," *ibid.*, p. 24.

could the Socialists hope to bring the working class to consciousness of its strength and its "mission."

Socialism was the next epoch of civilization into which the world was evolving. Neither feudalism nor capitalism had arisen or disappeared at a given date; nor would socialism replace capitalism on the world scene "at one stroke." The period of transition, Berger often wrote, would be gradual and would require two conditions in each country: the winning of a majority of the population by the Socialist Party, and a concentration of industry sufficient to make it "ripe for collective production." As with all Marxists in the days before the Russian Revolution, the idea of a successful revolution in an underdeveloped country was beyond Berger's imagination. Even in the United States, Berger was unsure that the second condition had been met. The trusts were already matured, he observed, but other industries, including farming, were not yet ready to be worked collectively and so should be left in private hands.[8]

Berger argued strongly against those Socialists who were constantly speaking of revolution, which he interpreted to mean a "catastrophe," as the path to socialism. He recognized and partially accepted Marx's statement that "force is the midwife at the birth of every new epoch," but saw in this "no cause for rejoicing." Looking for "another way out," Berger found it in the ballot, backed up by an armed people.[9] The proletariat "outnumbered the capitalist class most effectively," and thus had the "fate of every country in its hands," if it could "come to terms with the farmers." There was, of course, the danger that the capitalists would not recognize a working-class victory; but if the American people were fully armed, a peaceful transition would be assured. "An armed people," he frequently repeated, "is always a free people."[10]

The difference between Berger and left-wing Party members

[8] "How to Make a Change," *ibid.*, pp. 240-241.
[9] "Progress by Catastrophe or Common Sense," *ibid.*, p. 233.
[10] *Ibid.*, p. 234; see also "An Armed People is Always a Free People," in *Broadsides*, pp. 205 ff.

was indicated in an interview he and Debs granted Lincoln Steffens in 1908. At one point Steffens asked Debs what he would do with the trusts. "Take them," Debs replied. This greatly agitated Berger. No, he said, "I answer that we would offer to pay." This, he explained was not essentially a matter of justice, but of "tactics," and the tactic on this question had already been decided by the Party as a whole.

To justify his position, Berger explained that the Socialists were "the inheritors of civilization and all that is good in it." Art, music, buildings, public works, the sense of right and wrong— "not one of these shall be lost, and violence like that would lose us much." As an analogy, Berger pointed to the Civil War. Before that carnage some "tried to avert it by proposing to pay for the slaves," but "the fanatics on both sides refused." The result was four years of war at a cost of ten billion dollars and hundreds of thousands of lives. "We ought to learn from history," Berger concluded. "We will offer compensation" because "it seems just to present-day thought and will prove the easiest, cheapest way in the end."[11]

As a politician, Berger was unsurpassed in the Socialist Party. First elected to Congress in 1910, he was re-elected in 1918 but was refused a seat because of his antiwar activity. In a special election to fill the vacancy left by his unseating, Berger won again in 1919. Again he was unseated, and this time he failed of re-election until 1922, after which he remained in Congress until 1927. Editor of the *Milwaukee Leader,* Berger presided over the Milwaukee Socialists and guided them to their victories in 1910, 1916, and in the years that followed. An active trade unionist, he was president of his local of the Typographical Union and a perennial delegate to AFL conventions. Berger's belief that the Socialists could win control of the AFL if they worked within that organization made him a consistent foe of the IWW and of dual unionism. But his loyalty to the AFL did not keep him from opposing Samuel Gompers. He was convinced that the "Amer-

[11] Lincoln Steffens, "Eugene V. Debs," *Everybody's,* XIX, 4 (October 1908), 461-462.

ican labor movement will remain reactionary as long as [Gompers] has any influence."[12] At the same time, Berger shared some of Gompers' more reactionary attitudes on the race question and on the immigration of Orientals.

Sometimes associated with Berger, but more often characterized as a leader of the "Center," Morris Hillquit represented the pre-World War I orthodox Marxist tradition. A Russian immigrant, born in Riga, Hillquit grew to maturity on New York City's Lower East Side, where he spent his early radical years as an organizer and journalist for the United Hebrew Trades, a forerunner of the International Ladies Garment Workers Union.[13]

When he was 18, he joined the Socialist Labor Party, and as an outstanding young labor lawyer rose rapidly in party ranks. But Hillquit and Daniel De Leon soon differed over tactics, and a long and bitter fight began. By 1896, Hillquit found himself solidly opposed to the Party leader, especially on the question of the organization of the Socialist Trade and Labor Alliance as a rival to the AFL. He was chosen to head the opposition to De Leon within the Party. Then, in 1899, along with Max Hayes and Ben Hanford (both leaders of the International Typographical Union), and followed by a majority of the membership, Hillquit seceded and organized a rival party. It was this "Rochester" Socialist Labor Party[14] that fused with Berger's Social Democrats of Milwaukee and with Debs in 1901 to form the Socialist Party.[15]

As a leader of the Center tendencies in the Party, Hillquit often played the role of arbitrator in disputes between Left and Right, attempting frequently and often successfully to reconcile the positions of the contending groups. His efforts, however, were sometimes resented, especially by the Left, not so much because of differences in principle between Hillquit and the

---

[12] Quoted in Shannon, *op. cit.*, p. 24.
[13] Morris Hillquit, *Loose Leaves from a Busy Life* (New York, 1934), Chapters I, II.
[14] Named after the city where the secessionists convened in 1899.
[15] For Hillquit's version, see *Loose Leaves from a Busy Life,* Chapter III.

more militant Party members, but because his rhetoric was alien to their radical traditions. Ironically, Hillquit was fond of thinking of himself as an Americanizer of Marx, but his mild expositions of socialist principles were most infuriating to the indigenous left wingers of the Southwest and the Northwest. These native old-Americans had been reared in the rhetoric of class warfare, which they favored even when (as in the case of the ex-populists) the programs they advocated were no more radical than those put forward by Hillquit. On one occasion, for example, Hillquit commented that the workers alone, "especially the workers in the narrower sense of the term," were "neither numerous nor strong enough to successfully accomplish the Socialist revolution." They needed "the cooperation of persons from other classes, and," Hillquit believed, "that cooperation can be obtained."[16] In their election campaigns, especially where, as in many municipal contests, victory was possible, all Socialists except the followers of William D. Haywood acted on these assumptions and shaped their tactics accordingly. But only rarely would a left winger admit this in public.

Even Eugene V. Debs, who seldom involved himself in personal disputes, attacked Hillquit on occasion. When Hillquit debated Samuel Gompers on socialism and the labor movement, Debs charged him with exhibiting all "the cleverness of a pettifogging lawyer" who had sparred "all around the class struggle without touching it." Debs observed that Hillquit could have made a much stronger case had he not been restrained by "the fear of offending the American Federation of Labor."[17] In matters of principle, however, Hillquit's position rarely differed from that of Debs. Both advocated industrial unionism; both opposed dual unionism, sabotage, and violence; both actively opposed American participation in the First World War; and, as we shall see, both maintained the same attitude toward the Russian Revolution and the Third International.

[16] "The Task Before Us," *New York Call,* December 12, 1909.
[17] *The Rebel* (Halletsville, Texas), March 27, 1915.

The principles Eugene Debs and Hillquit held in common have led some historians to place them together as moderates.[18] But Debs' rejection of Socialist participation in the AFL and his rapport with the spirit of Western radicals qualify him as a left winger. Unlike any other Socialist leader, Debs was part of a central experience in American labor history. He came to socialism via the Woodstock jail and the ruins of his American Railway Union after the defeat of the great Pullman strike in 1894. A former Democratic member of the Indiana Assembly, a strong supporter of populism, and then of Bryan in 1896, Debs always retained a firm belief in political action. But his participation in politics as a Socialist was not based on a desire for office. "If there were any chance of my election," he once told Lincoln Steffens, "I wouldn't run. The party wouldn't let me." What Debs sought was a "majority of Socialists, not of votes," because "there would be no use getting into power with a people that did not understand, with a lot of office-holders undisciplined by service in the party, unpurged by personal sacrifice of the selfish spirit of the present system." Debs ran for President, he explained, "to teach social consciousness." When socialism was "on the verge of success," the Party would nominate "an able executive and a clear-minded administrator; not—not Debs."[19]

Debs opposed capitalism because "It's wrong. It's inherently unjust, inhuman, unintelligent, and—it cannot last." Graft, corruption, poverty, crime and cruelty were "evidences of its weaknesses and failure; the signs that it is breaking down."

"Why not wait, then, for it to break down?" Steffens asked.

"Because we have minds," Debs replied, "human intelligence

---

[18] See, for example, Link, *op. cit.*, p. 63. Debs' biographer, Ray Ginger, *The Bending Cross* (New Brunswick, 1949), treats Debs as a left winger. Ginger's treatment of Debs catches the spirit and power of the man. It is by far the best of Debs' biographies and will probably remain the definitive one. The book is weakest in the treatment of Debs' attitude to the Russian Revolution and the American Communist Party. Here the author fails to appreciate the close link between his subject and the leaders of the Right and Center who remained within the Socialist Party.

[19] Lincoln Steffens, "Eugene V. Debs," *loc. cit.*, p. 458.

is a force of nature. It could assist the process of evolution by searching intelligently for the root of all evils as they arise."[20]

Debs was more than the perennial standard bearer of the Party and its leading editorial writer. Aggressively class conscious, consistent champion of the oppressed, and implacable foe of the inequities of modern industrial capitalism, he personally embodied the unity of Populist, Christian, Marxist, and militant trade union traditions that fused to form the Socialist Party in 1901. To most Americans, Debs was the hero and the symbol of the movement, though he chose never to play a role in the Party organization commensurate with his popularity, preferring instead to remain above the organizational disputes. Not until his release from prison in 1922, when the Socialist Party was weaker than it had been when it was organized, did Debs take a seat on the National Executive Committee of the Party. This self-abnegation created an unfortunate situation in the prewar years, for Debs represented and expressed the mood of the largest sections of the Party. His absence from its organizational center at times created a discordance between the spirit (and the tactics) of the national leadership and the Party membership.

William D. Haywood represented the fourth and most distinct tendency within the Socialist Party. A one-time secretary-treasurer of the Western Federation of Miners, and general organizer of the IWW, Haywood, like Debs, had come to socialism through his experience as an industrial unionist. Unlike Debs, however, Haywood had no background of political activity in his early years in the mines and never developed any regard for its educational value. Haywood's concept of socialism and the manner in which it would come about was even more vague than that of Berger, Hillquit, and Debs. He was concerned almost entirely with fighting labor's immediate battles and with organizing the unorganized. His attitude toward political action flowed directly from this concern. Haywood urged

[20] *Ibid.*, p. 463.

"every workingman to use the ballot at every opportunity,"[21] and was himself a candidate for governor of Colorado in 1906. The real value of the ballot, in Haywood's eyes, however, was in the opportunity it offered to win administrative control of local government so as to "use the powers of the police to protect the strikers."[22]

Haywood's political theories were a composite of socialist and syndicalist ideas. He shared with the syndicalists a vision of society reorganized around the factories, mines, and other places of production—to be realized through a general strike. During a period of transition, however, Haywood believed it "absolutely necessary" that the workers also control the governmental machinery, which would be used to "inspire confidence and compel the wheels of industry to move in spite of the devices and stumbling blocks of the capitalists."[23] Haywood and his comrades in the IWW defined their theories as industrialism, rather than syndicalism. The syndicalists, or at least the Syndicalist League of North America, concurred.

Unlike Haywood and the IWW, which it opposed, the Syndicalist League rejected and "bitterly" opposed the "international Socialist Party," insisting that the labor unions alone represented the interests of the working class.[24] At the same time, the Syndicalist League opposed the dual unionism of the IWW, and sought to divert the mainstream of the American labor movement leftward by participating in the American Federation of Labor as a "militant minority."[25]

Haywood urged the worker to use the ballot, but he spoke to virtually disfranchised groups—nonferrous metal miners in the

[21] "What Haywood Says on Political Action," *International Socialist Review*, XIII, 8 (February 1913), 622.

[22] *Ibid.*

[23] *Industrial Socialism*, quoted in *ibid.*

[24] The League saw the Socialist Party as "an interloper and a parasite," that should be fought as an enemy. See Earl C. Ford and W. Z. Foster, *Syndicalism* (Chicago, 1912). Quoted in William English Walling, "Industrialism *vs.* Syndicalism," *International Socialist Review*, XIII, 9 (March 1913), 666-667.

[25] *Ibid.*

remote camps of the mountain states, lumber workers of northern Louisiana and the Northwest, migratory agricultural workers, and immigrant industrial workers. Unlike Debs, whose roots
were strongest among the workers in the older, more settled industries, Haywood's constituents existed on the edges of society.
The demands of his followers were more elemental than those
of other Party members because the conditions under which
they lived were more barbarous, and his hostility to reform followed largely from a belief that few reforms could effect the
conditions under which the membership of the IWW existed.

Similarly, Haywood did not share with Berger, Hillquit, or
Debs the view that capitalism might survive for a considerable
time. His was an apocalyptic vision of the revolution. Believing
that it could occur at any time,[26] he did not see the need to
develop long-term strategy.

These differences and the dual unionism of the IWW were the
real sources of the antagonism between Haywood and the center and the right-wing groupings of the Party. Haywood rarely,
if ever, advocated the use of violence during strikes. His leadership of the Lawrence textile strike was marked by the quiet
discipline he instilled in the strikers, and a policy of passive resistance was followed wherever possible. In Akron, Ohio, in
1913, Haywood advised striking rubber workers that their
"greatest weapon" was "to keep your hands in your pockets,"
and "let there be no violence . . . not the destruction of one
cent's worth of property, not one cross word."[27] But he did take
delight in proposing sabotage at speeches in New York City, the
heartland of Hillquit's influence. At Cooper Union in early 1912,
Haywood affirmed his hatred for the law and announced that
he was "not a law-abiding citizen." A few months later he
boasted, "I believe in sabotage, that much misunderstood
word."[28]

[26] See Haywood's "Socialism the Hope of the Workingclass," *International
Socialist Review*, XII, 8 (February 1912), 461-471.
[27] Mary E. Marcy, "800 Percent and the Akron Strike," *International
Socialist Review*, XIII, 10 (April 1913), 722.
[28] Quoted in Ira Kipnis, *The American Socialist Movement, 1897-1912*

These antics did not endear Haywood to the leaders in New York, but the IWW raids on locals of the Western Federation of Miners and the United Mine Workers did more to antagonize such Socialist trade unionists as Max Hayes, Berger, John H. Walker, and Adolph Germer. Since the Socialist Party did not officially enter union disputes, it would have been difficult to attack Haywood directly on this basis. Instead, at the convention in 1912, the Right and Center sponsored a successful amendment to the Party constitution which banned the advocacy of crime, sabotage, or other methods of violence—and in 1913 had Haywood recalled from his position as a member of the Party's National Executive Committee for violating the ban at a public meeting.

Haywood himself ceased being active in the Socialist Party after his recall from the National Executive Committee in 1913, but those who shared his views continued to exercise some strength in Minnesota, Washington, and in scattered areas throughout the West. They failed to achieve a more influential position in the Party because Debs agreed with Hillquit and Berger that tactics which involved "stealth, secrecy, intrigue and necessitate individual acts of violence for their execution" were unacceptable to the American working class,[29] and because Debs opposed the IWW after 1908. The adoption of the "anti-sabotage clause," Article II, section 6, of the Party constitution at the convention of 1912 marked the beginning of the decline of syndicalist influence in the Party. Yet many Haywood supporters retained both their membership and a smoldering hostility to Hillquit and Berger for their role in eliminating Haywood from the leadership. In 1919 this long-dormant resentment

---

(New York, 1952), pp. 386, 413. Haywood was also fond of anti-intellectual and anti-middle class demagogy. His "Blanket Stiff Philosophy" declared that the "scum proletariat" was composed of "lawyers, preachers, authors, lecturers and intellectual non-producers generally." These were an "even more dangerous element than the lumpen proletariat." *International Socialist Review*, XIII, 3 (September 1912), 258.
[29] Eugene V. Debs, "Sound Socialist Tactics," *International Socialist Review*, XII, 8 (February 1912), 483.

would break forth again and exacerbate the differences among American Socialists.

III

No brief summary, such as that above, can begin to present an accurate picture of the heterogeneity of early twentieth-century socialism in the United States. In addition to the major tendencies from Left to Right, there were several other group-ings, less familiar to historians, which swelled the ranks of the movement. The Populists, for example, were an important source of Socialist Party membership, in some states imparting a special flavor to the organization. In Texas, Oklahoma, Alabama, Louisiana, and Missouri, many former Populists found their way to socialism. A Texas Populist editor complained to Tom Watson in 1907 that while the older Populists were still all right, the younger men were "sliding into the Socialist party or what they think is such, but which is really an aggravated case of Popu-lism."[30] In Texas, both older and younger Populists transferred their allegiance to the new movement. Clarence Nugent, whose father was the Populist candidate for governor in 1892, was an active Socialist. In 1915 the young Nugent addressed the first meeting of Negro Socialists in Fort Worth, thus carrying on the Populist tradition of cooperation with the Colored Farmers' Al-liance.[31] Similarly, the publisher of the Halletsville *Rebel,* the major Socialist paper in Texas, was the son of the veteran Alli-ance and Populist leader, former judge E. O. Meitzen of Hallets-ville. Both father and son were Socialist converts. The younger

---

[30] Quoted in C. Vann Woodward, *Tom Watson: Agrarian Rebel* (New York, 1938), p. 404. Woodward sites similar reports from Alabama, Missouri, and other Southern and Midwestern states. He quotes the secre-tary of the Populist executive committee of Georgia as writing in 1905 that "most of the leading Populists of this section are Socialists," and the national organizer of People's Party clubs as reporting in 1907 that "some of our late Populist friends have gone over to Socialism." Pp. 404-405.
[31] *Rebel,* April 3, 1915. In 1916 Nugent was Socialist candidate for state comptroller.

Meitzen, a member of both the typographical and farmers unions, was Socialist candidate for governor in 1914.[32]

In Oklahoma, too, where the Populists had not merged with the Democrats in support of Bryan in 1896, they contributed heavily to Socialist strength.[33] Many local Socialist agitators and speakers were "ex-middle-of-the-road Populists" of old American stock. The one large contributor to Oklahoma's first Socialist newspaper, Steuben deKalb Wham, was a well-to-do farmer and a founder of the Populist Party.[34]

Many other leading Socialists were former supporters of populism. James H. Maurer of Pennsylvania, Victor Berger, and Charles Morrill, the long-term Socialist state representative in Massachusetts,[35] had supported the People's Party in 1892 and after. Populism, however, did not mold their characters; they were already Socialists or Single-Taxers when the People's Party was organized. In several of the Southern states, on the other hand, the entire socialist movement sprang out of populism and was flavored by it.

The Texas and Oklahoma Socialists were strong supporters of the Party's left wingers. They, and farmers like them on the hot plains of New Mexico, Arkansas, Kansas, and Missouri, came by the thousands to hear "Gene" Debs, Kate Richards O'Hare, Caroline Lowe, Arthur Le Sueur of North Dakota, and other Socialist spellbinders exhort them to fight for the cooperative commonwealth.[36] At these meetings the farmers spent their days

[32] *Rebel,* June 27, 1914.
[33] When the Populist Party disappeared, Oscar Ameringer, in *If You Don't Weaken* (New York, 1940), p. 260, writes that this "seething mass of discontent had nowhere to go," and so joined the Socialist Party when it was organized.
[34] *Ibid.,* pp. 65, 78, 264.
[35] James H. Maurer, *It Can Be Done* (New York, 1938), p. 110; Kipnis, *op. cit.,* p. 49; Charles H. Morrill to Carl D. Thompson, Haverhill, Massachusetts, December 20, 1912, Socialist Party Collection, Duke; Wachman, *op. cit.,* Chapter I.
[36] See, for example, *Rebel* (July 17, 24, August 7, 1915), which advertised Debs and O'Hare encampment dates in New Mexico, Texas, Oklahoma, and Arkansas.

reading socialist literature, eating barbecued beeves, and singing the old populist songs with new socialist words.[37] These farmers also admired Haywood; when he was recalled from the National Executive Committee in 1913, Texas voted more heavily against the move than any other state.[38] On the Negro question, too, the Oklahoma Socialists were closer to the positions of Debs and Haywood than to the racism of Victor Berger. Like Haywood, Tad Cumbie, a leader of the Oklahoma "intransigents," always took pleasure in flaunting his radicalism. At Party conventions Cumbie always wore a flaming red shirt. When Victor Berger likened the militant leftists at the Party convention in 1912 to the Hebrews, who carried bundles of hay on their journeys so as not to have to sleep on land contaminated by Gentiles, Cumbie responded by appearing the next day with a tiny bundle of hay pinned to his shirt.[39]

But if these Texas and Oklahoma Socialists were leftists, their stance often conflicted with orthodox Left positions. On the land question, for example, their program met the demands of the tenant farmers who constituted the bulk of their support—but contradicted traditional Marxism. To prevent speculation in land, and eliminate tenancy, the Oklahoma and Texas Socialists demanded that farm land not cultivated by the owners be taxed at its full rental value and that actual use and occupancy be the only basis of title to land. Land in the possession of the state, or later to be acquired, would be rented to landless farmers by the board of agriculture at prevailing rates of share rent. Payment was to cease when the total paid in equaled the value of the land. Thereafter, the tenant was to acquire for himself and his family in perpetuity the right of occupancy, with the land re-

[37] Ameringer, *op. cit.*, p. 265.
[38] Shannon, *op. cit.*, p. 78. The vote in Texas was 551 to 162 against. Haywood was recalled largely because of the vote in Pennsylvania, Massachusetts, New York, and Wisconsin, which went a little over three to one for the recall.
[39] Bell, *op. cit.*, p. 306.

verting to the state when it was no longer worked. Land for this purpose was to come from the public domain, enlarged through purchase and reclamation of arid land and land sold for taxes, and by the appropriation of segregated and unallotted Indian lands.[40]

In attacking this program at the 1910 Party congress, Victor Berger pointed out that there was nothing socialistic either in government encouragement of family farms or in leasing land. At best, Berger declared, such a program encouraged "State Socialism." Somewhat condescendingly, he referred to the program as Georgian, an accusation to which the Texas Socialists happily pleaded guilty.[41] Stressing their debt to Henry George, Texas Socialists even conducted a minor campaign to reconcile the Party with his spirit. Hostility to the single tax, wrote the *Rebel,* was not based on principle, but on George's denunciation of the Socialist Labor Party at the Syracuse convention of the United Labor Party of New York, in 1887.[42]

Texas-Oklahoma Socialists often took positions at odds with traditional doctrine. Unlike many left wingers, they shared with the "opportunists" a concern with reconciling Christianity and socialism—and with bringing ministers into the party.[43] In common with other left wingers, however, the Texans were astringently hostile to the "bureaucrats" in Chicago and to Morris Hillquit. They considered decentralization "the old Landmark and firm foundation" of Party organization.[44] In short, the ex-Populists were considered left wingers largely because of their hostility to the national organization; it would be impossible and pointless to place them firmly in any of the traditional ideological categories.

The Christian Socialists, likewise, are not easily categorized.

[40] "Texas Land Program" in William E. Walling, ed., *The Socialism of Today* (New York, 1916), p. 466.
[41] Victor Berger's remarks are quoted in *ibid.,* p. 471.
[42] *Rebel,* March 27, September 18, 1915.
[43] See *Rebel,* May 9, 1914, and *passim,* 1914-15.
[44] *Rebel,* October 6, 1913; May 1, June 5, 1915.

They were not close to the Haywood-IWW group or to the orthodox Marxists; and though they were warmly sympathetic to Debs, his views and theirs did not always coincide. Before the World War, two active Christian Socialist organizations existed: the interdenominational Christian Socialist Fellowship organized in Louisville, Kentucky in 1906, and the Church Socialist League, an Episcopal group formed in 1911. Neither affiliated directly with the Socialist Party, but many of their adherents were active Party members.

The smaller of them, the Church Socialist League, had an estimated 600 to 700 members in 1917, of which about 100 held Socialist Party cards.[45] For eleven years, from 1914 to 1924, the League published a quarterly journal, *The Social Preparation*, at Utica and Geneva, New York; while the Fellowship published a sometime weekly, sometime monthly, newspaper, the *Christian Socialist*, in Chicago.

The roots of Christian socialism in the United States went back into the 1870's and 1880's, and were intertwined with the National Socialist movement inspired by Edward Bellamy's *Looking Backward*.[46] The general secretary of the Christian Socialist Fellowship, the Reverend Edward E. Carr, had traveled the Bellamy route to socialism and had been a founding member of the Socialist Party.[47] Not all leading Christian Socialists were Party members. The Reverend Walter Rauschenbusch never joined the Party, though he shared the outlook of his fellows and became a Special Contributor to the *Christian Socialist* in 1914.[48] As the editors of that journal wrote, those joining the Fellowship, whether in the Party or not, did so "for one great, specific purpose, 'to permeate the churches and other

---

[45] Reverend A. L. Byron Curtis, "The Christian Socialists" in *American Labor Yearbook 1917-18*, ed. Alexander Trachtenberg (New York, 1918).
[46] See Howard H. Quint, *The Forging of American Socialism* (Columbia, South Carolina, 1953), Chapters III, IV.
[47] *Christian Socialist*, June 20, 1912.
[48] Dores R. Sharpe, *Walter Rauschenbusch* (New York, 1942). Rauschenbusch joined the staff of the *Christian Socialist* in March 1914 when Irwin St. John Tucker became the paper's managing editor.

religious organizations with the social message of Jesus, which in an age of machine production means Socialism, and nothing else.' "[49] The paper frequently urged its readers to join the Socialist Party and to be active in its affairs.[50]

In spirit the *Christian Socialist* was close to Debs and to E. R. Meitzen and his *Rebel* group; although an atheist, Debs' moral tone was close to that of these Protestants. In a "comment on Christ's words," Debs wrote that "Jesus taught that the air and the sea and the sky and all the beauty and fullness thereof were for all the children of men; that they should all equally enjoy the riches of nature and dwell together in peace, and bear one another's burdens and love one another, and that is what socialism teaches and why the rich thieves who have laid hold of the earth and its bounties would crucify the Socialists as those robbers of the poor crucified Jesus two thousand years ago."[51]

During the many bloody strike battles of the prewar years, the *Christian Socialist* exhibited a militant loyalty to the working class. After the Ludlow massacre, in which the Colorado militia shot up and then burned a strikers' tent colony (killing seventeen miners and their families, many of whom suffocated or were burned to death), the paper placed the blame squarely on John D. Rockefeller. Rockefeller controlled the Colorado Coal Company, against which the strike had been conducted, and financed the militia. "Contemptible as Rockefeller is," wrote Irwin St. John Tucker, the paper's managing editor, "he acts strictly in accordance with capitalist morality." The dead women and children of Ludlow were but "human sacrifices laid at the altar of his worship; he chants a hymn to capital as they die among the flames." Rockefeller had been widely condemned for his responsibility in the affair and had conducted his own investigation of it, after which he announced his innocence. Tucker commented: "His conscience is determined by his pock-

---

[49] *Christian Socialist*, April 1, 1914.
[50] See, for example, *ibid.*, December 15, 1913.
[51] *Ibid.*

etbook; and since his pocketbook prospers, his 'conscience acquits him.'" To Rockefeller, Tucker concluded, "deaths of the women and children in Ludlow are their own fault. They got in the way of his god; and his god crushed them."[52]

Like Debs (but also like Hillquit and Berger), Christian Socialists advocated industrial unionism, opposed the IWW,[53] and insisted on the primacy of political action. During a copper strike in Calumet, Michigan, someone (the strikers charged that it was a Citizens' Alliance man) called "Fire" while the strikers' children were having a Christmas party in the union hall. As the crowd rushed down the stairs to the doorway, deputy policemen blocked the exit and seventy-two strikers' wives and children were crushed to death or suffocated.[54] "Great is the patience of the poor," commented the editors. "Too great we often think." Yet, "their anger must be enlightened and directed toward political action, not insurrectionary violence. Workers who do not know enough to vote for their class on election day, will never be able to obtain their freedom any other way."[55]

On the Negro question the Christian Socialist Fellowship was somewhat in advance of the Party in general, and far ahead of Berger, Robert Hunter, and others close to the AFL. The Fellowship had many active Negro members and a special organization for work among Negro church groups. Its Secretary to the Colored Race was a Negro minister from Iowa, the Reverend George W. Slater, who wrote frequently for the *Christian Socialist*, and for Negro journals, which accepted articles about socialism from him.[56] Yet some ministers in the Fellowship took anti-Oriental positions, as did the Reverend J. Stitt Wilson, a contributing editor of the *Christian Socialist*, mayor of Berkeley,

[52] *Christian Socialist*, May 15, 1914.
[53] See, for example, *Christian Socialist*, June 8, 1911. Some Christian Socialists, such as Lewis J. Duncan, a Unitarian minister and mayor of Butte, Montana, from 1911 to 1914, were close to the IWW.
[54] The best account of this tragedy was given by Leslie H. Marcy, "Calumet," *International Socialist Review*, XIV, 8 (February 1914), 453 ff.
[55] *Christian Socialist*, January 15, 1914.
[56] George W. Slater in the *Christian Socialist*, July 1, 1913.

California, and a member of the Party's National Executive Committee. With many other California Socialists and trade unionists, Wilson supported the exclusion of Japanese and Chinese from the United States at the Socialist congress of 1910 and at the convention of 1912.[57]

Christian Socialists came to socialism through a belief that life on earth could approach the Kingdom of God—and by way of a search for means to make Christianity more meaningful to American workers. This "practical" socialism implied a commitment to seek amelioration of present inequities, but it did not mean only the improvement of material conditions; social morality was equally important. In 1901, Walter Rauschenbusch observed that some Socialists did not rally around ideals, but solely around narrow class interests. If this view prevailed, he warned, "if you can establish it that it is purely a matter of selfishness, and that the sense of justice, the ideal of brotherhood, the longing for a truer and nobler life count for nothing, you have cut the heart out of the social movement."[58] Debs, of course, understood this and always spoke in moral terms, of justice and brotherhood. It is probably for this reason that the Christian Socialists felt such a close kinship with him.

Before the World War, American socialism was diffuse geographically as well as in its tendencies. Until 1918 the greatest relative voting strength of the movement lay west of the Mississippi River, in the states where mining, lumbering, and tenant farming prevailed. New York, since 1917 the bastion of socialism in the United States, placed twenty-ninth and twenty-fourth in the percentage of Socialist votes in 1912 and 1916. Even in New York, the Party's greatest strength was upstate. Until 1917, Schenectady was the Socialist stronghold, electing the Reverend George R. Lunn as mayor in 1911 and 1915, and sending a Socialist to the state assembly in 1911.[59] The states

[57] See William E. Walling, ed., *The Socialism of Today*, p. 500.
[58] Rauschenbusch to the Rochester, New York, Labor Lyceum, February 24, 1901. Quoted in Sharpe, *op. cit.*, pp. 203-216.
[59] See below, pp. 116–117.

with the greatest percentages of Socialist voters in the prewar years were Oklahoma, Nevada, Montana, Washington, California, Idaho, Florida, Arizona, Wisconsin, and Texas. In that order, all appeared among the top dozen states in the Presidential elections of both 1912 and 1916.[60] Oklahoma had the largest and most complete organization: 12,000 Party members in 961 locals, 38,000 subscribers to the *Appeal to Reason*, 53,000 Socialist voters in the state in 1914. In that year, five Socialists were elected to the Oklahoma assembly and one to the state senate, along with more than 130 Socialist county and township officers.[61]

In other Western states, Socialists were less organized, but they more than held their own in relation to the East. From 1910 to 1918, the majority of Socialist state legislators were elected in Kansas, Nevada, Montana, California, Minnesota, Utah, New Mexico, Idaho, Washington, and Wisconsin.[62]

As in other American political parties, the geographic distribution of the membership of the Socialist Party corresponded to its political variations. The basic strength of Haywood and the Syndicalists came from timber workers in the Northwest, in upper Michigan and Minnesota, and from dissident groups in the Western Federation of Miners, spread out from Arizona to Butte, Montana. The former Populist tenant farmers, as has been noted, had their greatest impact on the Socialist movements in Kansas, Texas, and Oklahoma, with some influence in Washington, Missouri, and North Dakota. The Christian Socialists seemed to have had most of their following in Illinois, Iowa, Utah, Northern California, and upstate New York. On the other hand, the "constructive" Socialists, the followers of Berger and Hillquit, were strongest in the larger cities such as

[60] See *American Labor Yearbook, 1917-18* (New York, 1918), pp. 336-338.
[61] *Appeal to Reason*, September 25, October 9, 1915; Socialist Party of Oklahoma report on results of 1914 election in forty-nine of Oklahoma's seventy-seven counties, n.d. (1914), SPC, Duke.
[62] See Table 3, p. 118.

New York, Philadelphia, Milwaukee, Los Angeles, Boston, and Chicago, where success was more dependent upon stable organization and good working relations with the central labor councils of the AFL than it was in many of the smaller cities and towns where Socialists were active.

Geographical diversity contributed to the polarity in the minds of contemporary Socialists between "revolutionists" and "constructivists." But even here different self-images did not always mean different attitudes toward organization or program. Those who succeeded in building a stable electoral base, as did the Milwaukee Socialists under Victor Berger's leadership, the New Yorkers who followed Hillquit, and the left wingers in Texas and Oklahoma, given direction by Tom Hickey, E. R. Meitzen and others, emphasized programs of immediate relevance to their constituents and concentrated on precinct organization.[63] Those with less stable constituents (among migratory workers or immigrant women and children in the textile industry) often deprecated "practical" programs and emphasized apocalyptic, or "revolutionary" appeals. Yet the "revolutionists" made practical demands: higher wages, shorter hours of work, improved conditions—in short, those related directly to job conditions and directed against the employer. The "constructive" demands tended to be more political in that they were made against the state: maximum legal interest rates; state grain elevators; municipal ice, electric, and water plants. There was nothing incompatible in these two sets of demands, and in some places both were made; but since different constituencies were often involved, there was competition within the Party over which should be emphasized.

These differences were exacerbated by the parochial character of most Party leaders. Eugene V. Debs, because of the range of his experience, was the only truly national leader the Socialist Party ever developed. He was almost equally popular

[63] For a discussion of the Milwaukee and Oklahoma approach to organization and program see Shannon, *op. cit.*, pp. 21-25, 34-36.

among railroad workers spread out along the network of repair and maintenance shops in the Midwest and Southwest, among coal and metal miners, Christian Socialists, ex-Populists, IWW Socialists, and even among the brewery workers and garment workers who formed the backbone of Berger's support in Milwaukee and Hillquit's in New York. But since Debs evinced little interest in the organizational affairs of the Party, and since neither the Christian Socialists nor the ex-Populists were capable of winning national office, control of the Party organization fell into the hands of Berger, Hillquit, and their supporters. They were aided by their strategic location in the larger cities, where the national and many of the state offices were located (the national office was in Chicago). In addition, well-known writers or public figures, such as John Spargo, A. M. Simons, Robert Hunter, J. Stitt Wilson, often were the "constructivist" candidates for the National Executive Committee and this helped consolidate control by the Center and Right. Of those on the Left who ran for national positions, only Bill Haywood and Kate Richards O'Hare were well known throughout the Party. Thus Hillquit and Berger came to exercise a disproportionate influence over the Party organization.

2 ATTITUDES AND ACTIVITIES
1912-1917

During the decade ending with 1912, the Socialist Party of America enjoyed continuous growth and exerted a wide impact upon the political life of the nation. Starting with 10,000 members in 1901, the Party had grown to 118,000 by 1912, had elected some 1,200 public officials throughout the United States, and was publishing over 300 periodicals of all kinds. In the labor movement, and in many of the reform movements of the period, Socialists held positions of prominence and had won substantial followings. The steady growth of the Party filled many of its members with optimism. Convinced that the expansion would continue along the same lines in the years ahead, a large number of Socialists looked forward with confidence to the emergence of their Party as the dominant force in American politics. In the next decade, however, the Party not only ceased to grow but by 1922 it had all but ceased to exist.

Party leaders had not expected this leveling off. In the spring of 1912, Morris Hillquit and others envisioned a Party of 200,-000 or more members in the near future.[1] Instead, membership actually declined by about 22,000 in 1913; and although it rose slightly in 1914, it dropped to 79,000 in 1915.[2] This drop, along with Debs' high Presidential vote in 1912 and the departure of several thousand Syndicalists after Haywood's recall from the National Executive Committee in January 1913, sustain a widely

[1] Proceedings of the National Convention, 1912, p. 302.
[2] Membership of the Socialist Party, 1912, 1913, 1914, 1915, SPC, Duke.

held misconception that 1912 was the watershed of American Socialist history. Ira Kipnis, for example, ends his book *The American Socialist Movement* at 1912, when, he asserts, overcome by opportunism, racism, and the lack of inner Party democracy, the Socialist movement started on an irreversible decline.[3] Kipnis does not deny the viability of socialism as a political ideology in the United States, but simply argues that the expulsion of Haywood and the capture of the Party by the right wing so compromised the Party's principles that it disintegrated rapidly.

Daniel Bell agrees that "the eclipse of American Socialism took place in 1912," and that "the rest of the years were a trailing penumbra."[4] But in common with other liberal historians, Bell's implicit assumption is that the advent of Wilsonian liberalism in 1913 made socialism irrelevant in American political life. Because the Socialists rejected capitalism, Bell argues, the Party "could not relate itself to the specific problems of social action in the here-and-now, give-and-take political world."[5]

It is true that if any one year can be considered the high point of American socialism it is 1912. But 1912 was no great divide, for neither in its impact on American society nor in its internal development did the movement change fundamentally at that time. Nor will the theses of Kipnis or Bell stand close scrutiny. Contrary to Kipnis' thesis, "Left" activity and influence in the Party increased in the years after 1912, despite the departure of the Syndicalists in 1913. After Haywood's recall and departure from the Party, none of the well-known left wingers followed suit. Debs, Kate O'Hare, Louis Boudin, Charles E. Ruthenberg, Emil Herman, Ella Reeve Bloor, and Rose Pastor Stokes all remained Socialists. In the years after 1912, Socialists became more aware of the Negro, played a more active role in

[3] Ira Kipnis, *The American Socialist Movement: 1897-1912* (New York, 1952).
[4] "The Background and Development of Marxian Socialism in the United States," *op. cit.*, p. 291.
[5] *Ibid.*, p. 217.

trying to secure women's rights, and continued to play a major role in the trade unions. By the time of the emergency convention in 1917, the various Left tendencies were clearly in the ascendency. Furthermore, contrary to Bell's thesis, Party strength did not decline precipitously from 1912 to 1916, and during the war it increased despite continuous attacks on its organization and members.

A leveling off did occur after 1912. But with the departure of Haywood and many of his IWW followers, there was a reduction in the factionalism that had been, and remained, a by-product of the Party's heterogeneity. On every major political question, if not always on tactics, the years after 1912 saw a coming together in action. Of course, differences still existed; during the war they were to lead to a further split in Party ranks. But taken in the balance, the years from 1912 to 1917 were more nearly a period of consolidation than of disintegration. In this chapter we will explore various aspects of Party activity in these years.

Socialists and the Labor Movement

The dominant trend of the trade union movement in the United States, unlike that in most of the world, has been antisocialist throughout the modern history of the movement. The reasons for this have been thoroughly examined by labor historians from John R. Commons to the present, and will not be re-examined here. Today, and, in fact, ever since the early 1920's, socialist (including communist) influence in the labor movement has been so slight as to warrant little concern over the ideological commitment of the trade union rank and file on the part of the liberal leaders of our society.[6] This was not the case before the First World War, but even then Gompers suc-

[6] The Communists, of course, exerted considerable influence in the CIO from its inception through 1947, but at no time did they develop a mass socialist consciousness among the members even remotely reminiscent of that which existed in the pre-World War I period.

ceeded in impressing his ideology firmly upon the major trade
unions.

Gompers' membership in the National Civic Federation symbolized his acceptance of the framework of large-scale industrial capitalism and of labor's subordinate position within the
system. Sharing the essential elements of the dominant progressive ideology of these decades, Gompers differed only in his
emphasis on direct labor-business cooperation. In common with
corporation and financial leaders in the National Civic Federation, Gompers sought to bring "industrial peace and prosperity"
through mediation and conciliation between the unions and
the employers. In the words of the Civic Federation, they desired to "work out industrial problems through evolutionary
rather than revolutionary processes."[7] Representatives of both
capital and labor in the Federation appealed to enlightened
businessmen to recognize the growing demand of other groups
in society and to integrate them in an acceptable consensus. As
Herbert Croly wrote, both acted to prevent class divisions "from
dissolving society."[8]

The Socialists, of course, looked upon Gompers' refusal to
adopt an anticapitalist stance as nothing short of treason to
the interests of the working class. Gompers' membership in the
National Civic Federation, accompanied as it was by the active
participation of many top-ranking leaders of the AFL and the
Railroad Brotherhoods, symbolized an attitude of class collabo-
ration and so came under heavy attack by Party members in the
labor movement. At the convention of the AFL in 1911, for
example, Socialist delegates introduced and fought for a resolution condemning such membership. Duncan McDonald,
United Mine Workers delegate and prominent Socialist, expressed a point of view generally held by his comrades—that
the Civic Federation had been conceived "to chloroform the
labor movement into a more submissive mood." This was made

[7] Quoted in Marc Karson, *American Labor Unions and Politics 1900-1918*
(Carbondale, 1958), p. 126.
[8] From *The Promise of American Life,* quoted in Charles Forcey, *Crossroads of Liberalism* (New York, 1961), p. 27.

clear, McDonald asserted, by the presence among the Civic Federation's officers of directors of the United States Steel Corporation, a practitioner of the "vilest and most brutal methods in its treatment of workingmen."[9]

Debs often added his voice to those within the AFL who assailed Gompers for seeking the advice and friendship of such men as Andrew Carnegie, William H. Taft, Alton B. Parker, George W. Perkins, August Belmont, and "other trust magnates and labor exploiters bearing the Civic Federation label."[10] Joining Debs from the Left, Bill Haywood frequently offered his own expressions of contempt for the AFL and for its relationship with corporate leaders. In an attack on the Western Federation of Miners in 1914, Haywood declared that when that union rejoined the AFL, it had become "poisoned and polluted with the virus of the pure and simple trade union that has representatives on the Civic Federation proclaiming the identity of interests of capital and labor."[11] Within the internationals that made up the AFL, Socialists also campaigned steadily for bans on membership in the Civic Federation. In 1911 they scored a major victory when the United Mine Workers passed a resolution making membership in the Civic Federation a cause for expulsion from the union. As a result, John Mitchell, former UMW president, was forced to resign his position as chairman of the Trade Agreements Committee of the NCF.[12] The next year the Carpenters passed a similar resolution, and Ralph Easley complained that "We have had this spirit to contend with all through the labor movement in the crafts where the Socialists are strong. We have expected the Carpenters to take [President] Huber out for the last two years, as they practically control that organization."[13]

[9] Karson, *op. cit.*, p. 127.
[10] Debs, quoted in *Rebel*, March 27, 1915.
[11] William D. Haywood, "The Revolt at Butte," *International Socialist Review*, XV, 2 (August 1914), p. 9.
[12] Mitchell to Seth Low, n.p., February 15, 1911, Box 104, NCF papers.
[13] Ralph M. Easley to Walter Weyl, New York, September 28, 1912, Box 49, NCF papers.

Opposed as all Socialists were to Gompers' acceptance of capitalism and to his policies of cooperation, serious differences existed among them concerning the best path to a revolutionary labor movement. All agreed upon the need for industrial unions, although some, like Max Hayes of the Typographical Union, believed that for the present the American Federation of Labor was "the logical economic organization" for the United States.[14] In theory at least, Socialists also opposed dual unionism, but the sharpest divergences developed over the question of whether or not Party members should work within the AFL or should attempt to build a rival federation. Some believed it possible to win control of the AFL, or, even if not, that they should remain in the Federation to exert maximum influence in the mainstream of the labor movement. Others, such as Debs and A. M. Simons, believed a new union was the only hope, and for that reason participated in the organization of the Industrial Workers of the World in 1905.

Throughout his Socialist days, Debs favored the formation of a new federation of revolutionary industrial unions, believing it useless to attempt to change the AFL, which, he observed, subscribed to interclass harmony, while bringing workers into conflict with one another through its craft organization.[15] Any effort to influence the "rotten graft infested" Federation, he declared, would be "as useless as to spray a cesspool with attar of roses."[16] Max Hayes and Victor Berger, on the other hand, had refused to attend the IWW convention, preferring, in Hayes' words, not to "cut loose and flock by ourselves" to new "secession movements and fratricidal wars" between workers. Hayes preferred to "agitate on the inside of organizations now in existence," so as to "dump conservatism overboard."[17] Carry-

[14] Max S. Hayes, "Socialists in the Unions," *Appeal Socialist Classics*, No. 7 (Girard, Kansas, 1916), p. 36.
[15] See, for example, his "A Plea for Solidarity," *International Socialist Review*, XIV, 9 (March 1914), 535-536.
[16] Quoted in Karson, *op. cit.*, p. 160.
[17] Paul F. Brissenden, *The I.W.W.* (New York, 1957), p. 60; Karson, *op. cit.*, p. 153.

ing this argument further, Fred Heath, a Milwaukee Socialist and compatriot of Berger, suggested that Socialists concentrate upon capturing the AFL just as Party members had succeeded in doing in Milwaukee.[18]

Debs joined the IWW in the hope that it would organize the unorganized and become a socialist-oriented center for the existing industrial unions. He was disappointed in both expectations. Not even the Socialist-led, industrially organized United Brewery Workers joined the IWW; instead it returned to the ranks of the AFL in 1908.[19] At the same time, the IWW failed to build stable locals and a growing membership because of its refusal to bargain collectively during strikes or to sign time contracts when victories were won.[20] This, aggravated by the growing tendency to reject political action and to indulge in factional squabbling, prompted Debs quietly to drop his membership around 1908.[21]

The gap between Debs' concept of the ideal industrial union and the reality of the IWW widened further as the IWW's dual-union tendencies came to the fore between 1912 and 1915. During these years it battled more and more frequently, not to organize the unorganized, but to win workers away from established unions, and from the most militant of these.[22] The most notorious example of this occurred in 1914, when the headquarters of Local Number One of the Western Federation of Miners was dynamited in Butte, Montana. Responsibility for the dynamiting was never firmly established, but the *Miner's Magazine*,[23] organ of the Western Federation of Miners, blamed the IWW, and Haywood not only did not deny this but implied that it might well be so. Describing the WFM as a "one-time militant organization," Haywood asserted that it had betrayed

---

[18] Ginger, *Bending Cross*, p. 241.
[19] Karson, *op. cit.*, pp. 130-131.
[20] Brissenden, *op. cit.*, pp. 325-326, 332.
[21] Ginger, *op. cit.*, pp. 255-256.
[22] Brissenden, *op cit.*, pp. 321-326.
[23] July 2, 1914, p. 5.

the workers by adopting a system of time contracts after it rejoined the AFL in 1911. He attacked the union for this change
in its constitution and for signing a contract with the Anaconda
Copper Company. This, he said, had "destroyed Butte" and
justified the IWW attempt to build a rival union there.[24]

Debs had expressed his strong opposition to such dual unionism during a bitter coal strike in the Cabin Creek area of West
Virginia in 1913. While the strike was in progress, Governor
Glasscock declared martial law, closed down two Socialist newspapers, and threw fifty-two persons, including "Mother" Jones
and two Socialist constables, into the bull pen without trial.
Charges were hurled back and forth between the miners and
the governor,[25] who was accused by local Socialists of excessive
brutality and of illegally sending the state militia outside the
area of martial law to close down the Huntington *Socialist and
Labor Star*. To investigate the strike and the settlement reached
by the United Mine Workers, the Socialist Party National Executive Committee appointed a commission of three, made up of
Victor Berger, Debs, and Adolph Germer—himself a miner and
a leader of the United Mine Workers in downstate Illinois. Soon
after the committee began its investigation, the fifty-two prisoners were released from jail, and shortly thereafter the commission issued a report approving the new contract signed by
the United Mine Workers' officials. But two locals objected to
the settlement, apparently because a contract had been signed.
The editor of the Huntington paper attacked Debs for his role
on the commission, claiming that the Mine Workers' officials
had turned a "victory" into a "settlement."[26]

In an unusually sharp retort, Debs declared that he was an
industrial unionist, "but not an industrial bummeryite." Those
among the miners of West Virginia, he added, "magnifying
every petty complaint against the United Mine Workers and

---

[24] William D. Haywood, "The Revolution at Butte," *loc. cit.*, p. 93.

[25] By this time Governor Glasscock had been retired and Governor Hat-
field was in office.

[26] W.H. Thompson, "How a Victory was Turned into a 'Settlement' in
West Virginia," *International Socialist Review*, XIV, 1 (July 1913), 12 ff.

arousing suspicion against everyone connected with it" were "the real enemies of the working class." "The IWW-ists," Debs concluded, had "never done one particle of organizing" in the "dangerous districts" of the state, though the UMW had "been on the job for years." The UMW was a stable organization, "steadily evolving into a thoroughly industrial union," whereas "never in a thousand years" would the efforts of "these disrupters" succeed in unionizing the miners of West Virginia, or of "any other state."[27]

By 1914 Debs had long ceased to look with favor, or even sympathy, upon the IWW; but maintaining his belief in the impossibility of changing the AFL he remained an advocate of a new federation of revolutionary unions. When President Charles H. Moyer of the Western Federation of Miners suggested to the United Mine Workers convention of 1914 that the two unions amalgamate,[28] Debs quickly began campaigning for a new center of industrial unionism.[29] Praising the growing class consciousness and sense of class solidarity exhibited by the railroad workers who had refused to transport troops during the Ludlow strike in Colorado, Debs called upon the United Mine Workers and the Western Federation of Miners to pull out of the "Civic-American Federation of Labor," and form a new industrial union federation. At the same time he called for a unification of the Socialist and Socialist Labor parties.[30] Such an organization, Debs hoped, would draw to itself "all the trade unions with industrial tendencies," and thus would the "reactionary federation of craft unions be transformed within and without into a revolutionary organization."[31]

Many years later Debs' call for a new federation of industrial

---

[27] "Debs Denounces Critics," reprinted from the *New York Call*, *International Socialist Review*, XIV, 2 (August 1913), 105.
[28] *United Mine Workers Journal*, January 29, 1914.
[29] Eugene V. Debs, "Industrial Organization," *Miners' Magazine*, May 7, 1914; "A Plea for Solidarity," *International Socialist Review*, XIV, 9 (March 1914), 538; "Revolt of the Railroad Workers," ISR, XIV, 12 (June 1914), 736.
[30] Debs, "A Plea for Solidarity," *op. cit.*
[31] *Ibid.*

unions found partial fulfillment when the United Mine Workers took the initiative to organize the CIO, but at the time his suggestion elicited almost no active interest. The journal of the Western Federation of Miners published Debs' plea for amalgamation,[32] but the United Mine Workers, though friendly to Debs at the time,[33] did not look with favor on the proposal. The UMW found that the metal miners' union had organized only 17,000 of over 200,000 men in the industry, that the union was virtually bankrupt and would have to be defended by the coal miners from constant attack, and so declined to merge.[34] Despite Debs' hopes and efforts, therefore, the AFL continued to constitute the mainstream of the American labor movement. Insofar as Socialists succeeded in influencing organized labor after 1907, they did so within the ranks of the AFL.

While the Socialists never succeeded in winning a majority within the American Federation of Labor, their strength had become considerable by 1912. In that year Max Hayes received almost one-third of the vote running against Gompers for the presidency of the Federation, and William H. Johnston, a Socialist Machinist, received almost two-fifths in his contest for a vice-presidency. A majority of the delegates from the Machinists, the Brewery Workers, Bakers, United Mine Workers, Western Federation of Miners, Painters, Quarry Workers, and Tailors voted for the Socialist candidates.[35] The strength of the

[32] Debs, "Industrial Organization," *op. cit.*
[33] See, for example, Debs article on "Mother" Jones in the *United Mine Workers Journal,* March 26, 1914.
[34] See *Proceedings of the 25th Convention of the United Mine Workers,* Indianapolis, Indiana, 1916, pp. 38-41. The joint committee met twice, on October 12, 1914 and July 27, 1915. The UMW boasted of having organized 400,000 of 700,000 coal miners at this time, pp. 41, 236; on the financial condition of the WFM see *Proceedings of the Twenty-First Convention of the International Union of United Brewery Workers and Soft Drink Workers of America,* Houston, Texas, December 3-13, 1917, p. 70. The financial report included the information that the Mine, Mill and Smelter Workers (the new name of the Western Federation of Miners) was unable to pay the principal, or interest, of its $25,000 debt to the Brewers.
[35] American Federation of Labor, *Report of the Proceedings of the National Convention,* XXXII (1912), 374.

Socialists in the AFL at this time constituted a potential, if not immediate, challenge to Gompers' leadership and was greater than the standard generalizations about the ideology of American labor would lead one to expect.

Thus, while the general reasons advanced to explain the failure of socialism in the American labor movement may be valid, they do not increase our understanding of the fluctuations of Socialist strength within the AFL in prewar years. Nor do these generalizations explain the ebb of the tide of socialism in the Federation.

One Socialist historian concludes that the alleged sharp decline after 1912 followed from a policy of nonmilitance adopted by the right wing when it gained control of the Party. He sees the adoption of the antisabotage clause as part of the Party constitution in 1912, and the subsequent recall of Haywood in 1913, as evidence that the Party was corrupted with opportunism. The fruits of the policy are said to be a failure to oppose Gompers for the presidency of the AFL after 1912, a virtual cessation of agitation for industrial unionism, and a decrease in the financial support of strikes from $21,000 in 1912, to $400 in 1913, and to zero in 1914.[36]

The argument has several weaknesses. First is the equation of the IWW with industrial unionism and the apparent assumption that the rejection of syndicalism in 1912 also involved a renunciation of industrial organization. There is no evidence that this was so. Most Socialists shared the view expressed by the Party's Information Department in 1915 that "all Socialists believe in the industrial form of labor organization," but disagree with the IWW as to "the best method for bringing [it] about."[37] This had been the meaning of the return of the Brewery Workers and the Western Federation of Miners, both Socialist-led

[36] Kipnis, *op. cit.*, pp. 418-419.
[37] "The I.W.W. and the Socialist Party," Information Department, The Socialist Party, January 13, 1915; see also *Christian Socialist*, May 16, 1911, for the Christian Socialist Fellowship endorsement of industrialism, and *Rebel*, May 16, 1914 for the endorsement of the Texas party of industrialism.

and industrially organized, to the AFL in 1908 and 1911. Nor were the Right and Center groups opposed to industrialism. In New York, Hillquit's main strength after 1914 came from the Amalgamated Clothing Workers, while in Milwaukee, Berger's basic support came from the Brewers. Both the Clothing Workers and the Brewers were industrial unions.

Second, the Socialists' failure to challenge Gompers' presidency after 1912, or to agitate as consistently as before then for a formal endorsement of industrial unionism, might be attributed to a realization that the task was hopeless. After the election of Woodrow Wilson, the passage of the Clayton Act, and the appointment of a former UMW official, William B. Wilson, as the first Secretary of Labor, Gompers' position of leadership was greatly strengthened. In addition, by 1912, Catholic strength in the AFL had been mobilized solidly against the Socialists by the increasingly active Militia of Christ, organized by Father Dietz in 1909.[38] It does not necessarily follow that the Socialists ceased attempting to influence the AFL, but merely that their tactics changed. Marc Karson, most recent historian of the Federation in this period, writes that after 1912 the number of "progressive resolutions" passed at AFL conventions increased greatly, and that this reflected increased Socialist influence in the Federation.[39]

It is true, however, that the first Wilson Administration had

---

[38] Karson, *op. cit.*, p. 243. See Chapter 9 for a revealing discussion of the role of the Catholic Church in combatting socialism in the AFL.

[39] *Ibid.*, p. 131. As for Kipnis' contention about Socialist Party contributions to strikes, it can only be said that he is mistaken. In 1912 the Party did contribute about $21,000 to various strikes, including $18,630.97 to the IWW strikers at Lawrence, and $307.25 to the IWW Timber Workers in Louisiana. However, in 1913 and 1914 the Information Department of the Party reported contributions of approximately $40,000, including $30,912.45 to the Western Federation of Miners copper strikers at Calumet, Michigan, and $8,515.96 to the United Mine Workers strikers in Colorado. Reported by Conrad F. Nystrom, "Socialist Corner," *Galesburg* (Illinois) *Labor News,* June 25, 1915. I have found no other records of contributions. See also *The Appeal Almanac and Arsenal of Facts for 1915* (Girard, Kansas, 1915), p. 62, which gives a figure of $33,500 for 1913-1914.

some adverse effect on Socialist influence in the trade unions, as did the President's endorsement of the Adamson Act and his campaign for re-election in 1916 as the "man who kept us out of war." The International Association of Machinists, for example, had supported no candidate for the Presidency in 1912, but had exulted over the doubling of the Socialist vote that year. The election, commented the *Machinists Monthly Journal,* gave "splendid comfort to the pioneers of progress who are blazing the way toward the working class goal."[40] Yet in 1916, the Machinists supported Wilson for re-election and failed to comment either on the campaign of Allan Benson, the Socialist Presidential candidate, or, later, on the election of the Socialist Machinist leader Thomas Van Lear, as mayor of Minneapolis.[41]

Likewise, by 1916 the Western Federation of Miners, though still friendly to the Socialists, had begun to draw back from its position of close affiliation with the Party. President Charles Moyer explained that the political ties of the union had proved to be a detriment in organizing the miners, and that the regular injection of Party politics into the business meetings of the union had proven "disastrous."[42] After Wilson's victory, the *Miners' Magazine* expressed pleasure that the "candidate of peace" had won. At the same time, however, it commented that there was another party "that blazes the paths of progress, that sows the seed of human betterment, whose harvest is reaped by others." This party, "teaches the voiceless to speak and stirs the hopeless to action." It is "the Socialist."[43]

Although it had become clear by 1912 that the Socialists had no immediate prospects of capturing the leadership of the American labor movement, their activity in most internationals, and in state and local labor bodies, continued with at least as much

[40] *Ibid.,* XXIV (December 1912), 1093.
[41] *Ibid.,* XXVIII (November 1916), 1124; XXVIII (December 1916).
[42] Report of President Charles H. Moyer, *Official Proceedings of the Twenty-Second Consecutive and Second Biennial Convention of the Western Federation of Miners,* Great Falls, Montana, July 17-29, 1916, p. 39.
[43] *Miners' Magazine,* December 1916.

success as before. Probably the most important Socialist gain in these years was the organization of the Amalgamated Clothing Workers under Socialist leadership in 1914. The constitution of the new union expressed its Socialist orientation: "a constant and unceasing struggle is being waged between" capital and labor, and called for industrial organization, class-conscious political action and "inter-industrial" cooperation in order to put the working class in a position to take over industry in its own interest.[44] After its organization the Amalgamated grew rapidly, reaching a strength of 200,000 members during the World War and becoming one of the nation's largest industrial unions.

After 1912 the Socialists gained strength quickly in the International Ladies Garment Workers Union as well. Earlier, the union had been strongly anti-Socialist. At the 1912 convention of the AFL, for example, ILGWU delegates cast all their ballots for Gompers, rather than the Socialist Hayes. They also attacked the Socialist resolution favoring industrial organization.[45] However, after a change in leadership, the union announced in 1916 that "though by no means a political organization," it had "left the old path of no politics in the union of 1912." To make the point clear the convention then voted one thousand dollars to aid the 1916 Socialist campaign in New York City.[46]

Similarly, in 1912, William Johnston, an active Socialist, was elected president of the International Association of Machinists, a post he held for many years.[47]

In two major industrial state federations of labor Socialists also made substantial gains after 1912. Previously, no major state federation had been controlled by Socialists, but in that

[44] Preamble of the Constitution of the Amalgamated Clothing Workers of America, *Advance*, March 9, 1917.
[45] *Report of Proceedings* (1912), p. 374; *Ladies Garment Worker*, December 1919.
[46] *Ladies Garment Worker*, November 1916, p. 12.
[47] Karson, *op. cit.*, p. 130.

year James H. Maurer, an old-time Reading Socialist, began his long tenure as president of the Pennsylvania Federation of Labor. Maurer, a former Single-Taxer and Populist,[48] led the Party in central Pennsylvania and was elected to the Pennsylvania state assembly in 1910, 1914, and 1916. Under Maurer's leadership the state federation endorsed industrial unionism and woman suffrage and aided the IWW-led strike at Paterson, New Jersey, in 1913.[49]

The year following Maurer's election to the presidency of the Pennsylvania Federation, the Illinois Federation elected the Miners' leader John H. Walker as its president.[50] Walker was a resident of Danville, where he ran for mayor on the Socialist ticket in 1915.[51] Like Maurer and Max Hayes, he advocated full Socialist support of the existing trade unions, but unlike the more orthodox members of his Party, Walker also favored Socialist participation in a labor party to be patterned after the English model.[52] Walker remained president of the Illinois Federation until 1919; under his leadership Illinois delegates to the AFL conventions in 1914 and 1915 introduced resolutions in support of industrial unionism.[53]

Just as Socialists were active in the unions after 1912, so were trade unionists prominent in the Party. Following Maurer's and Walker's examples, many Party trade unionists participated in local and state politics. Probably their most important victory was the election in 1916 of Thomas Van Lear as mayor of Minneapolis. Van Lear, a business agent of the International Association of Machinists, received full support from both his Party and the organized labor movement in Minneapolis, and in a two-way race gained a clear majority of the votes.[54] In hun-

[48] James H. Maurer, *It Can Be Done* (New York, 1938), pp. 109-10.
[49] *International Socialist Review*, XIV, 1 (July 1913), 40.
[50] *Quincy Labor News*, October 25, 1913.
[51] *Ibid.*, July 23, 1915.
[52] *Ibid.*
[53] Kipnis, *op. cit.*, p. 419; *Report of Proceedings of the Thirty-Fifth Annual Convention of the American Federation of Labor* (1915), p. 299.
[54] *Duluth Labor World*, November 11, 1916.

dreds of smaller municipalities as well, Socialist trade unionists often led their Party tickets, frequently to victory. John Schield-knecht, a switchman on the Santa Fe Railroad and a member of the Brotherhood of Railway Trainmen, was elected mayor of Frontenac, Kansas, in April 1917.[55]

Despite the old canard that the Socialists elected to public office "were mainly ministers, lawyers and editors,"[56] trade unionists filled a good proportion of public offices held by Party members in the years from 1912 to 1920. Approximately 62 percent of Socialist state legislators, for example, were workers at the time of their elections, or had been workers for most of their lives, while another ten percent were farmers.[57] Twenty-five of these were union members. Among them were two members of the executive board of the Wisconsin State Federation of Labor, a business agent of the Brewery Workers, a general organizer of the AFL, a president of a Chicago Iron Moulders local, a secretary of a large Painters local in Chicago, an international vice president of the ILGWU, and the president of the Pennsylvania Federation of Labor. By trade they included seven machinists; five printers; four painters; three garment workers; two brewers, miners, barbers, and glassblowers; and one paperworker, moulder, bricklayer, rubberworker, and cigar maker. Of the nonworkers, there were eleven lawyers, six farmers, three businessmen, one dentist, and an engineer.[58]

[55] *Appeal to Reason*, April 28, 1917; *Rebel*, April 4, 1917. Schieldknecht won a majority of the votes, receiving 460 votes to 422 for his opponent. Although the Santa Fe allowed Shieldknecht to campaign, he was fired for winning the election.
[56] Ginger, *op. cit.*, p. 307.
[57] A total of eighty to eighty-five individual Socialists were elected to various state legislatures from 1912 through 1918.
[58] Compiled from information in *California Blue Book* (1913, 1915); *Illinois Blue Book* (1913); *Minnesota Legislative Manual* (1919); *New York Red Book* (1918); *Smull's Legislative Handbook and Manual for the State of Pennsylvania* (1915, 1917); *Rhode Island Manual* (1912); *Vermont Legislative Directory* (1917); *Washington Legislative Manual* (1913); *Wisconsin Blue Book* (1913, 1915, 1917, 1919); Information on two Kansas legislators from Everett Miller to Carl D. Thompson, Scammon, Kansas, December 17, 1912, George D. Brewer to Carl D. Thompson,.

A similar breakdown of Socialist mayors and other major municipal office holders cannot be made; but from the fragmentary information available it appears that in the smaller cities and towns the results would be substantially the same as with the legislators, while in the larger cities the proportion of ministers and lawyers would be greater.[59] Thus, for example, in Star City, West Virginia (where the Socialists elected their entire ticket for the fourth consecutive year in 1915), the mayor was a laborer and the other city officials were a carpenter and five glassblowers;[60] while in Schenectady, New York, George Lunn (elected mayor in 1915) was a minister, and his president of the council, Charles P. Steinmetz, was a well-known physicist.[61]

Pittsburg, Kansas, December 7, 1914, both in SPC, Duke; of the eleven lawyers, one had been a machinist, one a typographer, and one a teacher. I have listed them in both categories. Five legislators characterized themselves simply as workers, or listed so many trades that it is impossible to list them under any one. There was no biographical information available for the sixteen-odd Socialist legislators from Idaho, Kansas, Massachusetts, Montana, Nevada, New Mexico, Oklahoma, Massachusetts, and Utah. However, it is likely that the percentage of workers and tenant farmers would be even higher in these states, since in most of them Socialist strength was greatest among the metal miners, coal miners, and tenant farmers.

[59] This, however, is based on information from about 20 of more than 200 cities.

[60] Letter to editor, *American Socialist*, Star City, West Virginia, January 7, 1915, SPC, Duke.

[61] This pattern was evident also in Beatrice, Nebraska, where the Socialist mayor (1911) was a teamster; in Flint, Michigan, where the mayor (1911) was a cigar maker with twenty-eight years in the union; in Massillon, Ohio, where the mayor (1919) was a tinner (*St. Louis Labor*, April 8, 1911, November 8, 1919). In Newcastle, Pa., Walter V. Tyler, Socialist mayor (1911) was a railroad brakeman (*New York Call*, December 5, 1911). In Conneaut, Ohio, the mayor and director of public service (1913) were a railroad conductor and a day laborer (*Appeal Almanac*, 1915, p. 16). In St. Mary's, Ohio (1911) the mayor was a machinist and the president of the council and city treasurer were laborers (*ISR*, XII, 6 [December 1911], 576). In Muscatine, Iowa (1912) the alderman was a carpenter, and in Jamestown, New York (1912) a woodworker (*New York Call*, March 6, April 3, 1912). In Berkeley, California, on the other hand, J. Stitt Wilson (1911) was a minister, as was Lewis J. Duncan, Socialist mayor of Butte, Montana (1911-1913). In Los Angeles, the Socialist

Socialist administrations were most often elected in small or medium-sized railroad, mining, or industrial centers. Where the mayor was not a worker or trade unionist himself, others in the administration often were. In Butte, Montana, the Socialist mayor was a minister; the police judge and city treasurer elected with him in 1911 were miners.[62] In Lackawanna, New York, where a Socialist mayor (occupation unknown) was elected in 1919, the two Socialist councilmen were trade unionists.[63] Similarly, in Davenport, Iowa, which elected a Socialist doctor to the mayoralty in 1920, the Socialist city clerk was a machinist.[64]

Actively pro-labor, these Socialist administrations aided the unions in many ways. One of the first acts of the Socialist mayor of Eureka, Utah, for example, had been to arrest and fine a Pinkerton man for carrying a concealed weapon.[65] More substantial was the approach of Marshall E. Kirkpatrick, Socialist mayor of Granite City, Illinois (1911, 1913, 1917), a railroad and metal-processing suburb of St. Louis. During strikes, Kirkpatrick wrote, the city administration could not be neutral; true to his Socialist principles, he supported the workers. This could almost always be done by using the police power simply to allow a "fair fight." When three hundred metal workers struck, Kirkpatrick followed his own advice and refused a company request for police protection in running scabs through the picket line.[66] Similarly, during the Paterson textile strike of 1913, when IWW strikers were refused permission to speak in Paterson, the Socialist mayor of nearby Haledon invited the workers to

candidate for mayor in 1911 and 1913 was Job Harriman, an ex-minister and lawyer, but all nine council candidates were union men (*New York Call,* November 2, 1911).

[62] *St. Louis Labor,* April 8, 1911. *International Socialist Review,* XI, 12 (June 1911), 75.

[63] B.T. Saposs on Lackawanna in the David J. Saposs papers, Personal Interviews with Workers in the Steel Industry, II (1919), Wisconsin State Historical Society.

[64] *Davenport Democrat,* April 5, 1920.

[65] J. W. Morton, "How the Socialists Governed Eureka," *St. Louis Labor,* November 8, 1913.

[66] *St. Louis Labor,* October 25, 1913. For a similar incident during a garment strike in Milwaukee, see Kipnis, *op. cit.,* p. 361.

hold their meetings on his territory.[67] And during the IWW strike in Little Falls, New York, Mayor Lunn of Schenectady helped organize a relief committee to supply the nearby strikers with money, food, and clothing. For this aid, Bill Haywood praised the Lunn administration and noted that the strikers "deeply appreciated" what these right-wing Socialists had done, even though they could not vote Socialist, "as most of them are women and children."[68] Finally, in 1917, the Socialist mayor of Camas, Washington, appointed two strikers at Crown Paper as special deputies, and thereby lost his own job at the mills.[69]

In the years from 1912 to 1917, Socialist activity and strength in the trade unions seems to have remained at its earlier level or to have increased. The losses in the Western Federation of Miners and in the Machinists' union were more than offset by the gains in other internationals, and in state and local labor bodies. Socialist trade unionists played an increasingly prominent role in the Party in these years, and the Party seems to have developed a greater solidarity with the labor movement. If one is to find a substantial decline of socialism in the trade unions, it must be after the United States entered the war, in April 1917.

In his history of Marxian socialism in the United States, Daniel Bell comments that by opposing the First World War the Socialist Party "cut itself off from the labor movement and created widespread distrust of itself among the American people."[70] Certainly the Party's opposition to preparedness and later to participation in the war brought it into conflict with the policy of the American Federation of Labor. Gompers, who had previously played an ambiguous role on preparedness, became an ardent advocate in late 1916 after Herbert Hoover, Woodrow

[67] Alexander Scott, "What the Reds Are Doing in Paterson," *International Socialist Review*, XIII, 12 (June 1913), 854.
[68] William D. Haywood, "On the Picket Line," *International Socialist Review*, XIII, 7 (January 1913), 533ff.
[69] *Eye Opener*, December 8, 1917.
[70] Bell, *op. cit.*, p. 328.

Wilson, and Ralph M. Easley convinced him that if it wanted better treatment from the government, the trade union movement must support the national preparedness program.[71] In March, just before war was declared, most AFL affiliates agreed to a Gompers-sponsored pledge of loyalty to the government in the event of war. Only about a dozen internationalists did not attend the conference at which the pledge was given, among them the ILGWU, the Mine, Mill and Smelter Workers, the Typographical Union, Cloth Hat and Cap Makers, and the Railway Carmen.

After the United States entered the war, AFL leadership gave full support to the Administration, and a number of Federation and international union officers received appointments to some of the newly created wartime government boards. Early in 1918 the National War Labor Board was set up under the joint chairmanship of William H. Taft and Frank P. Walsh as an over-all arbitration board, on which labor and management had equal representation. The guiding principle of this board was that "there should be no strikes or lockouts during the war." In return for this pledge, workers were to have the right to bargain collectively through their representatives, and employers were to discharge workers neither for membership in unions, nor for "legitimate" trade union activities.[72] To Gompers these agreements were the result of his "broad-minded leadership." "At least during the war," he believed, labor's interests and welfare were "a part of the larger problem" represented in the establishment of "world democracy and human freedom."[73]

The Socialists, or at least those who supported their Party's position against the war, opposed the no-strike pledge and all forms of labor cooperation in the wartime programs. Viewing the war as a capitalist struggle over markets, they believed workers had no interest in supporting the government and that any form of cooperation was a departure from trade union

[71] Karson, *op. cit.*, pp. 92-94.
[72] *Ibid.*, pp. 94-99.
[73] Quoted in *ibid.*, p. 100.

principles. Within the AFL, Socialists agitated for opposition to conscription, for a declaration from President Wilson of war aims and of peace terms, and for the conscription of wealth. The pressures from government agencies and from the press, however, in addition to the practical problems facing unions engaged in vital wartime industries, made it extremely difficult for the top leadership to oppose the war openly, or even to give less than active public support. In some industries, unions grew rapidly, both as a result of new wartime jobs and of government recognition of the right to organize. This too, increased the pressure on trade union leaders, especially if they compared government treatment of the AFL with its attacks on the anti-war IWW—for not only did the administration launch a campaign of mass arrests involving hundreds of the top and secondary IWW leaders but in the Northwest lumber industry, it even organized a rival union.[74]

As a result of the many pressures upon them, not a single international union took a consistent antiwar stand. Most of the Socialist-led unions supported the war effort, at least officially; while in other internationals, such as the United Mine Workers Union, the wartime atmosphere weakened the position of Socialists in the top leadership, unless, like John Walker, they broke with the Party. Of the Socialist-led internationals, the Machinists seem to have backed the war effort and to have broken with the Socialist Party most fully. Others played more ambivalent roles. The Mine, Mill and Smelter Workers at first agreed with the Socialist contention that the war was the "logical outcome of the capitalist system," and that everybody who "approves of and supports the capitalist system is responsible."[75] In November of 1917, however, the *Miners' Magazine* unenthu-

---

[74] H.C. Peterson and Gilbert C. Fite, *Opponents of War, 1917-1918* (Madison, 1957), pp. 168-180, 235-236, 241, traces the campaign to eliminate the IWW. Robert L. Tyler, "The United States Government as Union Organizer: The Loyal-Legion of Loggers and Lumbermen," *Mississippi Valley Historical Review,* XLVII, 3 (December 1960), 434 ff.
[75] "Who Got Us In?" *Miners Magazine,* June 1917. In May 1917 the *Magazine* opposed conscription.

siastically gave its support to the "war to end wars,"[76] and by
the middle of 1918, after Wilson had presented his war aims
in the Fourteen Points, the union strongly supported the war
effort.[77]

Yet, even on the upper levels of the trade union movement,
support for the war was not universal, and estrangement from
the Socialists was a good deal less than unanimous. Like the
Machinists, the Quarry Workers pledged "wholehearted" support to the war effort; but unlike the Machinists, the union
journal continued to give as much space to the antiwar Socialists as to the pro-war. In May of 1917, the *Quarry Workers
Journal* reprinted sections of Hillquit's antiwar speech to the
St. Louis convention, in which he predicted that the war would
be "ended by the rebellious working class in Europe," and that
the American Socialists should oppose the war, so that when the
hour comes, "when the proletariat of the world finds itself," the
American movement would be "in a condition where we can
proudly take our place in the ranks of the rejuvenated International." Thereafter the *Journal* ran articles by pro-war Charles
Edward Russell, on how the war was to bring "real" socialism,
and answers by Job Harriman and Kate O'Hare. Throughout
the war the argument continued in the *Journal's* pages.[78]

Other union publications, notably Max Hayes' *Cleveland Citizen, The Tailor,* and the *Railway Carmen's Journal,* followed
the pattern of the *Quarry Workers Journal.*[79] Hayes supported
the pro-war Socialists and pushed the Liberty Loan in his paper,
but the news columns of the *Citizen* carried full reports of Party

[76] November 1917.
[77] *Miners' Magazine,* April 1918.
[78] *Quarry Workers Journal,* April 1917-December 1918.
[79] *The Tailor* (Chicago) infrequently ran political articles, but throughout
the war, and after, it continued to carry occasional pieces by Hillquit,
Debs, Scott Nearing, Daniel Hoan and others. See especially, April 17,
May 15, August 28, October 30, 1917; August 9, October 14, 1919. The
same is true of the *Railway Carmen's Journal,* whose editor, W. J.
Adames, was the only Socialist official in the union. Letter from Adames
to A. M. Simons, Kansas City, June 5, 1917, Simons papers, Wisconsin
State Historical Society.

activity in Ohio and the nation, and Hayes exulted in Party gains and lamented its losses throughout the war.[80]

The Brewery Workers took a somewhat ambiguous position on the war. The International acquiesced in the AFL programs, but the president of the union was dispassionate. At the union's convention in December 1918, he commented that the main effect of the war was that the workers had less money to spend on luxuries; as a result fewer people were buying beer. The wage-earner, he said, had no trouble keeping within the "appeal of Food Dictator Hoover" for the conservation of food, since earning power had not kept pace with "the ever-increasing cost of all the necessities of life."[81]

Among the international unions only those in the clothing industry gave open support to the Party during the war. The Amalgamated Clothing Workers commented that the St. Louis Manifesto "vindicated" American socialism. Its organ, *Advance*, urged Amalgamated members to vote for "Revolutionary Socialism and Woman Suffrage" in November 1917. Two of the seven Socialists elected to office in Rochester, New York, that year were the president and recording secretary of the local joint board of the union.[82] Similarly, the International Ladies Garment Workers Union gave strong support to the Socialist antiwar campaign in the fall of 1917. Elmer Rosenberg, first international vice president, was one of the ten Socialists elected to the New York assembly.[83]

In the state federations Socialists were also divided. James H. Maurer violated the stereotyped concept of Socialist labor leaders by taking an active part in the antiwar campaign of the Reading, Pennsylvania, Socialists in November 1917, and

[80] *Cleveland Citizen,* April 1917-December 1918.
[81] *Proceedings of the Twenty-First Convention of the International Union of United Brewery and Soft Drink Workers of America,* Houston, Texas, December 3-13, 1917, pp. 59-60.
[82] *Advance,* April 20, May 18, November 2, November 9, 1917. On April 20 the paper reprinted the entire St. Louis Manifesto.
[83] *Ladies Garment Worker,* November, December 1917.

by playing a leading role in the antiwar peace center, the People's Council.[84] As a result, Maurer faced the personal opposition of Gompers in his attempt at re-election as president of the Pennsylvania Federation in 1918. Despite Gompers' efforts, however, Maurer was re-elected by a vote of more than three to one.[85] In Illinois, as has been noted, John H. Walker, state federation president, supported the war, declaring in 1918 that there were no more pacifists, "only patriots and traitors."[86] But despite Walker's attempts to rally Illinois labor solidly behind the war, the Socialists retained their following in the state. At the end of the war, in early 1919, Walker was succeeded as president by Duncan McDonald, also a Miners' leader, who had remained a loyal Socialist throughout the war.[87] In his first presidential address, MacDonald commented that in wartime labor had been "assured on every hand that the war was for Democracy and that we were required to make sacrifices to carry it on." Now that the war was over, however, and "the workers seek to usher in the new Democracy," they found that the ideals alluded to during the war were "only a myth," and that instead of a democracy, business leaders had set up an oligarchy in industry "more arrogant than that enjoyed by the crowned heads of European monarchists."[88]

At conventions of other state federations of labor in 1917 and 1918, Socialists attempted to secure resolutions calling on the President to state his war aims and declare his peace terms, and they pressed for resolutions in opposition to conscription of men, and in favor of conscription of wealth. Greatest suc-

[84] Reading *News-Times,* November 5, 1917; Maurer, *op. cit.,* pp. 223-228.
[85] *Ibid.,* pp. 228-230.
[86] Quoted in *Galesburg Labor News,* June 7, 1918.
[87] *Ohio Socialist,* January 22, 1919. The *Ohio Socialist* at this time was the organ of the left winger, Charles E. Ruthenberg. The reference to MacDonald as a loyal Socialist indicates that he not only remained in the Party but also supported its antiwar stand.
[88] Illinois Federation of Labor, *Proceedings: Thirty-Seventh Annual Convention,* October 20-25, 1919 (Peoria, Illinois, n.d.), pp. 29-30.

cesses along these lines were in Wisconsin, where the 1917 convention of the state federation of labor adopted a resolution petitioning Congress to uphold freedom of the press, to repeal conscription and to announce the terms of peace.[89] At the same time, the Wisconsin Federation, following the lead of the Milwaukee Federated Trades Council, refused to join Gompers' American Alliance for Labor and Democracy or to associate with the Wisconsin Loyalty Legion.[90] In Minnesota, Socialists were less successful. Resolutions on war aims and against conscription were defeated handily, although a resolution demanding conscription of wealth was adopted by the Minnesota Federation at its 1917 convention and was readopted in 1918.[91] At the earlier convention, these workers in the heartland of "isolationism" passed a resolution sending greetings to the workers of all nations, "especially to the downtrodden workers of Ireland, India, Japan and Germany," in the hope that "the day may soon come when all the workers will unite and throw off their backs the parasite masters of industry from one end of the world to the other."[92]

Even in the South, Socialist antiwar resolutions were sometimes adopted. In Birmingham, Alabama, the local trades council adopted a resolution blaming the war on the munitions makers and declaring that since the war was one of property, "the owners of the property are the ones to do the fighting and dying." The author of the resolution, a Socialist Machinist

[89] Wisconsin State Federation of Labor, *Report on Proceedings of the 25th Annual Convention,* July 18-21, 1917, p. 97. The convention also went on record favoring nationalization of the coal industry, p. 94.
[90] On the attitude of the Milwaukee Federated Trades Council, see William B. Rubin to Samuel Gompers, Milwaukee, November 15, December 21, 1917, William B. Rubin papers, Wisconsin State Historical Society. In December the Federated Trades Council refused to endorse the Alliance with only five dissenting votes.
[91] Minnesota State Federation of Labor, *Proceedings: Thirty-Fifth Convention,* Faribault, July 16-18, 1917, pp. 55, 56, 57. The anticonscription resolution was introduced by the Machinists' delegates and was defeated 221 to 81; *Proceedings,* 1918, p. 66.
[92] *Proceedings, Thirty-Fifth Convention,* p. 57.

named Doyle, was described by the local labor paper as a "true-blue" union man who had "an utter horror of war."[93] Condemned by the Birmingham Typographical local, however, and under heavy pressure from the Birmingham press, the trades council reversed its stand.[94]

In several other areas there were indications that the labor movement was dissatisfied with the AFL position on the war. In the Moline-Rock Island-Davenport area, for example, the Tri-City Federation of Labor had a "big dispute" regarding the attitude of the labor movement toward the war.[95] Later, in the spring of 1918, the Socialists conducted an antiwar mayoralty campaign in Davenport and lost by only 24 votes in a total of 8,721. Their vote increased from 423 in 1916 to 3,326 in 1918.[96] In the next election, in 1920, the Socialists, supported actively by the Machinists' local, swept nine of fourteen local offices, including the mayoralty, and polled 5,008 of 10,351 votes cast.[97] In Indiana, also, the Socialists received heavy working-class support in November 1917. There the Socialists elected mayors in two small cities, in each of which, the *Indianapolis Star* reported, "the labor vote in the big factories predominates." It was, the *Star* concluded, "among the factory employees . . . that the Socialists made their gains."[98] Finally, indications of discontent with the AFL position on the war appeared even in the conservative Iron Moulders Union. A close friend of John P. Frey reported to him that among the delegates to the international convention of September 1917 "Socialism is gaining," even among the older delegates.[99]

---

[93] *Birmingham Labor Advocate,* March 31, April 7, 21, 1917.
[94] *Ibid.,* April 21, 1917.
[95] Charles MacGowan to Gompers, Rock Island, Illinois, May 4, 1917, Gompers papers, Wisconsin State Historical Society.
[96] *Davenport Democrat,* April 7, 1918; Buffalo *New Age,* May 4, 1918.
[97] *Davenport Democrat,* April 4, 1920.
[98] Quoted in "The Socialist Corner," *Galesburg Labor News,* December 7, 1917.
[99] William B. Rubin to John P. Frey, Milwaukee, September 11, 1917, William B. Rubin papers, WSHS.

Of course, examples of this kind are scattered and it is difficult to estimate precisely how prevalent such rank-and-file sentiment was. Pressure to conform was great, and while the official pro-war positions of the various internationals and state labor bodies received considerable attention in the press, expressions of anti-war or pro-Socialist feeling rarely received public notice. Nevertheless, it does seem likely that while the Socialist Party lost members and support from among the top ranks of labor, it held its own or gained among the rank and file during the war. At war's end Socialist strength in the labor movement, though undoubtedly less than before, was still considerable. It was not the war which isolated the Socialist Party from labor.

Women and Socialism

In her presidential address to the Buffalo convention of the Women's Christian Temperance Union in 1897, Frances Willard commented that the development of the trusts had proved that society was better off without competition. "What the socialist desires," she added, "is that the corporation of humanity should control all production." "Beloved Comrades," Miss Willard concluded, socialism "is the higher way; it enacts into everyday living the ethics of Christ's gospel. Nothing else will do it."[100] This appeal to the pre-laissez faire values of the socially conscious women who made up Miss Willard's following expressed the reassertion of corporate Christian ethics implicit in the theories of socialism. This affirmation of collective social responsibility, combined with the fact that the Socialist Party, in the words of a leading woman member, "was first among political parties to give women an equal vote with men in public affairs and an equal share in managing the movement,"[101] made

[100] Quoted in *The Socialist Woman*, II, 19 (December 1908); and in a Socialist Party pamphlet "Frances E. Willard on Socialism," Chicago (1913).
[101] Vida D. Scudder, "Woman and Socialism," *Yale Review*, III, 3 (April 1914), 459.

socialism particularly attractive to women in the early years of the century.

No other political party or organization embodied the social values of the various women's rights organizations as did the Socialist Party; no other group fought as consistently for the full enfranchisement of women. In return, women flocked into the Party, playing an active role in its affairs on many levels of the organization, from the lowest to the highest. In this respect, the Socialist Party is unique among American parties, past and present. After 1901, the organized movement attracted a wide variety of outstanding women into its ranks, including such prominent figures as Ella Reeve Bloor, Rheta Childe Dorr, "Mother" Mary Harris Jones, Helen Keller, Florence Kelley, Kate Richards O'Hare, Margaret Sanger, Anna Louise Strong, Lena Morrow Lewis, Ellen Gates Starr, and Rose Pastor Stokes.[102]

Although the Socialist Party recruited women of all classes and of many backgrounds, it had its greatest appeal among three fairly distinct groupings. The first consisted of old-American middle-class Protestants, often with a history of interest or participation in the nineteenth-century movements for women's rights. This group included Ella Reeve Bloor, Anna Louise Strong, Lena Morrow Lewis, Rheta Childe Dorr, and Florence Kelley.[103] The second comprised working-class or frontier farm women, many with early experience in the trade union movement (typically among machinists, miners, or railroad workers), such as "Mother" Jones, Kate Richards O'Hare, and Margaret Sanger.[104] The third group was made up of immigrant working-

[102] Frances Willard, though a devout Socialist, did not live to become a member of the Socialist Party. She died in 1898.
[103] See Ella Reeve Bloor, *We Are Many* (New York, 1940), Chapter I; Rheta Childe Dorr, *A Woman of Fifty* (New York, 1924), pp. 3-14; Dorothy Rose Blumberg, "Florence Kelley: Revolutionary Reformer," *Monthly Review*, XI, 7 (November 1959), 235.
[104] Mary Harris Jones, *Autobiography of Mother Jones* (Chicago, 1925), pp. 11-14. "Mother" Jones was born in Ireland around 1835, came to the United States in the 1840's, and was married to an iron moulder, an

class women who came to socialism through the sweatshops and factories of the large Eastern industrial centers. Of these, Rose Pastor Stokes was the best known.[105]

The ties, either organizational or ethical, between Christian reform and socialism were instrumental in bringing some of these women into the Party. Thus Ella Reeve Bloor came to socialism as a result of her early activity in the Women's Christian Temperance Union, which she joined shortly after meeting Frances Willard at an activity of her church group on Staten Island.[106] Lena Morrow Lewis also started out as a temperance advocate. Daughter of a Presbyterian minister, she served as a lecturer for the Women's Christian Temperance Union for six years following her graduation from Monmouth College in 1892. Then she entered the suffrage movement, and when the Socialist Party was formed, entered its ranks, where she played a leading role for over twenty years as an organizer in Alaska, Washington, and California.[107] Anna Louise Strong was also the daughter of a Protestant clergyman. An Oberlin graduate, she received a Ph.D. from the University of Chicago and then started work as an associate editor of a Protestant fundamentalist weekly. In 1915 she accompanied her father to Seattle, where she was elected a member of the Seattle school board with the solid backing of women's, civic, and good-government organizations. She had earlier been exposed to Socialist thinking while a supervisor of a child-welfare exhibit in Kansas City in 1911, but it was not until the United States was on the brink of entering the World War that she became active in the Party. Then she joined

---

active union man, in the 1860's. After her husband's death in 1867, Mrs. Jones moved to Chicago, where she operated a successful dressmaking shop until it was destroyed in the great fire of 1871. After the fire, she became involved with the Knights of Labor and by the 1880's was a full-time union organizer. On Kate O'Hare see below, pp. 56–57, and on Margaret Sanger, see *An Autobiography* (New York, 1938), Chapter I.

[105] Martha Gruening, "Rose Pastor Stokes," *Dictionary of American Biography*, XVIII, 68-69.

[106] Bloor, *op. cit.*, pp. 38-47.

[107] Harvey O'Connor, *Revolution in Seattle* (New York, 1964), p. 106.

the staff of a new Socialist daily, the Seattle *Daily Call,* and later became an editorial writer for the *Daily Union Record,* organ of the left-wing Seattle Central Labor Council.[108]

Florence Kelley was won to the movement after attending her first Socialist meeting in Zurich, Switzerland, where she was a graduate student. "It might," she later remarked, "have been a Quaker meeting. Here was the Golden Rule! Here was Grand-aunt Sarah."[109] Thousands of miles away, on the hot plains of Kansas, Kate Richards O'Hare underwent a similar experience. Daughter of a well-to-do rancher, Kate Richards first experienced poverty after the drought and panic of 1887 forced her father to sell his stock, dismantle his home, and move to Kansas City to seek work as a machinist. In Kansas City in 1888, the "sordid, grinding, pinching poverty of the workless workers and the frightful, stinging, piercing cold of the winter" made an indelible impression on the "child-woman," and she threw her whole being into church and religious work. But after a period of intense involvement in the temperance movement, she came gradually to realize "that prayers never fill an empty stomach or avoid a panic," and "that intemperance and vice did not cause poverty, but that poverty was the mother of the whole hateful brood." Dimly, she "began to realize" the need to "fight the cause and not the effects." Since "poverty was the fundamental cause" of the things she abhorred, that is what she studied. In place of religion she turned to Henry George and to Henry Demarest Lloyd.

During this time, Kate Richards had become a machinist in her father's shop and had been admitted to the union. It was as a unionist that her conversion to socialism became complete. When she heard "Mother" Jones speak at a Cigar Makers' ball, she "hastily sought out 'Mother' and asked her to tell what Socialism was," and how she could find the Socialist Party. Talking

---

[108] Robert L. Friedheim, *The Seattle General Strike* (Seattle, 1964), pp. 52-53.
[109] Blumberg, *op. cit.,* p. 236.

to "Mother" Jones proved "one of the mileposts" in her life, and brought her into the organized movement.[110]

Other women, Rheta Childe Dorr, for example, found socialism attractive for more immediate reasons. A feminist from childhood, and a leading reporter for *Hampton's,* Rheta Dorr was an ardent suffragist. In the course of writing her *What Eight Million Women Want* (a book that sold half a million copies), she discovered that the "full equalization of the laws governing men and women are a part of the Socialist platform in every country in the world."[111] Knowing this, and because she was frequently accused of being a Socialist by her readers, Mrs. Dorr eventually joined the Party.

Finally, many immigrant working-class women came to socialism as a result of their experiences in the textile and garment shops which relied heavily upon foreign-born female workers. Among these, Rose Pastor Stokes was best known, but not typical—for Rose Pastor started her socialist career as a cigar maker, rather than a garment or textile worker, and the cigar makers' tradition of paying a person to read aloud while they worked at their craft may have contributed to making her more articulate than her sisters in other industries. In any case, the young woman went from cigar maker to feature writer on the Yiddish language *Jewish Daily News* shortly after her family moved from Cleveland to New York in 1903. She met James Graham Phelps Stokes, millionaire Socialist, when he was living at the University Settlement House on the Lower East Side of Manhattan, and after marrying him became one of New York City's most prominent and exuberant Socialist women.[112]

Several of these prominent women Socialists devoted the major portion of their time to the reform activities in which they played leading roles and, therefore, are not often remembered as Socialists. Florence Kelley, for example, was so en-

[110] Kate Richards O'Hare, "How I Became a Socialist Agitator," *The Socialist Woman,* II, 17 (October 1908), 4-5.
[111] R. C. Dorr, *What Eight Million Women Want* (Boston, 1910), p. 70.
[112] Gruening, *op cit.*

grossed in her activity as general secretary of the National Consumers League and in organizing the National Child Labor Committee that she did not join the Socialist Party until 1912. Nevertheless, she was instrumental in helping reorganize the Intercollegiate Socialist Society in 1911, and served as an officer of the Society for many years, becoming president in 1918.[113] Likewise, Margaret Sanger spent most of her time and energy in her various campaigns for birth control and sex education, but she was a close friend of Bill Haywood, and an active member of her Socialist Party branch in New York City. She frequently wrote on many subjects for the *New York Call*, and it was there in 1912 that she published the first articles on birth control to appear in the United States. Like Ella Reeve Bloor and Elizabeth Gurley Flynn, Mrs. Sanger often toured the country speaking on sex hygiene and family limitation.[114] Rheta Dorr was even less active in the Party than Kelley or Sanger. Describing herself as a "high-brow Socialist," she remained a Party member until the United States entered the war, when she denounced the Party for its antiwar stand.[115]

Many women, on the other hand, were primarily concerned with the development of the organized Socialist movement. It was largely in response to their increased participation in its affairs that the Party expanded its activities among them after 1908. Beginning in 1907 the various women's committees published their own newspaper, *The Socialist Woman* (renamed *The Progressive Woman* in 1909), which was converted in 1913 to *The Coming Nation*, a magazine of general interest. At the convention in 1908, the delegates voted to employ a full-time organizer to direct propaganda among women, and the 1910

[113] Blumberg, *loc. cit.*, p. 240; Intercollegiate Socialist, VII, 2 (February-March 1919), 1.
[114] Sanger, *op. cit.*, pp. 77-78; Buffalo *New Age* (January 19, 1918; Oakland *World*, May 8, 1915. Miss Flynn spoke in Oakland on "Small families—a working class necessity." Mrs. Bloor in Buffalo on "How shall we teach sex hygiene?"
[115] Louis Filler, *Crusaders for American Liberalism* (Yellow Springs, Ohio, 1939), pp. 110, 373.

congress created the post of general correspondent of the Women's National Executive Committee with the task of implementing all the committee's decisions. As a result, in that year additional women's committees were organized in 156 locals and state committees organized in five states.[116]

After 1910, women also played a more prominent role in general Party activity. In that year Lena Morrow Lewis was elected to the National Executive Committee, as was Kate O'Hare in 1912, and Anna Maley in 1916 (while she was serving as manager of Thomas Van Lear's successful campaign for mayor of Minneapolis).[117] During these years the Party also hired a few women as general organizers, including "Mother" Jones and Ella Reeve Bloor. Mrs. Bloor was the Party organizer in Connecticut from 1905 to 1907, then an organizer in Ohio, and, during the coal strikes in 1914, she organized among the Colorado coal miners.[118]

In those states which admitted women to suffrage, the Socialist Party often nominated women for public office. Kate O'Hare, for example, ran for the House from the second district in Kansas in 1910, and was an unsuccessful candidate for the Vice-Presidential nomination in 1916.[119] In 1912, the Socialist Party of Washington nominated Anna A. Maley for governor. In California, Estelle L. Lindsay ran unsuccessfully for the state assembly in 1914, and was elected to the Los Angeles city council in 1915.[120] In 1916, Luella Twining was the Socialist choice for the House from California's Sixth District.[121] Similarly, in New York,

[116] Kipnis, *op. cit.*, pp. 263-265.
[117] *Ibid.*, p. 378; Socialist Party Monthly Bulletin, January 1912; *American Socialist*, May 27, 1916.
[118] Bloor, *op. cit.*, pp. 76, 131.
[119] *Progressive Woman*, IV, 39 (August 1910), 2; *Rebel*, December 4, 1915.
[120] State of Washington, *Twelfth Biennial Report of the Secretary of State* (Olympia, 1913), p. 186; *Miami Valley Socialist*, November 3, 1914, incorrectly claims election; *California Blue Book*, 1913-1915, p. 401; George W. Downing to Carl D. Thompson, Los Angeles, June 8, 1915, SPC, Duke.
[121] Oakland *World*, November 10, 1916.

in the first election after the suffrage victory of 1917, Ella Reeve Bloor was the Socialist candidate for Lieutenant governor and Jesse Wallace Hughan for state treasurer.[122] Even in Illinois, where women were not qualified for state office, they ran for those positions open to them. In Quincy, for example, three Socialist women, all wives of iron moulders, ran for local office in 1914.[123] Furthermore, elected Socialist officials occasionally appointed Socialist women to public positions. Thus, for example, the first woman police judge in California was appointed by the Socialist mayor of Daly City in 1912.[124]

Woman suffrage was the main concern of the Women's Committee in the Party, and a concern of the Party in general, especially after 1908. In all states where suffrage was denied, the Socialists campaigned for its adoption, and in the states where they had elected legislators, the Party introduced suffrage resolutions. Altogether, Socialist legislators introduced seven such resolutions in various states from 1907 to 1913.[125] In campaigning for the suffrage, Socialists played an important role in at least three states. In Nevada, where suffrage was victorious in 1914, the Party campaigned steadily for the reform and claimed credit for the victory. Nor does the claim seem unreasonable, since suffrage carried by a vote of 10,936 to 7,257, while the Party polled 5,451 votes in the general election. The only larger cities or towns to return suffrage majorities were the Socialist strongholds of Goldfield and Tonopah, and the heavily Socialist mining camps went overwhelmingly for the reform.[126] The Socialists also contributed to the victory in Kansas, where suffrage

[122] Buffalo *New Age*, July 6, 1918.
[123] *Christian Socialist*, March 1, 1914.
[124] Ira Brown Cross, "Socialism in California Municipalities," *National Municipal Review*, I (1912), 614.
[125] Ethelwyn Mills, *Legislative Program of the Socialist Party* (Chicago, 1914), p. 40.
[126] *Miami Valley Socialist*, November 13, 1914; *Biennial Report of the Secretary of State of Nevada*, 1913-1914, p. 49; *The Woman Protest*, VI, 1 (November 1914), 4.

was adopted in 1912. There, as in Nevada, the expected majorities failed to materialize in many non-Socialist counties; while in the Socialist strongholds of Cherokee, Crawford, Scott and Thomas counties, in the south, suffrage carried well.[127]

A climax in the movement was reached in 1917 when New York finally adopted suffrage after several bad defeats. During this campaign the Socialists devoted major effort to secure passage of the suffrage referendum. Morris Hillquit, candidate for mayor of New York City, spoke forcefully for the reform and urged his opponents to join with him in a joint plea to assure its passage. His request was denied. For the balance of the campaign, Socialists held nightly suffrage meetings throughout the city with heavy support from the two major Socialist unions, the Amalgamated Clothing Workers and the International Ladies Garment Workers Union. In upstate New York the Party also threw itself into the fight.[128]

On election day suffrage carried because of the large plurality for the reform in New York City, while upstate, where the Republicans opposed it, suffrage did well only in those areas where the Socialist vote was heavy.[129] The Rochester *Herald*, for example, lamented that in the recent campaign, "The forces of Socialism and its ally, antagonism to . . . the war, are more numerous and formidable than ever before, and their strength was enlisted solidly for woman suffrage. Wherever the Socialist . . . propaganda made headway . . . the suffrage vote was automatically increased."[130] In Rochester, the Socialists polled 20 percent of the vote, an increase over 1916 of fivefold.[131]

[127] May Wood Simon, "Suffrage and Socialism in Kansas," *Christian Socialist*, February 1, 1913; *Eighteenth Biennial Report of the Secretary of State of the State of Kansas:* 1911-1912, pp. 86-87.
[128] *New York Call*, October 11, 1917; *passim*, October 1917.
[129] *Handbook of the National American Woman Suffrage Association and Proceedings of the 49th Annual Convention, 1917* (New York, 1917), Delegate Vira B. Whitehouse, pp. 216-217.
[130] Rochester *Herald*, November 7, 1917.
[131] James Weinstein, "Anti-War Sentiment and the Socialist Party, 1917-1918," *Political Science Quarterly*, LXXIV, 2 (June 1959), 232.

Not every Socialist favored suffrage, however. Some expressed the opinion that many Catholic women would follow the Church in its hostility to the Socialist Party, and opposed the reform on that basis. Others, especially among the brewery workers, feared, with some sagacity, that suffrage might result in putting a large number of brewers out of work. Possibly for that reason, a Wisconsin referendum for suffrage was badly de-feated in the strongest Socialist wards in Milwaukee.[132] Indeed, when suffrage was won, the Socialists did not always benefit from the victory. In 1912, Ida Husted Harper, leading suffra-gette and historian of the movement, testified before the House Judiciary Committee that the Socialist Party was "the only one which declares for woman suffrage and thereby gives women an opportunity to come out and stand by it." This did not mean that women were naturally socialistic, Mrs. Harper implied, but merely explained "why there seem to be more Socialist women than Republican or Democratic."[133] That women with the vote could be a good deal less socialistic than their male counter-parts, even in Socialist strongholds, was proven in Chicago, in 1918, when William Rodriguez, Socialist alderman, was de-feated for re-election by the women. He received a 13-vote ma-jority among the men, but lost the women by 279.[134]

However, most Socialists were not primarily concerned with the practical results of suffrage. They believed that in the long run suffrage would strengthen the socialist movement, since capitalism worked even greater hardships upon women than it did upon men. As in their changing attitude toward Negro rights, the Party gained increasing awareness after 1912 of the need to lead the fight for women's rights. And women played an increasingly important role in the Socialist Party until the split in 1919.

[132] Walling, *op. cit.*, pp. 594-595.
[133] Ida Husted Harper, *History of Woman Suffrage, 1900-1920*, V (New York, 1922), p. 362.
[134] *Chicago Tribune*, April 3, 1918.

The Negro and the Socialist Party

In characterizing the progressive upsurge in the post-Populist South as "Progressivism for Whites Only,"[135] C. Vann Woodward has caught the dominant spirit of the era in the North as well; for the progressive and trade union movements were impregnated with racist ideology and shot through with hostility toward Orientals, Negroes, and Mexicans. The decades immediately preceding the World War saw a steady succession of racist victories both in the realm of ideology and politics. In the South, the Jim Crow system as it exists today was constructed. With the inauguration of Woodrow Wilson in 1913, segregation became the official policy in most government agencies, as the Administration placed its approval on the Southern caste system.[136] In part as a concomitant of America's entrance onto the stage of world power, racist theories were used to justify both expansion and reform, and were characteristic not only of the Democrats but of Progressive leaders such as Theodore Roosevelt, Albert J. Beveridge, and Hiram Johnson.[137] William Allen White explained America's greatness, including her recent impulse against corruption, in terms of the nation's "race life" and racial institutions. Extolling the American's "instinctive race revulsion to cross breeding" with "inferior races," White upheld

[135] C. V. Woodward, *Origins of the New South* (Baton Rouge, La., 1951), p. 369.

[136] See Arthur S. Link, *Woodrow Wilson and the Progressive Era* (New York, 1954), pp. 64-66. Albert Burleson initiated this move when he proposed segregation of all Negroes in the federal service. No one in the Cabinet raised a voice against this proposal.

[137] See William E. Leuchtenberg, "Progressivism and Imperialism: The Progressive Movement and American Foreign Policy, 1896-1916," *Mississippi Valley Historical Review* XXXIX, 3 (December 1952), 483 ff., especially pp. 498-499. In 1930, Franklin Delano Roosevelt was attacked by the *Amsterdam News* for his part, as Under-Secretary of the Navy, in the imposition of segregation in the Navy Department in 1916. See *Amsterdam News*, October 29, 1930.

the purity of the nation's "clean Aryan blood."[138] In the universities, also, racism was ascendent. Among American historians, for example, these years witnessed the unchallenged rise of Ulrich B. Phillips, with his frankly racist justification of slavery, and of William A. Dunning, with his anti-Negro attack on Radical Reconstruction.[139]

In the trade union movement racism was the justification for labor's protectionist policy of immigration restriction. The AFL in general, and Samuel Gompers in particular, vigorously promoted Oriental exclusion, and Gompers was the author of several anti-Chinese and anti-Japanese pamphlets, speeches, and resolutions. Gompers regarded Oriental immigrants, with their relatively low standards of living, as a threat to the gains made by the trade unions, and publicly gave his approval to the segregation of Japanese children in San Francisco's public schools, when this policy was initiated by E.Z. Schmitz, Union Labor Party mayor, in 1907.[140] The Negro also felt "the sting of Gompers' tongue and the discrimination of organized labor."[141] The AFL did little to organize Negro workers and openly violated its constitutional principle of racial equality; yet Gompers attacked Negroes for allowing themselves to be used as strikebreakers. In 1905 he warned that if the "colored man" continued to lend himself to the work of "tearing down what the white man has built up, a race hatred far worse than any ever known will result." "Caucasian civilization," Gompers concluded, "will serve notice that its uplifting process is not to be interfered with in any way."[142] It is in the context of these attitudes and events that the

[138] William Allen White, *The Old Order Changeth* (New York, 1910), pp. 128, 197, 253, cited in George Mowry, *The Era of Theodore Roosevelt: 1900-1912* (New York, 1958), p. 93.
[139] For an interesting summary of the attitude of American historians and others toward the Negro in the early years of the century, see Stanley M. Elkins, *Slavery* (Chicago, 1959), pp. 9-17.
[140] Marc Karson, *American Labor Unions and Politics, 1900-1918* (Carbondale, Illinois, 1958), pp. 137-138.
[141] *Ibid.*, p. 138.
[142] Quoted in *ibid.*, p. 139. This statement was extreme, even for Gompers.

relationship of the Negro to the Socialist Party must be understood.

Until the mass migration of Negroes into Northern industrial centers during the World War, the Socialist Party paid little attention to the Negro. Although women received special attention and a special program, Negroes were virtually ignored by the Party officialdom. Within the Party, at least in 1903 and 1904, attitudes toward the Negro ranged from the view of a Texas comrade that Socialists in the South should work to wipe out race prejudice, and that segregated locals should not be permitted, to the view that capitalism had produced "lynchable degenerates" among the Negro people.[143] In general, in the prewar period there was agreement that Negroes should have economic and political equality but that social equality was not the concern of the Party.

Those discussions which did take place in the Party on racial questions followed the controversy in the trade union movement about immigration restriction. Full debate on this question began at the 1908 Party convention; after failure to reach genuine agreement it was continued at the 1910 congress, and finally carried over to the 1912 convention. The discussion followed the adoption by the International Socialist Congress of 1907 at Stuttgart of a resolution conflicting with an earlier pronouncement of the American National Executive Committee calling on Socialists to "combat with all means at their command the willful importation of cheap foreign labor calculated to destroy labor organizations."[144] Condemning all measures designed to restrict freedom of immigration on racial or national grounds, the Stuttgart Resolution directly challenged the position of those in the American Party whose primary concern was not to offend the AFL or the anti-Asian groups on the West Coast.[145]

[143] See Kipnis, *op. cit.*, pp. 131-132, 133.
[144] Passed by the NEC, March 2, 1907. Quoted in Kipnis, p. 277.
[145] J. Stitt Wilson, for example, was active in local politics in Berkeley, where he was elected mayor in 1911 largely with non-Socialist support.

In the course of the discussion, three fairly distinct positions emerged. First, and clearly in the minority, was a group opposing immigration restriction and upholding the idea that "equality for all men regardless of race can only be accomplished by the Socialist Party."[146] In this group were Debs, Haywood, and other left wingers, joined occasionally by John Spargo. Second, and largest, was a loose grouping, led by Hillquit, which opposed immigration restriction based on nationality or race but supported legislation to prevent the mass importation of low-wage workers. Hillquit claimed that this compromise formula—which was adopted in 1910 by a vote of 55 to 50—was merely a summary of the Stuttgart Resolution.[147] The rephrasing, however, seems clearly to have been designed to win those who desired to straddle the issue rather than to resolve it. Thus Meyer London voted with Hillquit because the proposal rejected race as a basis of exclusion, while Robert Hunter did so because it enabled the Party "to do whatever is necessary to protect the class interests of the workers of America."[148] Finally, a group supported exclusion on openly racist grounds. Among these were Victor Berger, Ernest Untermann (known in the Party as a leading Marxist theoretician), Max Hayes, J. Stitt Wilson, and Joshua Wanhope—all of the Center or Right. They were joined by Herman Titus, semi-syndicalist left winger and editor of the Seattle and Toledo *Socialist*, who declared that racial incompatibility was a fact that could not be ignored. Berger proclaimed that only by keeping the United States a "white man's" country could socialism be victorious, and at one point went so far as to appeal for the defense of white womanhood against the invasion of "yellow men."[149] Early in the debate Berger warned

---

He was one of the strongest defenders of the exclusionist position in the Party debates.
[146] Barney Berlin at the 1908 Convention, quoted in Kipnis, p. 281.
[147] Kipnis, p. 286.
[148] *Ibid.*, p. 285.
[149] *Ibid.*, pp. 278, 286.

that the United States was already beset with one race problem and that if something were not done, "this country is absolutely sure to become a black-and-yellow country within five generations."[150]

In his history of the Socialist Party, Ira Kipnis reviews these attitudes and concludes that as the years passed, race prejudice apparently increased within the Party, and that Socialists "displayed a chauvinism seldom equalled by the most conservative AFL officers."[151] But in saying this, Kipnis supplies no evidence of growing anti-Negro sentiment after 1907, and little evidence with regard to Party attitudes toward Orientals after 1910. In fact, there is much evidence to suggest that exactly the opposite is true—that as the years passed the Party became more independent of the AFL on this question, and more conscious of the need to develop policies which would win Negroes to socialism.

It was not until April 1913 that the national office of the Socialist Party developed enough interest in its Negro membership to query the state secretaries as to the status of Negroes in their organizations. All secretaries from Northern states who replied reported Negroes in their organizations in mixed locals but could supply little information since membership records did not specify race.[152] Secretaries of nine Southern states and the District of Columbia replied. Florida, Georgia, and Mississippi reported Negro members either in segregated locals or as members-at-large. South Carolina reported no Negro members; the state secretary commented that strong racial feeling in the state made it unwise to permit Negroes to join white locals. Arkansas, Kentucky, Louisiana, Maryland, Tennessee, and the District of Columbia all reported that they allowed mixed locals. Of these, however, Arkansas had no known Negro members, and only Kentucky had more than a handful of active Negroes.

[150] *Ibid.*, pp. 278-279.
[151] *Ibid.*, pp. 134, 425.
[152] Shannon, *op. cit.*, p. 52.

In that state, the locals in the mining camps were mixed and the members of a Negro branch in Louisville attended local meetings with members of the other branches, while carrying on their own activity in the Negro community.[153]

In Texas, Negroes apparently belonged to mixed locals, and in 1915 and 1916 were urged to join the Party. Clarence Nugent and others addressed the first Socialist meeting for Negroes in Fort Worth, in 1915. And the *Rebel* published appeals to its Negro readers, including one from a Negro Socialist, to organize in Lavaca county. The *Rebel*, however, did not believe in social equality or intermarriage. It merely stood for full economic and political rights for Negroes, since they shared common problems and enemies with white tenant farmers and workers in Texas.[154] Several planks in the Texas platform, among them endorsement of industrial unionism, demands for old age pensions, free medical attention, employers' liability, and an end to child labor and the poll taxes, undoubtedly appealed to Negroes, as well as to whites. Neither these nor other planks, however, were aimed particularly at the Negro voter.[155]

In Oklahoma, on the other hand, the Party fought consistently for full enfranchisement of Negroes, and had been instrumental in defeating the proposed grandfather clause in the state consti-

[153] Florida, "Report on Negro Membership in the Socialist Party," n.d., n.p.; Max Wilk to Carl D. Thompson, Augusta, Georgia, May 16, 1913; Mississippi report, n.d., n.p., received May 19, 1913, reported 150 Negroes in segregated locals; William Eberhard to Carl D. Thompson, Charleston, South Carolina, May 15, 1913; Arkansas, n.d., n.p., received May 16, 1913; Walter Lansfersiek to Carl D. Thompson, Newport, Kentucky, May 17, 1913; W. F. Dietz to Carl D. Thompson, Lake Charles, Louisiana, May 26, 1913; Charles L. Miller to Carl D. Thompson, n.d., n.p.; Joseph Voss to Carl D. Thompson, Jackson, Tennessee, May 14, 1913, reported that no record was kept of race, but that Negroes were accepted as whites, and that they had had an all-Negro local in Nashville, now believed to be extinct; District of Columbia, n.d., n.p., also reported Negro members in white locals (3) and an extinct all-Negro local. All in SPC, Duke.
[154] *Rebel*, April 3, 24, August 24, 1915; May 13, 1916.
[155] *Rebel*, May 16, 1914.

tution in 1910.[156] Thereafter, Negroes participated with whites in Party activity.[157]

Occasionally, in the years before the war, the Party made official statements against the division of the working class on racial lines. The Tennessee platform of 1912, for example, declared that "the question of race superiority" had been "injected into the mind of the white wage-worker" only as a "tactical method" of the "capitalist class to keep the workers divided on the economic field." The platform called upon Negro workers to join the Party "on the political field as the only avenue of abolishing wage slavery, and the solution of the race question."[158] Again, in 1914, the *Socialist Congressional Campaign Book* stated that "capitalists exploit all of us in common, regardless of whether we are . . . black or white." It called on Negroes and whites "to stand solidly together as a United Working class," and attacked the man who appealed to racial prejudice as "an enemy of the working people."[159] These statements, however, were more notable for their rarity than for their courage. Until the war, most activity in behalf of Negro rights was carried on unofficially, by individual Socialists.

Both Bill Haywood and Debs were outspoken defenders of the Negro in the Party and in the organized labor movement. Haywood, at the founding convention of the IWW, was particularly critical of the racial policies of the AFL.[160] Later, as he

[156] Oscar Ameringer, *If You Don't Weaken,* p. 279. Ameringer writes that he was the author of a 2,500-word argument against the grandfather clause which, in accordance with a constitutional provision that each side be granted such a statement, was distributed by the state prior to the referendum on the question.

[157] Walling, *Socialism of Today,* p. 505.

[158] "Plank for State Platform of Tennessee Socialist Party, adopted July, 1912," n.d., n.p., SPC, Duke.

[159] *Socialist Congressional Campaign Book of 1914,* 426. Occasionally Negroes ran as Socialist candidates. In 1911, for example, one of nine candidates for councilman in Los Angeles was G. W. Whitley, a union man and secretary of the Afro-American League, *New York Call,* November 2, 1911.

[160] See Paul F. Brissenden, *The I.W.W.* (New York, 1957), pp. 84, 208.

did in the Louisiana lumber strikes of 1912, he fought consistently for the organization of Negroes, and also for Japanese and Chinese workers on the West Coast. Debs also spoke out forcefully for Negro rights. In 1903, for example, he toured the South urging Negroes to join the Party and to reject the "false doctrines" of meekness and humility. Again, in 1918, he wrote that the Socialist who would not speak out fearlessly "for the Negro's right to work, live and develop his manhood, educate his children, and fulfill his destiny" in equality with white men "misconstrues the movement he pretends to serve or lacks the courage to live up to its principles."[161] Individual Socialists also played a leading role in the organization and activities of the NAACP. William English Walling was instrumental in founding the association, as was the Socialist Mary Ovington White. In addition, Charles Edward Russell and Florence Kelley both served as directors of the NAACP after 1914, along with Walling and White.[162]

Despite the resignation from the Party of W.E.B. Du Bois in 1912 (he resigned to support Wilson),[163] the attitudes of Negroes to the idea of socialism (as well as to the Party) grew more favorable. Du Bois' criticism of the Party for "failure to face fairly the Negro problem and make a straightforward declaration that they regard Negroes as men in the same sense that other persons are," was motivated by a fear that the Party would move along the same path earlier followed by Southern radicals such as James K. Vardaman, Ben Tillman, Cole Blease, and Jefferson Davis. These men, Du Bois noted, combined "radical reform" with bitter and reactionary hatred of the Negro, and he wondered whether or not the Socialist Party would follow the same path in an attempt to win the Southern radicals to its banner.[164] By 1914, however, this apprehension

---

[161] Kipnis, op. cit., p. 133; Intercollegiate Socialist, VI, 4 (April-May 1918), 11.
[162] Crisis, VIII, 4 (August 1914), 184-188; IX, 6 (April 1915), 308.
[163] Shannon, op. cit., p. 53.
[164] W.E.B. Du Bois, "Socialism and the Negro Problem," New Review, I (February 1, 1913), 138.

had proven groundless, and Du Bois' *Crisis,* organ of the young NAACP, commented that "slowly but surely colored folk are beginning to realize the possible meaning of socialism for them."[165] In 1916 Du Bois wrote of the Socialist candidates as "excellent leaders of an excellent party," although he thought a vote for them would be "thrown away."[166]

Many other Negro newspapers and preachers, or so the Reverend George W. Slater, Jr. claimed, recommended the study of socialism at this time, and a leading Negro journal accepted articles by Slater on the subject. In 1913, Slater reported, the Florida Colored Baptist Convention spent an entire day discussing socialism and concluded by endorsing its teachings.[167]

Until 1917, there was no Negro Socialist periodical, but in that year A. Phillip Randolph and Chandler Owen began publishing *The Messenger,* a monthly that rapidly attained a circulation of 43,000.[168] In 1917 *The Messenger* supported Hillquit in his campaign for mayor of New York City, because Hillquit represented "the working people and 99 percent of Negroes are working people"; because "the Socialist Party, which Hillquit represents, does not even hold race prejudice in the South"; and because Hillquit believed that the war was about "exploitation of the darker peoples—the stealing of their land and labor—and is the only candidate who dares to say so." After the election, Randolph estimated that 25 percent of the Negro vote had gone to Hillquit.[169]

Probably as a result of the mass migration of Negroes northward during the war, the Party began to devote considerably more attention to working among them after 1917. In January 1918, the National Executive Committee of the Party voted to

[165] Review of Walling's *Progressivism and After, Crisis,* VIII, 4 (August 1914), 145.
[166] Editorial in *Crisis,* XII, 6 (October 1916), 268.
[167] Rev. George W. Slater, Jr., "The Negro and Socialism," *The Christian Socialist,* July 1, 1913.
[168] Minutes of the Joint Conference of the National Executive Committee and State Secretaries, Chicago, August 10, 11, 12, 1918, p. 161, SPC, Duke.
[169] *Messenger,* November 1917, pp. 16 ff. and January 1918.

make special efforts to organize Negro workers in the South;[170] in August the Party wrote a plank demanding full citizenship, including political, educational, and industrial rights for Negroes, into its congressional program. At the same time, the Party called for enforcement of the provision of the Fourteenth Amendment for the reduction of representation of those states denying Negroes the right to vote.[171] Meanwhile, in New York City a single Party branch had recruited one hundred Negro members, and the Socialists had nominated two Negro candidates for the state assembly and one for Congress.[172]

This new interest in the Negro continued through the split of 1919. In February of that year, *The Messenger* announced the formation of The National Association for the Promotion of Labor Unionism Among Negroes. The motto of the new organization was "black and white workers unite," and the emblem was a circle enclosing clasped black and white hands. Chandler Owen was president, A. Phillip Randolph served as secretary-treasurer, and the advisory board included in its membership Edward F. Cassidy, Morris Hillquit, Jacob Panken, James H. Maurer, Joseph Schlossberg of the Amalgamated Clothing Workers, Abraham Shiplacoff, Socialist state assemblyman, and Harold C. Keyes of the Brotherhood of Railway Trainmen.[173] Later in the year, at the emergency convention in early September, the Party again adopted a plank calling for enforcement of the Fourteenth Amendment in respect to Southern representation in Congress, and called for federal civil rights legislation. Once again, Debs proclaimed the "colored worker is as welcome in the Socialist party as the white worker."[174]

[170] Buffalo *New Age,* January 19, 1918.
[171] *Eye Opener,* August 1918.
[172] Minutes of the Joint Conference, pp. 158 ff. The conference condemned the policy of unions which denied Negro workers membership, and urged all unions to accept members without regard to color or creed.
[173] Reproduced in *The National Civic Federation Review,* IV, 11 (March 25, 1919), pp. 13, 20.
[174] Proceedings, 1919 Convention, p. 491.

In 1920 Randolph and Owen supported the Socialists as the best means of opposing colonialism and imperialism. "Socialism," *The Messenger* proclaimed, was the "only weapon that can be used to clip the claws of the British lion and the talons of the American eagle in Africa, the British West Indies, Haiti, the Southern States and at the same time reach the monsters' heart." This emphasis on anticolonialism was at least in part the result of the rapid growth of Marcus Garvey's Universal Negro Improvement Association, a nationalist organization that preached separation of the races and put forward the idea of an all-Negro party and a policy of pan-Africanism. Randolph and Owen rejected Garvey, despite his great popular appeal among Negroes; they identified with Bolshevism and with the American Socialist Party as the party that "has longest and consistently supported the Moscow government."[175] In 1918, *The Messenger* declared that Negroes should join the Party, that "no prejudice will be found anywhere and you will become a power to be feared and respected throughout this nation."[176] It repeated such appeals throughout 1919; in 1920, Randolph was the Socialist candidate for state comptroller, while Owen and three other Negroes, including a woman, ran for the state legislature.[177]

Increased activity among Negroes did not represent a change in the Socialist view that the Negro question was part of, and subordinate to, the position of the Negro as worker. Most of the activity among Negroes was in the North, in the new Negro ghettos, although, at that time, the vast majority of Negroes lived in the South in a semicolonial status. But even if the Party had arrived at a theoretical position directed toward the South, it would have made little difference, for by 1919 the Socialists

[175] W. A. Domingo, "Will Bolshevism Free America?" *Messenger*, IV, 8 (September 1920), 85-86; "Bolshevism and World Democracy," *Ibid.*, II, 1 (January 1918), 9; "The March of the Soviet Government," *ibid.*, III, 4 (May-June 1919), 8.

[176] "Negroes Organizing in the Socialist Party," *ibid.*, p. 8.

[177] *Messenger*, IV, 10 (November 1920), 138. Randolph polled 202,000 votes in the state, running only 1,000 behind Debs and well ahead of the rest of the ticket. *New York Legislative Manual* (Albany, 1920), p. 786.

had few locals remaining in the Southern states, and those were
feeble. In any case, the years since 1912 had brought a steady
and substantial improvement over the Party's earlier attitudes
and activity in relation to the Negro, one that hardly can be
characterized as increasing racism. By the end of the World
War, the Party was clearly on the road to assuming a major role
in the movement for Negro rights. And it had begun to win some
mass support among Negroes in Northern industrial centers.

Intellectuals, Muckrakers, and Socialism

Few active intellectuals avoided the challenge of socialism in
the early twentieth century. Whether accepted or rejected, the
questions raised and the solutions prescribed by Marx were an
integral part of the debates of the day. Walter Lippmann, for
example, began his career in 1911 as secretary to the Socialist
mayor of Schenectady. By 1914, in *Drift and Mastery*, he finally
rejected Marxism because, contrary to Marx's predictions, the
middle class had not disappeared but was in his view "the
dominant power expressing itself through the Progressives and
through the Wilson Administration."[178] Also in 1911, Walter
Weyl started writing his never-finished book, "The Class War,"
as a counterattack on the Socialist challenge to middle-class progressivism. By the time of his death in 1919, he had abandoned
"bourgeois reform movements," and, according to his widow,
had been ready to join the Socialist Party.[179] As Charles Beard
noted in 1913, the early twentieth century was an age when socialism was "admittedly shaking the old foundations of politics
the world over and penetrating our science, art and literature."
It would have been, he added, "a work of supererogation to attempt to prove that men and women presumptively engaged in

[178] Charles Forcey, *The Crossroads of Liberalism*, (New York, 1961), p.
169.
[179] *Ibid.*, p. 286; Forcey, "Intellectuals in Crisis: Croly, Weyl, Lippmann
and the New Republic," (unpublished Ph.D. dissertation, University of
Wisconsin, 1954), pp. 308, 586. Mrs. Weyl joined the Socialist Party in
1920, shortly after her husband's death.

the pursuit of knowledge should take an intelligent interest" in the subject.[180]

Beard's comment answered a query of the *Intercollegiate Socialist*, a sometimes quarterly of the Intercollegiate Socialist Society (ISS). The Society maintained its strength at about seventy chapters until after the United States entered the war in April 1917.[181] Then, because of disagreements among its leaders and restrictions on many campuses, the number of chapters declined to forty-two by late 1918.[182]

Students and intellectuals of all Socialist tendencies and many non-socialists participated in the activities of the ISS, which served as a forum for a wide range of views.[183] The *Intercollegiate Socialist* carried discussions of the "possible methods of socializing industry," the proper attitude of Socialists toward the Wilson Administration, the activities of Victor Berger in Congress, and other tactical matters. But there were few, if any, serious attempts to analyze the changes taking place in the political ideology of those who held power in the United States, or even of the theories of middle-class progressivism as expounded by Herbert Croly, Lippmann, and Weyl. Though many leading intellectuals participated in the activities of the Society, surprisingly little of substance appears to have been produced by it. Its journal did not go as deeply into current trends on the left as did the *International Socialist Review* or the *New Review*, to mention only two other Socialist publications, nor did it contain any significant essays on the relation-

[180] Letter from Beard to the *Intercollegiate Socialist*, I, 2 (Spring-Summer 1913), 3.
[181] Kipnis, *op. cit.*, pp. 259-260; Shannon, *op. cit.*, pp. 55-56; *Intercollegiate Socialist*, I, 1 (February-March 1913), 2; III (April-May 1915), 3-4; ISS letterheads, various dates, 1915-1918, J.G. Phelps Stokes papers, Columbia University. In April 1917, there were 70 college chapters.
[182] Harry W. Laidler to Stokes, New York, November 28, 1917, Stokes papers. In August 1917, ISS chapters had been reduced to 60. By December 1917, there were 38; by August 1918, 42.
[183] A survey of 580 members of the ISS, made in 1918, showed that 209 were Socialists, 210 non-Socialists, and 35 "anti-Socialist." *Intercollegiate Socialist*, VI, 3 (February-March 1918) 21.

ship of Marxism to the American experience. Indeed, the *Inter-collegiate Socialist* served primarily as a house organ for the Socialist student movement. If academic intellectuals were influenced by the writings of Marx and Engels, as in varying degrees they were, American Socialist theoreticians offered them little. Possibly for this reason, few academicians developed more than a flirting interest in the political movement in the United States. Many campus intellectuals participated in the activities of the ISS, but few played a role in the Party. It was the non-academic intellectuals, muckrakers, and writers who were drawn into practical political action.

As a group, muckrakers showed little interest in political theory, preferring, instead, simply to concentrate upon being "good reporters." William Hard was an exception among the muckrakers when he called for "intervention of the public authorities" to supervise industrial establishments, as had been done "in many of the countries of Europe."[184] For although some muckrakers, notably Lincoln Steffens, were aware of the German efforts at government intervention in behalf of social welfare, most of them were essentially unconcerned with the prescription of solutions. Or, if they were concerned, their usual appeal was to the good old days, to honest men (by which they typically meant businessmen) in office. Their analysis rarely went beyond moral indignation.[185]

Some, like Lincoln Steffens and Frederick C. Howe, concerned themselves with social theory and shared Herbert Croly's interest in the New Nationalism of Roosevelt and the New Freedom of Wilson. But Steffens, and even Howe, while

[184] William Hard, "Making Steel and Killing Men," *Everybody's Magazine*, XVII (November 1907), 579-596. Reprinted in Arthur and Lila Weinberg, eds., *The Muckrakers, 1902-12* (New York, 1961), p. 353.
[185] See, for example, Lincoln Steffens' comments in his autobiography (New York, 1931), p. 434; Ray S. Baker, *American Chronicle* (New York, 1945), p. 185; Ida M. Tarbell, *The History of the Standard Oil Company* (New York, 1904), II, pp. 288 ff.; Frederick C. Howe, *Confessions of a Reformer* (New York, 1925), pp. 176-181; Fremont Older, *My Own Story* (New York, 1926), pp. 339-340.

they supported particular men or movements, were primarily observers, uncommitted to a social theory. It was not until the postmuckraking years, with the emergence of the *New Republic*, that journalism created a group of politically oriented writers devoted to the development of a movement in behalf of progressive reform. Among the muckrakers, only the Socialists consistently attempted an explanation of social problems in terms of the structure of American society; only they offered more than particular solutions to particular problems. While most of the muckrakers looked longingly backward, the Socialists looked to the future. To young intellectuals, aroused by the literature of exposure, socialist ideas were stimulating and gave hope. As Louis Filler has pointed out, Socialists became the "outstanding educational force," to be found "in every field where reform was in progress."[186]

The relationship between the politics and journalism of these writers varied. Some developed deepened social consciousness as a result of literary explorations into the workings of their society. Others, animated by their socialist conviction, aimed directly at converting their readers to the movement. A third group apparently saw no direct connection between exposing social evils and building the political movement in which they participated. Thus Charles Edward Russell and Rheta Childe Dorr were converted to socialism by the experience of muckraking. In *Why I Am a Socialist*, Russell describes his conversion after discovering that the evils he encountered in the course of his reporting were not the fault of the individual capitalists involved. Low wages, brutal treatment, neglect of even the elements of safety, Russell writes, were forced on capitalists by competition. A kind capitalist, he concluded, would soon be an ex-capitalist. Like Victor Berger, Russell came to believe that capitalism, though still possibly a viable system, had ceased to

[186] Louis Filler, *Crusaders For American Liberalism* (Yellow Springs, Ohio, 1939), p. 124.

be a civilizing force. Only a reorganization of society along socialist lines could bring morality back into public life.[187]

Other writers, such as London, Sinclair, and Gustavus Myers, wrote primarily to expose the inhumanity of the system. Unlike the muckrakers who moved toward socialism in reaction to the evils they uncovered, these men almost inadvertently became leaders in the art of popular disclosure. Thus Upton Sinclair wrote *The Jungle* as an impassioned plea for socialism, and despite its eventual success, he was unhappy about its impact. Intending "to frighten the country by a picture of what its industrial masters were doing to their victims," he had aimed at the public's heart. But, he lamented, "by accident I hit it in the stomach."[188] Sinclair succeeded in sickening hundreds of thousands of Americans and in giving impetus to the movement for regulation and inspection of the meat-packing industry, but he made few converts to socialism. Like Sinclair, Gustavus Myers wrote his *History of the Great American Fortunes* as a lesson in the nature of capitalism. Myers attacked those muckrakers who "hold up the objects of their diatribes as monsters of commercial and political crime." Such writers, he lamented, gave "no explanation of the fundamental laws and movements of the present system, which have resulted in these vast fortunes."[189]

Still another group of writers divided their time sharply between literature of simple social protest and socialist exposition. Reginald Wright Kauffman, for example, wrote *What Is Socialism?*, which answered the question for the uninitiated, and the *House of Bondage,* which Louis Filler describes as the *Uncle Tom's Cabin* of white slavery, in the same year (1910).[190] Similarly, W. E. Walling wrote several books on the socialist

[187] Charles Edward Russell, *Why I Am a Socialist* (New York, 1910), pp. 298-301 and *passim.*
[188] Upton Sinclair, "What Life Means to Me," *Cosmopolitan,* XLI (October 1906), 591-601.
[189] Gustavus Myers, *History of the Great American Fortunes* (New York, 1937), p. 25. Quote from preface to 1909 edition.
[190] Filler, *op. cit.,* p. 290.

movement and several muckraking articles, one of which, "The Race War in the North," on the Springfield race riot of 1908, sparked the organization of the NAACP.[191]

Socialist muckrakers played an important role within the Party organization. Charles Edward Russell, for example, joined the Party in 1908, became the Socialist nominee for governor of New York in 1910, was nominated against Debs at the Socialist convention in 1912, and ran for mayor of New York City in 1913. Being well known both to the public and to Party members (a result of his regular publication in the muckraking magazine, *Everybody's,* and in the *Appeal to Reason*) facilitated Russell's rapid rise through Party ranks.[192] Other writers, John Spargo, A. M. Simons, W. J. Ghent, Robert Hunter, were all members of the Socialist Party National Executive Committee at one time or another, an indication of the great advantage held by writers in becoming known to the scattered membership. Of course, most of the best-known leaders in the Party, with the exception of William D. Haywood, were prolific writers.[193] Debs wrote regularly for literally dozens of Socialist publications; Kate Richards O'Hare was an editor and co-publisher (with her husband, Frank) of the popular *National Rip Saw,* a St. Louis monthly; Berger was the editor of the *Milwaukee Leader;* and Hillquit the author of several books on socialism.

The Socialist Party was not unique in this respect. It was an age when many leading politicians in all parties were editors or authors in their own right. The Socialist muckraker was unusual only in being able to ascend much more easily to top positions of Party leadership than were his progressive counterparts. The democratic structure of the Socialist Party organization made this possible, as did Socialist emphasis on what its

[191] W. E. Walling, "The Race War in the North," *The Independent,* LXV (September 3, 1908), 529-534.
[192] Shannon, *op. cit.,* pp. 9-10.
[193] Even Haywood wrote frequently. After 1912 he was an Associate Editor of the *International Socialist Review,* for which he wrote many stories of the strike battles in which the IWW was involved.

leaders said and believed, rather than on their ability to develop efficient electoral machines. The Socialist author who wrote frequently for the *Appeal to Reason* and one or two other leading Socialist publications had a captive audience of almost the entire Party membership. In such a situation he could, as several did, go from obscurity to prominence in the Party almost overnight. For the integrity of the movement this was as much a weakness as a strength, as events of 1917 would demonstrate.

A number of more intimate, informal forums where Socialists exchanged views with their progressive colleagues supplemented public meeting grounds. The rapid growth of the Socialist Party made socialism "almost a fad" in literary and academic circles after 1905.[194] In the dozen years from then until the United States entered the World War, a number of salons, luncheon clubs, and other informal institutions assembled and disbanded. Morris Hillquit described one such gathering, a three-day talkfest at the estate of Anson Phelps Stokes in Noroton, Connecticut, in 1906. Present at this seminar were Hillquit, Victor Berger, and John Spargo, representing the Socialist Party, and the journalists Arthur Brisbane, David Grahm Phillips, John Brisben Walker (editor of *Cosmopolitan*), Finley Peter Dunne, and Tom Watson of Georgia.[195] Another such group, organized in 1903 by W. J. Ghent, was the "X" club, which met weekly. Members included Lincoln Steffens, Norman Hapgood, and Samuel Moffet (of *Colliers*), Hamilton Holt and Edwin E. Slossen (of *The Independent*), Charles Edward Russell, Leroy Scott, John Dewey, Charles A. Beard, James T. Shotwell, Owen R. Lovejoy (secretary of the National Child Labor Committee), John B. Andrews (secretary of the American Association for Labor Legislation), Raymond Ingersoll, Walter Weyl, and Alfred J. Boulton. Socialist members included

[194] Morris Hillquit, *Loose Leaves*, p. 55. See also letters and papers in the Stokes papers, Box 25, Columbia University.
[195] *Ibid.*, pp. 57-58.

Hillquit, J. G. Phelps Stokes, Algernon Lee, W. E. Walling, and Leonard D. Abbott.[196]

Another, more modish, meeting ground for intellectuals and radicals of all varieties were the salons of socially conscious society matrons. The largest and best known of these was the weekly gathering at Mabel Dodge's fashionable apartment at 23 Fifth Avenue. That her salon was not unique is indicated by one of Mr. Dooley's "disserations," written several years before Mrs. Dodge began entertaining radicals. In the early days of American socialism, Mr. Dooley begins, socialism was none too popular. However:

'Tis far diff'rent now. No cellars f'r th' Brotherhood iv Man, but Mrs. Vanderhankerbilk give a musical soree f'r th' ladies iv th' Female Billyonaires Arbeiter Verein at her iligant Fifth Avnoo mansion yisterdah afthernoon. Th' futmen were dressed in th' costume iv th' Fr-rinch Rivolution, an' tea was served in imitation bombs. Th' meetin' was addhressed be th' well-known Socialist leader, J. Clarence Lumley, heir to the Lumley millyons. This well-known prolytariat said he had become a Socialist through studyin' his father. He cud not believe that a system was right which allowed such a man to accumylate three hundred millyon dollars. He had frequently thried to inthrest this vin'rable mossback in industhreel questions, an' all he replied was: 'Get th' money.' The ladies prisint cud appreciate how foolish th' captains iv industhree are, because they were married to thim an' knew what they looked like in th' mornin'. Th' time had come whin a fierce blow must be sthruck f'r human freedom. In conclusion, he wud sing th' 'Marsellaisy,' an' accompany himself on a guitar. Th' hostess followed with a few remarks. She said Socialists were not dhreamers, but practical men. Socialism was not a question iv th' hour, but had come to stay as an afthernoon intertainment. It was less expensive thin bridge, an' no wan cud call ye down f'r ladin out iv th' wrong hand. She had made up her mind that ivrybody must do something f'r th' cause. It was wrong f'r her to have other people wurrukin' f'r her, an' she intinded to free or bounce her servants an' go to live at a hotel.[197]

[196] *Ibid.*, p. 68.
[197] Finley Peter Dunne, "Socialism," in Louis Filler, ed., *Mr. Dooley: Now and Forever* (Stanford, 1954), pp. 252-254.

Mrs. Dodge's salon, organized in 1912 with the help of Lincoln Steffens, Hutchins Hapgood, and John Reed, drew as many as 100 people each week to participate in discussions led by radicals of many types.[198] William D. Haywood, John Reed, Margaret Sanger, W. E. Walling, and J. G. Phelps Stokes frequently led the discussions.

One typical evening was devoted to a debate between Bill Haywood, Emma Goldman, and W. E. Walling over the relative merits of the philosophies of the IWW, anarchism, and socialism. A large gathering, many in evening dress, included Walter Lippmann, Amos Pinchot and his wife, and Mary Austin. Another evening featured Frank Tannenbaum, a young IWW who had led a band of unemployed workers into the churches on lower Fifth Avenue in search of bread and Christian charity, but who had been thrown in jail instead. Tannenbaum and his comrades, "Chowder Joe" O'Brien, "Omaha Doc" Roth, and "Baldy" McSween, all attired in their cleanest gray sweaters, mingled with the ladies in evening gowns, while Bill Haywood explained the IWW program for the unemployed. The next day the *Brooklyn Citizen* commented: "I.W.W.. MEN STARVE AS LEADERS EAT."[199]

Some in the Party grumbled about preoccupation with wealthy reformers, accusing the leadership, from the early days through the split in 1919, of "toadying" to these elements.[200] A few historians, notably Ira Kipnis, have also tended to see disloyalty to Marxist principles in this mingling with nonproletarians, and have chided the Right and Center for its petty-bourgeois fawning. The Right and Center, however, clearly had no monopoly on participation in such affairs. Mabel Dodge's

---

[198] Mabel Dodge Luhan, *Movers and Shakers* (New York, 1937), pp. 95ff.; Steffens, *op. cit.*, 654-656.
[199] Luhan, *op. cit.*, pp. 96 ff.; Margaret Sanger, *An Autobiogarphy* (New York, 1938), pp. 72-73.
[200] See Kipnis, *op. cit.*, pp. 307-311; Also, Gustavus Myers, "Why Idealists Quit the Socialist Party," *Nation*, CIV (February 15, 1917), 181-182; Leon Trotsky, *My Life* (New York, 1930), pp. 274-275.

salon, the largest and most elegant of all, was a forum primarily for left wingers and syndicalists: John Reed, W. E. Walling, Margaret Sanger, and Bill Haywood. Of course, taking part in these gatherings was not evidence of betrayal of working-class ideology, either on the part of the Left or the Right. They are merely evidence of the extent to which the ferment of the progressive era stirred interest in social questions among all classes of American society. Present-day observers are amused or disturbed by such activity depending on the way in which they are affected by the cult of proletarianism, which came to full fruition in the 1920's and 1930's. But the self-conscious participation in these affairs by radicals of many stripes was simply an attempt to enlist the intellectual or financial support of members of other social classes in reaching the goals of the socialist movement.

Of the meeting grounds between Socialists and intellectuals described here, only the Intercollegiate Socialist Society survived American participation in the World War, and it declined after 1917. Muckraking declined rapidly after 1912, largely, but not entirely, because of the pressure on the muckraking magazines organized by the National Civic Federation and groups of creditors.[201] Socialists continued to write exposures of

---

[201] See letters from F.G.R. Gordon, an ex-Socialist and self-styled "industrial expert," to Harry Payne Whitney, Theodore Roosevelt, and to a number of the larger companies, such as Hudson Motor Company, Campbell Soup Company, that advertised in the *Metropolitan Magazine*. Gordon tells these manufacturers of the alleged support given socialism by *Metropolitan Magazine*, and urges them to review their policy of advertising therein, since an application of these policies would lead to confiscation of the companies' property (Box 82, NCF papers, March, April 1915). In reply, the president of the Beech-Nut Packing Company promised to "study much more carefully the editorial policy of the *Metropolitan Magazine* in the future," and blamed his past advertising on the advertising agency (Bartlett Arkell to F.G.R. Gordon, Canajoharie, New York, April 29, 1915, *ibid.*). On the other hand, see L. Olwell to F.G.R. Gordon, Detroit, April 30, 1915. Olwell, who was first vice president of the Chalmers Motor Company, wrote that the "editorial policy doesn't interest us particularly as we think they have a right to run their magazine in their own way," and no advertiser has a right to use his adver-

the evils of capitalism, but more and more they were restricted
to publishing in the Party press. Few of the informal clubs and
salons continued for long. Mabel Dodge's, for example, lasted
about two years, ending in 1914. Those, like the "X" club, that
were still in existence in 1917, divided hopelessly and with hostility over the question of American participation in the war.[202]
Over-all, in the years from 1912 to 1917, socialism remained a
central concern of intellectuals and their organized connections
with the movement did not change drastically. When America
entered the war, the ISS was considerably stronger than it had
been in 1912, but this was balanced by the increasing interest
and participation by journalists and intellectual reformers in
the concerns of Wilsonian liberalism. Even so, as we shall see,
it was the war that disrupted the relationship of the Party and
its intellectuals.

The Socialist Press

The Socialist press, which was the main vehicle of Party propaganda and education, reached its high point in terms of the
number of periodicals published in 1912 through 1913. At that
time the Party claimed some 323 English and foreign language
daily, weekly, and monthly publications.[203] Reflecting both the
scope and political character of the Socialist movement, the
fortunes of these newspapers and magazines roughly paralleled
that of the Party until the United States entered the war.

From 1912 to 1918, the Socialist press was diverse in nature
and function. Socialists published weekly and monthly popular
newspapers and magazines of national circulation, daily and
weekly local newspapers, trade union newspapers, various for-

---

tising "as a club over" any magazine. See also Richard Hofstadter, *The
Age of Reform* (New York, 1960), pp. 195-196; Filler, chapter XXVIII,
pp. 359 ff.
[202] Hillquit, *Loose Leaves*, p. 70.
[203] "Report of National Secretary John Work to the 1912 Socialist Convention," Socialist Party, *Proceedings of the National Convention, 1912*,
p. 221.

eign language dailies and weeklies, as well as several theoretical, cultural, and special group publications. The nationally read publications included the *Appeal to Reason,* one of the most widely circulated weekly newspapers in the world; the *International Socialist Review,* an illustrated monthly of news, views and polemics; and the *National Rip Saw,* a monthly aimed primarily at the Socialist farmer. Daily and weekly local newspapers ranged from the *Milwaukee Leader,* with a daily circulation of 35,000, to the little weeklies in Oklahoma towns with populations of from 200 to 600 people. The variety of trade union papers included such as Max Hayes' *Cleveland Citizen,* official organ of the Cleveland Central Labor Council; the *Miner's Magazine,* organ of the Western Federation of Miners; the *Quarry Workers Journal,* voice of the Vermont Quarry Workers; and the *Laborer,* of Dallas, Texas, an independent labor paper edited by Socialists.

Total circulation of this press probably exceeded two million copies in 1913, although an accurate estimate cannot be made with the data available. Of this, the *Appeal to Reason* alone had an average weekly circulation of 761,747; the *National Rip Saw* fluctuated around 150,000; the *Jewish Daily Forward* had 142,000; the *International Socialist Review* 42,000; the *National Socialist* 35,000 and the Halletsville, Texas *Rebel* 26,000.[204]

Although Socialist periodicals reflected the different tendencies and factions in the Party, the most striking aspect of the Socialist press before 1920 is the attention devoted to mass Socialist education and the emphasis on the common goals of the Party. Unlike the Communist and Socialist house organs of the post-1919 period, the main function of the prewar Socialist press was to reach and convert the masses, to bring the message of socialism to the greatest number of people. To do this a combination of Socialist muckraking—that is, the exposure of the inherent evils of capitalism—and popular exposition of Marxist theories was used; it was this, plus news of

[204] See Table 1 below, pp. 94–102.

the Socialist, labor, and farmers' movements, which dominated most Socialist organs of all tendencies. Intra-Party disputes, although not neglected by many Socialist publications, generally received secondary space and attention.[205]

Unlike the *Appeal to Reason,* which explicitly declined to join in factional disputes, many of the most interesting smaller journals participated warmly in the debates on tactics and strategy for the movement. Even those most given to upholding a particular point of view, however, followed the *Appeal* in opening their pages to contributors of many tendencies. No one considered it strange that Debs should be an editor of both the semi-populist *National Rip Saw,* and the neutral *Appeal,* as well as a regular contributor to both the *Christian Socialist* and Victor Berger's *Milwaukee Leader.* Nor did anyone question the practice of the *International Socialist Review* in featuring among its contributors non-Socialist reformers, such as Frederick C. Howe and Clarence Darrow; moderate Socialists, such as Carl Sandburg, Charles Edward Russell, Gustavus Myers, and Upton Sinclair; and left-wingers of assorted views, such as Debs, Margaret Sanger, Jack London, William D. Haywood, S. J. Rutgers, Louis Fraina, and Sen Katayama.[206] Even the *New Review,* organ of the left-wing theoreticians from 1913 to its merger with the *Masses* in 1917, opened its pages to a wide range of Socialist and non-Socialist writers.[207] This heterogeneity is an indication of the factional fluidity which existed before

[205] There were exceptions, of course, such as the *Christian Socialist's* campaign against J. Mahlon Barnes in 1911 and 1912; the attacks of the *Rebel* on "centralization" of Party power in 1915, and the articles in the *International Socialist Review,* by Henry Slobodin and others, attacking the vote-chasing proclivities of the national leadership. But these were exceptions. Thus, for example, one can read through the Buffalo *New Age,* a weekly newspaper, of late 1918 and early 1919, when the Party was splitting in three and the Buffalo local was going "Left," and hardly glean the fact that a factional dispute was raging in the local.
[206] These contributors appeared in the *Review* in the period from July 1914 through January 1917.
[207] In 1915 and 1916, the *New Review* carried articles by reform-oriented Socialists such as John Spargo, J.G. Phelps Stokes, Harry W. Laidler, Eduard Bernstein, and Charles A. Beard, as well as the regular contributions of left-wing theoreticians such as Louis B. Boudin, Louis C. Fraina,

1919, and a reflection of the absence, or at least the tentative nature, of differences in principle between the several groupings and tendencies. Searching and open debate was characteristic of the Socialist press in these years, not as a tactical maneuver, but because no group could assert with confidence that it had found the answers to all the problems besetting the movement.

Another reason for the multiformity of the Socialist press is that few papers or magazines were Party owned or operated. Until 1914, when the Party constitution was amended to allow the "Party Builder," a weekly bulletin, to become the weekly *American Socialist*, there was no official Socialist national newspaper.[208] Even after 1914, the *American Socialist* was only one among scores of Party newspapers. Many weeklies were owned and operated by various Party locals. In New Jersey, for example, most of the newspapers were Party owned.[209] The leading publications, however, were all privately operated. The *Appeal to Reason* was founded in 1895 by J. A. Wayland, and remained firmly in his control until his death in 1912. Thereafter the *Appeal* was published by Wayland's sons, until purchased by Louis Kopelin, then editor, and E. Haldeman-Julius, in 1919.[210] Similarly, the *National Rip Saw* was published and edited by Oscar Ameringer from 1904 until 1912, and thereafter by Frank and Kate O'Hare, of St. Louis. The *International Socialist Review* was the organ of the Chicago publisher of Marxist classics, Charles H. Kerr.[211]

Other Socialist newspapers, notably the *Milwaukee Leader*

Paul Kennaday, and Austin Lewis. Stokes was a member of the Advisory Council of the *New Review* and enjoyed cordial relations with Louis Fraina. In 1916 he contributed $10.00 per month to the magazine's sustaining fund. See J.G. Phelps Stokes to Louis Fraina, n.p., April 8, 1916, Stokes papers, Columbia University.

[208] Walling, ed., *Socialism of Today*, pp. 231-232.
[209] Report to Carl D. Thompson, June 7, 1913, n.s., SPC, Duke.
[210] *Appeal to Reason*, May 24, 1919.
[211] Theodore Draper, *The Roots of American Communism* (New York, 1957), 48, makes a factual and the interpretive error in seeing the private publication of the *International Socialist Review* and the *New Review* as exceptional and as an indication of the "estrangement of the Left Wing." In fact, this condition was typical.

and *St. Louis Labor,* were owned by companies in which most of the stock was held by trade union locals. The stock of *Labor* and the *Leader* was held by Brewery Workers and Teamsters' locals, in the main. Still another arrangement was that of the Pittsburg, Kansas, *Workers Chronicle,* which was owned and operated jointly by District 14 of the United Mine Workers and the Socialist local.[212] Finally, there were the journals of Socialist-led unions, such as those of the Western Federation of Miners, the Quarry Workers, and the Amalgamated Clothing Workers. These devoted considerable space to news of the Party and to the educational material it supplied.

In Daniel Bell's attempt to illustrate the rapid decline of the Socialist movement after 1912, he strikingly asserts that of the 262 Socialist periodicals published in 1912, only 42 remained in business in 1916.[213] If this claim were correct, it would certainly indicate a serious and rapid decline in the vigor and influence of the movement. But his figures are wrong at both ends. First of all, there were 323 Socialist periodicals publishing in 1912, of which 262 were English language weeklies.[214] Of this latter number, however, over 150 should be initially discounted; for, according to National Secretary John Work, these were cooperatively published papers, a highly transistory experiment in party journalism lasting no more than three or four years. Begun in 1911 and 1912, the experiment quickly failed. In Arkansas, the Party secretary complained in 1913 that publishing their own papers had "left the locals busted financially," drained the movement without returns, and left the comrades "disgusted" and "sore."[215] In 1912, four locals in Arkansas advanced the required amount of money but found it impossible either to gather one page of material a week, or

[212] Letterhead dated December 7, 1914, SPC, Duke.
[213] Bell, *op. cit.,* p. 309.
[214] "Report of National Secretary John Work to the 1912 Socialist Convention," *loc. cit.*
[215] Ida H. Callery to Carl D. Thompson, Bonanza, Arkansas, June 5, 1913, SPC, Duke.

to handle the distribution. To make matters worse, the "principal feature" of the papers themselves had been "a picture of the printing plant."[216]

One Socialist cooperative publishing company in Iola, Kansas, printed fifty-nine local papers in 1913.[217] By early 1915, so many had dropped off that the company ceased publishing Socialist weeklies.[218] In 1917, only three of the original fifty-nine papers survived.

Assuming the experience of the Iola company to have been typical of cooperative publishers, about 95 percent of the 150-odd cooperative papers should be discounted from Work's figure of 323 for 1912. If this is done, about 170 noncooperative publications remain. I have found 162 of these for 1912, of which 133 remained in business in 1916 or had been replaced by new Socialist periodicals.[219] The rate of failure of the noncooperative papers of which traces remain, in other words, was about 18 percent, as opposed to 95 percent for the cooperatives. But the general rate of decline of American weekly newspapers in the years from 1914 to 1920 was greater than 10 percent.[220] Thus, Bell to the contrary, the performance of the noncooperative Socialist press was only slightly worse than that of the commercial press in these years.

It is true, however, that the flux of the Socialist press was greater than the over-all totals would indicate, especially among the small town newspapers. In Oklahoma, for example, there were eleven Socialist weeklies in 1913, twelve in 1916, and nine in 1917. But of the original eleven, only four survived until 1916, the difference being made up by six new papers and two

---

[216] *Ibid.*

[217] List in letter from M. F. Wiltse to Carl D. Thompson, Marshalltown, Iowa, June 4, 1913, SPC, Duke.

[218] J. H. Bard to Carl D. Thompson, Iola, Kansas, March 2, 1915, SPC, Duke. Not all the papers had failed, but enough so that it was no longer profitable to publish the remaining ones, Bard wrote.

[219] See Table 1, pp. 94–102.

[220] Edwin Emergy and Henry Ladd Smith, *The Press in America* (New York, 1954), pp. 514, 517.

which changed their political affiliation to Socialist (see Table
1). A good portion of the small-town Socialist weeklies were
like those in Oklahoma. Most began publishing between 1910
and 1914, and few lasted more than five years. Always marginal, these semirural weeklies suffered from rapidly rising costs
after 1914, as well as from the hostility of local bankers and
advertisers.

Among the larger Socialist publications, circulation did not
decline sharply from 1913 to 1917. The *Appeal to Reason*
showed the greatest drop, from 761,747 to 529,132, but the
National Rip Saw maintained a steady 150,000 in these years,
while the *Milwaukee Leader,* the *New York Call* and the *American Socialist* gained circulation (see Table 1). Some important
Socialist papers appeared as late as 1917. The *Seattle Daily Call,*
edited by Lena Morrow Lewis, was the first new English language daily to appear since 1911; the *Messenger,* edited by A.
Phillip Randolph, which claimed to be the only magazine of
"scientific radicalism" in the world published by Negroes, attained a circulation of 43,000 by 1918.[221] Others included *Advance,* militant Socialist weekly organ of the Amalgamated
Clothing Workers Union; the Duluth, Minnesota, *Labor Leader*
(later *Truth*), a left-wing weekly; and *The Class Struggle,* theoretical journal of the new Left Wing movement, organized in
Boston in 1915.

Wartime hysteria and Government suppression, rather than
faltering support, disrupted the Socialist press. Within five
months after war had been declared, every leading Socialist
publication had been suspended from the mails at least once,
and many were barred for weeks at a time. Second-class mailing
privileges were denied Socialist periodicals by Postmaster General Albert Burleson, who used his powers under the Espionage
Act of 1917 to destroy political opposition to Government pol-

[221] Minutes of the Joint Conference of the National Executive Committee
and State Secretaries, Chicago, August 10-12, 1918, p. 158, SPC, Duke.

icies.[222] Burleson went so far as to prevent the *Milwaukee Leader* from sending or receiving first-class mail, a move for which he had not even a semblance of legal sanction.[223] Correspondence of the *Leader* had to be sent to the homes of individual employees, and this was kept secret, lest the Postmaster General stop it, too.[224] In addition to pressure applied by the federal government, Socialist papers in dozens of small towns and cities faced the wrath of vigilance committees organized by local chambers of commerce and boards of trade. In Seattle, for example, the *Daily Call* printing plant was smashed by a mob led by three drunken sailors on January 5, 1918, and a few months thereafter the paper ceased publishing.[225] In many of the smaller towns in the West and Midwest, Socialist newspapers were particularly vulnerable to Government attack. In these areas Socialist antiwar strength tended to come from the farmers, or from small mining camps and railroad yards outside of town, while the commercial centers themselves were strongly pro-war. Since the papers were published in the towns, they were often isolated from their supporters and were unable to survive in the face of a combination of hostile pressures. By late 1917 or early 1918, a majority of these papers had either been forced out of business or had capitulated and assumed pro-war stances.

[222] See H. C. Peterson and Gilbert C. Fite, *Opponents of War: 1917-1918* (Madison, Wisconsin, 1957), pp. 95 ff., 164.

[223] See Oscar Ameringer, *If You Don't Weaken* (New York, 1940), pp. 316-318. According to Ameringer, pressure from Washington forced even the express companies to stop delivering the *Leader* to the countryside.

[224] *Ibid.*

[225] Seattle *Post-Intelligencer*, January 7, 1918; Interview with Harvey O'Connor, Madison, Wisconsin, November 6, 1961; O'Connor to the author, Boerne, Texas, January 22, 1962. O'Connor was managing editor of the *Call*. He relates that the newspaper ceased publishing on April 22, 1918, two days before the *Seattle Union Record* became a daily. Sam Sadler, a Socialist, was on the *Call* board of editors, and also on the *Union Record* committee. He helped make the decision to end the *Call's* existence so as not to compete with the new labor daily. See also Seattle *Post-Intelligencer*, April 24, 1918.

Probably the greatest loss to the antiwar Socialists was the desertion, in December 1917, of the *Appeal to Reason*. Following Wilson's apparent adoption of the Socialist demands of "no annexations, no indemnities," the *Appeal* changed its name to the *New Appeal,* and threw its support behind the President with the declaration that Wilson had "heard the voices of humanity that are in the air."[226] Characterized by Daniel Bell as "the final blow, perhaps," in the transformation and decline of the Socialist Party,[227] the defection certainly weakened the Party and its antiwar activity. But contrary to Bell's implication, the paper was not permanently lost. Even during early 1918, when it was clearly pro-war, the *New Appeal* gave prominent space to the Tom Mooney frame-up, to Leon Trotsky's new book, *Bolsheviki and World Peace,* and to the hesitantly antiwar Socialist Congressman Meyer London.[228]

As soon as the war ended, the *Appeal* moved steadily back toward its old alliance. In November 1918, it began a campaign for amnesty for political prisoners and conscientious objectors, exposing the brutalities perpetrated against IWW's and Socialists at the Leavenworth prison. In January 1919, it ran the full text of Debs' speech to the jury at his Canton trial.[229] Finally, on March 1, 1919, the *New Appeal* changed its name back to the *Appeal to Reason,* with a special amnesty issue of which 900,000 copies were distributed. Headlining the question "Shall Gene Debs Lie in Jail While the Plutes and Profiteers Defy Public?" the editors answered by demanding from President Wilson "peace and democracy at home," as well as abroad. Next, the *Appeal* favorably reviewed John Reed's *Ten Days That Shook the World,* calling it the "truth about Russia." Finally, on May 24, 1919, the newspaper explicitly returned to Socialist ranks by initiating a campaign for Debs' nomination for President and Kate R. O'Hare's nomination for Vice President on

[226] *Appeal to Reason,* December 15, 1917.
[227] Bell, *op. cit.,* p. 313.
[228] *New Appeal,* January 26, March 23, 1918.
[229] *Ibid.,* November 16, 1918; January 4, 11, 1919.

the 1920 Socialist ticket.[230] To make matters complete, the *Appeal* also implicitly disavowed its former pro-war policy in an announcement that Louis Kopelin and E. Haldeman-Julius had bought the paper from J. A. Wayland's son. Calling attention to the recent reappearance of the paper's "old revolutionary spirit," the new owners declined to assume responsibility "for anything done in the past . . . whether in a business or editorial sense."[231]

The experience of the *Appeal*, however, appears to have been unique. Most Socialist publications had simply been forced out of business, and only a few were replaced by new ones. In Seattle, the *Daily Call* was replaced by the *International Weekly* in 1918, and in Duluth the *Labor Leader* was replaced by *Truth*, but these were exceptions to the rule.[232] By the middle of 1918, the Socialist press consisted almost entirely of periodicals published in the larger cities—those not dependent upon the mails for distribution. Newspapers such as the *New York Call*, the *Milwaukee Leader*, the *Miami Valley Socialist*, *St. Louis Labor*, the Oakland (California) *World* had held their own or increased circulation despite all the harassment they had had to endure. But the Socialist press in the West and Midwest had been decimated.

Socialist Electoral Strength, 1912-1918

If 1912 represented the high point of the Socialist movement in any area, it was in electoral strength; in that year Debs polled 6 percent of the total Presidential vote, a figure never again equalled by a Socialist candidate. At the same time, Party members held their greatest number of public offices—some 1,200

(*continued on p. 103*)

[230] March 8, 1919; May 24, 1919.

[231] May 24, 1919. The editors revealed that they had purchased the paper on April 7, 1919.

[232] The *International Weekly* published only until 1919. It was "padlocked" by the Department of Justice after it got out an issue with a headline in boxcar type: "CAPITALISM TOTTERING." The editor of paper recalls that "it was we who tottered." Letter to the author from Harvey O'Connor, Chicago, October 30, 1961.

TABLE 1

Socialist Periodicals 1912-1918[233]

y=publishing at the time
x=known to be out of business
d=daily; w=weekly; m=monthly; s=semi

State	City	Name	Founded	1913	1916	1917-18	Frequency
Alaska	Fairbanks	Alaska Socialist	1913	y	y	y	s-m
Ala.	Girard	Ala. Soc. Dem.	1914	–	y	x	w
Ariz.	Phoenix	Ariz. Soc. Bul.	?	?	y	y	w
Ark.	Clarendon	Monroe Co. Soc.	?	y	?	?	w
	Hot Springs	H. Springs Clarion	?	y	?	?	w
	Huntington	So. Worker	1901	y	y	800	m
	Jonesboro	Revolutionist	?	y	?	?	?
	Judsonia	White Co. Worker	?	y	?	?	w
	Little Rock	Pulaski Co. Soc.	?	y	?	?	?
	Pine Bluff	Jeff. Co. Agitator	?	y	?	?	w
	Rogers	People's Friend	1909	y	y	x	w
	Van Buren	Crawford Co. Star	?	y	y?	?	w
Calif.	Fresno	Abarez (Armenian)	1908	y	y	1250	w
	Llano	Colonist	1916	–	y	y	w
	Los Angeles	Cal. Soc. Dem.	1911	11,600	y	4900	w
		Western Comrade	1913	y	5200	5200	w
	Oakland	World	1905	4300	y	2500	w
	San Francisco	Vorwarts (German)	1910	y	y	y	w
Colo.	Denver	Colorado Worker	?	y	?	?	m
		World for the Workers	?	y	?	?	w
		Miners Magazine	1900	2750	2750	2750	w&m

State	City	Publication	Year	1914	1917	1918	Freq.
Conn.	New Haven	*Criterion*	1917	–	–	y	w
	Waterbury	*Weekly Worker*	1915	–	y	x	w
Idaho	Moscow	*The Palouser*	?	y	?	?	?
Ill.	Canton	*Socialist*	1913	y	x	x	w
	Chicago	*Amer. Socialist*	1914	–	y	60,000	w
		Arbeiter (German)	1876	15,000	y	15,000	d
		Christian Soc.	1904	19,000	y	18,000	w&m
		Eritassard Hayastan (Armen.)	1904	y	y	5000	bi-w
		Eye Opener	1912	y		y	m
		Int. Soc. Review	1900	42,000	26,000	25,000	m
		Parola Proletaria (Italian)	1906	3000	y	4500	w
		Proletarec (Sloven)	1904	4250	y	3100	w
		Radnicka Straza (Cr)	1908	2700	y	y	w
		Revyen (Scand)	1894	5000	y	4500	w
		Rovhost Ludu (Slovak)	1907	5500	y	9500	w
		Spraredelust (Bohem)	1905	12,000	y	11,000	w
		Svenska Soc. (Sw)	1905	3900	y	7000	w
	Granite City	*Tri-City Leader*	1911	900	y	x	w
	Moline	*Rock Is. Co. Soc.*	?	y	?	?	w
	Quincy	*Quincy Socialist*	?	y	?	?	w
	Waukegan	*Free Press*	1910	y	y	x	w
Ind.	Marion	*Econ. Intelligencer*	1913	y	x	x	w

[233] It would be almost impossible to annotate each periodical listed here, since there were many sources, and some publications had to be traced and verified through several, each of which produced a part of the information included in a particular listing. The major source was *N. W. Ayer's American Newspaper Annual and Directory* for the years 1914, 1917, and 1918. *Ayer's Annual* lists a very large proportion of all the newspapers and magazines published in the United States and gives information which includes the year of original publication, frequency of publication, circulation (where available), political affiliation, and names of editor and publisher.

State	City	Name	Founded	1913	1916	1917-18	Frequency
Iowa	Valparaiso	Social Educator	?	y	?	?	m
	Albia	Monroe Co. Leader	?	y	?	?	w
	Boone	Boone Co. Searchlight	?	y	?	?	w
	Cedar Rapids	Linn Co. Searchlight	?	y	?	?	w
	Centerville	Voice of the Toilers	?	.y	?	?	w
	Charles City	Floyd Co. Soc.	?	y	?	?	w
	Clinton	Clinton Co. Soc.	?	y	y	y	w
		Merry War	19_4(?)	—	y	y (Rep.)	w
	Council Bluffs	Council Bluffs Soc.	?	y	y	y	w
	Davenport	Scott Co. Soc.	?	—	y>	—	w
	Grinnell	Tribune	1918	y	—	y>	w
	Lyons	Clinton Co. Soc.	?	y	?	?	w
	Marshalltown	Marshall Co. Tocsin	?	y	?	?	w
	Mason City	Cerro Gordo Leader	1912	y	?	?	w
	Muscatine	Muscatine Co. Soc.	1913	y	—	—	w
	Ottumwa	Ottumwa Referendum	1912	y	y	y	w
	Perry	Dallas Co. Worker	?	y	—	—	w
	Waterloo	Vanguard	?	y	?	?	w
Kansas	Chanute	Chanute Leader	?	y	?	?	w
	Dexter	Dispatch	1905	850	y	900	w
	Girard	Appeal to Reason	1895	761,747	y	529,132	m
		Natl. Socialist	1912	35,000	y	—	m
	Iola	Iola Co-operator	1912	200	—	—	w
	Lawrence	Prog. Herald	1911	y	—	—	w
	Leavenworth	Leavenworth Soc.	?	y	—	?	w
	Newton	Harvey Co. Searchlight	?	y	?	?	w
	Pittsburg	Workers' Chronicle	?	y	y>	y>	w
	Pleasanton	Linn Co. Searchlight	1911	y	y	?	w
	Salina	Salina Co. Soc.	?	y	?	?	w

State	City	Paper	Year				Freq.
	Sedan	News and Views	?	y	?	?	w
	Topeka	Shawnee Co. Soc.	1913	y	—	—	w
	Wichita	Socialist	1910	y	—	—	w
La.	New Orleans	Rebellion	1915(?)	—	y	?	?
	Shreveport	Southern Light	1912	y	—	—	w
Maine	Portland	The Issue	1911	2100	2000	2000	m
Mass.	Boston	Hairenik (Armen.)	1889	y	y	5000	w
		New International	1917	—	—	y	w&m
		Laisve (Lith.)	1911	5000	y	y	w
	Fitchburg	Leader	1912	y	y	11,000	w
		Raivaaja (Finn.)	1905	6500	y	10,000	w
		Strahdneeks (Lett.)		6500	y	13,000	bi-w
Mich.	Ann Arbor	Call	?	y	y	—	w
	Detroit	Michigan Socialist	?	?	y	y	?
	Flint	Flashes	?	y	(Ind.)	(Ind.)	w
	Grand Rapids	The Commonwealth	1918	—	—	y	m
	Hancock	Call	?	y	—	—	w
	Holland	Tyomes (Finnish)	1903	y	y	y	d
		Prog. Worker	1911	y	y	y	w
	Kalamazoo	Billy Goat	?	y	y	—	m
		People's Paper	1911	y	—	—	w
		People	1915	—	y	y	w
	Manistee	Workers Advocate	?	y	y	—	w
	Saginaw	Socialist	?	y	y	—	w
Minn.	Badger	Herald Rustler	1896	700	y	480	w
	Bemidji	Examiner	1911	1102	—	—	w
	Crookstown	Eye Opener	1911	y	—	—	w
	Duluth	Socialisti (Finn.)	1910	y	5243	y	d
		Labor Leader	1917	y	y	y	w
	Faribault	Referendum	1899	1400	y	y	w
	Minneapolis	Forskaren (Sw.)	1893	2500	y	y	m

State	City	Name	Founded	1913	1916	1917-18	Frequency
	Two Harbors	Gaa Paa (Nor.)	1904	4500	4000	4000	w
		Minn. Socialist	1910	y	-	-	w
		New Times	1910	y	y	y	w
		Rights of Man	1897	y	-	-	w
		Socialist	1913	y	752	900	w
Mo.	Benton	Scott Co. Kicker	1902	1200	1200	1200	w
	Hyati	Critic	1912	4000	-	-	w
	Independence	Soc. Democrat	?	y	?	?	w
	Joplin	Socialist	1912	y	y	-	m
		The Question	?	y?	y??	y??	w
	Kansas City	Socialist	?	y	-	-	w
	Kennett	Justice	?	y	?	y?	w
	St. Joseph	People's Appeal	?	y	?	?	m
	St. Louis	Natl. Rip Saw	1904	150,000	150,000	150,000	m
		Melting Pot	1913	y	y	y	m
		St. Louis Labor	1900	6000	6000	6000	w
		Arbeiter Zeitung	1898	3000	3000	3000	w
Mont.	Butte	Montana Soc.	?	y	y	?	w
	Helena	Montana News	1902	4000	-	-	w
	Sheridan	Forum	1911	y	y	y	w
Neb.	Byron	Advocate	1912	y?	-	?	w
	Lincoln	Neb. Worker	1910	7000	y	11,391	m
Nev.	Ely	White Pine Worker	?	y	y?	?	?
	Fallon	Ballot Box	1911	y	-	-	w
N.J.	Camden	Camden Co. Soc.	?	y	?	?	?
		Voice of Labor	1916(?)	-	y?	y?	w
		Morris Co. Educator	?	y	?	?	?
	Dover	Issue	1911	y	2800	2800	w
	Elizabeth		?	y	2800	2800	w
	Gloucester	Gloucester Soc.	?	y	?	?	?

State	City	Publication	Year				Freq.
	Orange	*Socialist*	1911	300	–	–	w
	Paterson	*Issue*	1911	y	y	y	w
	W. Hoboken	*Soc. Review*	?	y	–	–	w
N.Y.	Buffalo	*Arbeiter Zeitung*	1886	7750	7500	7500	w
		New Age	1912	y	y	y	w
	Brooklyn	*Laisve* (Lith)	1911	y	14,850	14,850	w
	Jamestown	*Free Press*	1915	–	y	y	w
	New York	*Advance*	1917	–	–	y	w
		Call	1909	22,200	y	60,000	d
		Elore (Hung.)	1900	9250	y	23,003	w
		Intercol. Socialist	1913	y	4000	19,000	quart.
		Masses	1911	10,000	y	4500	m
		New Review	1913	y	y	17,000	w, m, bi-m
		Messenger	1917	–	y	–	m
		Novy Mir	1910	y	14,000	14,415	d
		Obrana (Bohem)	1910	y	y	y	w
		The Class Struggle	1917	–	–	y	bi-m, quart.
		The Hotel Worker	1917	–	–	y	m
		The Fur Worker	1916	–	–	y	w
		Jewish Daily Forward	1897	142,000	130,000	198,000	d
		Pilot	1911	y	y	–	w
		Young Soc. Mag.	1908	y	y	y	m
		Zukunft	1892	69,000	69,000	69,000	m
	Schenectady	*Citizen*	1910	5000	5000	5000	w
	Utica	*Centr. N.Y. Soc.*	1911	925	–	–	w
N.D.	Devils Lake	*N.D. Call*	1911	y	y	–	w
	Milnor	*Sargent Co. Teller*	1883	750	750	(Rep.)	w
	Minot	*Iconoclast*	1912	y	y	–	w
Ohio	Akron	*Summit Co. Soc.*	1911	y	y	y	w
	Cleveland	*Citizen*	1891	y	12,000	13,000	w
		Socialist News	1911	y	1500	3000	w
	Columbus	*Socialist*	1910	y	–	–	w

State	City	Name	Founded	1913	1916	1917-18	Frequency
	Conneaut	Ashtabula Co. Advance	1913	y	(Dem.)	–	w
	Dayton	Miami Valley Soc.	1912	y	2500	2400	w
	Hamilton	Searchlight (Soc.)	1910	y	y	y	w
	Lorain	Lor. Co. Pol. Outlook	1912	y	–	–	w
	St. Marys	Socialist	1910	y	–	–	w
	Zanesville	Socialist	1911	y	–	–	w
Okla.	Alva	Constructive Soc.	1910	y	–	–	w
	Boswell	Submarine	1912	y	–	–	w
	Carter	Beckman Co. Advoc.	1913	y	y	y	w
	Goltry	News (Eagle)	1901	700	y	(Ind.)	w
	Hobart	Woodrow's Monthly	1915	–	y	–	m
	LaVerne	Beacon Light	1912	(Prog.)	y	y	w
	May	Record	1911	y	1400	y	w
	McAlester	Pitts. Co. Hornet	1911	y	–	–	w
	Okemah	Sledge Hammer	1912	y	–	–	w
	Okla. City	Social Democrat	1912	y	–	–	w
	Rosston	Review	1915	–	y	(Ind.)	w
	Shattuck	Ellis Co. Socialist	1914	–	y	y	w
	Snyder	Otter Valley Soc.	1914	(Loc.)	y	y	w
	Strong City	Herald	1912	y	y	600	w
	Sugden	Clarion	1911	2727	–	–	w
	Sulphur	New Century	1911	–	y	y	w
	Taloga	Times	1915	y	y	y	w
	Tishomingo	News	1913	y	y	y	w
	Okla. City	Oklahoma Leader	1914	–	y	y	w
Oreg.	Astoria	Oregon Ballet	1912	y	–	–	w
	Milwaukee	Toveri (Finnish)	1907	4548	4000	4000	d
	Portland	Alliance	1912	2000	–	–	s-m
	Portland	Voice of the People	?	y	y	y	w
Penna.	Charleroi	Union de Travailleurs	1901	1500	1500	–	w

State	City	Title	Year				
	Erie	*Truth*	1911	y	y	y	w
	Lancaster	*Lanc. Co. Socialist*	1911	y	–	–	w
	New Castle	*Free Press*	1908	y	–	–	w
	Oil City	*Venango Co. Soc.*	1910	y	2000	y	w
	Philadelphia	*People's Press*	1915	–	2000	2000	w
		Socialist	1912	46,444	–	–	m
	Pittsburgh	*Gornik Polski*	1912	y	y	y	w
		Justice	1911	y	y	–	w
	Pottstown	*Social Educator*	1911	y	y	y	w
	Rochester	*Saturday Journal*	1911	y	y	y	w
	Reading	*Labor Advocate*	1900	1500	1500	1500	w
	Smitmill	*Pick and Plow*	1917(?)	–	–	y	w?
S. D.	Mitchell	*Co-Op Commonwealth*	1914	–	y	y	m
	Sisseton	*Co-Op Commonwealth*	1914	–	350	500	m
	Sturgis	*Call to Action*	1913	(Prog.)	y	y	s-m
Tenn.	Memphis	*Social Democrat*	1910	y	y	y	w
Texas	Anson	*Frying Pan*	1914	–	y	y	w
	Corpus Christi	*Socialist*	?	y	y?	?	w
	Corsicana	*Plain Dealer*	?	y	?	?	w
	Dallas	*The Laborer*	1904	515	1350	–	w
	Halletsville	*Rebel*	1911	26,145	25,000	25,000	w
	Hillsboro	*Hill Co. Worker*	?	y	?	?	w
	Longview	*Gregg Co. Red Ball*	?	y	?	?	w
	Marshall	*Harrison Co. Soc.*	?	y	?	?	w
	Mt. Pleasant	*Eye Opener*	?	y	?	?	w
	San Antonio	*Amigo del Pueblo*	1908	y	y?	?	w
	Taylor	*Searchlight*	?	y	y?	–	w
	Teague	*Freestone Co. Truth*	?	y	?	?	w
	Temple	*Bell Co. Socialist*	?	y	?	?	w
	Terrell	*Kaufman Co. Soc.*	?	y	?	?	w
	Texarkana	*Texarkana Soc.*	?	y	?	?	m
	Thornton	*Limestone Co. News*	?	y	?	?	w

State	City	Name	Founded	1913	1916	1917-18	Frequency
Utah	Tyler	Common Sense	?	y	?	?	w
	Myton	Dawn	1912	y	5000	5000	m
	Salt Lake City	Inter. Mt. Worker	1912	y	y	y	w
Vt.	Barre	Quarry Workers Journ.	1904	4500	4500	4500	m
Va.	Brookneal	Union Star	1906	y	3000	3147	w
Wash.	Aberdeen	New Era	?	y	?	?	?
	Centralia	Lewis Co. Clarion	1912	y	?	?	?
	Everett	No. West Worker	1911	4500	2400	2400	w
	Kelso	Socialist News	1911	y	y	y	w
	N. Yakima	No. West Forum	1905	y	—	—	w
	Seattle	Call	1917	—	—	y	d
		Herald	1912	y?	5600	6000	w
		Internatl. Weekly	1918	—	?	y	w
		World	1916	—	y?	y	w
		Truth	1912	y	y?	y?	?
	Tacoma	Labor Argus	1905	y	—	—	w
W. Va.	Charleston	W. Va. Leader	?	y	?	?	?
	Clarksburg	Soc. & Labor Star	?	y	?	?	?
	Huntington	Socialist	1912	y	—	—	w
	Parkersburg	Majority	1907	7000	7000	7000	w
	Wheeling	Leader	1911	35,000	37,201	y	d
Wisc.	Milwaukee	Leader	1911	—	y	y	w&m
		Wisc. Comrade	1914	—	12,131	y	d
	Superior	Tyomes (Finnish)	1903	y	y	y	s-w
	Two Rivers	Reporter	1905	y	y	y	

in 340 municipalities from coast to coast, among them 79 mayors in 24 states.[234] In 1916, the Socialist Presidential vote declined from 897,000 to 590,000, and the percentage dropped even more sharply. Similarly, after 1912, the number of Socialists elected to local office decreased progressively. The number of Socialist mayors,[235] for example, dropped from 74 elected in 1911 to 32 in 1913, 22 in 1915, and 18 in 1917. The Presidential figure is most often cited as proof that the history of the party after 1912 is that of a "trailing penumbra."

Social reforms and a more sophisticated approach to conservative trade union leadership did operate to circumscribe Socialist influence during Wilson's first administration. Many Party leaders anticipated a continued rise in Party strength; at the 1912 convention, Hillquit spoke of a Party of 200,000 members in the near future. Others viewed the 1912 vote as a rock-bottom Socialist core from which the Progressive Party had already scraped the decayed organic matter.[236] Yet some also understood that more reforms were coming, and that these would include government regulation of industry. The *International Socialist Review* commented that "the clearest thinkers among the capitalists and their politicians" realized that if American manufacturers were "to compete with Germany in the world market," they must have "the same sort of help from the government in conserving the labor supply which the German employers get." In this the editors found "no ground for anxiety on the part of Socialists," explaining that the " 'Progressive' reforms that are coming will be, so far as they go, a good thing for 'all the people.' " Child labor laws and other progres-

---

[234] *National Municipal Review,* I (1912), 492 ff.; Grady McWhiney, "The Socialist Vote in Louisiana, 1912 (unpublished Master's Thesis, Louisiana State University, 1951), p. 6; *International Socialist Review* XIII, 12 (June 1913), 854.
[235] This term is used here to include all top municipal officers; where there were no mayors, for example, presidents of village boards, city commissioners, chairmen.
[236] "Editorial," *International Socialist Review,* XIII, 7 (January 1913), 561.

sive reforms, they concluded, were good for both capitalist and labor.[237]

The left wingers on the *International Socialist Review* understood this better than Hillquit. In an exchange of letters with Ralph Easley of the National Civic Federation over the Federation's sponsorship of workmen's compensation acts, Hillquit had charged that the game played by the businessmen's organization was "the shrewdest yet devised by the employers of any country." As Hillquit observed, the Federation understood that to ignore the movement would be to "face the danger that this agitation may give rise to a powerful labor movement along Socialist lines." But he would not admit that the Federation's activity in behalf of compensation had improved matters. Instead he accused it of seeking "to divert the movement of the workers into the shallow channels" of reform. In reply, Easley insisted that the workers had a right to better conditions in the present, and read Hillquit (who was open to the charge) to mean that improvement could only come after the Socialists had captured power.[238] Hillquit did not see, or would not admit, that the Federation could distinguish "between proposals and direct undertakings" which were "socialistic and anarchistic in principle," and those which Socialists "would naturally favor, although not necessarily in conflict with the underlying principles of the existing industrial order."[239]

The *International Socialist Review* not only admitted this but went further to observe that the "next step" would be for the businessman "to act on the discovery that he can carry on cer-

[237] "Editorial," *ibid.*, XIII, 6 (December 1912), 495. The *Review* commented further, "All Socialists, even opportunists, agree that revolution, the overthrow of the capitalist system, should be our ultimate aim. The *Review*, on the other hand, is willing to concede that the enactment of some reforms may be on the whole advantageous to the working class . . ."

[238] Morris Hillquit and Ralph Easley, *Socialism and the National Civic Federation* (n.p. 1911).

[239] Memorandum Concerning the Policy to be Pursued by the Department of Industrial Economics of the National Civic Federation, Box 84, NCF papers [1914?]

tain portions of the productive process more efficiently through *his* government than through private corporations." "Some muddleheads," the *Review* continued, "think that will be Socialism, but the capitalist knows better." The right of "wageworkers to organize and to control the conditions under which they work— that is the issue that must be fought out between the two great opposing classes."[240]

The reforms that came during Wilson's first term were impressive. In 1913, the Sixteenth and Eighteenth amendments, authorizing the income tax and providing for the direct election of senators, were finally adopted, and labor gained representation in the Cabinet with the appointment of William B. Wilson as the first Secretary of Labor. In 1914, Congress adopted the Federal Trade Commission Act, for which the National Civic Federation had agitated since 1907, and the Clayton Act, hailed by Gompers as "labor's Magna Charta." Then in 1915, the La Follette Seaman's Act, sponsored by the International Seaman's Union, became law. Finally, in 1916, the Federal Farm Loan Act and the Child Labor Law were passed. These reforms entailed no substantial change in the lives of most workers, but their cumulative impact was sufficient to halt the steady growth which the Socialist Party had enjoyed during the previous four years.

In 1916, even such leading Socialists as A. M. Simons and Gustavus Myers voted for Wilson.[241] Casting his first Presidential ballot in 1916, John Reed expressed the classical dilemma of minority party supporters: whether to support the party in whose principles they believe or to use their ballots to achieve immediate practical results. Reed decided he would vote for Wilson "as considerably the lesser of two evils," revealing at the same time his superficial understanding of the President by

[240] "Editorial," *International Socialist Review*, XIII, 6 (December 1912), 495.
[241] Shannon, *op. cit.*, p. 92.

commenting that "the only real principles he has (few enough) are on our side."[242]

However, Debs' refusal to run for re-election in 1916 was also instrumental in the decline of the Socialist vote. Ill, and desiring to give a younger man the opportunity, Debs stepped aside, and for the first time since the organization of the Socialist Party of America, was not the Party standard bearer. In his place the Socialists nominated Allan L. Benson, a journalist, in a Party referendum. Compared to Debs, Benson was not only unknown, even within Party ranks, but he campaigned poorly and ran badly. Debs had generally run well ahead of the ticket; Benson trailed his running mates in almost every state.[243]

Early in the campaign the Socialists had optimistically looked forward to receiving two million votes for their Presidential candidate and to electing ten congressmen and a United States senator.[244] Before election day, however, there were many indications that Benson would fall well short of this mark, although, at the same time, the Party's popularity did not appear to have diminished substantially, if at all, since 1912. The *Literary Digest*, for example, in a pre-election forecast considerably more

[242] John Reed to the National Executive Committee, New York, October 13, 1916, SPC, Duke.

[243] On Benson's campaign see Shannon, *op. cit.*, p. 91. Benson ran 50% behind the congressional vote in Oregon. In Nevada the Socialist candidate for the Senate ran ahead of him by 300%, while in North Dakota Benson ran 40% behind the Socialist senatorial vote, 35% behind in Massachusetts, 33% behind in New York, 25% behind in New Jersey, and 5% behind in Pennsylvania. In Minnesota, Benson ran 30% behind the gubernatorial candidate, and ran 10% behind in Wisconsin. In Tennessee he ran 50% behind the Socialist candidate for railroad commissioner. Illinois seemed to be a major exception to this trend, as Benson ran 9,000 votes ahead of the Socialist candidate for governor. But even here he ran behind; for in the Presidential election in Illinois women voted, whereas they did not have a vote for governor. Actually, Benson polled 2.8% of the Presidential vote in Illinois, while the Socialist candidate for governor polled 4.35%. Election statistics compiled from various Blue Books, reports of secretaries of state, official registers, legislative manuals, etc.

[244] Bakersfield (California) *United Labor Journal*, October 21, 1916. The Party expected to elect congressmen in New York, Oklahoma, Wisconsin, Nevada, and Indiana, where Debs was a candidate for the House. The senator was expected in Nevada.

accurate than its attempt two decades later, predicted that the labor vote would go heavily for Wilson.[245] At the same time, the *Digest* found "a widening undercurrent of strength" for the Socialists, and suggested that "on some occasions" Wilson was preferred "only because in the way of actual accomplishments he can do more for the Socialists than Mr. Hughes."[246] In a later report on three thousand local communities, the *Digest* predicted that while Benson would carry only forty-seven, their informants "not infrequently noted" that the local Socialist vote would be stronger than it had been in 1912.[247]

In fact, although they failed to achieve their goals, Socialists did fare better in legislative and local elections in 1916 than they had in 1912. The Party elected Meyer London to Congress in 1916, whereas no congressman had been elected in 1912.[248] They also came closer to electing a United States senator in 1916 than ever before, when Grant A. Miller polled 30 percent of the vote for that office in Nevada.[249] In elections to the various state legislatures, the Party also surpassed its record of 1912, electing twenty-nine legislators compared to twenty, four years before.[250] Fusion against them, not a decline in their voting strength, led to some Socialist defeats in 1916. In California, both Socialist legislators lost to fusion candidates, despite an increase in their vote.[251]

In municipal elections the Socialist vote increased in 1916

---

[245] "A Presidential Straw Vote of Union Labor," *Literary Digest*, LIII, 15 (October 7, 1916), 871 ff. The pollsters asked 457 labor leaders how they believed their members would vote; 332 believed the majority of their membership would vote for Wilson, 47 thought theirs would vote for Benson, and 43 that theirs would vote for Hughes.

[246] *Ibid.*, p. 872.

[247] "Political Reports from 3000 Communities," *Literary Digest*, XIII, 18 (October 28, 1916).

[248] Victor Berger had been elected in 1910, but lost to fusion in 1912. London was elected for the first time in 1914. He was re-elected in 1916, and again in 1920.

[249] Miller lost to Key Pittman by 9,507 to 12,765. *Biennial Report of the Secretary of State of Nevada—1915-1916*, p. 40.

[250] The high was reached in 1914, when 33 Socialists were elected to legislatures in 14 states. See Table 3, p. 118.

[251] Oakland, California, *The World*, November 17, 24, 1916.

in several major cities. Most prominent were Minneapolis and Milwaukee, both of which elected Socialist mayors by majority votes. The victory in Milwaukee was most significant because Emil Seidel, elected mayor in a three-way race in 1910, had been unable to overcome fusion in 1912 and 1914. In 1916, Daniel Hoan finally succeeded in winning a majority and began his long tenure as mayor of the city.[252]

The decline in the number of Socialist municipal office holders after 1911 had several causes. In part, it was a result of the Party's earlier emphasis on the pressing need for reform in American cities and towns. Even Woodrow Wilson had commented on this aspect of Socialist popularity. In *The New Freedom,* Wilson inquired of his readers if they had "noticed the growth of socialistic sentiment in the smaller towns." Not many months before, Wilson explained, he had stopped in a small town in Nebraska and met the mayor, who was a Socialist. "What does this mean?" Wilson asked. "Does this mean that this town is socialistic?" "No Sir," replied the mayor; "I have not deceived myself; the vote by which I was elected was about 20 percent socialistic and 80 percent protest."[253]

After 1911 the old parties showed an increasing willingness to adopt many of the reforms advocated by the Socialists, who were severely limited in what they could do when in control of a municipality. They could not bring socialism to one city while the rest of the country remained capitalist. Furthermore, even if charter restrictions permitted (which they rarely did), Socialists could not put through reforms which would seriously impinge upon business interests, lest industry be driven from their city. In practice, a Socialist administration could press for public ownership of utilities and transportation facilities; increase social, recreational, and cultural services; and adopt a friendly attitude toward unions, especially in time of strikes.

[252] *Wisconsin Comrade,* III, 1 (March 1916), 1. Hoan polled 33,863 to 32,106 for his opponent.
[253] Woodrow Wilson, *The New Freedom* (New York, 1913), p. 26.

But some or all of these things could be done, and at times were done, by non-Socialist reformers such as Tom Johnson and Newton D. Baker in Cleveland, Samuel Jones in Toledo, and John Peuroy Mitchel in New York, and by business groups under city manager charters.

On a municipal level, Socialist administrations often met with the approval, implicit if not explicit, of the larger and more sophisticated business interests. This was brought home in dramatic fashion to David I. Nelke, editor of the anti-Socialist Catholic magazine, *The Common Cause*, when he went to see Charles A. Coffin, president of the General Electric Company, in February 1912. Nelke had gone to Coffin to ask for support for his anti-Socialist venture at the suggestion of Ralph Easley. After Nelke had waited for "some little time," Coffin rushed into the room, "evidently very much excited," and without even asking Nelke to be seated, "he began roaring about [the] magazine." Coffin attacked the statements against socialism it had made, and said that as far as he was concerned "Dr. Lunn was the best man that had ever been Mayor of Schenectady," and that he (Coffin) was "going to work hand in glove with him." Nelke "was unable to get in a word in any way whatsoever," and Coffin "kept edging toward the door, evidently with the desire of leaving." At the door, Coffin turned to Nelke and stated that he was "simply tearing down socialism and offered nothing in the way of reforms."[254]

The ability of some progressive administrations to match Socialist demands, or the failure of municipal Socialist platforms to go beyond reform, gave rise to many criticisms of the leadership from within the Party. The Left took the lead in these attacks, but it was not alone. Some complained that the old parties were "only too anxious to copy this weak stuff."[255] Walter Lippmann, on his first job as secretary to Mayor Lunn, wrote

[254] David I. Nelke to Ralph Easley, New York, February 15, 1912, NCF papers.
[255] John J. Scholtes to Carl D. Thompson, Alliance, Ohio, November 6, 1913, SPC, Duke.

Carl D. Thompson suggesting that the Socialists include in their platforms only those planks which the progressives could not steal. He was highly critical of the administrations both in Milwaukee and in Schenectady for failing to follow this path, and was perturbed by the reluctance of the Socialists in Schenectady to raise the tax rate and thereby "expropriate private capital for social use."[256]

Unfortunately, neither Lippmann nor any of the other critics offered real alternatives. Nor were their critiques well directed, for, as Berger had pointed out, with each reform won it was the responsibility of the Socialists to go on to the next demand. Only thus could the Party retain its popular following while it moved on toward socialism. In fact, in local elections, left wingers gave implicit support to this approach and espoused programs indistinguishable from those of the Right. In 1912, for example, the Cleveland left winger Charles E. Ruthenberg admitted that "it was on municipal reform issues that most of the Ohio victories were won."[257] When appealing for votes on a local level, both Left and Right pointed to the miserable conditions created by capitalist government, and both promised, if elected, to solve their city's most pressing problems.

Debs also looked with mixed feelings on the early municipal victories, fearing that the Party would attract reform elements it could not assimilate. He believed that Socialists should seek only to register the "actual vote of Socialism," and criticized members who regarded "vote-getting as of supreme importance." To Debs, socialist propaganda was not "bait for votes" but a means of education, and the only meaningful election victories were those which would occur when the workers developed a solid socialist consciousness.[258]

[256] Walter Lippmann to Carl D. Thompson, n.p., October 29, 1913, *ibid.*
[257] *New York Call,* July 30, 1912, quoted in Theodore Draper, *The Roots of American Communism* (New York, 1957), p. 44.
[258] *Socialist Review,* XI, 7 (January 1911), 413.

In this view of political action, Debs was further from Haywood and the IWW than were Berger and Hillquit. Debs tended to believe only in the educational value of the ballot, while Haywood believed it had only practical value. Berger, on the other hand, saw both aspects, believing that election campaigns provided the dual opportunity to conduct mass socialist education, and to win the chance to demonstrate in practical terms the civilizing values for which the Socialists stood.

Eventually, even the right wingers came to share Debs' fears. In 1915, four years after Debs had warned of false victories, Oscar Ameringer issued a similar injunction. Observing that in many cities Socialists had disguised themselves as reformers, "sneaked into the camp of the enemy and yelled 'victoria,'" Ameringer went on to relate that when the foe "woke up," he "kicked us out of camp." The lesson to learn, Ameringer stated, was that the "revolution in the economic world must be reflected in the brains of the workers." Agreeing with Debs, he concluded that "every campaign must be a campaign of education first," since power without mass consciousness "is weakness."[259]

This attitude on the part of Socialists of all tendencies led Party members to value the number of votes received above the election of officials, and even to look upon fusion against them as a positive blessing which allegedly placed the issue of capitalism versus socialism squarely before the voters. Thus, when the Socialists were defeated for re-election in Milwaukee in 1912, they claimed a victory because in a "straight vote" against a combined capitalist enemy they had increased their percentage.[260] Nor, if one can project oneself back into the spirit of those years, does the explanation appear to have been concocted entirely of sour grapes.

But if Debs' position had no ideological foundation at variance with that of his comrades to the right, there was a differ-

---

[259] Oscar Ameringer, "Go Easy," *Wisconsin Comrade*, II, 3 (May 1915).
[260] *Social Democratic Herald*, April 13, 1912, cited in Kipnis, *op. cit.*, p. 361.

ence of mood, a greater degree of alienation, which Debs shared with many left wingers in the Party. This hostility to their society reflected itself in an attitude which made the idea of Socialists holding public office under capitalism almost unbearable, and which caused many to view any practical activity of elected Socialists with extreme suspicion. In many places Socialists were expelled or hounded to the point of resigning from the Party simply because they had performed their normal duties. In Ashtabula, Ohio, for example, W. E. Boynton, Socialist president of the city council, resigned from the Party after he had been attacked by the "reds" in his local for voting in favor of a commission charter which included proportional representation, and was, therefore, fully in accord with Party policy.[261] Similarly, in Duluth, Minnesota, Socialist State Senator Richard Jones was expelled from his local, dominated by an IWW-oriented Finnish branch, apparently only because he managed to get himself elected.[262] In Pittsburg, Kansas, two Socialists were brought up on charges of diluting Socialist principles in the "quest for mere election" because they accepted Trades and Labor Council support as well as Socialist endorsement.[263] Finally, in Los Angeles, the Socialist councilman was forced to resign from the Party for voting for a Democrat for council president, there being no Socialist member other than himself.[264]

Many Socialist officials were expelled once they reached office, and it appears that most of them were victims of the alien-

[261] W. E. Boynton to Carl D. Thompson, Ashtabula, September 12, 1913, SPC, Duke. Ashtabula was the first American city to adopt proportional representation. See *Proportional Representation Review*, Third Series (October 1915), p. 3. According to Boynton, other Socialist councilmen were expelled from the Party for voting dry.
[262] Richard Jones to Carl D. Thompson, Duluth, September 29, November 15, 1914, SPC, Duke.
[263] Report of Clarence A. Lewis to the State Executive Committee of Kansas, Pittsburg, Kansas, April 16, 1913, SPC, Duke.
[264] G. W. Downing to Carl D. Thompson, Los Angeles, June 7, 1915, SPC, Duke.

ation of their comrades, rather than of their own misdeeds. This, of course, was not always the case. Some were expelled for violating Socialist principles—e.g., H. K. Davis, a Socialist state assemblyman in Nevada, who voted against woman suffrage.[265] Others were expelled for more practical reasons, as in Ashtabula, where a councilman voted "dry" when the local was "wet"; or as in the case of school board members in Edmonds, Washington, who refused to appoint a Socialist as principal of the local high school.[266] On the whole, however, left wing Party members were quick to expel their elected comrades for reasons that now appear quite flimsy.[267]

While the Party debated the correct approach toward municipal elections, municipal reformers came to life after 1911. Of national scope and highly successful, the commission and manager movements swept the country after the adoption of commission government by Des Moines, Iowa, in 1907, and the victory of a manager charter in Dayton, Ohio in 1912. Designed to rationalize city government and to enable municipalities to meet some of their more pressing commercial and social needs, these plans were the adaptation, under the guiding hands of local chambers of commerce, of corporate methods to city government.[268] For the first time, in hundreds of cities throughout the United States, organized business threw its support behind civic reformers, adopted programs that often differed little from

[265] Justus E. Taylor to Carl D. Thompson, n.p., February 11, 1913, SPC, Duke.
[266] W.E. Boynton to Carl D. Thompson, *loc. cit.*; n.s. to Carl D. Thompson, Edmonds, Washington, July 9, 1912, SPC, Duke.
[267] By 1913, Socialist state legislators had been expelled in North Dakota and Nevada; mayors in Sheboygan, Wisconsin, Two Harbors, Minnesota, Lima, Canton and Lorraine, Ohio; and aldermen in Ashtabula, Reno, Devil's Lake, North Dakota, Brainerd, Minnesota, Chicago, and Dayton. Ralph Korngold to Carl D. Thompson, Spring Lake, Michigan, May 10, 1913; and *passim*, SPC, Duke.
[268] For a full discussion of this movement see James Weinstein, "Organized Business and the Commission and Manager Movements," *Journal of Southern History*, XXVIII, 2 (May 1962), 166 ff.

those of the Socialists on municipal issues, and carried the day for reform.

Under these new charters, the likelihood of Socialists gaining office was lessened both by the strength of the new coalition of business and traditional reform groups, and by the mechanics of commission and manager government. The number of elected city officials was sharply reduced, and ward representation was replaced by a commission, usually of five, elected on a city-wide vote. This often meant the elimination of minority representation, since minorities, racial, national, and political, were usually concentrated in specific wards. In Dayton, for example, the Socialists had polled 25 percent of the vote in 1911 and elected two councilmen and three assessors, but after the adoption of the manager charter, they elected no one, although their vote rose to 35 percent in 1913 and to 44 percent in 1917. The "nonpartisan" ballot, a standard feature of commission and manager charters, acted against the Socialists in the same manner as fusion. Under this feature of the plans only two sets of candidates competed in the final election; where the Socialists had formerly been able to win with slightly more than one-third of the vote, they now needed an absolute majority.

In cities without commission or manager charters, direct fusion was commonly used to prevent reelection of Socialists. Here, also, the Socialist vote often increased while the number of elected officials declined. In 1915, for example, in the face of an increase in their vote in each case, Socialist administrations lost to fusion of Republicans and Democrats in Coshocton, Hamilton, and Martin's Ferry, Ohio.[269]

Over-all, Socialist electoral strength varied unevenly from 1911 to 1917. The Presidential vote dropped sharply in 1916

[269] *Cleveland Citizen,* December 4, 1915. The same happened in St. Mary's, Ohio, in 1913 (*St. Louis Labor,* November 8, 1913); and in Granite City, Illinois, in 1915 (Marshall E. Kirkpatrick to Carl D. Thompson, Granite City, April 29, 1915, SPC, Duke); and, as has been noted above, in Milwaukee in 1912 and 1914.

(although it made a comeback in 1920 when Debs polled 923,-000 votes from his cell in Atlanta penitentiary).[270] In legislative elections the Party reached its high point in 1914, yet the decline through 1918 was slight. In 1918, for example, thirty-two Socialist state legislators were elected, compared to twenty in 1912, thirty-three in 1914, and twenty-nine in 1916. There was, however, a reduction after 1914 in the number of states electing Socialist legislators, from fourteen in 1914, to nine in 1916, to four in 1918. Finally, in municipal elections, 1911 and 1917 were high points, although there was a change in the pattern of the vote in these years. In 1911, Socialist strength was greatest in many semirural towns and small cities (see Table 2), whereas, as we shall see, the Socialist vote in 1917 increased principally in the larger cities of the industrialized East and Midwest.

What emerges is a patchwork pattern which does not lend itself to generalizations. The period of more or less steady growth that characterized the Party in its first dozen years obviously came to an end at least by 1914. Yet the years after 1912 did not constitute a period of break-up and decline as most historians have asserted.

After the low Socialist vote in 1916, the *Nation*, recognizing the specific circumstances, commented that "the future of the Socialist Party should not be predicated from its showing at the last election."[271] Only a few months later the United States entered the war, and soon after, the world entered a new era of revolution. Caught up in this stormy course, the Socialist Party was to emerge battered and torn. But during the war, the Party made a rapid comeback at the polls, as the *Nation* had prophesied.

[270] Debs' vote in 1920 has been looked on traditionally as purely a personal tribute to the aging warrior, but, as we shall see, it was not only that.

[271] *Nation*, January 18, 1917, pp. 65-66.

TABLE 2

Cities and Towns Electing Socialist Mayors or Other Major
Municipal Officers, 1911-1920

State	City	State	City
	1911 (74)	Ohio	Amsterdam
Arkansas	Winslow		Ashtabula
California	Berkeley		Barnhill
	Watts		Conneaut
Colorado	Nederland		Fostoria
	Victor		Lima
Idaho	Coeur d'Alene		Linden Heights
Illinois	Davis		Lorain
	Dorrisville		Martin's Ferry
	Grafton		Mineral City
	Granite City		Mineral Ridge
	O'Fallon		Mount Vernon
	Thayer		Osnaburg
Iowa	Madrid		St. Marys
Kansas	Arma		Salem
	Curransville		Sugar Grove
	Girard		Toronto
Michigan	Flint	Oklahoma	Antlers
	Greenville	Oregon	Coquille
	Kalamazoo	Pennsylvania	Broad Top
	South Frankfort		Township
	Wilson		Hazeldell
Minnesota	Crookstown		New Castle
	LaPorte		North Versailles
	Pillager		Roulette
	St. Hillaire		Wheaton
	Ten Strike	Utah	Cedar City
	Two Harbors		Eureka
Missouri	Buffalo		Mammoth
	Cardwell		Murray
	Gibson		Stockton
	Minden Mines	Washington	Edmonds
Montana	Butte		Tukwila
Nebraska	Beatrice	West Virginia	Star City
	Red Cloud	Wisconsin	Manitowoc
	Wymore		Milwaukee (1910)
New Jersey	Rockaway		West Salem
New York	Schenectady		**1912 (8)**
North Dakota	Deslacs	California	Daly City
		Florida	Gulfport
		Louisiana	Winnfield

116

State	City	State	City
New Jersey	Haledon	New Jersey	Haledon
West Virginia	Adamston	West Virginia	Star City
	Miami	Wisconsin	Manitowoc
	Star City		
Wisconsin	Manitowoc		

1915 (22)

State	City
Alabama	Birmingham (Commissioner)

1913 (32)

State	City	State	City
Arkansas	Chant	California	Eureka
	Hartford	Illinois	Canton
Colorado	Buena Vista		Eagle River
	Edgewater		Jerseyville
	Grand Junction		Lincoln
	Lafayette		Phelps
	Longmont		Riverton
Connecticut	Naugatuck		Torrino
Illinois	Canton	Indiana	Hymeria
	Granite City		Clinton
Michigan	Harbor Springs	Michigan	Gustin
Missouri	Liberal	Minnesota	Cloquet
Minnesota	Brainerd	New York	Schenectady
	Crookstown	Ohio	Conneaut
	Eagle Bend		Krebs
Montana	Butte		Cleveland
New Jersey	Haledon	Pennsylvania	Pitcairn
North Dakota	Minot (1 Commissioner)		Williamsport (Commissioner)
	Rugby	Virginia	Brookneal
Ohio	Canal Dover	West Virginia	Star City
	Conneaut	Wisconsin	Manitowoc
	Coshocton		
	Hamilton		

1916 (6)

State	City

	Martins Ferry	Michigan	Traverse City
	Shelby	Minnesota	Minneapolis
	Talent	New Jersey	Haledon
South Dakota	Sisseton	Vermont	Barre
Washington	Burlington	Wisconsin	Milwaukee
	Hilyard		West Allis
West Virginia	Hendricks		
	Star City		
Wisconsin	Manitowoc		

1917 (18)

State	City
Illinois	Buckner

1914 (5)

State	City	State	City
			Granite City
			Sylvis
Florida	Lakeworth	Indiana	Elwood
Montana	Missoula (2 Commissioners)		Gas City
		Kansas	Frontenac
			Hillsboro

State	City	State	City
Minnesota	Duluth (Commissioner) Dawson	Wisconsin	Milwaukee

1919 (5)

State	City	State	City
Ohio	Byesville Jenera Piqua	New York	Buffalo (High vote for Councilman-at-Large) Lackawanna
Pennsylvania	Garrett McKeesport (Controller)	Ohio	Byesville Massillon
	Pitcairn Union City	Wisconsin	Sheyboygan (assessor, municipal judge)
Utah	Eureka		
Washington	Camas		

1920 (2)

1918 (2)

State	City	State	City
Illinois	Mascoutah	Iowa	Davenport
		Wisconsin	Milwaukee

TABLE 3

Socialist State Legislators, 1910-1920

State	1910/11	1912/13	1914/15	1916/17	1918/19	1920/21
California	1	1	2			
Idaho			1			
Illinois		3	2			
Kansas		3	1	2		
Massachusetts		1	1	1	1	
Minnesota	1	1	3	2	4	2
Montana		1	2			
Nevada		2	2			
New Mexico			1			
New York	0/1		0/1	2/10	3/5	5
North Dakota	1					
Oklahoma			6	1		
Pennsylvania	1		1	1		
Rhode Island	0/1					
Utah			1	1		
Vermont				1		
Washington		1				
Wisconsin	13	7	9	10	22	10
TOTALS	19	20	33	29	32	17

118

3 THE SOCIALISTS AND THE WAR
1914-1918

When war came to Europe in 1914, the majority of Socialists in almost every country turned their backs on the positions adopted at the Stuttgart and Copenhagen congresses of the Second International in 1907 and 1910, and supported their governments at war.[1] This reversion to nationalism disrupted the Second International and created a crisis in the internal life of the European parties. In the United States, the failure of European socialism to oppose the war led to considerable disillusionment.[2] Unlike the Europeans, however, the vast majority of American Socialists opposed the war both before and after the United States became a belligerent. The American equivalents of Scheidemann, Ebert, Vandervelde, Hyndman, and Guesde were not the top Party leaders, as in Europe, but a group of leading Socialist intellectuals who failed to sway much of the membership to a pro-war position: men such as J. G. Phelps Stokes, William English Walling, W. J. Ghent, A. M. Simons, Charles Edward Russell, Winfield Gaylord, John Spargo, and Upton Sinclair.

[1] The Italian Socialists opposed the war and are credited with preventing Italy from entering on the side of the Central Powers in 1914. See Merle Fainsod, *International Socialism and the World War* (Cambridge, 1935), pp. 36-37. The parliamentary Socialists in Russia and Bulgaria also opposed the war and voted against war credits.
[2] See, for example, M.E.M. (Mary E. Marcy), "Socialist Unpreparedness in Germany," *International Socialist Review,* XV, 4 (October 1914), 245, quoted in Shannon, *op. cit.,* pp. 82-83.

The initial reaction of the American Socialists to the outbreak of war in Europe was one of shock and disbelief, followed by great confusion and a tendency to excuse the majority Socialists of Germany and the Allied Powers for their support of the war. In August 1914, the *New York Call* admitted that the German Socialists had "failed," but stated that their European comrades had "done their best" in a confused situation. In the minds of the German Socialists, the *Call* explained, support of German imperialism and militarism was a lesser evil than invasion by reactionary Russia.[3] This rationale was reiterated by Morris Hillquit: The Socialists of Austria and Germany had had no opportunity for mutual consultation, but had "spontaneously" supported their governments, acting on impulse "which broke through with elemental force."[4] Later, Hillquit extended his defense to include the actions of Socialists on both sides, adding that the international Socialist movement had actually suffered nothing "spiritually or morally" from the conduct of Socialists in the war.[5]

Hillquit's claim was an attempt, typical of many Party leaders in the United States, to evade the issues raised by the action of the European parties. In fact, the American Party suffered both a loss of prestige with the general public and considerable demoralization within its own ranks. Evasion only intensified this, and Party membership dropped sharply in the first six months of 1915. During these months following the beginning of the war in Europe, average membership fell to 79,-000, compared to 103,000 for the same period a year earlier.[6]

Although the tendency to excuse the European comrades persisted among the leaders of the Right and Center, the Party gradually regained its equilibrium, associated itself with the antiwar leaders in Europe, and moved to a position of strong opposition to American involvement. After Karl Liebknecht

[3] Quoted in W.E. Walling, ed., *Socialists and the War* (New York, 1915), p. 380.
[4] Quoted in *ibid.*, p. 380.
[5] *Ibid.*
[6] Membership records in SPC, Duke, for corresponding years.

broke with the majority Socialists in Germany to vote against the second war loan, the leading American organs endorsed his actions. The *Call* did so in September 1914, and the official Party organ, the *American Socialist*, followed suit in January 1915. Lauding Liebknecht, and declaring that the world Socialist movement needed the courage and consistency he exhibited, the *American Socialist* commented: "If some of the Socialists of Europe have for the moment been won to participation in the blood feast, their acts are inconsistent with the teachings of Socialism." It was not, the paper concluded, quoting the German leftist approvingly, "our principles which have failed, but the representatives of those principles."[7]

Meanwhile, the Party's National Executive Committee had been working out a tentative peace program that placed the blame for the war on "imperialist" rivalry between the capitalist powers in Europe, and implied that no conflict of interest existed between the workers of the various nations engaged in the war. The peace-terms sections of the program contained two planks: no indemnities, and no annexations without popular consent. In addition, the program called for the extension of democracy through "social changes in all countries to eliminate the economic causes of war." These were to include socialization of national resources, public utilities and basic industries; elimination of unearned income; and the immediate and progressive amelioration of conditions of labor. A subsection called for the abolition of secret diplomacy and the extension of suffrage to all, including women. Another plank, written by Allan Benson, future Presidential candidate, called for a Constitutional amendment requiring a popular referendum in order to declare future "offensive" wars. Finally, a section on disarmament called for the abolition of private profits in arms manufacture and a freezing of armaments at present levels until an international police force had sufficient power to enforce total disarmament.[8]

[7] *Call,* September 12, 1914; *American Socialist,* January 9, 1915. Quoted in Walling, *op. cit.,* pp. 390-391.
[8] W.E. Walling, *op. cit.,* pp. 466-470.

In the discussion that followed, A. M. Simons led the attack on the provision allowing armaments for defense until such time as an international police force could effectuate international disarmament. The idea of an international police force, Simons wrote, was visionary, and even if possible, would be disadvantageous as long as the capitalists controlled the major sources of power. Similarly, he characterized the attempt to differentiate between defensive and offensive wars as the indulgence in a "piffling distinction" which had allowed Socialists in all warring countries to excuse their support of the war. "Shall we prepare the same pitfalls for our own footsteps?" he asked. Simons' conclusion, filled with irony, considering his future role as chairman of the literature department of the Wisconsin Loyalty League, called on Party members to "quit trying to get support from 'patriots' while posing as Socialists."[9]

Simons was answered by John C. Kennedy, secretary of the Illinois Party and a member of the committee that had drafted the tentative program. Pointing out that it would be neither feasible nor desirable for the United States to disarm unilaterally, lest the country be placed at the mercy of "an autocracy such as Russia," Kennedy asserted that disarmament could be accomplished only through international agreement. He failed, however, to indicate the role of the international socialist movement in bringing about such an agreement. On the distinction between offensive and defensive wars, Kennedy admitted some difficulty, but concluded that the problem was simply one of defining "offensive" better than had been done in the past. Perhaps, he suggested, the term "wars of invasion" might be sub-

---

[9] *American Socialist,* January 9, 1915. See also Simons to Carl D. Thompson, Milwaukee, January 20, 1915, SPC, Duke, where Simons comments that "this is the fight of my life. A Socialist Party with such a program is no more of a Socialist Party than a Party that should stand for rent, interest and profit as sacred. It is a betrayal of everything I have worked for . . .

"This program was written to accord with the position of bourgeois peace bodies and not with Socialist principles. I am willing to work with such bodies as far as they go in opposition to war, but I am not willing to give up Socialism in order to do this."

stituted, but as W. E. Walling pointed out, this was exactly the criterion used by the German Socialists to rationalize the support they gave their war government.[10]

The mood of the Party, however, was clearly one of non-involvement, and with each debate the Socialists moved nearer to an unequivocal antiwar stand. Interestingly, in the early debates the final roles of many of the key leaders were reversed. Several Party members who, like Simons, later gave vigorous support to American involvement, took the most uncompromising positions against preparedness; others, such as Hillquit and Berger, who would later be the most prominent antiwar campaigners, took equivocal positions. John Spargo, for example, declared late in 1915 that he was irreconcilably opposed to militarism, and that he regarded it as the "most pressing duty" of American Socialists "to vigorously oppose the sinister attempt to commit this nation to militarism under the misleading title of 'preparedness.' "[11] Hillquit, on the other hand, had publicly evaded taking a principled stand against preparedness, relying instead on the argument that America was immune from attack by European or Asian powers. In addition, Hillquit tended to line up with Berger, Kennedy, James H. Maurer, and J. Stitt Wilson in favor of international, rather than unilateral, disarmament.[12]

The changes in the tentative program from the time it was drafted by a committee composed entirely of Center and Right Socialists to the time it was adopted by the membership in its final form reflected the growing strength of the Left in the Party.[13] As approved, the program contained a third peace term:

[10] *American Socialist*, January 9, 1915, Walling, *op. cit.*, p. 477.
[11] John Spargo, Old Bennington, Vermont, December 25, 1915, SPC, Duke.
[12] Isaac A. Hourwich, "The Gardner-Hillquit Debate," *New Review*, III, 5 (May 1915), 12-13, discusses Hillquit's position. Carl D. Thompson to Hillquit, Chicago, January 21, 1915, SPC, Duke, reveals that the *Appeal to Reason* and the Left were aligned with Allan Benson and Simons.
[13] On this see Ludwig E. Katterfeld, "The 1915 National Committee Meeting," *International Socialist Review*, XV, 1 (July 1915), 56-57. Katterfeld comments that the trend toward centralization of 1912-1914 was

self-determination of colonial countries, and it settled the question of armament by providing that Socialists should oppose all appropriations for military or naval purposes. This latter provision received special emphasis when the membership adopted a constitutional amendment by a vote of 11,041 to 782, making mandatory the expulsion of any elected Socialist who voted either for war or war credits.[14] The program as it now stood remained the basis of the Socialist position on peace throughout the war; the Party would later boast that it had been first to formulate the peace terms: no indemnities, no forcible annexations.

Soon after the program was adopted, the lone Socialist congressman, Meyer London, introduced a resolution in the House calling for a conference of neutral nations to discuss ways of ending the war in accord with the Socialist demands. Shortly thereafter, London joined Hillquit and James H. Maurer in a delegation to the White House, where they presented their plan to President Wilson.[15] Even before the White House interview, however, Wilson had presented his armaments program to Congress in a speech which initiated the preparedness campaign and the President's open advocacy of the need for legislation to suppress "disloyal activity."[16] Thus, by December 1915, preparedness was the official policy of the Administra-

---

reversed, and that the Left gained all its objectives, though still unable to win organizational control. See also L. B. Boudin, "The Mind of an Opportunist," *New Review*, IV, 4 (April 1916), 99-100. Boudin observed that the "once famous . . . curiosity of Socialist literature," Section Six, was "now dead and forgotten."

[14] *American Labor Yearbook: 1916*, ed. Alexander Trachtenberg (New York, 1917), p. 126.

[15] Maurer, *op. cit.*, p. 215; Hillquit, *Loose Leaves*, p. 160; Walter Lansfersiek to Hillquit, Chicago, December 23, 1915, Hillquit papers, WSHS. The National Executive Committee originally selected Debs as part of the three-man delegation, but he apparently declined, and London took his place. Hillquit papers.

[16] On Wilson's role in the suppression of civil liberties see Harry N. Scheiber, *The Wilson Administration and Civil Liberties* (Ithaca, N.Y., 1960).

tion, while the Socialists lined up almost solidly in opposition.

Within the Party, antiwar sentiment was so strong that the membership nominated Allan Benson as its Presidential candidate in 1916 solely on the strength of his vigorous antipreparedness articles in the *Appeal to Reason*. Previously a virtual unknown, Benson's popularity shot upward after he repeatedly advanced his favorite panacea—Constitutional requirement of a popular referendum to declare war. As Hillquit commented privately, the proposal, and especially its provision that those who voted in the affirmative should be the first to serve in the army, was "perfectly wild." But it so caught the mood of the membership that it won Benson the nomination in a referendum against James Maurer and Arthur Le Sueur (of North Dakota), both of whom were better known and better qualified for the honor.[17] Although Benson's position on the war was popular with the membership, he had no following with the electorate at large. As we have seen, he ran poorly against Wilson, in a campaign in which the President was widely heralded as the man who had "kept us out of war."

Soon after the election, the nation moved swiftly toward involvement in the European conflict. By March 1917, the entrance of the United States into the war was imminent. The Socialist Party National Executive Committee, determined not to be caught in a position similar to that of their European comrades, called an emergency convention in St. Louis for April 7 to formulate a wartime program. Almost two hundred delegates converged on St. Louis for the convention, arriving not a moment too soon; by the time the meeting convened, Congress had already declared a state of war between the United States and Germany. The Party now faced the test its European counterparts had failed, but in a vastly different mood. Kate Richards O'Hare expressed the dominant attitude

[17] Shannon, *op. cit.*, pp. 90-91; Hillquit to Carl D. Thompson, New York, January 20, 1915, SPC, Duke. Similarly, in the Vice Presidential contest, George Kirkpatrick of New Jersey, best known for his antiwar speeches and pamphlets, defeated Kate Richards O'Hare.

of her comrades: "I am a Socialist, a labor unionist and a be-
liever in the Prince of Peace *first,* and an American second,"
she declared. "If need be," she added, "I will give my life and
the life of my mate, to serve my class, *but never with my consent will they be given to add to the profits and protect the
stolen wealth of the bankers, food speculators and ammunition
makers."*

She was, she assured her readers, "not pro-English; not pro-
German; not pro-American," but simply *"pro-working class."*[18]

That the Party shared her spirit was made clear when the St.
Louis convention chose Mrs. O'Hare to chair the Committee
on War and Militarism. Made up of fifteen members representing all the major groups within the Party, the committee
conducted the main business of the convention. Its majority
resolution, written by Morris Hillquit, his close associate Algernon Lee, and the militant Cleveland left winger Charles
E. Ruthenberg, symbolized the new unity of Left and Center
that had been developing since 1914. The resolution branded
the congressional declaration of war "a crime against the people
of the United States," and proclaimed allegiance to the principle of international working-class solidarity. Characterizing
the war as one of capitalist interests fighting over colonial markets, the resolution called on workers of all countries to stand
in opposition to it, and pledged that "in support of capitalism,
we will not willingly give a single life or a single dollar." In
conclusion, the resolution promised "continuous, active and
public opposition" to conscription, as well as "vigorous resistance" to censorship of the press, restriction of free speech, and
limitations on the right to strike.[19]

The majority resolution was signed by eleven of the committee of fifteen, including Kate O'Hare, Hillquit, Lee, Ruthenberg,

[18] Kate R. O'Hare, "My Country," *Social Revolution,* April 1917, p. 5. For
a similar statement see Mary E. Marcy, in *International Socialist Review,*
XVII, 9 (March 1917).
[19] "Special Convention on War," *International Socialist Review,* XVII, 11
(May 1917), 670 ff.

Victor Berger, Job Harriman, Dan Hogan, and Patrick Quinlan. In addition, Louis B. Boudin wrote a slightly different antiwar resolution, signed also by Kate Sadler of Washington and Walter Dillon of New Mexico. John Spargo submitted a report calling for cooperation with the government in the hope of obtaining concessions during the war and the best possible terms of peace.[20]

In the convention, the majority resolution received 140 votes to 31 for Boudin's and only 5 for Spargo's pro-war report; the membership then ratified the convention decision by an overwhelming vote of 21,639 to 2,752.[21] Almost every Socialist publication followed the lead of the St. Louis convention and strongly denounced the war. Thus, even the right-wing *St. Louis Labor*, one of the few Socialist papers which had been friendly to Samuel Gompers, hailed the antiwar stand.[22] The only major exception to this trend was Max Hayes' *Cleveland Citizen*, which, as we have seen, endorsed the war effort, though remaining friendly to the Party.[23]

However, even the strongly antiwar tone of the St. Louis Manifesto did not completely satisfy all Socialist opponents of the war. The left-wing Louis Boudin, for example, attacked the manifesto as a collection of "soap-box immaturities and meaningless generalities; assertions which cannot be defended when taken literally," and which must therefore be "taken with mental reservations which render them utterly worthless as a definitive statement of position." In addition, Boudin complained that the convention had failed to grapple with important theoretical questions, such as the relation of nationalism to international-

---

[20] *Ibid.*
[21] *New York Times*, July 8, 1917; *American Labor Yearbook: 1917-18*, p. 338, gives a figure of 21,000 to 350. The discrepancy results from the fact that each section of the manifesto was voted upon separately.
[22] *St. Louis Labor*, May 5, 1917.
[23] Of course, the organs of various Socialist-led International unions supported the war. See, for example *Quarry Workers Journal, Miners Magazine*, and *The Tailor*; Brookneal, Virginia, *Union Star* also supported the war.

ism, the defense of small nations, and how far class-conscious workers should go in joining hands with other social groups in defense of democracy. But Boudin's attack on the convention was largely misdirected. His report differed little, especially in its theoretical aspects, from that of the majority. In fact, the convention had represented a triumph of "Left" views; for not only had the delegates taken a strongly antiwar position but they had also overwhelmingly voted to repeal the "anti-sabotage clause" of 1912, and had unanimously adopted Boudin's own draft of an address to the Socialists of belligerent countries, after Victor Berger withdrew his version.[24]

In an attempt to find a right-wing villain, Boudin and his fellow editors of *The Class Struggle* concentrated their fire on Berger, whom they attacked both for being pro-German in his neutrality, and for being privately pro-war.[25] Boudin claimed that, in committee, Berger, Job Harriman, and Dan Hogan had supported Spargo's pro-war position, but had voted with the majority and finally signed the Hillquit-Ruthenberg draft.[26] In this, however, Boudin was on shaky ground. The criticism of pro-Germanism came closer to the mark, for Berger's neutrality may very well have been strengthened by his closer identification with the German Socialists than with those of the Allied Powers. Even here, however, the imputation served primarily as a device, since, along with most of the Party, Berger inclined increasingly toward the Liebknecht-Mehring antiwar group in the German Party.[27] As we shall see, the war drove Berger steadily leftward, and he remained a consistent advocate of

[24] *Proceedings, Emergency Convention of the Socialist Party of America at St. Louis,* April 7-14, 1917 (n.p., n.d.), April 13, 1917, afternoon session. L. B. Boudin, "The Emergency National Convention of the Socialist Party," *The Class Struggle,* I, 1 (May-June 1917), 41-48. Boudin treats Berger's withdrawal as a most suspicious maneuver.
[25] "The Task Before Us," *op. cit.,* pp. 1-14, criticizes Berger and others as pro-German.
[26] Boudin, "The Emergency National Convention . . .," p. 46.
[27] The Wisconsin Party organization, in which Berger was a leading light, also associated itself with Liebknecht in general after the war began, quoting him often on many subjects. See, for example, Ameringer's "Go Easy . . ." on Socialist education.

immediate peace and total nonsupport of the war in his public utterances.[28]

But if Boudin's shaft missed Berger, it came closer with respect to Harriman and Hogan. Harriman urged Party members to vote for the Spargo report although he had signed the majority resolution. After the adoption of the antiwar resolution by referendum, he again reversed himself and upheld the Party position against attack from the pro-war Charles Edward Russell.[29]

II

Unlike Harriman, most of those who shared Spargo's view resigned from the Party and supported the war with vigor and often with venom. Pro-war Socialists were few in number, as the vote at St. Louis indicated, but many of the best known public figures and almost all the nationally prominent journalists and intellectuals were among them. Some had supported the Allied Powers since early in the war. Jack London had been most bellicose until his death in early 1917, even favoring American occupation of Mexico at a time when Socialists and trade unionists were virtually unanimous in their opposition to Wilson's intervention against the Mexican revolution.[30] Charles Edward Russell and Upton Sinclair had urged United States support for England in 1915.[31] Others, among them A. M. Simons, Spargo, and Allan Benson, had been the most outspoken

[28] Berger did testify that he secretly bought $600 worth of Liberty bonds. But this did not become public knowledge until after the war. See *Hearing Before the Special Committee Concerning the Right of Victor L. Berger to be Seated as a Member of the Sixty-Sixth Congress*, II, 303. Berger was asked if he bought bonds. He replied: "Well, I did. Occasionally, as a Mohammedan drinks wine."

[29] Harriman, "Shall We Commit Suicide?" *Cleveland Citizen*, May 5, 1917; *Quarry Workers Journal*, July 1917. In answer to Russell, Harriman argued that the war was a struggle for the commerce of the world in which Socialists opposed fighting and killing their brothers with whom they had no differences.

[30] Phillip S. Foner, *Jack London: American Rebel* (New York, 1947), pp. 114 ff.

[31] Ginger, *Bending Cross*, p. 330.

opponents of war until the United States entered; then they became super-patriots and condemned the antiwar Socialists as foreign born and pro-German.[32]

The pro-war Socialists corresponded in their politics and ideology to the right-wing majority of the Second International in Europe, but within the Party they did not come from the Right alone. All tendencies were represented. W. E. Walling, Henry L. Slobodin, Rose Pastor Stokes, Frank and William Bohn were left wingers; W. J. Ghent, Winnfield Gaylord, Robert Hunter came from the Right; Charles Edward Russell, Upton Sinclair, John Spargo, A. M. Simons occupied the Center. Their exodus did not affect over-all Party membership, which increased by 13,384 in the three months after war was declared;[33] but the impact on the leadership was considerable, not only among journalists, but also in trade union ranks. As we have seen, John H. Walker of Illinois, William Johnston of the Machinists, and others became strong Administration supporters. Among the trade unionists were several local leaders, such as B. F. Ginther, State Secretary of the Virginia Socialist Party, mayor of Brookneal, and managing editor of the *Union Star*, a local labor paper. Like many others who supported the war, Ginther did not condemn the Party on principle, but saw the St. Louis Manifesto as a "blunder" that would hinder positive action for socialism during the war.[34] Pro-war Socialists argued that the war would inevitably advance the cause of socialism, and that they could

[32] See, for example, "The Socialist As Patriot," *Literary Digest*, June 16, 1917, pp. 1836-1837; "Divergent Effects of War on the Socialist Movement," *Current Opinion*, (August 1917), p. 74; Shannon, *op. cit.*, pp. 100-102. Benson did not resign from the Party until the summer of 1918, when he did so "in protest against foreign born leadership." His thesis at the time was that "both the people and the Government have welcomed part of the [Socialist] philosophy but have kicked out the Party." See "Why Mr. Benson Has Resigned From the Socialist Party," *Current Opinion*, (August 1918), p. 85, and Benson, "What the War Has Done to Socialism in America," *ibid.*, pp. 82-85.
[33] *New York Call*, July 8, 1917. Membership rose from 67,788 in April to 81,172 in June. The *Call* predicted that it would be over 100,00 for July.
[34] B.F. Ginther, to J.G. Phelps Stokes, Brookneal, Virginia, April 7, 1917; May 3, 1917, Stokes papers.

contribute to social progress by cooperating with the Administration and exerting pressure for reform from within. They shared with Croly, Lippmann, and Weyl "a vision of the United States spreading American ideals throughout the world," while at home the government would intervene in the economy to plan and regulate.[35] Charles Edward Russell, for example, argued that the war would bring "real socialism," such as government management of the railroads.[36]

Some pro-war Socialists, notably John Spargo, participated in the American Alliance for Labor and Democracy as their contribution to "wartime socialism." Organized to counteract the activities of the antiwar Peoples' Council for Peace and Democracy, a coalition of pacifists and Socialists that was suppressed by late 1917, the American Alliance was the creature of the National Civic Federation and George Creel's Committee on Public Information. The idea for the Alliance originated in Ralph Easley's office, at a meeting with Samuel Gompers, and Easley advanced the first seven hundred dollars to get it started.[37] Thereafter, Creel supported the Alliance with money from President Wilson's special $100 million fund. As Creel told the League of National Unity, "we have formed an alliance for labor and democracy by Mr. Gompers."[38] Spargo assisted in the formulation of policy in this organization during the war as his contribution to socialism.[39] Other Socialists, such as Charles Edward Russell, went to Russia on the Root Commission wearing old clothes so that they could talk the Bolsheviks out of their revolution.[40]

[35] Forcey, *Crossroads*, p. 560.
[36] Charles Edward Russell, "War to Bring Real Socialism," *Quarry Workers Journal*, June 1917.
[37] Easley to Vincent Astor, New York, November 14, 1917; Easley to Gompers, July 12, 1917, NCF papers.
[38] Minutes of the League for National Unity, September 12, 1917, p. 6, NCF papers.
[39] Frank P. Walsh to George Creel, Kansas City, August 30, November 10, 1917, Walsh papers.
[40] Ronald Radosh, "American Labor and the Root Commission," *Studies on the Left*, III, 1, pp. 34 ff.

In general, pro-war Socialists, both in and out of the labor movement, encouraged cooperation of labor with the several wartime commissions and agencies on which the unions had representation. Antiwar Socialists, and Senator La Follette, condemned profiteering during the war, and Victor Berger published profit reports of 287 corporations comparing prewar profits with those of wartime that showed vast increases during the war.[41] In contrast, V. Everitt Macy, President of the National Civic Federation and Chairman of the Shipbuilding Labor Adjustment Board, revealed what labor had gained from its cooperation. "It is safe to say," Macy told the executive committee of the Federation, "that if these various boards had not been established, there would have been constant interruption of production, an immensely increased labor turnover, much higher wages . . ."[42]

The war proved how little influence the pro-war liberals and Socialists had on the decisions of the Administration and on the actual course of events. But even the more sophisticated among them were deluded with a sense of power and participation. In May 1917, Walter Lippmann wrote to J. G. Phelps Stokes that the United States stood "at the threshold of a collectivism which is greater than any as yet planned by the Socialist Party." He was convinced that "the war has really carried already beyond the stage of merely national socialism."[43] Almost alone among intellectuals, Randolph Bourne knew better. The pro-war liberals, he wrote, had accepted—in the "vain hope of conscious guidance and control—almost every program that the bigoted unsocialized patriot has demanded." Although their motives may have been very different, their actions served simply to give "their reactionary opponents a rationalization for the

[41] Included in remarks of Wheeler P. Bloodgood to the Executive Council Meeting of the NCF, October 11, 1918, NCF papers.
[42] Minutes of the Meeting of the Executive Committee, December 2, 1918, NCF papers.
[43] Lippmann to Stokes, New York, May 1, 1917, Stokes papers.

war." As Bourne sorrowfully noted, the "real control" was "taken over by the reactionaries who pull the strings of power." Liberals, Bourne concluded (and he could have included the pro-war Socialists), had helped lead the United States into "a hateful and futile war, with a fatal backwash and backfire upon creative and democratic values at home."[44]

The sharp and often bitter hostility between pro-war and antiwar Socialists had its greatest impact on Party relations with middle-class social reform groups and in the structures of the trade union movement. Virtually all avenues of debate that had existed between Socialist and non-Socialist before the war were closed, except for the Intercollegiate Socialist Society. At its ninth annual convention in 1918, for example, the left-wing stalwart Louis Boudin defended the Party's antiwar stand; the semi-syndicalist Frank Bohn, until late 1917 an editor of the Left *International Socialist Review,* justified his resignation from the Party and spoke in support of American participation in the war; the right-wing National Executive Committee member George Goebel explained that he remained loyal to the Party, while disagreeing with its position on the war; and the non-Socialist reformer Frederic C. Howe suggested that after the war the United States should so reorganize its economic system as to "give to the workers essentially the product of their toil."[45] But even the ISS suffered a serious decline, as we have seen, and within it unity was not maintained. In July 1918, unable to acquiesce in a mixed list of speakers for a Society conference, J. G. Phelps Stokes resigned as president of the ISS.[46]

[44] Randolph S. Bourne to Van Wyck Brooks, n.p., March 27, 1917, Bourne papers, Columbia University; Max Lerner, *Ideas for the Ice Age* (New York, 1939), p. 130.
[45] *Intercollegiate Socialist,* VI, 3 (February-March 1918), 18.
[46] Stokes to Harry W. Laidler, n.p., July 15, 1918, Stokes papers. Stokes had attempted to resign in 1917, but remained president after Laidler assured him that the Society had maintained strict neutrality on the war. Laidler to Stokes, New York, November 28, 1917, Stokes papers.

III

In the months before the United States entered the war, Socialist antiwar propaganda struck a responsive chord in many Americans. Wilson had been re-elected as "the man who kept us out of war," but he moved rapidly toward involvement. Members of his Administration spoke openly of the imminence of hostilities, and privately of the necessity for universal service and the need to "unify sentiment in the nation."[47] Although Gompers and the majority of AFL leaders supported preparedness, and despite the ineffectiveness of the pacifist organizations, such as the American Peace Society, the American Union against Militarism, and others, most farmers and workers opposed participation in the war. As John Hays Hammond, prominent Republican and wealthy mining engineer, told the annual meeting of the National Civic Federation in January 1917, ". . . some influence or combination of influences has certainly brought about a weakening of the patriotic spirit in this country when we find that neither the workingmen nor the farmers—the two great groups upon which our national life depends—are taking any part or interest in the efforts of the security or defense leagues or other movements for national preparedness."[48] As if to emphasize Hammond's remarks, the newly elected Nonpartisan League-dominated legislature of North Dakota petitioned Wilson in the first days of January 1917 to maintain neutrality. Calling the drive toward war the result of propa-

---

[47] Howard E. Coffin, Chairman of the Committee on Mobilization of the National Council of Defense at the Annual Meeting of the National Civic Federation, January 23, 1917, NCF papers; Coffin to the Executive Council of NCF, February 6, 1917, *ibid*. This latter speech was marked "Strictly Confidential," and Coffin requested that no notes be taken. See also George W. Perkins to W. S. Rainsford, n.p., January 6, 1917, in which Perkins comments that "our spirit of patriotism has well nigh oozed out, and we need a most thorough reawakening religiously, patriotically, morally." Perkins papers, Columbia University.

[48] Annual meeting of the National Civic Federation, January 23, 1917, NCF papers.

ganda on the part of munitions and armor plate makers, the legislature suggested that Congress give the President authority, in the event of war, to seize and operate without compensation all manufacturing plants, shipyards, armor plate mills, and flour mills, "so that citizens of wealth may be enabled and compelled to contribute to the common welfare and need of their country on the same terms as the enlisted soldiers and sailors who give their lives and their all."[49] And on the eve of the declaration of war, the Seattle Central Labor Council added its voice by unanimously adopting a resolution pleading with Wilson and the state's congressional delegation to avoid war.[50]

When President Wilson asked for a declaration of war against Germany on April 2, 1917, only a handful of senators and congressmen argued against it. Senator George W. Norris warned that "we are going to war upon the command of gold," and argued that munitions makers and bankers had been instrumental in putting the country in a position where war was inevitable. "I feel," he said in desperation, "that we are about to put the dollar sign upon the American flag." Senator La Follette also spoke out forcefully. Pointing out that our commercial policies had been pro-British "from early in the war," La Follette asserted that Germany had been patient with us before January 31, 1917, when she resumed full-scale submarine warfare. Before that date, he reminded his colleagues, the United States had thrown its "neutrality to the winds by permitting England to make a mockery of it to her own advantage."[51]

Fifty congressmen and six senators voted against the declaration of war, and it was said that more would have done so had they voted their convictions,[52] but once the United States en-

[49] Walsh papers, Box 133. Walsh to Dante Barton, Kansas City, February 2, 1917. Here Walsh comments that the resolution "appealed to me strongly."
[50] Harvey O'Connor, *Revolution in Seattle*, p. 84.
[51] Congressional Record, 65th Congress, First Session, April 4, 1917, pp. 212, 214, 234. Also quoted in H. C. Peterson and Gilbert Fite, *Opponents of War* (Madison, 1957), p. 5.
[52] *Ibid.*, n. 19, p. 307.

tered the war public opposition on the part of major party politicians virtually ceased. A few men, such as La Follette and Congressman William E. Mason of Illinois, continued to criticize the lack of a democratic war program and wartime profiteering, but they received no support from their party organizations.[53] Nevertheless, large numbers of Americans remained dubious of the necessity of American participation in the conflict, and even greater numbers strongly resisted the draft.

Opposition to the war and to conscription took many forms, ranging from widespread attempts to evade service to armed rebellion. Initially, many Americans simply failed to register, as local newspapers occasionally reported.[54] Then, when the induction process began, large numbers of registrants failed to appear for their physical examinations. In Donora, Pennsylvania, 40 percent of the men who registered gave their draft boards fictitious addresses, such as vacant lots. Apparently they registered only to obtain draft cards. In Erie, where one registrant in six was a "slacker," the *Dispatch* proudly reported that Erie men were "showing a greater willingness to serve than in most Pennsylvania cities." One district in Chicago reported that of 345 men called, 139 did not appear.[55] In the month of August alone, 2,500 slackers were reported in Cleveland. In October, 4,000 were reported in Akron.[56] And as late as June 1918,

---

[53] *Ibid.,* pp. 22, 67-72, 77-78; *New York Times,* July 9, 1917.

[54] For example, the *Reading* (Pennsylvania) *News-Times* reported on August 2, 1917, that the Department of Justice was receiving from one hundred to two hundred letters a day giving substantially correct information of men who had not registered. The *New Castle* (Pennsylvania) *Herald,* September 18, 1917, reported the arrest of three unregistered men; *The Youngstown* (Ohio) *Vindicator,* October 22, 1917, revealed that many men registering to vote were found to be "shy of serial numbers."

[55] Allentown *Democrat,* August 8, 1917; Erie *Dispatch,* August 26, 1917. On November 1, 1917, the *Dispatch* reported: "Slackers multiply. No Men To Go Friday." Minneapolis *Journal,* August 8, 1917.

[56] Dayton *News,* August 20, 1917; Akron *Beacon-Journal,* October 3, 1917.

30 delinquents were picked up and inducted and 16 deserters found in a two-week period in Minneapolis.[57] Even among those who did appear for their physical examinations, large numbers were reluctant to serve. In New York City, said to be a center of interventionist sentiment, 70 percent of those who appeared filed exemption claims. And in Philadelphia, several draft boards exhausted ten times the number of exemption blanks originally provided; the Government was unable to keep up with the demand for these forms.[58]

In addition to these efforts to avoid personal military service, there were many more general attacks on the draft and the Administration's war policies. In some cities, for example, draft lists were stolen to delay the induction process. On the night before the first draft in Indianapolis, the lists for the entire county were stolen,[59] and a few days later a similar incident occurred in New York City.[60] On August 7, the Minneapolis *Journal* reported that antidraft sentiment had "infected large areas of Minnesota" and was "fast spreading." Protest meetings were reported in many places, and merchants and bankers who supported the war were boycotted in Hutchinson, Glencoe, and New Ulm.[61] Similarly, in Georgia, as Senator Hardwick later told his colleagues, "there was undoubtedly general and widespread opposition (to) . . . the draft law. Numerous and largely attended mass meetings in every part of the state protested against it."[62] The outstanding leader of this opposition was Tom Watson, whose energetic activity against the war brought him renewed prominence in Georgia politics. In his newspaper, *The Jeffersonian*, Watson attacked the "dictatorial powers demanded by the President." Nor did he hesitate to attack the Administration's motives in leading America to war. Watson twitted

[57] Minneapolis *Journal*, June 15, 1918.
[58] *New York Times*, August 8, 1917; Philadelphia *Public Ledger*, August 15, 1917.
[59] Reading *News-Times*, August 3, 1917.
[60] *New York Times*, August 6, 1917.
[61] Minneapolis *Journal*, August 6, 7, 22, 1917.
[62] *Congressional Record*, 65th Congress, 2nd Session, May 2, 1918, 5941.

"our sweetly sincere President" for saying "The world must be made safe for democracy." "What he meant," Watson explained, was "that the huge investment which our blood-gorged capitalists had made in French, Italian, Russian, and English *paper* must be made safe.

"*Where Morgan's money went, your boys' blood must go, else Morgan will lose his money.*"[63]

In June, July, and August, Watson appealed for funds to challenge the constitutionality of the Conscription Act. Checks in small amounts, totaling $100,000, poured in from Atlanta, Chattanooga, Danville, Virginia, and numerous towns throughout the South. Every week Watson published a list of contributors several columns long—until in mid-August, *The Jeffersonian* was banned from the mails.[64]

In the South, Watson's voice was not alone. Charles S. Barrett, president of the Farmers Educational and Cooperative Union, and himself a Georgia farmer, told the League for National Unity early in September that antiwar sentiment was prevalent among Southern farmers. In New Orleans, he reported, a State Farmers Union convention of 350 delegates had adopted a resolution "dictated by an agent of the German Government," with only nine dissenting votes. Asked what was in the resolution, Barrett replied: "If you have heard anything about what appears in papers like Watson's *Jeffersonian* and the *Appeal to Reason*" you will know. "It was general criticism, condemnation." A few days after the New Orleans experience, Barrett attended a convention of 1,500 to 2,000 farmers in Dallas. There one in fifty supported the war. "There is," he added, "a great deal of indifference in North Carolina," and "a great deal more in Virginia that I thought for."[65] The response to Barrett's report on the part of Rabbi Stephen S. Wise was one of relief, rather than shock. He had, he explained, wondered

[63] C. Vann Woodward, *Tom Watson*, pp. 453-455.
[64] *Ibid.*; Philadelphia *Public Ledger*, August 5, 1917.
[65] Minutes of the League for National Unity meeting of September 12, 1917, Washington, D.C., NCF papers.

whether he was the only one "unfortunate enough to meet this faint heartedness." Rabbi Wise observed that the "inexplicable failure to understand the meaning of this war" was not among his constituents, but among "the representatives of the oldest American stock," in the Adirondacks and in the Middle West.[66]

This hostility to America's involvement in the European war led many to forceful resistance, especially in the South. In Dallas, Texas, six men were arrested with arms in their possession. In North Carolina, the farmers of Chatham County organized an "armed revolt" against the draft.[67] Outside of Toledo, Ohio, someone fired on a troop train, wounding three soldiers. In California, twenty-five men, allegedly a band of IWW's, cut off the last two cars of a troop train and fought the soldiers.[68]

The most dramatic, and certainly the most pathetic, antiwar action occurred in eastern Oklahoma, where an armed uprising, known as the Green Corn Rebellion, took place in early August. The rebels were some eight hundred to one thousand poor tenant farmers, the vast majority of old American stock, who were deeply opposed to war. These farmers referred to President Wilson as "Big Slick," out of resentment over what they considered his betrayal in failing to keep the United States out of war.[69] The rebellion was organized by the Working Class Union, a syndicalist organization which had its greatest strength among the Socialist farmers of Arkansas and eastern Oklahoma. The farmers, believing that there were groups of men under arms in many states, planned to march on Washington, seize the government and end the "Rich Man's War."[70]

In only six counties of Oklahoma did groups of men actually assemble. A few of these set about cutting telegraph wires and attempting unsuccessfully to burn railroad bridges, while the

[66] *Ibid.*
[67] *New York Times*, August 4, 5, 1917.
[68] Toledo *News-Bee*, September 16, November 4, 1917.
[69] See Charles C. Bush, "The Green Corn Rebellion" (unpublished master's thesis, University of Oklahoma, 1932), pp. 1, 11, 26.
[70] *Ibid.*, pp. 6, 9, 17.

encamped "army" waited with growing restlessness for its four million promised allies to materialize. After two days of waiting and eating barbecued beef and green corn, realization came: They were alone. Demoralized and without leadership, the "army" scattered at the approach of a local posse. By August 16, the last of the known conspirators had been rounded up, and some 450 frightened men rested in Oklahoma jails. The "revolution" was stillborn.[71]

IV

Meanwhile, the Socialist Party was the only major national organization officially to condemn American participation in the war. This made the Socialists highly vulnerable to attack from old and new enemies, but it also presented them with an unprecedented opportunity. In the months that followed the St. Louis convention, Socialists campaigned vigorously to rally the various antiwar elements under their banner. The Party was, of course, unable to mobilize all opponents of the war. Its potential as a center of opposition was limited both by its radical nature and by a deficiency of press and organization. In many states, however, Socialists were "in evidence almost everywhere,"[72] speaking against continuation of the war and against conscription.

During the first year of war, Socialists of all tendencies actively and openly opposed American participation as they had promised to do at St. Louis. In the spring and summer of 1917, mass meetings and parades organized by the Party met with warm responses from the public and with increasing hostility and violence from federal, state, and local officials as well as from vigilante groups organized by local chambers of com-

[71] *Ibid.*, p. 50. Oscar Ameringer, *If You Don't Weaken*, p. 351, writes that although the rebellion was limited to the eastern counties, opposition to the war "was just as strong in the western half of the state. And there the bitterest opponents were . . . the Democrats who had cast their ballots for the man who 'kept us out of war' . . . only being better situated and educated, they saw the futility of opposing the war by force."
[72] Dayton *News*, August 18, 1917.

merce and commercial clubs.[73] On July 1, more than eight thousand Socialists and trade unionists, led by the left-wing Lettish federation, paraded in Boston with banners and placards demanding peace with "No Forcible Annexations" and "No Punitive Indemnities." As they marched, organized groups of soldiers and sailors attacked them. Hundreds of fights broke out, the Socialist headquarters was ransacked, and the police arrested ten of the paraders.[74] A quieter gathering took place in Chicago when three thousand pacifists heard addresses by Congressman William E. Mason and six Socialist speakers, and then called upon the Administration to seek immediate peace talks based on the Socialist demands for "No Annexations, No Indemnities."[75] In Evansville, Indiana, Frank Lamonte, Socialist candidate for mayor, had a "thrilling escape" from a group of vigilantes after "flaying" the draft before a large crowd.[76] And on New York street corners countless radicals spoke against the war. So many were jailed on Blackwell's Island that the *New York Call* facetiously suggested that the prisoners might request a local charter.[77]

In the Midwest, Socialists were particularly effective. In Minnesota, for example, Party members spoke at mass meetings throughout the state, attracting huge crowds and bringing upon themselves the wrath of state officials. On July 25, Thomas Van Lear, mayor of Minneapolis, denounced conscription before 7,500 farmers at New Ulm at a meeting jointly presided over by the mayor and the local college president.[78] Two weeks later Van Lear addressed a meeting in Glencoe, "where 6,000 persons gathered for a protest against sending American troops to

[73] For a full discussion of these attacks see Peterson and Fite, *Opponents of War.*
[74] *New York Times*, July 2, 1917; *New York Call*, July 2, 1917; Peterson and Fite, *op. cit.*, pp. 45-46; Maurer, *op. cit.*, pp. 225. Maurer gives a figure of 30,000 demonstrators. He describes a group of sailors burning books and furniture in the street while the police stood by.
[75] *New York Times*, July 9, 1917.
[76] Dayton *Journal*, August 7, 1917.
[77] September 6, 1917.
[78] Minneapolis *Journal*, August 6, 22, 1917; Peterson and Fite, *op. cit.*, p. 37.

France." Petitions against sending conscripts overseas were signed by 4,500 demonstrators, while Van Lear "hinted" that the nations fighting Germany were doing so for private gain, and demanded a statement of war aims, declaring that the people had a right to know for what they were fighting. Another speaker declared his opposition to the Kaiser, but added that the war was being fought "for Wall Street interest . . . not for democracy."[79]

The success of these meetings led to the arrest of many Socialist leaders, and inspired "loyalty" meetings throughout Minnesota. Among those arrested was J. O. Bentall, a farmer, a former editor of the *Christian Socialist* and one-time Socialist candidate for governor. In a letter written from jail, Bentall described some of the meetings:

At Hutchinson at least 10,000 came—some 20 or 30 miles—full of enthusiasm and eagerness. I never saw anything like it. In the middle of my speech the postmaster rushed up on the platform and struck me in the face. He was promptly reduced to quiet by some big farmers, and I talked another hour and a half. People are falling over each other to hear about Socialism these days. They are no longer afraid of it, and the farmers are most radical and fearless . . . Eight thousand attended a meeting at Dale, including two sheriffs, three judges, and several U.S. deputy marshals and a number of plain clothesmen . . . I never talk against the war, all I do is talk peace.[80]

At the first big "loyalty" meeting in Minneapolis, Governor Burnquist gave his answer to the critics of the war. He warned that if "anti-American meetings" could not be stopped by local officials, "every resource at our command will be used to punish offenders and prevent such meetings from being held." If, by means of such action on the governor's part, "bloodshed and loss of life will result," he added ominously, "the responsibility therefor will rest on those who are back of and support, by their presence, these un-American demonstrations."[81]

The governor's warning failed to stop the peace meetings,

[79] Minneapolis *Journal*, August 8, 1917.
[80] *International Socialist Review*, XVII, 3 (September 1917), 188.
[81] Minneapolis *Journal*, August 7, 1917.

however, so early in September he placed a blanket ban on Socialist meetings in most counties of the state.[82]

Governor Burnquist's attitude toward expressions of antiwar sentiment, although extreme, was by no means unique. Most active interventionists, typified by Theodore Roosevelt, saw in every opponent of war "the Hun within our gates;"[83] the press followed this line almost unanimously.

The atmosphere generated by these attacks was such that officers of the armed services as well as local officials felt secure in enforcing "loyal" opinion even where no public acts were involved. Thus in Lewiston, Idaho, an Army captain arrested several of the Socialist officers and members of the Central Labor Council for remarks made in the heat of a private argument with their fellow trade unionists. The secretary of the Oregon Socialist Party, who came to Lewiston to organize a branch of the antiwar People's Council, was arrested "for no reason whatsoever."[84]

These incidents fulfilled an often-quoted lament made by President Wilson on the eve of the declaration of war that he feared the American people would quickly "forget there ever was such a thing as tolerance."[85] Yet it was the President himself who took the lead in creating the atmosphere of hostility in which such violence against dissenters flourished. Under Wilson's guidance the "loyalty" plank of the 1916 Democratic platform was written to condemn every organization tending "to divide our people into antagonistic groups and thus destroy that complete agreement and solidarity of the people . . . so essential to the perpetuity of free institutions."[86] After war was declared, Wilson promoted a series of security measures including the Espionage Act of June 15, 1917. In Congress, debate

[82] *International Socialist Review,* XVII, 4 (October 1917), 209; *New York Call,* September 14, 1917.
[83] Peterson and Fite, *op. cit.,* p. 81.
[84] C. O. Young (General Organizer for the AFL) to Samuel Gompers, Boise, Idaho, September 24, 1917, AFL papers, Wisconsin State Historical Society.
[85] Quoted in Peterson and Fite, *op. cit.,* p. 11.
[86] Scheiber, *op. cit.,* pp. 8-9.

centered around the President's demand that the Act include a section on press censorship, the main feature of which was a provision for a heavy fine and imprisonment for persons convicted of publishing information the President might proclaim to be useful—or possibly useful—to the enemy. Unlike the other provisions of the Act, however, this section was universally condemned by the American press and was defeated in the House, despite Wilson's firm stand in its behalf.[87] Nevertheless, the President achieved his purpose under another provision of the Espionage Act giving the Postmaster General the right to withhold from the mails matter urging "treason, insurrection, or forcible resistance to any law of the United States."[88]

The initial, and in the long run the most damaging, attack upon the Socialists by the Administration came from the Postmaster General. Unable to restrain himself, Burleson began seizing Socialist papers even before Wilson signed the Espionage Act. His first victim was the Halletsville *Rebel*, which he removed from the mails with the issue of June 9, 1917. Himself a Texan, Burleson may have been influenced against the *Rebel* by the fact that the paper had exposed the eviction of tenant farmers and their replacement by unpaid prison labor on some land that he owned.[89] But, if this is so, Burleson quickly demonstrated that he could be equally repressive where his immediate personal interests were not involved. Among the dozen or more Socialist publications he barred from the mails (for one or more issues) in the weeks after the Act became law were the *Masses; Appeal to Reason; American Socialist; International Socialist Review; Social Revolution* (formerly *National Rip Saw*); *The People's Press*, Philadelphia; *Socialist News*, Cleveland; *The Michigan Socialist*, Detroit.[90]

[87] *Ibid.*, p. 18.
[88] *Ibid.*, p. 19.
[89] Ameringer, *op. cit.*, pp. 318 ff; Halletsville *New Era*, June 12, 1917. The Espionage Act was signed and became law on June 15.
[90] "Divergent Effects of War on the Socialist Movement," *loc. cit.*, p. 75; *International Socialist Review*, XVII, 2 (August 1917), 125; *American*

As the attacks on the Party mounted on many fronts, Socialists found it increasingly difficult to carry on their antiwar agitation through normal channels. In many places vigilante groups put pressure on the proprietors of meeting places to deny Socialists the use of their halls, in others Party meetings were simply outlawed, and in still others Socialist speakers were tarred and feathered by night riders. In South Dakota, for example, the police broke up the state convention of the Party and forced some delegates to leave town.[91] In Kentucky, across the river from his Cincinnati home, the Reverend Herbert S. Bigelow was seized by a mob as he was about to give an antiwar speech, driven some twenty miles away, stripped to the waist, whipped and abandoned.[92] In this atmosphere even electoral activity became perilous for Socialists; but Bigelow, who was a recent convert to the Party, and had been president of the Ohio Constitutional Convention in 1912, hoped that the government would "have to heed the Socialist votes." If, he added sanguinely, "there are as many as we expect, the war will end."[93] So it was that although there were only municipal elections in 1917, Socialists turned to these campaigns as the best remaining forum for public discussion of the issues raised by the war.

V

Even before the Party officially ratified its antiwar program, Socialists had begun to receive substantial increases in their vote in many cities. Thus, in the April elections in Illinois, many people turned to the Socialists, apparently to protest the United States' imminent involvement in the war. In Chicago the So-

---

Labor Yearbook: 1919-1920, p. 401. *The American Socialist,* for example, had its June 16, 23, 30 issues seized.

[91] *New York Call,* January 29, 1918.

[92] Peterson and Fite, *Opponents of War,* p. 79.

[93] Hoyt Landon Warner, *Progressivism in Ohio, 1897-1917* (Columbus, 1964), pp. 313-315; *Akron Beacon-Journal,* October 4, 1917.

cialists elected two aldermen in April, raising their total to a new high of three.[94] At the same time the Socialists elected a mayor in the town of Buckner and the president of the village board in Sylvis. In Granite City, Marshall E. Kirkpatrick was reelected to his third term, after having been defeated by a fusion in 1915.[95] In Rockford, Oscar Ogren, Socialist candidate for mayor, received 30 percent of the vote, compared to 7 percent for Benson in 1916.[96]

After the April elections, the Socialists carried their antiwar campaign into the August and September nonpartisan primaries in Ohio, Pennsylvania, and New York. The first full test of the popularity of the Socialist position on the war came in Dayton, Ohio, home of Governor James Cox. During the campaign the Dayton newspapers virtually ignored the Socialists, concentrating instead on a battle between the Democrats and the "nonpartisan" Citizens' Committee. Yet Socialists from all over Ohio converged on Dayton to aid their comrades. They presented the Party's demands for a statement of war terms and repeal of the draft at street meetings in the working-class wards and in the pages of the one small Socialist weekly newspaper.[97] On primary day, August 14, the Socialists amazed even themselves by sweeping nine of Dayton's twelve wards. The Citizens' Committee carried the remaining three, while the Democrats, supported by Governor Cox's *News*, carried none. Winning by an absolute majority and a record plurality, the Socialists received

[94] *Chicago Daily News Almanac and Yearbook for 1918* (Chicago, 1917), p. 624. Charles Johnson was elected in the Ninth ward in a three-way race. John C. Kennedy polled an absolute majority in the Twenty-Seventh ward.

[95] *American Socialist*, April 28, 1917. Silvis was a Rock Island Railroad maintenance center. Fred Hartline, the Socialist board president, was elected by a vote of 288 to 222 (*St. Louis Labor*, April 21, 1917). Kirkpatrick was elected by a vote of 1,961 to 1,904.

[96] Rockford *Register-Gazette*, April 18, 1917. Ogren received 4,700 votes of some 16,000 cast; Benson had received 1,298 in 1916 (*American Socialist*, April 28, 1917). Five Socialist aldermen were chosen in a field of sixteen, an increase of three.

[97] Joseph Sharts in *New York Call*, September 2, 1917; *Chicago Tribune*, August 18, 1917.

11,017 votes, the largest primary total ever recorded in Dayton. In doing this, they spent only $395, compared to the $28,058 spent by the Democrats and Citizens' Committee.[98]

Overjoyed, Joseph Sharts, local Socialist leader, declared that the victory had been won "squarely on the antiwar issue, and any attempt to minimize the significance of the victory is an effort to hoodwink the rest of the country. . . . The workers registered their protest against the war and voted for peace."[99]

Governor Cox's paper admitted that the vote resulted from the disaffection of Democrats, many of whom were "inimical to the war." At the same time the *News* called for a "combined fight" against the Socialists in the November election to defeat those "cowardly" opponents of the war who, although "afraid to proclaim their convictions to their fellows," were still capable of enjoying the "sensation of the silent stab of the ballot."[100]

The Dayton primary was "an inspiration" for the Party; with growing enthusiasm Socialists campaigned in the remaining primaries available to them. In September, for example, Pennsylvania Socialists nominated their four council candidates in the Reading primary; in Allentown, the one Socialist council candidate, R. J. Wheeler, a local Machinist leader, ran first in a field of eight nominees; in New Castle, Walter Tyler ran second in a similar election; and in Erie, the Socialists unexpectedly nominated one of their four candidates for council.[101] Similarly, in Toledo, Ohio, the Socialist candidate was among three nominees chosen to run for mayor.[102] In the next month, Buffalo Socialists came within a few votes of surpassing the Republicans. Increasing their vote over the previous election from 13 to 32

---

[98] Dayton *News*, August 15, 25, 1917; *Call*, September 2, 1917.
[99] *Ibid.*
[100] Dayton *News*, August 15, 1917.
[101] Reading *News-Times*, Allentown *Democrat*, New Castle *Herald*, Erie *Dispatch*, all September 20, 1917. In Erie the nomination of Ralph Tillotson was called the "zenith" of many surprises in the election.
[102] Toledo *News-Bee*, September 12, 1917. The Socialist ran a poor third in a large field of candidates.

percent, the Party lost a place on the ballot for mayor by 14,341 to 14,695.[103]

After the news of the large primary vote in Buffalo, the *New York Call* rejoiced. "The world is sick of war; it is sick of bloodshed and destruction," the *Call* commented. *"The world wants peace! The world wants socialism."* In a burst of premature enthusiasm, it added: "The great victories that we are winning and that we are going to win are the most significant political events of the century . . . it is not a political revolution. It is *the* political revolution."[104]

Support for the Socialists appeared to be developing so rapidly at the time that this seemingly incredible view is not entirely inexplicable. Several weeks earlier, a Wisconsin newspaper (the *Plymouth Review*) commented that "probably no party ever gained more rapidly in strength than the Socialist party is just at the present time." Expressing the opinion that the Socialists could "carry Sheboygan county by three to one against the two old parties together," the *Review* observed that "thousands assemble to hear Socialist speakers in places where ordinarily a few hundred are considered large assemblages." The revulsion in political sentiment was "simply amazing," for not only were "rock-ribbed Democrats" deserting their Party, but (and this was truly "astounding" to the Progressive-Republican *Review*), people were "going back on the Republican party as well." The paper, a strong supporter of Senator La Follette, saw "a war-sick world" turning to the Socialists, and concluded that if the Republican Party must depend "on such leadership as the Roots, the Lodges and others of that stamp," then "the sooner the party goes down the better." "It is time," the *Review* ended with flourish, "for men to rule and not the 'money bags.' "[105]

---

[103] *Call,* October 18, 1917; Paul H. Douglas, "The Socialist Vote in the 1917 Municipal Elections," *National Municipal Review,* VI (March 1918), 135.
[104] October 19, 1917.
[105] *Plymouth* (Wisconsin) *Review,* August 29, 1917.

In Ohio, the sentiments expressed by the *Review* were echoed by C. L. Knights' conservative Akron *Beacon-Journal,* which commented on September 7 that there was "scarcely a political observer whose opinion is worth much but what will admit that were an election to come now a mighty tide of Socialism would inundate the Middle West" and "maybe all other sections of the country." The *Beacon-Journal* believed that the United States had "never embarked upon a more unpopular war," and that "the vast majority of the people" had "never been convinced that war was necessary either to sustain our honor or to protect our interests." This being so, the *Beacon* concluded, people "vote the Socialist ticket as a means of protest."

While the Socialist record in the various nonpartisan primaries in which they participated was an impressive one, the number of cities involved was small, and, except for Buffalo, no major cities had been tested. By the end of September, however, the fall election campaigns were in full swing in cities from New York to Chicago. Of these campaigns, the one in New York City ranked first in national significance and served as a prototype for almost all the others. In New York, a four-cornered race developed, with the incumbent, John Peuroy Mitchel, a highly irregular Democrat, running as a fusion candidate after unexpectedly losing the Republican primary to William M. Bennett.[106] Against Mitchel, Tammany, under heavy pressure from William Randolph Hearst, had nominated John F. Hylan, a singularly obscure and undistinguished judge from Brooklyn. Morris Hillquit ran on the Socialist line.

Mitchel seized the initiative in the campaign. Disregarding his excellent record on municipal matters, he chose to campaign on all-out support of the war. The tactic played directly into Socialist hands, since the war was the issue the Party wanted most to test. Similarly, Tammany turned the issue to its advantage by adopting a position of ambiguity. Nevertheless, Mitchel

---

[106] Mitchel had originally been declared the victor in the Republican primary, but lost after irregularities were discovered during the recount.

flung the challenge of "Americanism" versus "Kaiserism" at his opponents.

In the early weeks of the campaign, Mitchel concentrated his fire on Judge Hylan. Since Hylan was Hearst's candidate, and Hearst was a well-known Anglophobe whose papers had expressed pro-German sentiments, Hylan quickly became the "Kaiser's candidate." "Hearst, Hylan, and Hohenzollern" became Mitchel's war cry,[107] while campaign posters depicted Mitchel in a doughboy's uniform, rifle in hand, bayonetting the Tammany Tiger. In this posture Mitchel received the support of powerful politicians, of whom Theodore Roosevelt was the loudest and most prominent.[108] Some of Mitchel's supporters attempted to focus the campaign on local issues, but with no success.[109] As the *Nation* observed, Mitchel "not only wrapped himself in the American flag, but declared that a vote for Hylan was a vote for the Kaiser and every vote for Hillquit a vote for treason."[110]

Press support for Mitchel was almost unanimous, and interest in his campaign nationwide,[111] but it was Hillquit for whom there were amazing manifestations of popular support. Rather than carrying on the "usual propaganda campaign" which Hillquit had expected,[112] the Socialists rapidly imparted a spirit of religious revival to the campaign. For the first major Socialist meeting, 20,000 people jammed in and around the old Madison Square Garden. At the "magic" words, "We want peace," the throng rose in its place and "for five minutes the shouting,

---

[107] New York *World*, October 2, 1917, and *passim* September through November 6, 1917.

[108] Charles E. Hughes, Alton B. Parker, Henry Morganthau and Oscar Straus also supported Mitchel actively.

[109] Governor Whitman, in announcing his support of Mitchel, tried to make Tammany and corruption the main issue (*World*, October 15, 1917).

[110] November 8, 1917, p. 500.

[111] See "National Aspects of the Mayorality Contest in New York City," *Current Opinion*, November 1917, pp. 293 ff.

[112] Hillquit, *Loose Leaves*, p. 293.

whistling and stamping of feet beat in waves upon the scarlet-decked platform from which the demand had come."[113]

Morris Hillquit set the tone of the Socialist campaign as he declared:

We are for peace. We are unalterably opposed to the killing of our manhood and the draining of our resources in a bewildering pursuit of an incomprehensible "democracy" . . . a pursuit which begins by suppressing the freedom of speech and press and public assemblage, and by stifling legitimate political criticism.[114]

Hillquit called not for a separate peace but for the immediate convocation of an international conference to end the war on the Socialist principles of no annexations, no indemnities. Meanwhile, Hillquit made clear, the Socialists refused to support the war, and in keeping with the St. Louis Manifesto he announced that he would not buy Liberty Bonds. This caused a storm of indignation; Mayor Mitchel declared that "any man who will not buy a Liberty bond when he can afford them is not fit to be a citizen of the United States."[115] Theodore Roosevelt and Charles E. Hughes joined the attack on this issue, but Hillquit retorted that those who wanted to aid the soldiers should contribute to a fund to end the war.[116]

In Washington, President Wilson considered an indictment of Hillquit for his "outrageous utterances about the Liberty Loan," but decided that the government would "only be assisting Mr. Hillquit by apparently making him a martyr" if it "should pay any attention to his remarks."[117]

Hillquit's refusal to buy bonds increased popular enthusiasm for his candidacy, and throughout October Socialist meetings on the East Side drew great masses of people. One night, for example, fifteen thousand admirers "surged through the streets,"

[113] *Call,* September 24, 1917.
[114] *Ibid.*
[115] *World,* October 26, 1917.
[116] Robert W. Iversen, "Morris Hillquit, American Social Democrat" (unpublished Ph.D. dissertation, University of Iowa, 1951), p. 204.
[117] *Woodrow Wilson, Life and Letters,* ed. R.S. Baker, VII (New York, 1939), 333.

following Hillquit from hall to hall and breaking into spontaneous demonstrations as Hillquit repeatedly asked the crowd: "War or peace? How will you decide?"[118] In a straw poll conducted by the *Herald,* "Scores of ballots were returned with the words written, 'They are all crooks but Hillquit.' " A meeting at which Hillquit had been "followed by thousands who cheered until they were hoarse" was described by this conservative newspaper as a "typical Socialist reception."[119]

The greatest· manifestations of popular support came after Postmaster General Burleson initiated proceedings to revoke the second-class mailing privilege of the *Call.* Although in the long run Burleson's tactics greatly weakened the Party, the immediate effect was to rally non-Socialist support to Hillquit. Several pro-war liberals, including Amos Pinchot, Dudley Field Malone, J. A. H. Hopkins, Allen McCurdy, and Harry Hopkins, supported Hillquit's candidacy as a protest against the actions of the Post Office, which they characterized as "Burlesonism." Most of them also endorsed the Socialist demand for a statement of war terms including no indemnities, no annexations.[120]

Meanwhile, despite the intense barrage from Mayor Mitchel and the press, Judge Hylan maintained a discreet silence on the war. Tammany saw Mitchel's arrogant superpatriotism alienating him from the voters and came to view the growing strength of Hillquit as its main concern. On October 21, the *World* reported that Hillquit had "gained strength at an alarming rate," and that Tammany, "trying to cut the ground from under the Socialistic program," was giving "paramount importance to the municipal ownership pledge and other vagrant features of the Socialistic doctrine." Instructions had been given the leaders "to star municipal ownership and the high cost of living and to *evade any agitation of patriotism or other issues resulting from war conditions."* (Italics added.)

[118] *New York Times,* New York *World,* October 19, 1917.
[119] *Herald,* November 1, 1917.
[120] *New York Times,* October 15, 27, 29, 1917; New York *American,* November 5, 1917, advertisement; Robert E. Sherwood, *Roosevelt and Hopkins* (New York, 1948), p. 25.

The Business Men's League of the City of New York had also come to view Hillquit's candidacy as "not a joke but a dangerous menace." The League, consisting of "business men of standing in this community," was normally opposed to Tammany and friendly to Mitchel, but they warned that businessmen were "confronted with this condition: *the next Mayor of New York will either be Hylan, a Democrat, or Hillquit, a Socialist,*" adding that businessmen "must be guided accordingly."[121]

With the exception of the Hearst papers, the commercial press followed Mitchel in attacking nonsupport of the war as alien and non-American. The *Tribune,* for example, had "Morris Hillquit of Riga" as its subject in the October 28 number of its series on "Who's Who Against America." Hillquit was described as "a Jew, Born at Riga, the Milwaukee of Russia, 48 years ago. Now he is rich and lives on Riverside Drive." The *Herald,* too, ran a cartoon on page one showing a hook-nosed man named "Hillkowitz or Hillquitter" waving a flag inscribed "Peace at any price" at a smiling "Kaiser."[122]

Colonel Roosevelt seized the lead in condemning dissenters. In a speech in support of Mitchel, Roosevelt bellowed: "I don't like the Hun outside our gates, but I tell you, I like the Hun inside them still less. (Applause) And even worse than the Hun is the man who cringes before them!" (Shouts: "Traitors!" Applause.)[123]

In the end, even the liberal *World* joined the pack. On Hillquit, Hylan, and Mitchel it editorialized: "Today's election will determine whether New York is a traitor town, or a quasi-Copperhead town or an American town devoted to American

---

[121] Business Men's League of the City of New York to New York business men, New York, n.d. [October 1917], Hillquit papers.

[122] November 2, 1917. This anti-Semitism appeared to confirm fears previously expressed by several conservative Jewish leaders. The pro-Mitchel *American Hebrew* protested: "It is regrettable that the shortsighted policy of making the Jew the scapegoat for all radical movements, having been abandoned by the reactionary Russian press since the outbreak of the Revolution, has been adopted now by some of our New York dailies." Quoted in *World,* November 5, 1917.

[123] *Herald,* November 1, 1917.

ideals and pledged without reservation to the war policies of the United States government."[124]

On election day, Mayor Mitchel's militantly pro-war campaign ended in disaster. Hylan swept in, receiving the greatest plurality in the history of the city, while Hillquit finished almost even with Mitchel. The vote was 313,956 for Hylan, 155,-497 for Mitchel, 145,332 for Hillquit, and 55,438 for Bennett. Two-thirds of the vote had gone either to the candidate widely accused of disloyalty or to the one openly opposed to the war. Hillquit's 21.7 percent represented a nearly fivefold increase over the normal Socialist vote. For the first time the Party put candidates on the board of aldermen, electing seven. The Socialists also elected a municipal court judge and ten assemblymen, an increase of eight over their previous high.[125]

Hillquit hailed the result as a repudiation of Administration politics. But Hylan "proclaimed his loyalty" the day after the election, and newspapers the country over that had attacked Hylan as the Kaiser's candidate took this belated declaration as proof that Hylan's victory was no reflection of peace sentiment.[126] "New York is not against the war," the *Tribune* wrote. "It is not ready to accept the programme of surrender which Mr. Hillquit so boldly preached."[127] The Des Moines *Register* echoed: "Whatever satisfaction the Kaiser got out of the New York election will be due to the large minority vote cast for the Socialist candidate."[128] It was left for the *Survey* to state the obvious: that although "Hillquit polled much of the anti-war vote . . . some non-Socialist pacifists voted for Hylan as more practical."[129]

[124] November 6, 1917.
[125] *Call*, November 8, 1917; *Annual Report of the Board of Elections in the City of New York: 1917*. One other Socialist candidate for the assembly was tied until the soldier vote was counted; an aldermanic candidate lost by 11 votes.
[126] *Literary Digest*, November 17, 1917, p. 12; *Herald*, November 8, 1917.
[127] November 7, 1917.
[128] Quoted in *Literary Digest, loc. cit.*
[129] November 10, 1917, p. 144.

As in New York, so in most other cities, the war was the main issue projected by the Socialists.[130] In Reading, Pennsylvania, for example, James Maurer told the voters: "On election day you have on one side a party which has plunged you into war . . . on the other hand you have the Socialist party which is opposed to the war and demands an immediate peace."[131] And in Cleveland, C. E. Ruthenberg, under indictment for inciting resistance to the draft, campaigned vigorously along the same lines. Calling Ruthenberg "the Hillquit of Cleveland," the *Plain Dealer* wrote that should this "candidate of Prussianism" be given a respectable showing, Cleveland—"200 percent city in patriotism"—would be "shamed before the world."[132]

In Toledo, where a two-way race developed,[133] Robert T. Haworth, the Socialist candidate, was a locally prominent leader of the Machinists' union, and was described by the local labor paper as the "workingman candidate for mayor." He received support from Senator La Follette, who attacked war profiteers at a meeting also addressed by the Socialist candidate.[134] After La Follette endorsed Haworth, the senator was attacked by Charles Edward Russell. Calling the senator "a perjurer and a traitor," who sympathized with Germany, Russell suggested La

---

[130] Eureka, Utah, was an exception (Eureka *Reporter,* October 26, 1917), as was Blairsville, Pennsylvania. In Blairsville the main issue seemed to be that the Socialist candidate, Reuben Einstein, was the richest man in town. Einstein was accused of being himself a parasite, and was chided for his Socialist ideals. Conceding his parasitic nature, Einstein explained that "the actual difference between me and the other parasites is this: They want to stay on your backs and continue to live off you, while . . . I am willing to get entirely off your backs just as soon as you have enough sense to keep others off . . . [Until then] I refuse to join your ranks and starve . . ." (Blairsville *Courier,* October 25, 1917, advertisement.) Einstein received 45 percent of the vote, but lost against fusion.

[131] Reading *News-Times,* November 5, 1917.

[132] November 3, 1917.

[133] The third nominee died several weeks before the election.

[134] *Toledo Union Leader,* September 28, 1917. Haworth was a delegate to the Ohio Federation of Labor Convention, and to the People's Council. See also Toledo *News-Bee,* September 24, 1917; and New York *Tribune,* November 7, 1917.

Follette should "go live there."[135] Meanwhile, the Toledo *News-Bee,* concerned over the possibility of Haworth's election, warned "that to elect a Socialist mayor at this time would be to encourage sedition and treason, to stimulate German intrigue, to aid in dividing our own people when we should stand together as one man."[136]

At the same time, in Dayton, the Democratic governor actively supported the Citizens' Committee campaign. Attacking the Socialists, Governor Cox argued that in opposing the war they "insolently assume that our people are not opposed to war in the abstract." Following this non sequitur, Governor Cox explained that "everybody knows that the war is being fought to prevent wars in the future; that when the Kaiser is destroyed the great menace to peace shall have been destroyed."[137] The Dayton *Journal,* organ of the Citizens' Committee, was also deeply concerned at the prospect of Socialist victory. It quoted the New York Socialists' declaration that a Socialist victory *"will be a clear mandate to the government of the United States to open negotiations for an immediate peace."* The prospect was more than the *Journal* could bear. "When the votes are counted," it declared, "we are going to know, for a truth, whether we really have a nation, or as Colonel Roosevelt expresses it, 'only a polyglot boarding house.' "[138]

In Hamilton, Ohio, too, where the Socialist candidate for mayor faced a single opponent, the *Evening Journal* noted that many intended to vote Socialist "as a means of saying they want the war to stop." But, the *Journal* argued, "such a vote cannot stop the war. If every man in Hamilton voted the Socialist ticket it would and could have no effect on our nation at war . . . The

[135] *News-Bee,* November 6, 1917.
[136] November 3, 1917.
[137] Cleveland *Plain Dealer,* November 4, 1917. The governor also challenged the Socialists to "produce one Socialist leader that had bought a war bond."
[138] November 1, 1917.

only thing a vote for the Socialist ticket can do is say you . . . are in sympathy with the Kaiser."[139]

On election day, November 6, Socialist mayors were elected in only eleven small municipalities, two in Indiana, one in Minnesota, three in Ohio, four in Pennsylvania, and one in Utah.[140] Yet the Party made unprecedented gains in the larger industrial cities in which they had campaigned (see Table 4). The most sweeping gains were recorded in Ohio, where the Party received 30 percent of the vote or more in at least seven cities and two towns. All told, the Party received from 20 to over 50 percent of the vote in a dozen of the largest municipalities in Ohio, in ten cities and towns in Pennsylvania, in six cities in Indiana, and in four in New York. It received 34 percent of the vote in Chicago (see Table 4). A large number of minor officials were elected to municipal offices in Ohio, Indiana, Pennsylvania, New Jersey, New York, Minnesota, and Kentucky.

Throughout the country the press commented on the large Socialist vote in New York City, while ignoring or minimizing it elsewhere. In reporting the results in Chicago, for example, the *New York Times* exulted because the " 'anti-war, anti-Wilson, anti-American' judicial ticket of the Socialists" had been snowed under "in a blizzard of ballots."[141] But the Socialist defeat in Chicago was decisive only because the Democrats and Republicans had united in a single opposition slate. Actually, the 34 percent which the Socialists won represented almost a tenfold increase over their normal vote; and the Party carried nineteen of twenty-nine Cook County towns outside of Chicago. Indeed, the large Socialist vote induced Roger Sullivan, Chicago Democratic leader, to suggest that it might be "time to amal-

[139] November 5, 1917.
[140] These victories were in small cities or towns. McKeesport, Pennsylvania has been included in the list although the Socialists elected a controller there. Apparently there was no contest for mayor.
[141] November 8, 1917.

gamate the Republican and Democratic parties in the nation in a new lineup of conservatives and radicals."[142]

In further deprecation, the press widely attributed the Socialist vote in these elections to the foreign born. The Philadelphia *Public Ledger,* for example, declared that Hillquit's vote was "almost entirely due to . . . alien discontent, intensified by conditions peculiar to foreign populations of New York in wartime."[143] Summing up for the press, the *National Municipal Review* attributed the large Socialist vote in New York City, Buffalo, Cleveland, and Chicago to the "immense foreign influence" in those cities.

Indeed, in many cities Socialists won large sections of the immigrant populations to their banner. In New York City, Hillquit's strength was greatest in the Jewish working-class districts on the East Side of Manhattan.[144] But contrary to popular belief, this was not typical. In many cities with few foreign born, the Socialists received heavy popular support, and on the whole, there was no correlation between the number of foreign born in the population and the Socialist vote (see Tables 4 and 5). Hamilton and Dayton, Ohio, for example, each gave the Socialists 44 percent of the vote, yet they had foreign-born populations of only 6.7 and 8.6 percent, very low figures in this period. And in Indiana there was actually a negative correlation between the percentage of foreign born and the Socialist vote (see Table 5). Nor did the foreign-born population necessarily support the Socialists. In Reading, Pennsylvania (where the Party received 33 percent of the vote), the *News-Times* wrote that the "election dispelled another fallacy. It proved that the German-

---

[142] Paul H. Douglas, "The Socialist Vote . . .," p. 139; *Nation,* November 27, 1917, p. 712; Milwaukee *Leader,* November 8, 1917. Election figures, *Chicago Daily News Almanac and Yearbook: 1918,* p. 624.
[143] November 9, 1917.
[144] Harry Best, "Melting Pot in the United States," *Social Forces,* May 1936, pp. 591 ff. Best, however, considers the heavy Socialist vote among the Jewish immigrants as proof that these foreigners had failed to become "Americanized."

American citizens were absolutely loyal, for they voted almost as a unit against the Socialist candidates."[145]

The truth is simply that the Socialist vote was heaviest in working-class districts. Thus most of the small cities and villages in which the Socialist Party elected candidates were factory towns, railroad maintenance centers, or coal mining camps, while in the larger cities they received their heaviest vote in working-class wards.[146] Consequently, in those cities with large numbers of working-class immigrants, such as Chicago, Cleveland, Buffalo, Rochester, and New York City, the Socialist vote came predominantly from the foreign born, while in small cities and towns in Indiana, Ohio, and Kansas, their vote came from native-born workers.

VI

After the election, the New York *Evening Post* commented that "The Socialists have won admission, as it were, to the family of political parties,"[147] a sentiment confidently echoed by Debs and other Party leaders.[148] These statements, however, reflected the lack of comprehension in the Party, even after more than six months of unprecedented harassment, of the rapid changes taking place in American society as a result of the war.

[145] November 7, 1917.
[146] For example, the Socialists captured the factory towns of Granite City, Illinois, Elwood and Gas City, Indiana, and McKeesport, Pennsylvania, as well as the railroad centers of Sylvis, Illinois, Frontenac, Kansas, and Pitcairn, Pennsylvania, and the mining towns of Garrett, Elk Lick and Hooversville, in Somerset County, Pennsylvania.
[147] Quoted in Douglas, *loc. cit.*
[148] Debs commented that "the tremendous and unprecedented Socialist gains" had resulted from the fact that the campaign was waged on issues arising from the war, adding that there was "nothing in all its past career to be compared to the sweeping political victory achieved this year," *Eye Opener*, December 1, 1917. This opinion was widespread. Thus, for example, the comment of John C. Sjodin in "The Socialist Corner" of the Galesburg, Illinois *Labor News* that "perhaps the most wonderful election in the United States will be credited to the year 1917," November 23, 1917.

Just before the election the liberal Dayton *News* had indicated more accurately what was in store for the Party. "Ever since the outbreak of the war," observed the *News*, "we have heard sedition preached and it has been allowed to pass in the name of free speech." Now, the paper continued, "we see riot and disorder encouraged in political campaigns by Socialist candidates, who hope thereby to collect under their banner all who have grievances . . ." But, concluded the *News*, tolerance has its limits: "Action must take the place of forebearance."[149]

Some weeks earlier, George Creel had revealed that "action" was coming. President Wilson, Creel told the League for National Unity, had been forced to reject a proposal for a national junketing tour "to whip up support for the war," because "he saw this country sectionalized as perhaps never before." Instead the Administration had proceeded piecemeal, Creel explained. "We have a Loyalty League in Wisconsin," and in general try "to find centers of disaffection, and then fight it on its ground." But this had not been enough. "You will find," he went on "in Georgia and parts of South Carolina; you will find in Arkansas; you will find in many parts of the West, an indifference that is turned into a very active irritation that borders on disloyalty." The piecemeal approach envisioned in the formation of such organizations as the Wisconsin Loyalty Legion or the Alliance for Labor and Democracy had to be supplemented. "We feel," Creel explained, "that we must go further . . . that we must take on the whole country."[150]

In the months that followed, the Federal Government moved against the Socialist and IWW opponents of the war through a series of indictments under the newly enacted Espionage Act. These were returned not only against Party leaders but even against rank-and-file members in many communities.[151] Some of

[149] November 3, 1917.
[150] Minutes of the League for National Unity, Meeting September 12, 1917.
[151] For a full discussion of this see Scheiber, *op. cit.*, and Peterson and Fite, *op. cit.*, Chapters V, XV, XVII.

these indictments were obviously designed directly to hamper the Party organization and activity, as was the indictment of Victor Berger in the middle of his campaign for senator in Wisconsin in March 1918. Others seemed aimed simply at terrorizing and intimidating individuals, as in the conviction and ten-year sentence of A.L. Hitchcock, a Cleveland Socialist, who was arrested on the complaint of a person not present for a remark he was alleged to have made while visiting a sick friend in his home.[152] In Seattle, Hulet Wells, a former president of the Central Labor Council, Sam Sadler, an editor of the Seattle *Daily Call* and the *Union Record,* and Joe and Morris Pass were indicted for circulating a leaflet against conscription. Union support for Wells and Sadler was substantial, and their first trial resulted in one of the few hung juries during the war. But at the second trial all four were convicted and sentenced to two years. Emil Herman, Washington state secretary, was less fortunate; he was convicted and sentenced to ten years imprisonment for violation of the Espionage Act.[153] In some places these Government actions threw the Party into panic, inflicting permanent damage to its organization. Out of fear of the possibility of the prosecution drawing a connection between the Green Corn Rebellion and the activities of the Party leadership, the Socialist Party of Oklahoma formally dissolved after Berger and four other national leaders were indicted.[154]

Meanwhile, vigilante activities continued to increase, especially in the smaller cities and towns where Party members were known, could not work anonymously, and did not dare work openly. All in all, in the last year of the war, some 1,500 of the more than 5,000 Socialist Party locals were destroyed, mostly in small communities.[155] This, in addition to the suppression of

---

[152] Hitchcock to Seymour Stedman, Cleveland, May 28, 1918, SPC, Duke.
[153] O'Connor, *Revolution in Seattle,* pp. 105, 115-118; Friedheim, *The Seattle General Strike,* pp. 10-11.
[154] Ameringer, *If You Don't Weaken,* p. 351.
[155] Seymour Stedman at the National Convention of the Socialist Party, August 30, 1919, Chicago. *Proceedings,* p. 13.

those Socialist publications dependent on the mails, greatly weakened the Party on the West Coast and in the Midwest. At the same time the rapid growth of the Party in the larger industrial cities shifted both the geographical pattern of Socialist strength and the national composition of its membership.

VII

Another event halfway around the earth, however, had an even more profound impact on the Socialist movement in the United States. The day following the November 1917 elections, the Bolsheviks seized power in Russia. Hailed joyfully by all Socialists at the time, the Russian Revolution, and the events it precipitated, was soon to influence the attitude of many Socialists toward continuation of the war, as, in the long run, it was to change their attitudes toward the nature of the Socialist movement in the United States. More immediately, the Russian Revolution impelled President Wilson to enunciate, early in December 1917, the principles he would soon embody in his Fourteen Points. At the same time, the Bolshevik triumph in Russia undoubtedly strengthened the resolve of many Administration leaders to crush Socialist opposition at home.

The President's espousal of the Socialist principles of no annexations, no indemnities, in his December 8 address to Congress and in the Fourteen Points, enabled many wearying opponents of war to change gracefully to supporters of the Administration. Among the first of these, as we have seen, was the *Appeal to Reason*, which threw its support behind Wilson on December 15. On that date, also, the New York local decided not to sponsor an antiwar meeting in Madison Square Garden or to arrange another peace meeting.[156] Yet, despite the hesita-

---

[156] Minute Book, Executive Committee, Socialist Party Local New York, December 15, 1917, p. 95, Tamiment Library. Also cited in Melvin Dubovsky, "Organized Labor in New York City and the First World War, 1914-1918," *New York History*, XLII, 4 (October 1961), p. 393, which draws implications not in the minutes themselves.

tion of the New York local, the Party remained overwhelmingly antiwar for several months following Wilson's new declaration of principle. The enthusiastic reception of the Fourteen Points, both in the United States and among the Allied Powers, convinced some Socialists, notably those who, like Dan Hogan, had hesitated to adopt a strongly antiwar position in the first place, that "a great principle," the "right of self-determination," had "grown out of the war." Believing that the Allies were now committed to this principle past "the possibility of repudiation," Hogan (at the time the Socialist candidate for governor of Arkansas) insisted in the spring of 1918 on the right to support the government's war policies.[157]

Other Socialists considered the future attitude of the Allied governments toward Soviet Russia as "of first importance." These Party members argued that the Bolsheviki, despite the treaty of Brest-Litovsk, were the genuine opponents of the German government, which they viewed as "the most dangerous exponent of reactionary capitalism."[158]

The strong feeling of the need to protect the Russian Revolution convinced many Socialists of all tendencies of the necessity, or at least desirability, of German defeat. Joseph Freeman, for example, relates how the Treaty of Brest-Litovsk changed the attitude of many radicals to the war. This "victory of German autocracy over the workers' revolution" made the defeat of Germany seem "essential for the defense of the workers' republic." As a result, along with many of his radical friends, Freeman joined the R.O.T.C. at Columbia University in early 1918.[159]

Freeman's changing attitude toward the war reflected a general condition among Socialist and non-Socialist radicals. William J. Robinson, a well-known pacifist, had steadfastly opposed

[157] Dan Hogan, "Socialist Pacifism Repudiated," *Quarry Workers Journal*, June 1918.
[158] J. C. Sjodin, "The Socialist Corner," *Galesburg Labor News*, May 17, 1918.
[159] Joseph Freeman, *American Testament* (New York, 1926), pp. 111, 124-25.

the war until February 1918. But Germany's attack on the
Soviets appeared "so incredible, so horrible, so treacherous, so
unprecedented, that the mind staggers and the blood runs
cold." Russia, Robinson wrote, was "begging for peace," but
Germany was "determined to crush" her, "to dismember her, to
drink her last drop of blood."[160] Under such circumstances, Germany must be defeated. The Amalgamated Clothing Workers
also praised Wilson's Fourteen Points in January 1918, as evidence that the President, unlike other Allied leaders, was
friendly to the Soviets. By March the union had come to believe
that the role of "heroic Russia" in "this frightful world tragedy"
gave the "struggle against German militarism new meaning."
German militarism now stood as "the brigand of the world."[161]
Max Eastman echoed these ideas at his sedition trial in April.
Wilson, he announced, had "placed himself directly beside the
Russians" with respect to annexations and indemnities. The Germans, on the other hand, ignored these principles and were gain-
ing ground in Russia. Eastman now supported the Allied
Powers.[162]

These sentiments gained ground rapidly in Socialist ranks in
the spring of 1918. In early March, Algernon Lee had signed a
cable begging the German Socialists "vigorously to oppose"
their "rulers' efforts to crush the Russian revolution."[163] And in
April, Lee and five other Socialist aldermen in New York voted
to support the third Liberty Loan. By June, Thomas Van Lear
had announced his support of the war in Minneapolis, the three
Chicago aldermen had voted for a loyalty resolution, and the
eighty-four-year-old "Mother" Jones had announced that for the

[160] William J. Robinson, typescript statement, February 27, 1918, J.G.P.
Stokes papers, Columbia University.
[161] *Advance*, January 18, March 22, 1918.
[162] *New York Call*, April 21, 1918.
[163] Reprinted in *Revolutionary Radicalism, Its History, Purpose, and
Tactics: Report of the Joint Legislative Committee Investigating Seditious
Activities,* filed April 24, 1920 in the Senate of the State of New York
(Albany, 1920), I, 636.

first time she was urging working men and women to buy government bonds.[164]

Meanwhile, as so often before, Debs reflected the feeling in the Party's ranks, this time of uncertainty. In May, Debs called for a convention to reformulate the Party position on the war. Declaring the St. Louis Manifesto no longer adequate, Debs wrote that the role of the German Socialists in supporting the Kaiser's invasion of Russia revealed that they were "base nationalists." This action on the part of the Germans raised a question about the ability of the Soviets to survive, which, Debs declared, necessitated a new look at the Party's position on the war.[165] By the middle of June, however, Debs had backtracked on the implications of his position, declaring that there was still only one war in which he would enlist; that of the workers of the world against the exploiters of the world. He still called for a convention to determine the feelings of the Party, but not for a new look at the Party's basic attitude toward the war.[166]

The problems involved in holding a convention during the war were so great that the idea never received serious consideration. Instead, a Conference of State Secretaries and Party Officials met in Chicago from August 10 through 12. In the midst of considerable confusion over what policy to adopt, the conference reaffirmed the Party's long-standing opposition to the Kaiser, but did not alter the Party position on the war. The reasons for this decision, aside from constitutional inhibitions, were expressed in a "Proclamation on Russia," issued by the conference. In this proclamation, the Party welcomed the Soviets as "an advanced form of democracy," and praised the Russians for having "cast aside the false idols of secret diplomacy and imperialism." "Economically and socially, as well as

[164] Minutes of the Central Committee of the New York Local of the Socialist Party, April 13, 27, 1917; *Quarry Workers Journal,* June 1918; *Galesburg Labor News,* May 14, 1918.
[165] Debs, "The Socialist Party and the War," *The Social Builder,* May 1918.
[166] Buffalo *New Age,* June 15, 1918.

politically," the conference declared, "the Russian Socialist Federated Soviet Republic is a government of the workers, by the workers and for the workers," which the "forces of capitalism and reaction throughout the world" were "determined to crush."

Since both sides were intent on destroying the Russian Revolution, the Party declined to choose between them. "German imperialism," the proclamation continued, "has attempted to crush Russia from the West," after wresting the Russian border provinces and the Ukraine from Russia under a "brigand's peace." But "imperialists in the countries at war with Germany have adopted an attitude toward Russia similar to that of the Prussian junkers," and were "demanding an invasion of Russia" and the "crushing of the Soviet Republic by Allied armies." Condemning both sides, the Party called on Americans to join with it in urging the Administration to recognize the Soviet Republic. "The Socialist Party of America," the proclamation concluded, "declares itself in accord with Revolutionary Russia and urges our government and our people to cooperate with it," to the end that the "democratic forces of the world may be victorious and autocracy and imperialism banished forever."[167]

Not all party leaders had wavered in their attitudes toward the war in spring and summer of 1918; nor was there any meaningful division along factional lines. Thus, while some leaders of all tendencies exhibited confusion, others remained staunchly anti-Administration. In late December 1917, William Bross Lloyd told a meeting of the People's Council for Peace and Democracy that "we fight to export our surplus products, for the profit of their makers and exporters." Lloyd quoted a statement of William Gibbs McAdoo that "we fight first of all for America's vital rights, the right to the unmolested and unobstructed use of the high seas, so that the surplus products of our farms, our mines and our factories may be carried into the harbors of every friendly nation in the world." But, Lloyd pointed out,

[167] "Proclamation on Russia," adopted by the Conference of State Secretaries and Party Officials, August 10-12, 1918. Typewritten, SPC, Duke.

other nations fight for the same reasons, and so peace cannot be gotten by war, but only by ending commercial rivalry: "by removing the causes of war."[168]

Right-wing Victor Berger emerged as the Party's most consistent and effective opponent of further American participation in the war. When in December 1917, Daniel Hoan was reported to have said that he could no longer support both the Constitution and the St. Louis Proclamation, Berger answered sharply. Giving "plain notice to all Party members, and especially to those who are seeking office," Berger warned that anyone who could not accept the official Socialist position, "be that man a mayor or a constable," must "get out of the Party in justice to himself and the Party."[169] Berger often reiterated his support of the St. Louis Manifesto, and made it clear in the Milwaukee mayoralty election in April 1918, that the "great issue is peace or war." The Socialist Party in Milwaukee, "as elsewhere," Berger wrote, would give the voter a chance "to register his vote in favor of an immediate, general and democratic peace . . . or for a bloody, long-drawn-out plutocratic war."[170]

Berger explained America's entrance into the war as a result of the "close partnership" of "our capitalist class" with the English capitalists in the struggle against their German counterparts for control of world markets. "All the rest," he frequently commented, was "hypocrisy and humbug," and, as he later observed, one of the "biggest humbugs and most contemptible lies" was the phrase "this war was fought to make the world safe for democracy."[171]

In April 1918, when a special election for United States sen-

---

[168] *Peace, Now You See It, Now You Don't* (n.p., 1918?), pamphlet. Lloyd's speech was made in Chicago on December 21, 1917.
[169] *Milwaukee Leader,* December 28, 1917. Quoted in *Hearings Before the Special Committee Concerning the Right of Victor L. Berger to be Sworn in as a Member of the Sixty-Sixth Congress,* II, 579. Referred to hereafter as *Berger Hearings.*
[170] *Milwaukee Leader,* January 12, 14, 1918. Quoted in *Berger Hearings,* p. 64.
[171] Speeches delivered March 30, 1918, Milwaukee, and June 8, 1919, New York. Quoted in *Berger Hearings,* I, 65, 92.

ator was held in Wisconsin, Berger became the Socialist candidate. Running against him were Joseph E. Davies, who received strong support from President Wilson and the pro-war press, and Irvine Lenroot, supported by Senator La Follette. Although one of Wisconsin's two congressmen who had voted for the declaration of war (nine voted against it), Lenroot was attacked by the Democrats for having a record which did not square with the "interests of the nation," as well as for his acceptance of La Follette's aid.[172]

Berger campaigned on a platform calling for an immediate, general peace, without forcible annexations or punitive indemnities, but with the right of all nations to self-determination; he promised, if elected, to introduce a resolution for an immediate peace conference. He also demanded the return of American troops from Europe, and a system of taxation of war industries which would "take every penny of profits derived from the sale of war supplies."[173] During the campaign fifty billboards in Milwaukee announced that "WAR IS HELL CAUSED BY CAPITALISM. SOCIALISTS DEMAND PEACE. READ THE PEOPLE'S SIDE. MILWAUKEE LEADER. VICTOR L. BERGER, EDITOR."[174] Outside Milwaukee, however, Berger had difficulty hiring halls in which to speak; Socialists distributing literature were arrested without cause and meetings were broken up by mobs organized by the vigilante committees of local chambers of commerce and commercial clubs.[175] In the middle of the campaign, Berger was indicted under the Espionage Act. Among the 500-odd newspapers in Wisconsin, only the *Milwaukee Leader* supported Berger, and that paper could circulate only in and near Milwaukee, being banned from the mails even as first-class matter.

Lenroot, described often as a 50 percent war candidate,[176] won the election over the 100 percent pro-war Davies, by a vote

---

[172] *Milwaukee Journal,* April 1, 1918.
[173] *Berger Hearings,* I, 340.
[174] *Ibid.,* pp. 312-313.
[175] *Milwaukee Leader,* April 3, 1918.
[176] See, for example, *Milwaukee Leader,* April 4, 1918; and *Milwaukee Journal,* April 3, 1918.

of 163,980 to 148,713, while Berger polled 110,487. Despite the tremendous odds against him, Berger won 26 percent of the vote, a fourfold increase over the normal Socialist vote in the state.[177]

Later, in November, the Socialists elected their entire county ticket in Milwaukee, re-elected Berger to Congress from the Fifth District for the first time since 1910, and polled 42 percent of the vote in the Fourth District. At the same time they increased the number of Socialist state legislators in Wisconsin from 13 to 22.[178]

The gains in Wisconsin did not represent a general trend in 1918, although in that year, Socialists did run unusually well in parts of Minnesota, Iowa, Michigan, and South Dakota.[179] In Minnesota, in June, Thomas Van Lear campaigned jointly with Charles A. Lindbergh, Nonpartisan League candidate for governor in the Republican primary. A "loyalty ticket" was put up against the radical pacifist and the Socialist, and the Minneapolis *Journal* urged the people of Minnesota to "let Lindbergh know that he cannot preach sedition and treason, and yet aspire to the chief magistry of the state." Van Lear was told that "stirring up class feeling will not avail to return him to the seat he does not deserve, and that his acceptance of the disloyal St. Louis platform was emphatically 'a local issue.' "[180] Repression

---

[177] *Milwaukee Journal,* April 10, 1918. The Socialists polled 27,856 votes for President in 1916 in Wisconsin.

[178] *Milwaukee Leader,* November 6, 1918; *Milwaukee Journal,* November 6, 7, 1918. Berger was refused his seat after a House hearing. Re-elected in a special election in 1919 by an increased plurality, he was again refused a seat. In 1920 he lost, but finally won and was seated in 1922.

[179] In St. Paul the Socialists increased their vote from 1,308 in 1916 to 7,205 in April 1918 (*Cleveland Citizen,* May 4, 1918). In Iowa the Socialist mayorality candidate in Davenport polled 3,326 votes (38%) in the April election, losing by only 24 votes, an increase from 430 in 1916. In Muscatine the Socialist lost by only 215 votes (*Davenport Democrat,* April 7, May 4, 1918). In Kalamazoo and Grand Rapids, Michigan Socialists elected commissioners and councilmen for the first time (*New Age,* May 18, 1918). In South Dakota the Party elected a judge against fusion in Hutchinson county. The war was the main issue (*Eye Opener,* November 1918; *South Dakota Manual,* 1919, p. 133).

[180] *Minneapolis Journal,* June 15, 1918.

in the campaign was so intense that Lindbergh was forced to conduct at least one meeting in the state of Iowa.[181] Yet he received 43 percent of the primary vote, while Van Lear won renomination. In November, Van Lear lost to J. E. Myers by 27,652 votes to 28,967, but the Socialists increased their number of aldermen in Minneapolis from three to seven; and in the state, two Socialists were elected to the assembly and two to the senate.[182]

Riding on the crest of its heavy gains of 1917, the Party had expected to continue increasing its vote in 1918. With the slogan "on to Washington," a million-dollar fund drive had been initiated early in the year, but by the summer this had bogged down.[183] Government and vigilante attacks had disrupted the Party organization in most areas, and in the fall elections only Berger was elected to Congress. Meyer London failed of reelection from his Lower East Side district, but his loss did not indicate a decline in Party strength there: it was the price he paid for his insufficient militancy against the war.[184] In general, the Party held its own or gained in those areas where its organization was still intact. In many cities, however, the wartime attacks had taken their toll, and even where the locals had not been entirely disrupted, their energies were often dissipated in defending their right to exist.

VIII

When the United States entered the war, the Socialist Party had become the only one among the warring countries of the world which, in the words of the Amalgamated Clothing Workers organ, "was not caught in the treacherous swamps of jingo-

[181] Peterson and Fite, *op. cit.*, pp. 189 ff.
[182] *Minneapolis Journal*, June 19, 23, November 7, 8, 9, 13, 1918.
[183] Buffalo *New Age*, January-July, 1918.
[184] See, for example, *The Class Struggle*, II, 5 (December 1918), 621, 622. London's loss is thankfully received, but the loss of Hillquit, Joseph Whitehorn, Scott Nearing, and Abraham Shiplacoff, in their congressional races, is lamented.

ism and murder—patriotism."[185] At the end of the war the "singular" position of the American Party was again affirmed by E. M. Dutton, secretary of the Virginia Party organization. The war, Dutton wrote, had left the American movement in unique "harmony with the new spirit" of world socialism. The conservatives had "bolted," but had failed to disrupt the Party.[186] Although differences in approach had developed during the war, no group within the Party could claim superiority in its anti-war militance or consistency—unless it was Victor Berger's.

The decline in factional differences within the Party was well illustrated at a meeting in Chicago just after the November election. Present were Berger and Seymour Stedman representing the Right, J. Louis Engdahl, William F. Kruse and William Bross Lloyd, a part owner of the *Chicago Tribune*, representing the Left, Irwin St. John Tucker of the *Christian Socialist*, and Alexander Stoklitsky, translator-secretary of the Russian Language Federation of the Party. Introduced as a good Socialist "because he can show his indictments," Berger expressed his sympathy for the Russian Revolution and his hostility toward the Administration. "They are afraid of Bolshevism," he said, but "all Socialists are pro-Bolshevik today." The capitalists, Berger added, "are not afraid of Germany, but they are afraid of Bolshevism in Europe. They are afraid 2,000,000 soldier boys will be affected by it." After being told by Berger to "Stand by your colors—the flag—your ideas—and when I say the flag I mean the international flag," the meeting adopted several resolutions. The first extended "the hand of fellowship to the revolting working class of Europe" and expressed accord with "German comrades under the leadership of Karl Liebknecht"; the second demanded the immediate recognition of the Russian Socialist Soviet Republic; the third attacked the Sisson documents, which purported to prove that the Bolsheviks were German agents, as libelous; and the fourth demanded im-

[185] *Advance*, April 20, 1917.
[186] E. M. Dutton, "Virginia Bulletin," *Ohio Socialist*, January 22, 1919.

mediate withdrawal of United States troops from Europe.[187] In the United States, the Scheidemanns had not controlled the Party as in Europe: they had either resigned or been expelled. Like W. J. Ghent, Charles Edward Russell, William English Walling, and Henry Slobodin, they had become the most rabid enemies of the Party.[188]

Most Socialist publications and a good many Party locals had been destroyed or disrupted during the war by the actions of the federal government and of local vigilantes. Indeed, the mass of indictments, the refusals of the right to hold meetings in public, the removal of newspapers from the mails, the tarrings and featherings, and even lynchings[189] suffered by Socialists and other radicals during the war so far exceeded what during the 1950's came to be known as the terrors of McCarthyism as to make the latter appear to be an era of tranquillity. But in the face of this the Party increased its membership and held its own at the polls. When peace and an end to the government-encouraged attacks finally came, there was good cause for optimism; not only had the Socialists survived their greatest trial but their position on the war was rapidly to be vindicated by the diplomats at Versailles. In Kansas, the *Appeal to Reason* began its steady movement back to the Party, and in Texas, Tom Hickey, editor of the defunct Hallettsville *Rebel,* and Covington Hall, militant left-wing Southern Socialist, made plans to start a new paper in Dallas.[190] Debs, Berger, and Hillquit looked to the future hopefully, and labor leaders such as Duncan McDonald pointed to the hollowness of the democratic pretensions of the Wilson administration. In July 1919, for example, *Advance* (organ of the Amalgamated Clothing Workers) expressed the disillusionment of many others in the labor move-

[187] *Chicago Tribune,* November 18, 1918, under the headline: "Socialists Out in the Open for the Bolsheviki."

[188] See, for example, Lawrence Goldman, "W. J. Ghent and the Left," *Studies on the Left,* III, 3 (Summer 1963).

[189] Peterson and Fite, *Opponents of War, passim.*

[190] Tom Hickey to Frank P. Walsh, Brandenburg, Texas, December 6, 1918, Walsh papers. The paper's name was *The Voice of the People.*

ment who, like *Advance,* had warmly greeted Wilson's Fourteen Points in 1918. In the "Fourteen Points Brought Up to Date," the union journal commented that the League of Nations had turned out to be a new security "for the kings not overthrown by the war-made revolutions," and listed the Fourteen Points as they had been translated into reality:

1. Secret diplomacy: Secret covenants secretly arrived at.
2. Clique of Nations.
3. Annexations.
4. Indemnities.
5. Self determination of nationalities whenever allowed.
6. International relations: Blockade and Militarism.
7. Domestic situation: Repression, espionage, censorship, raids, deportation, militarism.
8. End the one great war and continue twenty-three small ones.
9. Victory without peace.
10. Peace treaty: The first step toward the next war.
11. Camouflage.
12. Hate.
13. Revenge.
14. Prepare for the war that is to come.

To those Socialists who had lived through the trying days of wartime America, the early postwar months were ones of hope and expectation. But the dream of a revived Socialist movement was to be shortlived.

TABLE 4
The Socialist Vote in 1916 and 1917
and Percentages of Foreign Born in 1920[1]

State	1917	1916	Elected Socialist Officials, 1917	Percent Foreign Born
Ohio[2]				
Byesville			Mayor and others	7.0
Hamilton	44.1%	15.5%	1 Councilman	6.7
Dayton	44.0%	6.5%	None	8.6
Toledo	34.8%	5.9%	3 Councilmen	15.7

[1] Foreign-born percentages compiled from *U. S. Census, 14th Census* (1920), III.
[2] Figures for 1916 from *Annual Report of the Secretary of State of Ohio* for 1917 (vote for Governor, 299ff). Figures for 1917 from Douglas, *loc. cit.,* pp.

State	1917	1916	Elected Socialist Officials, 1917	Percent Foreign Born
Piqua	33.0%	8.1%	Mayor, 2 Councilmen	3.9
Sandusky	48.9%	4.7%	1 City Commissioner	11.7
Massilon	29.6%	10.2%	1 Councilman	12.5
Springfield	30.0%	3.6%	?	4.5
Canton	21.0%	3.8%	?	16.9
Cleveland	22.4%	4.5%	2 Councilmen, 1 Member School Board	30.1
Lima	19.9%	3.7%	None	4.6
Akron	16.3%	3.8%	8 Assessors, 1 Constable	18.2
Cincinnati	11.9%	2.9%	None	10.7
Columbus	5580	1044(2.1%)		
Crestline	129	29(3.1%)		
Jenera			Mayor, and full ticket	
Marietta	509	164(4.7%)		
Marion	637	209(3.5%)		
Montpelier		23(2.8%)	2 Aldermen	
Pennsylvania[3]				
Garrett		33.0%	Burgess (Mayor)	?
Pitcairn		134(15%)	Mayor, Councilman	6.8
Union City		9(1%)	Mayor	4.4
McKeesport	3543	398	Controller	25.4
Allentown	4151	513	1 Councilman (of 4)	11.7
Slatington	42.3%	5.0%	?	8.2
Blairsville	45%	11.3%	None	7.3
Reading	32.6%	14.3%	None	8.9
Erie	3403	702	None	22.5
New Castle	1488	307	None	19.3
Maryland[4]				
Hagerstown	15%	1.6%	None	1.5

136-137; Hamilton *Evening Journal;* Dayton *News;* Toledo *News-Bee;* Piqua *Leader-Dispatch;* Sandusky *Register;* Massilon *Evening Independent;* Cleveland *Plain Dealer;* Lima *News;* Akron *Beacon-Journal,* all November 7 or 8, 1917; Oakland *World,* December 7, 1917; Galesburg *Labor News,* November 3, 1917.

[3] Figures for 1916 from *Smull's Legislative Handbook and Manual for the State of Pennsylvania: 1917,* 667ff, vote for President. For 1917 from New York *Call,* Allentown *Democrat,* Blairsville *Courier,* Reading *News-Times,* Erie *Dispatch,* New Castle *Herald,* all November 7 or 8, 1917. *Oakland World,* December 7, 1917.

[4] For 1916, *Maryland Manual: 1915-1916,* p. 249, vote for governor. For 1917, Hagerstown *Globe,* November 7, 1917.

State	1917	1916	Officials, 1917 Elected Socialist
New York[5]			
Buffalo	30.2% (Primary)	2.6%	None
Schenectady	3150(23.7%)	1268	None
New York	21.7%	4.5%	10 Assemblymen, 7 Aldermen, 1 Municipal Court Justice
Rochester	19.5%	3.4%	3 Constables, 2 Aldermen, 2 Supervisors
Gloversville	18.7%	?	None
Syracuse	11.9%	3.0%	None
Olean	597	100	?
Albany	965(4%)	208	None
New Jersey[6]			
Passaic County	14.0%	7.5%	None
Hudson County	13.2%	3.7%	None
Camden County	8.3%	4.8%	None
Newark	12.0%		None
Rahway	16.8%	3.9%	None
Bayonne			Justice of the Peace
Illinois[7]			
Chicago	34.7%	3.6%(1915)	2 Aldermen
Granite City	50.7%	10.0%	Mayor
Rockford	29.8%	7.0%	5 Aldermen
Connecticut[8]			
Bridgeport	1299(7%)	582	None
Utah[9]			
Eureka	36.4%	6.9%	Mayor, City Treasurer, Alderman

[5] For 1916, *Manual for the Use of the Legislature of the State of New York: 1917*, 898ff, vote for governor. For 1917, Douglas, *loc. cit.*, pp. 133-135; New York *Call*, October 18, November 7, 8, 1917; New York *Tribune*, Albany *Times-Union*, Rochester *Democrat and Chronicle*, Gloversville *Herald*, Syracuse *Herald*, all November 7, 1917.

[6] Douglas, *loc. cit.*, p. 134; *Manual of the Legislature of New Jersey; 1916, 1917*, vote for assembly. New Jersey State Department, *Result of the General Election*, 1916-17, pp. 82, 78.

[7] For 1915 see Douglas, *loc. cit.*, p. 315. For 1916, *Blue Book of the State of Illinois, 1917-1918*, pp. 585-586. Figure for Granite City is an estimate. The Madison County figure is 3.9%. Total Socialist vote in the county for 1916 was 808, Granite City Socialist vote in 1917 was 1,961. For 1917, *Chicago Daily News Almanac and Yearbook*, p. 624; Rockford *Register-Gazette*, April 18, 1917; *St. Louis Labor*, April 21, 1917.

[8] For 1916, *Connecticut Register and Manual, 1917*, p. 582, vote for President. For 1917, New York *Call*, November 7, 1917.

[9] For 1916, *State of Utah Report of the Secretary of State*, 1915-1916, p. 109. For 1917 *Eureka Reporter*, November 9, 1917.

TABLE 5
The Socialist Vote and the Percentage of Foreign Born
in Indiana Cities in 1917[1]

City or Town	Percentage of Vote	Percentage of Foreign Born
Gas City	40.4 (elected mayor)	4.9
Elwood	38.9 (elected mayor)	4.2
Marion	30.9	2.2
Anderson	29.1	3.2
Elkhart	22.5 (2 councilmen)	6.3
Fort Wayne	19.6 (1 alderman)	7.7
Kokomo	18.3	3.9
Evansville	17.3	3.7
Columbus	13.6	1.5
Bedford	12.1	3.3
Princeton	11.6	1.2
Alexandria	11.3	5.3
Clinton	11.3	21.3
Goshen	10.9	3.1
Logansport	10.3	4.9
Gary	6.2	29.7
South Bend[2]	5.2	18.9
Mishawaka	5.1	15.2
Indianapolis	4.0	8.5
East Chicago	2.8	40.0
Hammond	? (1 alderman)	?

[1] Election figures compiled from *Yearbook of the State of Indiana for the
Year 1917.* Foreign born compiled from *U. S. Bureau of Census, 14th
Census,* 1920, III.
[2] Douglas, *loc. cit.,* p. 138.

4

THE TWO INTERNATIONALS AND THE SPLIT OF THE SOCIALIST PARTY 1918-1919

The war, and then the Russian Revolution, moved the Socialist Party's center of gravity leftward, and served to unite the Party's various wings and tendencies and to reduce earlier hostilities. Hillquit, Lee, and Ruthenberg's joint authorship of the antiwar St. Louis Manifesto had symbolized this unity, and the emergence of Hillquit and Victor Berger as the most widely-known Socialist opponents of the war reinforced it. The Left, although still distrustful of these leaders, occasionally paid tribute to their antiwar militance.[1] In turn, Berger and Hillquit became more tolerant of their former antagonists. Berger, for instance, changed his attitude even toward the IWW, which he had attacked unsparingly in the prewar years. The wartime experience of the American Party should not have led it toward further division, but the Party in the United States was not immune to repercussions from the failure of the Second International, or from the split of the European movement. By the beginning of 1919 it faced a crisis of its own.

In part, the leftward movement of the Center and Right groups during the war came about as a result of the militant support of the Administration on the part of the American Federation of Labor. After the United States entered the war, even such right-wing Socialist organs as *St. Louis Labor,* which had been conciliatory toward Gompers in the prewar years, attacked

[1] See, for example, Ludwig Lore, "The Elections," *The Class Struggle,* II, 5 (December 1918), 621.

him as a "fifth wheel on [the] capitalist war chariot." Gompers, the St. Louis newspaper charged, was "used by our own capitalist war crowd" as Scheidemann was used by the Kaiser.[2]

Similarly, Berger's attitude toward the AFL and the IWW shifted during the war. He did not now approve the tactics of the IWW; yet, he now insisted that the IWW was a valid expression of industrial unionism. In May 1918, Berger sent a contribution to one of the leaders of that organization's defense fund, with the comment that he thought the IWW, "or some organization that will inherit its matchless spirit," was "destined to take the place of the American Federation of Labor."[3] Later, during the House hearings to determine whether or not he should be allowed to take his seat, Berger rejected the advice of his attorney to dissociate himself from the IWW.[4] In these hearings, Berger testified that he believed the IWW had "stood the test of being a class organization infinitely better than the trade unions," and observed that Gompers and his "cohorts" had in the main proved to be the tail of capitalism.[5] His testimony in these hearings was a running reaffirmation of the St. Louis Manifesto and of the most militant antiwar positions the Party had taken, tempered only by his interjection that the Party had never physically interfered with the conduct of the war.

At one point, for example, the Committee counsel asked whether or not Berger believed the portion of the St. Louis Manifesto that said "our entrance into the European war was instigated by predatory capitalists in the United States." Berger replied that he had believed it when it was written and believed it still. "We have devoted two days to telling the committee about that," he added. "This sentence not only expresses the true facts of the case, but also the philosophy of our movement, and there it ends. We gave you a whole lot of evidence to prove

[2] May 12, 1917.
[3] Berger to A. Wouri, Milwaukee, May 6, 1918, *Berger Hearings*, II, 575.
[4] Berger to Hillquit, Milwaukee, August 20, 1919, Hillquit papers.
[5] *Ibid.*

that," Berger concluded, "and we are going to give you a good deal more before we get through."

Asked if he would have considered the war honorable if it had been approved by referendum, Berger replied that "this imperialistic war would have been criminal, even if a referendum had been in favor of it." The referendum would only have "shown the sentiment of the people," but would not have made the Socialists "enthusiastic supporters of the majority." "Personally," Berger explained, "I have for a long time been a minority man."[6]

As in their attitudes toward the war, so in their attitudes toward the revolution in Russia, there was little difference between Left and Right. From November 7, 1917, almost all Party members and organs praised the Russians for what they had achieved. Three months after the revolution, the National Executive Committee of the Socialist Party rejoiced in the fact that "the revolution in Russia threatens the thrones of Europe and makes the whole capitalist structure tremble." Commenting on the ability of the Bolsheviks to accomplish their revolution "with hunger stalking their midst, without credit, without international recognition, and with a ruling caste intriguing to regain control," the NEC welcomed the Soviets' "message of proletarian revolution," and gloried "in their achievement and inevitable triumph."[7]

This sentiment was echoed by almost every Socialist leader. Debs had early praised the Bolsheviks, and by 1919, when he was an editor of *The Class Struggle*, averred that "from the crown of my head to the soles of my feet I am a Bolshevik, and proud of it."[8] Hillquit, in June 1918, saw Russia standing "in the vanguard of democracy, in the vanguard of social progress, in the hands, all through from top to bottom, of the people

[6] *Berger Hearings*, I, 297-298.
[7] Socialist Party National Executive Committee Statement on the Russian Revolution, adopted February 4, 1918, SPC, Duke.
[8] Ginger, *Bending Cross*, pp. 355, 369; *The Class Struggle*, III, 1 (February 1919), 4.

themselves, of the working class, the peasants."[9] Berger, too, praised what the Bolsheviki had done in Russia. On the first anniversary of the revolution, Berger wrote that "the Russian people love the Soviets. They are the Soviets. Here is a government of the people and for the people in actual fact. Here is a political and industrial democracy." Berger did not know how long the Soviet republic could survive against "the opposition of the capitalist world," but the fact remained "that it has lived one year in spite of the hatred of every other government in the world." The Soviets' survival, "in the face of all attacks," proved that "it has satisfied its own people. It has fitted their immediate needs, it has maintained their interests, and they are with it."[10]

Berger's view coincided with the official Party position, expressed in a proclamation on the coming peace that was sent to all members of Congress a few days before the armistice. In the proclamation, the Party demanded that the people of Russia be granted "complete freedom to solve their internal problems and that the integrity of Russian territory, as well as that of Finland, the Baltic provinces, Poland, Lithuania, Ukraine and other border provinces be preserved."[11]

Even some of those Socialists who had supported the war, or who had been equivocal about the Party's antiwar stand, showed enthusiasm for the Russian Revolution. Max Hayes, for example, wrote in his *Cleveland Citizen*, in May 1919, that the Soviets were the "most extreme democratic government that has yet been inaugurated."[12] Several months later, at the emergency convention of the Socialist Party in late August and early September, Dan Hogan took it for granted that all Socialists gave

[9] Hillquit, "Labor's Progress in Spite of the War," an address to the International Convention of the ILGWU, Boston, May 1918. Quoted in *The Ladies' Garment Worker*, June 1918; See also Hillquit in the *Quarry Workers Journal*, February 1918.

[10] "The Bolshevik Birthday," *Milwaukee Leader*, November 7, 1918.

[11] *Milwaukee Leader*, November 5, 1918. See also, *Messenger*, July 1918.

[12] May 7, 1919. See also, T. F. Allen in the *Bakersfield* (California) *Union Labor Journal*, January 4, 18, 1919.

"unqualified support to Soviet Russia." But, he pointed out, "the psychology of American workers is different than that of Russian workers:" Socialists "must not appear to support Russian methods for America." To do so, he warned, "would isolate us."[13]

By the time Hogan voiced this insight, large sections of the Party had already done what Hogan warned against. Hogan had merely expressed one aspect of the issue over which the Socialist Party split in the spring and summer of 1919, for, although almost all English-speaking Party members shared Hogan's view, his position conflicted sharply with the imperatives of the Russian Revolution, as the Russians perceived them, and flew directly in the face of the psychology of the Party's foreign-language federations. This, together with the latent hostility of the old Left groups, revived and brought to fever pitch by the panic-stricken actions of the national leadership in May and June, had made further Socialist unity impossible.

II

In Russia, Lenin had succeeded in convincing his comrades to move toward insurrection only after assuring and reassuring them that their action was to be but a prelude to revolution in Germany and the West. Lenin firmly believed that "if we act now we shall have on our side the whole of proletarian Europe."[14] After the revolution, the Bolsheviks continued to believe not only that an uprising in Western Europe was imminent, but that it was a condition for the survival of the Soviets in Russia. When the Third International was organized early in 1919, its program was one of immediate world-wide revolution. In his "Letter to American Workingmen," Lenin emphasized this point, commenting that the Bolsheviks were "in a beleaguered fortress, so long as no other international socialist

[13] Proceedings of the National Convention of the Socialist Party, 1919, p. 573.
[14] Quoted in Isaac Deutscher, *The Prophet Armed: Trotsky: 1897-1921* (New York, 1954), p. 293.

revolution" came to their assistance with its armies. "We know full well," he wrote, "that the outbreak of the European proletarian revolution may take many weeks to come," but, he added, "we are counting on the inevitability of the international revolution."[15]

At the same time, as Theodore Draper points out, Lenin expressed fewer illusions about the future of the Socialist movement in the United States than did his American imitators. "We know," he commented, that "it may take a long time before help can come from you, comrades, American Workingmen, for the development of the revolution in the different countries proceeds along various paths."[16]

Most American-born Socialists shared Lenin's last insight, but the small minority of native-born Party members who saw revolution in the United States as the first order of business for Socialists were joined by the overwhelming majority in the foreign-language federations, especially the Russian and Eastern European. These federations had constituted 35 percent of Party membership in 1917, but by 1919 there were 57,000 foreign-language Socialists, or 53 percent of the Party. The relative increases of the foreign-language federations were in part the result of wartime decimation of the Party organization in the West and South. Before the war, Oklahoma alone had twelve thousand Party members in nine hundred locals. Almost all of these were lost when the state Party was dissolved after the Green Corn Rebellion. Most of the fifteen hundred Socialist locals destroyed by wartime attacks were in the rural and mining states between the Mississippi and the Rockies. They were the smallest locals, the ones most dependent on the mails and the most exposed to vigilante and government attack. They were also almost solidly native-born. At the same time, the upsurge of Socialist sentiment among workers in such industrial

[15] V. I. Lenin, "A Letter to American Workingmen," *The Class Struggle*, I, 5 (December 1918), 532-535. Sequence of quotations altered.
[16] *Ibid.*, Draper, *op. cit.*, p. 133.

centers as Chicago, Buffalo, Cleveland, Detroit, and New York during the war rapidly shifted the balance between native and foreign born, since most industrial workers in these cities were recent immigrants.[17]

The Russian Language Federation, which had not been organized until 1915, grew most rapidly, its ranks filled with recently arrived Mensheviks who lived more in the turbulent events of revolutionary Russia than in the United States. As late as the beginning of 1918, there were only 792 members of the Russian Federation of the Party, but a year later there were 3,985. When Gregory Weinstein, editor of the Russian organ, *Novy Mir*, was nominated for the New York Socialist state committee in January 1918, he was ruled ineligible because he had not been a Party member the requisite two years.[18] Yet, as Draper points out, the Russian Federation in general, and Weinstein in particular, "became the most arrogant and vociferous force within the Left Wing" for a Russian-style Party.

Unable to vote, excluded from most trade unions, forced into the worst slums and sweatshops, these newly arrived immigrants easily identified with the demands of the IWW-oriented Americans. They readily rejected political action, immediate demands, and work within the established trade unions. Retaining close ties to their Eastern European homelands, and with little knowledge of the mood or traditions of American-born workers, the members of the foreign-language federations accepted the slogans of the new revolution as their own and responded eagerly to its entreaties for international action.

Allied loosely with the foreign-language federations, a group of old Party left wingers, especially on the West Coast, looked with lingering distrust on the followers of Hillquit, Berger, and the other leaders of the Party bureaucracy. Although they had differed little, if at all, with the national leadership in their

---

[17] *American Labor Yearbook*, 1917-1918, p. 340; Draper, *op. cit.*, pp. 137-138.
[18] *Ibid.*

approach to the most important issues facing them since the beginning of the war, these Socialists considered the Hillquit and Berger groups to be reformist and nonproletarian.[19] Not all of them participated in the movement toward a split in 1919, but they were a force helping to lead toward dispersal and disintegration.

In *The Roots of American Communism*, Theodore Draper traces the beginning of the movement for a split to the activities of Louis Fraina and the new left wing in Boston in 1915. Yet he recognizes that at this time there was little or no internal pressure for repudiation of the Party leadership, much less for a split in the movement. Fraina's prominence in the new left-wing movement indicates how peripheral it was until shortly before the split actually took place, for Fraina had been a Party member for only six months—in 1909, when he was fifteen years old. By 1915, when he was writing regularly for the *New Review*, he had been through the Socialist Labor Party and the IWW as well. What concerned Fraina most was the crisis of socialism—in Europe. He devoted his major attention to attacks on the Second International and to a campaign for a Third.[20]

Other early left-wing advocates were interested in European events even more exclusively than Fraina. The Socialist Propaganda League, organized in October 1915, was led and dominated by the Lettish Socialist Federation, and the Letts, in turn, were as much a part of European politics as American. Originally, simply an American branch of the Latvian Party, the Lettish Federation had formally affiliated with the American Socialists in 1908, but had retained their European connection. Their closeness to events in Latvia is indicated by the fact that their leader, Fricis Rozins, returned to his homeland shortly after the Russian Revolution to become the head of the first revolutionary Latvian government.[21]

[19] Interview with Harvey O'Connor, Madison, November 6, 1961.
[20] Draper, *op. cit.*, pp. 62-64; see also *New Review*, 1914-1916, *passim*.
[21] Draper, *op. cit.*, pp. 67, 132. Rozins later became an Executive Officer of the All Russian Central Executive Committee of the Russian Socialist Federated Soviet Republic. See, *Revolutionary Radicalism*, I, 261.

By the fall of 1918, the new left wing had two solid organs, the semiweekly and weekly *Revolutionary Age,* of Boston, and *The Class Struggle,* a bimonthly journal published in New York. Draper writes of these organs as the corporealization of the movement toward a Communist party. In a sense he is correct; with the emergence of these publications there is the first direct organizational tie to the new parties of September 1919. Yet, in order to understand the nature of the split and the manner in which it occurred, two things must be kept in mind: First, that these organs, and the movement they spoke for, were marginal to the life of the Socialist Party; second, that the organs themselves represented no self-conscious movement for a new party until after February 1919, at the earliest. The movement for a split in the Socialist Party, in other words, did not develop in the manner, or for the reasons, that it did in Europe. It sprang forth suddenly, and with little or no internal impetus, in the spring of 1919. Let us trace the emergence of a conscious policy of splitting in the *Revolutionary Age* and in *The Class Struggle.*

The Letts still controlled the left wing in Boston when that group won control of the local in 1918. When the *Revolutionary Age* appeared a few months later as Boston's official organ, it reflected the Lettish preoccupation with European events. Subtitled "A Chronicle and Interpretation of Events in Europe," the *Revolutionary Age,* under Fraina's editorial guidance, was true to its promise for several months. The first two issues contained not a word of events in the United States,[22] and when the first article on American affairs did appear, it was not a comment on the state of the Socialist Party, but on the decision of the Supreme Court refusing a new trial in the Mooney case —an article similar to those appearing in many Socialist publications, and even in non-Socialist labor papers.[23] Indeed, for the first fifteen issues, or until February 1919, only a handful of

[22] Draper, *op. cit.,* p. 132, mistakenly writes that the first four issues contained no word about events in the United States.
[23] See, for example, the February 1, 1919 issue of the *Bakersfield* (California) *Union Labor Journal.*

articles on American conditions appeared in the left-wing organ. These give no impression of any burning issues dividing the Party.

However, in retrospect, two articles had significance in relation to the coming split. On November 30, 1918, the *Age* reported a resolution of Local Boston on "The Crisis in the Socialist Party," calling for an emergency convention at which the Party should "unify itself" and "formulate policy expressing the requirement of the crisis." This referred not to an internal struggle in the Party, but to the need to counteract "the campaign of the imperialistic press for armed intervention in Russia."[24] Of course, the proposal in no way contradicted Party policy. Second, and more consistent with later charges, an article in the issue of December 11 attacked the *New York Call*, Hillquit's unofficial organ, for its alleged refusal to take a position on the Constituent Assembly *versus* the Soviets. Actually, the *Call* had not upheld the Constituent Assembly, as the *Revolutionary Age* charged, but had merely printed a letter from Joseph Shaplen that did. Shaplen's letter, in fact, attacked the *Call* for favoring the Soviets.[25] Thus, although the *Revolutionary Age* had raised an issue which the Left would make central in the coming battles, it had misunderstood the *Call's* position on it.

The *Revolutionary Age* also published a call for a general amnesty for political prisoners, on the theory that the war was over, and whatever the necessity of the Espionage Act "during the war, even that alleged necessity exists no longer." This, of course, was also fully in accord with Party activity. In addition, the *Age* carried an open letter from Debs to Charles H. Moyer, attacking the Mine Mill leader, and an article on the development of the labor parties in the United States. The latter piece took the mild position that while the labor parties should not be supported uncritically, they should be studied seriously by Socialists. Finally, on December 28, the *Revolutionary Age*

[24] *Revolutionary Age*, I, 5 (November 30, 1918).
[25] *Call*, December 6, 1918; *Revolutionary Age*, December 11, 1918.

published Lenin's Letter to American Workingmen. However, not even Lenin hinted at a split. On the contrary, he affirmed the judgment of the right-wing *St. Louis Labor* that Gompers, rather than Berger or Hillquit, was the American Scheidemann.[26]

The first indication of an intention to split the Party came in February 1919, when Nicholas I. Hourwich, a leader of the Russian Federation, discussed "The Left Wing in the American Socialist Party." This article was of great importance, not only because it was the first to call for a split, but also because it reveals the process of reasoning involved. Hourwich raised none of the issues which actually or allegedly divided the Party. He did not even intimate that the Right had really supported the war, that they had opposed the Soviets, or even that they opposed propaganda for immediate revolution. Instead, he began by tracing the splits that had been necessary in the European parties, which had been divided in *their* response to the war and patriotism. He then observed that the split in the German and Russian parties had been necessary preconditions for the revolution in those countries, and concluded that a "united" Socialist Party is "the chief weakness of the Socialist movement and is a continual burden to the revolutionary wing of the party." Since the split in Russia strengthened the Party, Hourwich wrote, "the same task lies before the American Socialist party."[27]

Like the *Revolutionary Age, The Class Struggle* came into being under the guidance of European-oriented Socialists. Unlike it, however, the latter journal concerned itself with Amer-

[26] Lenin's letter was dated August 20, 1918. On January 21, 1919, he wrote "A New Letter to the Workers of Europe and America." In this he repeated his equation of Gompers with Scheidemann. "No sincere Socialist," Lenin wrote, "can fail to see what shameful treason against Socialism was perpetrated by those who, in line with the Renaudels of France, and the Vanderveldes in Belgium, with the Hendersons and Webbs in England and with Gompers and Co., in America, supported 'their' bourgeoisie in the war of 1914-1918." Quoted in *Revolutionary Radicalism*, I, 669.

[27] February 1, 1919.

ican as well as European affairs. Edited, when it appeared in May 1917, by Louis B. Boudin, Louis C. Fraina, and Ludwig Lore, *The Class Struggle* was conceived at a meeting in Brooklyn the previous January at which the Russian revolutionaries outnumbered the American. At the meeting the new American left wing was represented by Lore, Boudin, Fraina, and John D. Williams, of the Boston Socialist Propaganda League, while the Russians were represented by Leon Trotsky, Nikolai Bukharin, Mme. Alexandra Kollontai, and V. Volodarsky, all of whom were soon to play leading roles in the Bolshevik Revolution, and by Grigorii I. Chudnovsky. Called to discuss "a program of action for Socialists of the Left, for the purpose of organizing the radical forces in the American Socialist movement," the meeting was dominated by Bukharin and Trotsky.[28] Bukharin proposed an immediate split in the Party. Trotsky, who had arrived in the United States only twenty-four hours earlier, argued that the Left should stay in the Party, but should start an independent organ to develop its own position. Both agreed on the need for a new publication, and the debate around the split was decided in Trotsky's favor.[29]

When the revolution broke out in Russia, Trotsky, Bukharin, and other Russians hastily departed, depriving the remaining leftists of their leaders.[30] When *The Class Struggle* appeared in May, therefore, it was edited by the Americans alone.

In its outlook the new journal was militantly Left, but within the tradition of the Left in the Socialist Party. *The Class Struggle* opposed the war unswervingly, attacked the AFL for its belief in "harmony between labor and capital," and opposed cooperation of the Socialist Party with the antiwar People's

[28] For a full discussion of this meeting see Draper, *op. cit.*, pp. 80-81.
[29] *Ibid.*
[30] Both Lore and Katayama, the only two to write of the January 1917 meeting, looked upon Trotsky as the leader of this group. See Ludwig Lore, "Leon Trotsky," in *One Year of Revolution* (Brooklyn, New York, 1918), pp. 7-8, cited in Draper, p. 410, n.l.; and Sen. Katayama, *Revolutionary Age,* July 26, 1919.

Council, which Fraina attacked as "a bourgeois organization" that "does not square with our revolutionary aims."[31] The first two positions did not differ with the dominant Party position, and the last fell into the traditional pattern of IWW-oriented attacks on coalition.[32] In that sense it was a link between the old and the new, although, interestingly, Scott Nearing, later one of the original editors of the *Revolutionary Age,* was chairman of the People's Council.

The Class Struggle's three editors themselves represented different traditions and exhibited different temperaments. Boudin was highly critical of Berger, Hillquit, and other Party leaders, while presenting a reasoned "Marxist" analysis of issues, in substance not very different from Hillquit and Berger. His hostility to Berger, as we have seen, was so great that he accused him, simultaneously, of being pro-war and pro-German in his neutrality.[33] Lore, on the other hand, as late as December 1918, commented that the militant stand against the war and government suppression taken by Berger, and the "aggressive attitude of the Socialist movement in Wisconsin under this leadership," had convinced most Socialists that Berger, rather than London, should have been in Congress during the war. At the same time, Lore expressed his thanks for London's defeat in the November election, but deplored the losses of Hillquit, Scott Nearing, Joseph Whitehorn, and Abraham Shiplacoff in their efforts to win election to Congress in New York. "Men of their calibre," Lore remarked, "would have laid a good foundation for the more numerous Socialist congressional delegations of the future," a statement thoroughly in accord with the traditional American Socialist view and totally contrary to the program

[31] "The War and American Unionism," I, 2 (July-August), 120; Louis C. Fraina, "Labor and Democracy," I, 3 (September-October 1917) 61-62; *passim,* 1917-1918.

[32] Actually, the Party was not affiliated with the People's Council, although Hillquit, James H. Maurer and other Socialists were prominent in the organization.

[33] See above, p. 128.

of the left wing in which Lore was to participate only three months later.[34] Of the three editors, only Fraina exhibited genuine hostility to the Party organization, which was not strange considering that he had spent most of his political life in the IWW and the Socialist Labor Party. Fraina not only attacked the Party for its cooperation with non-Socialist groups but saw in the American Party a repetition of the European model. In February 1918, Fraina wrote that before the proletarian revolution could conquer capitalism in Europe it "had to conquer the dominant Socialism." This was so, he added, because the dominant Socialism "had become part of the governing system of things, indirectly its ally and protector." The same was true in the United States, Fraina concluded, for the Party here had "no clear call to accept the new purposes and tactics of the revolutionary Third International."[35]

Fraina raised an issue which had at least partial validity, for the attitudes of the Hillquit-Berger-Debs groups differed from those of the left wing toward the Third International, as we shall see. But Fraina did not explain how the American Socialists could be considered "part of the governing system of things." Like most of the foreign-language federations, Fraina revealed a good deal of ignorance of American reality. The response of the federations to specific issues illustrates this.

Early in 1919, the National Executive Committee of the Party called an amnesty convention for the spring, the purpose of which was to organize the various forces working to secure the release of the thousands of Socialists, IWW's, and conscientious objectors from federal prisons. Five foreign-language federations refused to participate in the convention plans. The reason given by the Ukrainian branch of the Cook County (Illinois) local was that the demand for amnesty made by Socialists and

[34] Ludwig Lore, "The Elections," *The Class Struggle,* II, 5 (November-December 1918), 338.
[35] Louis C. Fraina, "Problems of American Socialism," *The Class Struggle,* II, 1 (January-February 1918), 30-33.

liberals together, "on the basis of 'Democracy' and 'constituted rights' " was "in direct contradiction of our declarations that our comrades are class war prisoners," and that "there are no 'rights' and 'immunities' which the Government of the United States will recognize." In support of this stand, which in its original form was sectarian but not necessarily irrational, the Boston left-wing local opined that the true purpose of the convention was "to use the Socialist Party as an instrument in securing the release of the Bourgeois 'conscientious objectors' and to abandon the imprisoned victims of the class struggle."[36] Why the Party should be interested in securing the release of non-Party conscientious objectors but not in freeing Debs, Kate O'Hare, J. O. Bentall, and hundreds of other Socialists, Local Boston did not bother to explain.

The discussion around the proposal for a new national Party headquarters reveals even more clearly the mentality of many of the Eastern European Party members. In late 1918 and early 1919, the Party appealed for funds to buy a building in Chicago to house the national office. Many left wingers refused to contribute to the fund, and the Lithuanian paper, *Musu Tiesa*, explained why the Lithuanians refrained. "We all know," the paper commented, "that the party is in the control of Social-patriots and opportunists . . . And so long as we are not sure of the lefts' control in the party, we must be on our guard that our donation shall not become a tool against ourselves." Socialists such as then controlled the Party, *Musu Tiesa* warned, "would not scruple to arm the Party Home with machine guns against the international Socialists, [just as] the German Social-patriots have made of the Party Homes armories against the Sparticides."[37]

[36] Resolution for Referendum to prevent amnesty conference, spring 1919. Adopted by the Ukrainian branch of Local Cook County, April 6, 1919, SPC, Duke; Resolution adopted by Local Boston, *Revolutionary Age*, July 12, 1919.
[37] "The Party's Home," *Musu Tiesa*, No. 3 (March 22, 1919), translation in SPC, Duke. Punctuation altered in last sentence.

III

The self-conscious movement toward a split in the Socialist Party developed after February 1919. Before then, the organized left wing was restricted to Boston, where the Socialist Propaganda League (and later, the local, under Left control) was heavily dominated by the Lettish Federation, and Chicago, where the Communist Propaganda League was organized and dominated by the Russian Federation.[38] In 1918, the English-speaking leftists on the "theoretical magazine" of the new left wing, as Draper calls *The Class Struggle,* were still publishing articles by such "social-patriots" and "opportunists" as Florence Kelley, James Oneal, Joseph Whitehorn, and Adolph Germer.[39] The theoretical need for a split and for hostility toward the Right and Center was not brought home to large sections of the English-speaking membership until after the organizing committee for the Third International sent out its call in January 1919.

The call for a Third International went out from Moscow on January 24. Among other things, it called on the proletariat to take power "at once," and to establish through "mass action of the proletariat" a "dictatorship of the working class." This task was to be accomplished by a "combat without mercy" against the right-wing elements of the old International, and by using against the Center the tactic of "separating out the revolutionary elements, in a pitiless criticism of its leaders and in systematically dividing its adherents."[40] Of course, in the

---

[38] The Communist Propaganda League was organized in November 1918.
[39] Draper, *op. cit.,* p. 87; Florence Kelley, "Changing Labor Conditions in Wartime," *The Class Struggle,* II, 2 (March-April 1918); James Oneal, "The New 'Americanism,'" *ibid.,* II, 3 (May-June 1918), 289; Joseph Whitehorn, "A War Legislature," *ibid.,* I, 2 (July-August 1917), 36; Adolph Germer, "Samuel Gompers," *ibid.,* II, 1 (January-February 1918), 9. James Oneal was then a member of the National Executive Committee; Joseph Whitehorn was a Socialist state assemblyman from New York City; Adolph Germer was the Party national secretary.
[40] Quoted in *Revolutionary Radicalism,* I, 418. Quotes taken out of order.

American Party, there were virtually no right wingers in the European sense: i.e., supporters of the war and of the postwar attacks on the Soviet Republic. But, as we shall see, the left wing converted the European reality into a universal formula. If the facts did not fit the formula, in the United States, so much the worse for the facts.

The first formal step in the establishment of the left-wing organization in New York occurred just before the Third International issued its call. Julius Gerber, executive secretary of Local New York, precipitated this development by refusing to allow left wingers to voice their criticisms of the Socialist aldermen who had voted for the fourth Liberty Loan and for the erection of a temporary victory arch in Madison Square.[41] After being refused the floor, a group of leftists bolted the meeting and organized a City Committee of Fourteen to draw up a manifesto and begin a campaign to win over the rank and file.

The manifesto of the City Committee clearly showed the influence of the revolutionary movements taking place in Europe, and of the new militancy of the entire Socialist movement in the United States. It called for new policies and tactics, including "year round agitation" in support of the Soviet Republic and the Sparticides, and called on Socialists to be ready to take leadership of the revolutionary proletariat "when the hour strikes"—adding, "and it will strike soon." The manifesto also emphasized the need for agitation in favor of industrial unionism, among the craft unions. On political action, the City Committee took a position influenced both by the Bolshevik left and the IWW. Although favoring participating in elections, the manifesto declared that since the attempt to capture the state was "merely for the purpose of destroying it," the nature of parliamentary activity "should be purely destructive." At this point, the City Committee apparently did not consider the Party leadership to have the characteristics of the European Right. Thus, the introduction to the manifesto declared: "First

[41] Draper, *op. cit.*, p. 144.

of all, be it understood we are not a secessionist movement, nor do we contemplate splitting the party."[42] However, upon revision by Fraina at the left-wing convention on February 15, this disclaimer was omitted.[43]

The formal organization of a left-wing section of the New York local struck a chord of immediate response from locals in many parts of the country. By April, the manifesto had been published in the *Soviet World* of Philadelphia, and in *Truth* of Duluth, Minnesota, while the Left had gained control of locals Cleveland, Toledo, Akron, Buffalo, Oakland, San Francisco, Seattle, Detroit, Philadelphia, Newark, Queens, the Bronx, and Brooklyn, as well as the Hungarian, Lithuanian, Lettish, Russian, Polish, South Slavic, and Ukrainian federations.[44] To Max Hayes, writing less than two weeks after the Left had captured Local Cleveland, it was obvious that the "moderate-left wing fight" was spreading all over the country, and that a split was inevitable.[45]

Despite these developments, Party leaders had little awareness that a split was impending before the spring of 1919. Indeed, the National Executive Committee had planned to put major effort into an amnesty campaign,[46] and planned to use its available funds for the purchase of a new national headquarters. Its outlook was to re-establish its organization rather than to defend itself from a divisive attack. At the end of 1918, Debs had laid out the task before the Party. In an article entitled "We Must Organize Now," Debs referred to the government attacks on the Party during the war and optimistically declared that it had "lost nothing" but had "gained much." The people, he explained were "readier for Socialism than they ever were

---

[42] "Manifesto and Program of the Left Wing," *The Revolutionary Age*, February 8, 1919. The Program of the Chicago Communist League appeared in the same issue and was similar in character.
[43] See Manifesto of Left Wing Section, Socialist Party Local Greater New York, *Revolutionary Radicalism*, I, 706 ff.; see also Draper, *op. cit.*, p. 145.
[44] *Revolutionary Radicalism*, I, 680; Shannon, *op. cit.*, p. 135.
[45] *Cleveland Citizen*, April 12, 1919.
[46] The campaign was called off because of the hostility of the federations.

before. We have but to proceed without delay to build our organization."[47]

Similarly, Hillquit had little reason to believe that he would soon be under attack as the main barrier to revolution in the United States. Hillquit had given active support to the new Soviet regime. In October 1918, Santeri Nuorteva, later one of the left wingers most influential in the formation of the Communist Party, wrote Hillquit for aid in carrying out his duties as American representative of the short-lived "People's Republic" of Finland. In January 1919, both Hillquit and Nuorteva were appointed to head departments of the Russian Soviet Government Information Bureau, set up in the United States by Ludwig C. A. K. Martens. The Information Bureau had been organized on instructions from the Soviets in January 1919,[48] and had published May Day greetings from Russia in the *New York Call* on May 1, 1919. As late as July 1919, Nuorteva paid tribute to Hillquit's activity in behalf of the Soviets. "I shall never forget," he wrote Hillquit, "that it was you who most readily and ably stepped in to help me in the performance of duties new and strange in the annals of the Socialist movement." "Your understanding of the nature of the class struggle, and your unflinching devotion to the cause of the international proletarian movement," Nuorteva continued, "strengthened my efforts to discharge my duties in accordance with the interests of international class solidarity of the workers." After additional praise along the same lines, Nuorteva concluded: "There is no other man in the American Socialist movement who from the very outset of the establishment of the workers' rule in Russia has more clearly than you understood what Russia meant, and who more unreservedly was willing to defend it against all attack."[49]

Of course, by the time Nuorteva wrote his last letter to Hillquit, the split had been all but formalized. The letter indicates,

[47] Oakland *World,* November 29, 1918.
[48] *Revolutionary Radicalism,* I, 643.
[49] Nuorteva to Hillquit, n.p., October 23, 28, 1918; July 31, 1919, Hillquit papers, Wisconsin State Historical Society.

however, how rapidly and unexpectedly the development took place. As late as May, Fraina wrote that although the development of the left wing was the "most vital fact in the Socialist Party at this moment," it was "not yet definite and organized."[50] From the opposite camp, Adolph Germer, Party national secretary, wrote Hillquit in April that the Left would not capture the Party, although in some places it had "succeeded in converting our most active locals into mere debating societies with the result that attendance at meetings is getting smaller and the membership is decreasing."[51]

As it turned out, Germer's estimate was wrong. Since the foreign-language federations constituted a majority of the Party, the prospects of the Left sweeping the elections for the new National Executive Committee then in progress were extremely good. This prospect, and the formal organization of the new International in late March, gave added impetus to the formation of a unified national opposition movement within the Socialist Party. In mid-April, Local Boston issued a call for a national left-wing conference, to be held in New York on June 21, 1919.[52]

IV

Meanwhile, the old leadership in Chicago suddenly awakened to what was happening around them. The result was panic and a resort to bureaucratic action to prevent the majority from gaining control of the Party machinery and treasury. Their situation was not an easy one: They understood that the Left intended either to capture the Party and convert it into an effigy of the Russian original—in which case the followers of Hillquit and Berger would certainly have been expelled—or to pull out and organize their own party. But even so, their course of action, and especially their haste and their failure to engage the Left

[50] Louis C. Fraina, "The Left Wing," *Class Struggle*, III, 2 (May 1919).
[51] Germer to Hillquit, Chicago, April 9, 17, 1919, Hillquit papers.
[52] See *Revolutionary Radicalism*, I, 683.

in debate over the issues involved, played into the hands of the splitters and lost the old guard thousands of members who agreed with them in principle and shared their concepts of party organization and political action.

To retain control of the Party organization was no easy task; in the elections for National Executive Committee in the spring, the Left captured twelve of fifteen seats and elected four of five international delegates.[53] To keep control, the elections had to be invalidated. For that purpose a special meeting of the old Executive Committee was called in Chicago at the end of May.

Of the ten members present at the National Executive Committee meeting, only two—Ludwig Katterfeld and Alfred Wagenknecht—were left wingers. By a vote of eight to two, the National Executive Committee voted to suspend the seven language federations affiliated with the left wing, and in more or less open revolt against the Party leadership. Then, by a vote of seven to three, the Committee voted to expel the entire state organization of Michigan, which had not joined the left wing, but had recently amended its constitution to provide for the expulsion of any Michigan Socialist who advocated "immediate demands," such as were part of the national platform, and had passed a resolution requiring Party members in the state to discuss religion "on the basis of the materialist conception of history." The expulsion was voted despite the fact that the Committee had not yet received official confirmation of the Michigan convention action, and although the convention decisions had not been ratified by a state referendum as required by the Michigan constitution.[54] After this beginning, the Committee took the decisive action of declaring the recent elections to

[53] The international delegates elected were John Reed, C. E. Ruthenberg, Louis C. Fraina, Kate O'Hare, and Hillquit, who ran a poor fifth.
[54] Shannon, *op. cit.*, pp. 135-137; *Eye Opener,* May 1919. The expulsion of Michigan and the suspension of the federations was followed by the expulsion and reorganization of the Massachusetts Party, after that group expressed its opposition to the action of the NEC by voting to send two delegates to the left-wing conference in New York on June 21.

the National Executive null and void, on the ground that irregularities had occurred in the tabulation of the vote. Several irregularities were alleged,[55] but whether or not there was evidence that the total number of fraudulent ballots could have changed the results of the election was not disclosed.[56]

The result, far from aiding the advocates of unity, was to strengthen the secessionists. Most important, among the followers of Debs and Kate O'Hare, who had long opposed the bureaucracy of the old guard, the issue of inner Party democracy had been revitalized to the serious disadvantage of the old leadership. Kate O'Hare, in prison at the time, was one of the four left-wing candidates elected as international representatives. She remained a Socialist despite the old guard's voiding of her election, but, as she told the Party national secretary ten months later, she received many furious letters from the rank and file condemning the old guard for its actions. One letter was "so hot it scorched the envelope." This comrade, O'Hare explained, "was one who went 'Left,' and with him as with thousands of others, it was a mere matter of emotional reaction, not reason at all." Another Socialist wrote Party National Secretary Adolph Germer in June that in Michigan he had heard "nothing but condemnation of the method adopted by the NEC."[57]

The action of the NEC quickly became the most prominent issue used against it by the left wing, and in the process the principled differences between those who would remain S₋-

[55] Irregularities appearing to have substance included a charge that in locals of the suspended federations, voters had been given marked ballots to sign, that some locals had reported straight Left slate votes, although the ballots had shown split voting, and that some locals voted twice their membership.

[56] See, for example, the discussion at the National Convention of the Socialist Party at Machinists' Hall, August 30, 1919, Proceedings, pp. 352-375; also Shannon, op. cit., p. 138.

[57] Kate O'Hare to Otto Branstetter, Jefferson City, Missouri, February 24, 1920, SPC, Duke; Nathan L. Welch to Adolph Germer, Detroit, June 6, 1919, SPC, Duke. Similar letters of condemnation came in from all over Michigan. When Local Cuyahoga (Ohio) instituted a national referendum to rescind the action on the NEC, hundreds of seconds came in from locals in two weeks from June 16 to 31, 1919.

cialists and those who became Communists were virtually obscured. A week after the expulsion meeting, for example, Alfred
Wagenknecht sent an impassioned appeal for support of the
Left to all Party members and locals. In his letter, Wagenknecht
failed to raise any of the issues which had given rise to the left-
wing movement. Instead, he wrote that "*No minority of seven
Socialists, even if they do happen to be National Executive
Committee men, shall assume the power to throw out of our
organization nearly 40,000 members.*"[58] Similarly, the *Ohio Socialist*, organ of C. E. Ruthenberg and the Ohio Left, gave
greater priority to this issue than to others that would have been
less persuasive to many rank-and-file Party members.

The importance of this issue was further demonstrated by
John C. Taylor, a candidate for delegate to the August 30 convention. Taylor, who later led California's six-man delegation to
the emergency Socialist convention and then into the Communist Labor Party, promised that if elected he would do his
"utmost to undo the murderous work of the despotic seven and
maintain our organization intact that it may be the greatest
possible force for the revolution." He also called for the elimination of immediate demands from the Party program, and for
the rapid establishment of the dictatorship of the proletariat,
but the issues of democracy and unity were dominant.[59] Thus
the Left was given an issue of great emotional intensity capable
of uniting both the old and new opponents of the old guard.

Of course, inner Party democracy was not the only issue that
drew native Americans to the Left. The unprecedented strikes
of early 1919, the Seattle general strike, and the Butte copper
strike, as well as the establishment of Soldiers', Sailors' and
Workers' Councils in Seattle, Butte, Portland, Oregon, and other
cities, led many to believe that they were witnessing "the beginning of the flood," as John Dos Passos would later write,

[58] A. Wagenknecht to all members and locals of the Socialist Party,
Brecksville, Ohio, June 6, 1919, SPC, Duke.
[59] "Statement of Nominees for Delegates to National Socialist Party Convention, August 30, 1919," Oakland *World*, July 25, 1919.

"instead of the beginning of the ebb."[60] To the Left this series of strikes, which culminated in the Boston police strike and the great steel strike in September, appeared to "verge on revolutionary action."[61] The strikes gave some semblance of reality to the imperative call of the Bolsheviks for revolutionary support.

In addition to seeing the revolutionary potential in the United States through the scarlet-colored glasses of the Russian Revolution, some left-wingers saw a positive need for a break "with American methods and American ideals." C. E. Ruthenberg commented that this need had been brought about by repression in the United States during the war. The Socialists, he argued, had endeavored to educate the voters to an understanding of their view of the war through public meetings and in election campaigns; as a result "they went to prison by the thousands." In the city of Cleveland the Party elected three men in 1917, pledged to the Socialist view of the war. If the old theory of American institutions were valid, Ruthenberg insisted, these men had a right to express their views. Even in autocratic Germany, Ruthenberg reminded his readers, Karl Liebknecht had remained unmolested in Parliament after speaking and voting against war credits. But when the Cleveland Socialists refused to pledge support to the war, they were expelled from the council. "If the Socialists are seeking new weapons," Ruthenberg concluded, "it is because the ruling class has taught them the need of new weapons."[62]

Arguments based on the American experience, such as Ruthenberg's, were rare. Most left wingers simply tried to squeeze the American Party into the pattern of the Bolshevik experience. They assumed that the United States was ripe for revo-

[60] Quoted in William E. Leuchtenberg, *The Perils of Prosperity: 1914-1932* (Chicago, 1958), p. 69.
[61] See "Manifesto of the Left Wing Section Socialist Party Local Greater New York," in *Revolutionary Radicalism*, I, 711. It should be noted that this estimate was made after the Seattle and Butte strikes, but several months before the steel and police strikes; that is, in February 1919.
[62] C. E. Ruthenberg, "News and Views," *Ohio Socialist*, April 9, 1919.

lution because Lenin had said that the revolution in Russia was only the first stage of the world revolution and that the Bolsheviks could not survive alone.

V

In the month following the expulsion of the language federations and the Michigan Party, the Left worked feverishly to make a success of the national conference of June 21. Attendance was impressive for a first meeting of the left wing, but in itself there was little indication that this group would sweep over half the membership of the Party along with it in the next six to eight weeks. In all, twenty states were represented, but except for John Reed, Ruthenberg, Wagenknecht, and William Bross Lloyd there were no widely known Socialist leaders present.[63]

Even before the conference met it was plain that a basic divergence would develop on the issue of splitting the Party. The call to the conference had declared the purpose of the meeting to be the formation of a national, unified left wing, which would attempt to "conquer the Party for Revolutionary Socialism."[64] However, at the conference, Dennis Batt of the expelled Michigan group fought to organize a new party immediately and Nicholas Hourwich of the Russian Federation supported him. The policy of waiting and of attempting to capture the old Party organization was defended by John Reed, Benjamin Gitlow, James Larkin, Bertram D. Wolfe, and Fraina. Ruthenberg and other veteran Party members present upheld the Reed-Gitlow position. The division on the question was 55 to 38, with almost all the English-speaking members, other than those in the Michigan group, voting with the majority against an immediate split.[65]

[63] Draper, *op. cit.*, pp. 166-167; *Revolutionary Age,* July 5, 1918; *Revolutionary Radicalism,* I, 684.
[64] *Revolutionary Age,* April 26, 1919.
[65] *Revolutionary Age,* July 5, 1919.

In the face of this defeat, thirty-one delegates, led by Hour-wich, left the conference and issued a call for a convention on August 30 in Chicago to organize a Communist party.[66] This decision had been in the making for several weeks before the left-wing conference met. Agitated by the arrival in the United States of the first publications of the new International, as well as by the expulsion of Michigan and the suspension of the seven federations, these groups took literally Gregory Zinoviev's instruction that "the dictatorship of the proletariat is the order of the day throughout the civilized world."[67] The first issue of the organ of the Communist International arrived in the United States some time in May. In its pages were assurances that "before this year is over, Europe will be one great Soviet Re-public," and that in the United States "working men are com-ing into the streets in readiness for a decisive struggle."[68] Dom-inated by the Russian Federation, the groups represented by the secessionist minority of thirty-one were ready to assume their revolutionary responsibility.

Of course, America was not really like Europe, and the Amer-ican Socialist Party was not like the European. When the Man-ifesto of the Third International declared a "merciless fight" against the "social patriots" to be "absolutely necessary," and called for pitiless criticism of the leaders of the Center in order to "separate the revolutionary elements,"[69] it was declaiming in terms that had little meaning in the United States. After splitting with the left-wing majority, however, this problem was solved by the minority simply by shifting the European labels

[66] *Ibid.;* Draper, *op. cit.,* p. 167; *Revolutionary Radicalism,* I, 685 ff. Actually, the Michigan Party had already issued such a call from its emergency state convention, held just after the expulsion of the state organization and just before the left-wing conference convened.
[67] G. Zinoviev, "Vistas of the Proletarian Revolution," *The Communist International, Organ of the Executive Committee of the Communist Inter-national* (Petrograd), I, 1, (May 1919), 98.
[68] "Long Live the First of May," *Ibid.,* 26.
[69] Quoted by Alexander Stoklitsky in "On the Party Horizon," *The Com-munist* (Chicago) I, 1 (July 19, 1919).

one notch leftward, and then applying them to the American Party. "The Right, the social traitors," declared Alexander Stoklitsky of the Russian Federation, were "headed by Berger and Hillquit, and permeated with the rottenness of the Second International," while the Center emerged as the "accidental majority of the Left Wing Conference." In a style that was to become characteristic of the American Communist Party, Stoklitsky reserved his heaviest fire for the Center. "Here as everywhere in Europe," he wrote, the Center "has learned nothing." They, too, were "irresolute, they too vacillate, temporize and remain stupid." He wished them "God Speed," because the new Left, "headed by the Russian Communistic Federations and the Socialist Party of Michigan," viewed the split in the Party as *nothing less than an echo of the death rattle of the Second International; it is the direct result of a growing revolutionary ferment in the great masses of the American people, which only the panic-stricken N.E.C. and the irresolute Center with all their followers cannot or do not want to see.*"

Although the new "Extreme Left," as they called themselves, had learned well the lesson of irresolute struggle against the Right and Center, they had paid less attention to the needs of carrying out a revolution. Stoklitsky, therefore, felt it necessary to remind his readers that while "striking the opponents of revolutionary socialism one death blow after another from without, we must not for one moment forget the direct and ultimate aim of our struggle against the capitalistic structure."[70]

Those who remained in the new "Center," that is, the majority of the left wing, were somewhat less concerned with carrying out their revolutionary mission of splitting the Party and somewhat more concerned with bringing on a revolution against the existing system. The difference, however, was more of mood than of program. Although the majority group voted to remain in the Party until the emergency convention, they were as determined as the Russian-led minority to form a Communist

[70] *Ibid.* Sequence of quotations altered.

party, even if to most of them the concept of a "Leninist party" was unknown. Yet, in their backgrounds, the two groups differed substantially. Many in the majority were experienced radicals, with roots in both the Socialist movement and the IWW. They were overcome by the siren call of the Third International, but they retained some consciousness of the relative strength of the IWW and the AFL, and they were aware of the difficulties facing a revolutionary movement in the United States. This was reflected in the majority manifesto.

The manifesto began with a declaration that the world was in crisis, and that capitalism was in the process of disintegration and collapse. "Out of its vitals," the manifesto proclaimed, "a new social order" was developing. "The struggle between this new social order and the old" had become the "fundamental problem in international politics." Following this introduction, the manifesto traced the origins of the war to imperialism, then discussed the character and role of "moderate socialism" and the proletarian revolution triumphant in Russia. Finally, coming to American socialism, the manifesto insisted that the upsurge of "revolutionary Socialism" in the American Party was "not simply a product of European conditions," but also of the "experience of the American movement." The Left Wing had merely "been invigorated by the experience of the revolutions in Europe."

The American Socialist Party, the manifesto asserted, was dominated by the "moderate Socialism of the International," and followed a policy of uniting "all the people" against the trusts and big capital. "In short," the manifesto charged, "the official Socialist Party actually depended on the *petite bourgeoisie* for the realization of Socialism." Attacking the trade union policies of the Party, the manifesto also asserted that the dominant moderate socialism had "rejected industrial unionism and openly or covertly acted against the I.W.W." while uniting "with the aristocracy of labor and the middle class." Finally, the American Party was charged with following an "*official* policy" of "petty bourgeois pacifism" in alliance with the People's Council during the war, and of rejecting the "revolutionary implications" of the St. Louis Resolution by "repudiating the policy of the Russian and German Communists and refusing affiliation with the Communist International."[71]

The difficulty in following the policy of the Russian and German Communists, however, was admitted in the very next paragraph, in which the manifesto noted that the war had "aggrandized American Capitalism, instead of weakening it as in Europe." However, not to be deterred by this hard reality, confidence was expressed that although now "all-mighty and supreme, Capitalism in the United States must meet crisis in the days to come." This condition modified the Left's "immediate task," but did "not alter its general character." Admittedly, "not the moment of revolution," the Manifesto declared that the time was still "the moment of revolutionary struggle."[72]

VI

To the groups that were to remain in the Socialist Party, all this talk of revolution was meaningless, at best. As Ralph Korngold, a leading Socialist pamphleteer, commented, these "revolutionary romanticists" wanted a revolution in the United States, and wanted it "right away." They were "tired of voting," and "tired of teaching the masses how to vote." The problem was that they did not know how to bring this revolution about. Finding education and electoral politics too slow, they proposed "hysteria." "As far as anyone is able to make out," Korngold explained, the revolution was to be brought on by "the general strike, supplemented by general rioting."

To illustrate his point, Korngold quoted a statement of William F. Dunne, which the *Liberator* had carried "with evident approval." Dunne, a leader of the electrical workers in Butte, Montana, had been elected to the state legislature in 1918 on

[71] "The Left Wing Manifesto," in *Revolutionary Radicalism*, I, 716-727.
[72] *Ibid.*, p. 728.

the Democratic ticket although a member of the Socialist Party. A left winger, he was editor of Butte's labor newspaper, the *Butte Daily Bulletin,* and was to bring the Butte local into the Communist Labor Party when the split took place in September 1919. Compared by the *Liberator* to Lenin (there were many left wingers eager to assume the mantle), Dunne had said: "I don't know what I am. . . . But I'll tell you what I think is going to happen. . . . Craft unionism is out of date; it's too late for industrial unionism; mass action is the only thing—mass action." This insight was followed by the prediction that "unemployment will increase, there'll be starvation, and some day the banks will fail and the people will come pouring out on the streets and the revolution will start."

This, said Korngold, was simply a romantic attempt by the Left "to shape the workers and farmers of America to fit their theories," rather than "fitting their theories to the American workers and farmers." "Lenin," he added, "would never have made that mistake."[73]

Other Party leaders were equally contemptuous of the manner in which the Left attempted to transplant Russian conditions in the United States. Victor Berger, for example, commented that he was "sick and tired" of the inner-Party disputes. "If there is to be a revolution some day," he wrote to Hillquit, "I and my crowd will surely be there." But the continuous talk of revolution reminded him of a man who was constantly brandishing a revolver which was not loaded. Revolution in Russia had been one thing, Berger pointed out. She was "a beaten country," both on the military and economic fields. By the time of the revolution, the first line of her military forces "were either dead or prisoners," while the second line was "honeycombed with propaganda." In addition, the Socialists "absolutely controlled the trade unions and the landless, starved and hungry peasants had no other place to go than to the Bolsheviki."

[73] Ralph Korngold, "Revolutionary Romanticists," *Cleveland Citizen,* May 19, 1919.

"None of these conditions prevail in America," Berger observed. On the contrary, the war "seems to have strengthened capitalism, reaction and *treason* within the *working class.*" Berger reiterated his support of the Bolsheviki in Russia, and pledged that he would "fight like a tiger" against American intervention in Soviet affairs. "But while we can learn from them," he concluded, "we cannot transfer Russia to America."[74]

Hillquit stressed the same points made by Berger. The United States, he wrote, had emerged from the war "the strongest capitalist country in the world," and offered dim prospects for revolution, since the system had emerged "less shaken in the United States than in any of the advanced countries of Europe."[75]

In speaking to the convention of the ILGWU, Hillquit also stressed the idea that the "working class movement in the United States" had remained, on the whole, "the most backward in the world." Organized labor, Hillquit believed, had "learned nothing" from the war. So far, the "great new vision which the workers all over the world have exhibited," has had "little appeal in this country."[76] Hillquit believed the Left "wrong in their estimates of American conditions, their theoretical conclusions and practical methods"; nevertheless, he viewed Communists as "still socialists," and hoped that they, like the Socialists, would "center the whole fight on capitalism."[77]

[74] Berger to Hillquit, Milwaukee, August 20, 1919. The National Executive Committee, or at least a majority of it, agreed with Berger. In a letter to the state secretaries of the Party, the Commitee commented that the left wing was attempting "a transplantation in detail of methods used by the comrades in the second Russian Revolution, with an utter disregard for the difference of conditions in this country." "Letter to all State Secretaries of the Socialist Party," Chicago, May 31, 1919, Hillquit papers.
[75] Letter from Hillquit in *New York Call,* May 21, 1919.
[76] Hillquit, "Labor's Progress in Spite of the War," *The Ladies' Garment Worker,* June 1918.
[77] Hillquit, "We are all Socialists," *Eye Opener,* October 1, 1919. See also *Justice,* September 27, 1919, in which Hillquit is quoted as saying "I don't agree with the Communists, but I don't consider them enemies of the Socialist movement."

Similarly, Debs rejected the call of the Left, and appealed instead for united action against the capitalist enemy. Emotionally, Debs was with the Bolsheviks, as we have noted, but when it came to the tactic of splitting he had "no time for that sort of business." Debs wrote that the Socialist Party "deserves better than this at the hands of its professed supporters," and expressed the earnest hope that all efforts would be made to find "common ground" and to resolve differences on a basis of "united action." "Failing in this," Debs warned with accuracy, the situation "which ought at this time to be promising as never before," would become "more and more demoralized," the "capitalist oppressor more and more impudent and despotic," and the movement itself "discredited and brought into odium."[78] A year later, from prison, Debs reiterated his plea for unity, this time around the Socialist Party program. Lamenting that some of his "most dear friends" were in other factions and parties, Debs expressed confidence that they would "some day realize" they were mistaken in their tactics, and that the Socialist Party was "best adapted for emancipating the American working class."[79]

L. B. Symes, a Socialist pamphleteer, argued that the Left was really but an extension of the old syndicalist and anarchist traditions, and that that explained the new opposition to an educational party.[80] But the left wing was only in part an off-spring of the traditional antipolitical tendencies in the American Socialist and labor movements. Although influenced by syndicalist thinking, their rejection of the old methods of politi-

---

[78] From Debs reply to a request from the left wing for support, *Cleveland Citizen*, May 3, 1919.
[79] "Press Telegram from Atlanta," quoted in Otto Branstetter to Hillquit, Chicago, July 3, 1920. Earlier, Debs had commented that "the psychology of the American workingman is different from that of workers of other countries," in that "they will not respond to any appeal that has a suggestion of violence." See "A Message from Comrade Eugene V. Debs," *St. Louis Labor*, September 6, 1919.
[80] L. B. Symes, "The Socialist Position Justified," Oakland *World*, January 16, 1920.

cal action was based primarily on the euphoria created by
Bolshevik success, and the consequent belief that they faced
a revolutionary opportunity, which led them to accept the need
for an insurrectionary monolithic party. But, as Algernon Lee
had charged, "Lenin was a realist," while the Left in the United
States was "trying to burlesque" him.[81] Like the American Left,
Lenin had been not in the least averse to opposing the majority
within his Party or within the Soviets. Unlike the Americans,
however, Lenin moved toward insurrection only after he became convinced that the majority of the people had no place
else to go. He followed a policy of splitting only when he
thought it was necessary to break with his comrades in order
to maintain or increase his following among the Russian
masses.[82] The American Left, on the other hand, simply followed Lenin's rhetoric in a situation totally unlike that which
inspired it. The "Right," as we have seen, did not hesitate to
point this out.

VII

But the walkout of Hourwich and his minority from the left-
wing conference was more persuasive than the arguments of
the old guard to the majority of the left wing. The bulk of the
70,000 members expelled or suspended by the Socialist leadership were in the foreign-language federations, and Hourwich
and his thirty-one delegates represented about two-thirds of
these. Among the various federations, Hourwich's Russians were
dominant, both because of their numerical strength and because
of the almost mystical prestige in the Left of anything Russian.
In early July, the Hourwich group called for a convention on

[81] Quoted by Louis C. Fraina, "A Discussion of Party Problems," *Revolutionary Age*, May 24, 1919. Fraina took Lee's charge to mean that if
Lenin were in the United States he would not be a left winger. To this,
his answer was simple. Lenin was always a left winger in Russia, *ergo*, he
would be one in the United States, too.
[82] See, for example, Lenin, "The Bolsheviks Must Assume Power"; "Marxism and Uprising," in *Collected Works*, XXI (New York, 1932), 221, 226.

September 1, 1919, in Chicago to form a Communist party. This stole the thunder of the National Council of the left wing, and, against their better judgment, most of the original majority proved unable to withstand the stigma of being "Centrists," and so surrendered their position to that of the Russian Federation. On July 28, 1919, five of the seven members who had been elected to the majority National Council at the June conference reversed themselves. Voting to go to Chicago on September 1 to form a Communist party, Ruthenberg, John Ballam, I. E. Ferguson, Bertram D. Wolfe, and Maximilian Cohen aligned themselves with the Russian Federation. They were quickly joined by Fraina.[83]

Gitlow and James Larkin held out, and were joined by John Reed, Wagenknecht, and Eadmonn MacAlpine, of the *Revolutionary Age*.[84] This latter group attended the Socialist convention in Chicago on August 30. When some of their delegates were refused seats, Reed and Gitlow led a secession movement and organized their own convention. Since there was a Communist Party convention going on in another part of the city, this group named itself the Communist Labor Party.[85]

VIII

From August 30 through the first week in September, three conventions met in Chicago: the Socialist, the Communist, and the Communist Labor. Among these three conventions, charges and countercharges filled the air, but the decisive one was whether or not the Third International's estimate of the revolutionary potential in Europe was valid in the United States. The refusal of the Socialists to agree that revolution was imminent in the United States led the Communists to equate them

[83] Draper, *op. cit.*, pp. 174-175; Emmet Larkin, *Jarmes Larkin, Irish Labor Leader, 1876-1947* (Cambridge, 1965), pp. 232-233.
[84] Draper, *op. cit.*; Larkin, *op. cit.*, p. 333.
[85] For a detailed account of the three conventions, see Draper, *op. cit.*, Chapter II; Shannon, *op. cit.*, Chapters VI, VII.

with the right-wing parties in Europe opposed to the Russian Revolution. Then, in a triumph of formal logic over reality, the Communists read back into the wartime activities of Hillquit and Berger all the characteristics exhibited by the Scheidemanns and Guesdes in Germany and France.

In the manifesto adopted at its convention, the Communist Party insisted that "the problems of the American worker are identical with the problems of the workers of the world."[86] Like the Communist Labor Party, however, the Communists conceded that the war had strengthened American capitalism and that, therefore, the moment of "actual revolution" had not quite arrived. Nevertheless, even more urgently than the Communist Laborites, the Communists proclaimed that the United States was in "a moment of struggles pregnant with revolution."[87] In these struggles, "parliamentarism" was to be of only secondary importance, since communism did "not propose to 'capture' the bourgeois state," but to "conquer and destroy it."[88] Apparently, however, the Party intended to participate in elections, although it did not actually do so until 1922. The manifesto pledged that Communist "parliamentary" representatives "shall not introduce or support reform measures," but would "analyze" such proposals "as evasions of the issue and as of no fundamental significance to the working class."[89] In conformity with the position that the "uncompromising character of the class struggle must be maintained under all circumstances," the manifesto declared that the Communist Party would not cooperate with the Socialist Party, the Labor Party, the Non-Partisan League, the People's Council, Municipal Ownership leagues, or any other group "not committed to the revolutionary class struggle."[90]

Revealing a mixture of IWW and Bolshevik ideology, the Communist Party pledged that its "major campaign" would

[86] Quoted in full in *Revolutionary Radicalism*, I, 776.
[87] *Ibid.*, p. 782.
[88] *Ibid.*, p. 783.
[89] *Ibid.*, p. 788.
[90] *Ibid.*

be the "great industrial struggles of the working class." Communists were to participate in strikes, not only to achieve the immediate purpose of the strike, but "to develop the revolutionary implications of the mass strike" and the "latent" tendency toward the "general mass strike." Their isolation from any actual labor movement was so great, however, that to carry out these policies, Communists were instructed to "establish contact" with "shops, mills, and mines," where they would then propagandize for industrial union organization. This was to be done not simply as a "means for everyday struggle against capitalism," but as a factor in the "final mass action for the conquest of power."[91]

The Communist Labor Party proposed a similar course of action, as John C. Taylor, chairman of the California delegation, pointed out. There was, he wrote, "no practical difference in the platform written by them and ourselves." But the two conventions and the two parties were necessary because the Communists "seemed imbued with the idea that the mantle of Elijah had been cast down upon them" and would not deal with the Communist Laborites on a basis of equality.[92] "The Russian Comrades," the Communist Laborites charged, "do not want unity, they want unconditional surrender."[93]

Almost all the English-speaking Communists went into the Communist Labor Party, and most of these came from the syndicalist tradition of the IWW. The delegations of California and Washington, for example, heavily influenced by the rapid growth of IWW strength on the West Coast during the war, joined the Communist Labor Party. Similarly, William F. Dunne led the IWW-oriented Butte local into the same Party. These groups had been opponents of the dominant Socialist tendencies for many years, and not a few must have felt that in helping

[91] *Ibid.*, pp. 788-789.
[92] John C. Taylor, "Report of the National Convention at Chicago," Oakland *World*, September 26, 1919.
[93] "Join Us," *Communist Labor Party News*, September 1919.

split the Socialist Party, they were but avenging the recall of Haywood from the National Executive Committee in 1913.[94]

The Western left wingers were poor Communists. They had even less understanding of the Leninist concept of Party organization than did their Russian Federation comrades. Instead, their hostility to the old right wingers stemmed from the belief, as expressed by Hulet Wells of Seattle, that the "real line of demarcation" between Right and Left was "the class philosophy of Marx." The new slogans created by the Bolsheviks were harder to handle, as an article in the Oakland *World* (then controlled by the Communist Labor Party) revealed. "Mass Action," the *World* admitted, "is one of those terms which some workers are stumbling over." Some choose to think of the term "as pertaining to a mob of men armed with clubs and guns." But, the paper explained, "in the true acceptance of the term that would *not* be mass action—it would be purely mob action." Mass action, the *World* continued, "is indicative of organization —necessarily organization of workers," but it did not imply organization of workers into an army for military purposes. "We have just had one of those," the *World* went on, "and we are extremely glad to see it being disbanded." It was in conjunction with industrial organization that they used the words mass

[94] The *Communist Labor Party News*, September 1919, claimed that each of the two Communist parties had about 30,000 members, but that whereas the Communist Party drew 26,000 of its members from the foreign language federations, headed by the Russians with 6,500 followers, the Communist Labor Party had only 9,000 foreign language members, most of them German (and, therefore, of longer Socialist affiliation). The CLP claimed 3,000 members in Ohio, 2,500 in New York, 2,000 in California and in Illinois, 1,500 in Washington and in Oregon, 1,000 in Indiana, 800 in Minnesota and New Jersey, and 500 in Arkansas, Colorado, Kansas, Kentucky, Missouri, Rhode Island, Utah, and West Virginia. These figures appear highly inflated, since they were apparently compiled by crediting the CLP with the entire membership of those states and locals whose leaders joined the Party. In reality many of these members remained in the Socialist Party, while even more simply dropped out of activity in the confusion. The Communist Party figures were given as follows: Russian Federation 6,500; Ukrainian 3,500; South Slavic 3,000; Lithuanian 6,000; Lettish 1,500; Hungarian 2,400; Polish 2,000; American 4,000.

action—"mass action of the workers or, turning it over—action of the masses of workers through industrial organization."[95]

Confusion among the members of the Communist Labor Party was equally great on the question of political action.[96] When John C. Taylor returned to California from the convention, for example, he reported that the CLP would hold a convention in 1920, at which time he believed the new Party would nominate Debs and Kate O'Hare for President and Vice President. Again, at the state convention for the California Party organization in November, the chairman of the resolution committee read a demand that the CLP lay greater stress on the ballot as an instrument "of tremendous assistance to the workers in their struggle for emancipation." He was told, however, that the national convention had adopted a program which "defines that the ballot is practically worthless as an instrument of emancipation," and that the Party must look to "organizing the workers industrially as our great weapon of offense and defense."[97] The latter statement was, of course, a correct one. But, apparently, neither the chairman of the state delegation, nor of the resolution committee of the first state convention knew this. In such a situation, the confusion among the rank and file must have been considerable.

Those in California who "defined" the ballot as practically worthless were within the IWW tradition. They identified almost exclusively with the "OBU" (One Big Union) movement, which had swept up the West Coast and into Canada in the years from 1917 to 1919. Even in attempting to reconcile their industrial program with events in the United States and in California, however, the advocates of the One Big Union ran into difficulties. James H. Dolsen, first state chairman of the California CLP, for example, saw the steel strike of September 1919 as placing the United States "trembling upon the verge

[95] "The Revolution Via Mass Action," *World*, October 3, 1919.
[96] This question did not arise in the Communist Party, largely because only an infinitesimal percentage of the membership was eligible to vote.
[97] *World*, September 26, 1919; November 14, 1919.

of a struggle between Capital and Labor" such as the world had "never yet seen." But as Dolsen himself noted, the steel workers were trying only to achieve what workers in many other industries had already secured: "the primary right of all workers to the principle of collective bargaining." It was hardly a revolutionary aim. Even more disturbing to the advocates of the OBU and of "smashing" the AFL was the fact that "the very contradictions inherent in capitalist society" were "compelling the leaders of the AFL to align their organizations on a fighting basis." Dolsen noted still further problems for the advocates of the One Big Union in the developments of the California telephone strike of 1919. It seems that the telephone girls, whose work was "of a rather distinct kind," themselves preferred "a separate organization."[98]

IX

Meanwhile, at the Socialist Party convention in Chicago, the remnants of the Party were attempting to formulate a program and lay the basis for rebuilding a militant organization. Adolph Germer, the Party's national secretary, declared the purpose of his Party to be to unite the working class of the United States, "that we might follow the splendid example set by our comrades in Russia." He stressed, however, that differences in the social conditions prevailing in the United States and in Russia would make the methods of American Socialists "somewhat different." It was on this, Germer declared, that the division occurred.[99]

[98] James H. Dolsen, "Prohibiting the Social Revolution," *World,* October 31, 1919.
[99] Adolph Germer, Introductory Remarks, "Proceedings of the National Convention," Chicago, August 30, 1919, 2-3. Germer added in defense of the Party, that the Socialists in the United States had been as true to its revolutionary principles as "any Socialist party on earth," and that in testimony to the Party's loyalty "hundreds, yea! thousands of our members are in prison today." Had they, in fact, been a party of Scheidemanns and Eberts, Debs would not be in prison and Berger would not be under a twenty-year sentence, nor would Congress refuse to seat him, Germer added.

Following Germer, Seymour Stedman of Chicago reviewed the Party's antiwar activity and the government persecution of the Party, its press and leaders. After the war, Stedman said a new group grew up rapidly within the Party ranks. "Influenced by the rapid changes taking place in Russia and Europe," this new Left believed that in "the richest creditor nation in the world," with a working class "discontented, but by no means revolutionary," it was not only possible to follow the Russian example, but mandatory. The new left wing, Stedman declared, thought "they alone hold the secret of success," and that it was their duty "to impose it upon the party," or to launch a new party.[100]

Other Socialists tried to formulate a program for postwar America. One of the more coherent attempts to do this was made by two leaders of the St. Louis local, William M. Brandt and G. A. Hoehn. "At a time like this," they wrote, "it is well for the Socialists to free themselves of Utopian illusions and hallucinations," and to take "constructive action along the lines of scientific revolutionary socialism." Hoehn and Brandt believed that American capitalists were "intensely interested" in the efforts of the Left "to divide the advance guard of the militant proletariat." After reviewing the "uncompromising attitude against the war taken by our Socialist party," and the "extremes" to which the Government went in outlawing and persecuting active Socialists, Hoehn and Brandt took note of the social revolution "tearing Europe from one end to the other." True, the "American ruling classes" feared that the revolution might "spread to this side of the Atlantic." Nevertheless, the "counter-revolution" was "already at work," as the recent crushing of the Communist regime in Hungary proved.

The times demanded a "solidified Socialist party movement that will be in constant feeling and cooperation with the Organized Labor Movement": one whose members would "participate in the daily battles and struggles" of the workers. So-

[100] Proceedings, pp. 12-16.

cialists, they wrote, must at all times "endeavor to advance the unity, integrity and solidarity of the Proletarian movement"; only by such cooperation and aid, and by "consistent educational efforts," would the Party be placed in a position to "strengthen and solidify" the movement for socialism. At the same time, Socialists should seek to strengthen the trade unions to which they belonged by advocating industrial organization, or the amalgamation of unions in related trades. But in all these efforts "the main aim should always be the strengthening of the unity and militancy of the Proletarian movement."[101]

On most issues in this convention there was agreement in principle, although the views were far from homogeneous. On the question of the fraudulent voting for the National Executive Committee, and even on the expulsion of the federations, for example, such a left winger as J. Louis Engdahl, future editor of the *Daily Worker,* conceded that drastic action had been necessary to prevent the "anarchists" from destroying the Party. It was not the result that disturbed Engdahl and others, but the arbitrary and hasty manner in which the NEC had acted.[102]

The manifesto adopted by the convention, similarly, met with almost unanimous approval. Alexander Trachtenberg, who along with Engdahl and others was to leave the Socialist Party and help organize the Workers' Party in 1922, praised the manifesto. It would "certainly bring back to the party those Socialists who were anxious to get back but were deluded" as to the true nature of the Party by "obstructionists and misrepresentations."[103]

The manifesto began with the statement that "the capitalist class is now making its last stand in its history," that capitalism had become "a dangerous impediment to progress and human welfare," and that "the working class alone" had the power to

---

[101] "Suggestions for National Socialist Platform and Program," *St. Louis Labor,* August 23, 1919.
[102] *Proceedings,* pp. 547-548.
[103] *Ibid.,* p. 565.

"redeem and save the world." Attacking the "mad era of capitalist imperialism," it went on to describe the subjugation of Asia,
Africa, Central and South America, where "hundreds of millions of peaceful inhabitants were forcibly parcelled out into
colonies" of the "capitalist conquerors." The rivalry of imperialism led to the great war, and even now was continued by the
"executive committee" of the capitalist governments in the "so-
called League of Nations."

The manifesto then went on to the issues which divided
Socialists from Communists. "The people of Russia, like the
American Colonists of 1776," it declared, "were driven by their
rulers to the use of violent methods to obtain and maintain their
freedom." In the United States this might also be necessary,
the manifesto implied, but the Socialist Party called upon the
workers "to do all in their power to restore and maintain" civil
rights, to the end that the "transition from capitalism to Socialism may be effected without resort to the drastic measures made
necessary by autocratic despotism."

Since the Socialists did not see any immediate revolutionary
potential in the United States, they saw no need for a sharp
break with the methods employed in the prewar period. "To
win the American workers from their ineffective and demoraliz-
ing leadership, to educate them to an enlightened understanding of their own class interests, and to train and assist them to
organize politically and industrially on class lines in order to
effect their emancipation," was the task the manifesto set out
for the Socialist Party.[104]

But all was not harmony at the convention. On one issue real
disagreement existed: whether or not to affiliate with the Third
International. Some comrades, Engdahl reported, wanted to
leave the way open for a possible future return to the Second
International; another group stood for affiliation with the Third.
In the course of the discussion in committee, the pro-Second
International platform was dropped and two alternative posi-

[104] Reprinted in *Revolutionary Radicalism*, pp. 618-624.

tions emerged. The majority report declared the "Second International is no more." It called for the "speediest possible convocation of an International Socialist Congress," to reconstitute a functioning International that would include only those parties which declared "strict adherence by word and deed to the principle of the class struggle," such as "the Communist parties of Russia and Germany." It would exclude any party "which participates in a government coalition with the parties of the bourgeoisie."

Engdahl and a minority of the committee opposed this statement and presented instead a call for affiliation with the Third International, "not so much because [the Socialist Party of the United States] supports the 'Moscow' programs and methods," but because: (a) "Moscow" is doing something which is really challenging world imperialism; (b) "Moscow" is threatened by the combined capitalist forces of the world simply because it is proletarian; (c) under these circumstances, whatever we may have to say to Moscow afterwards, it is the duty of the Socialists to stand by it now because its fall would mean "disappearance of Socialist hopes for many years to come."[105] The dilemma the Party faced on the question of international affiliation was apparent, but was made explicit by Abraham Beckerman, a leader in the ILGWU. For Beckerman there was no question of choosing between the Second and Third International. "Moscow," he explained, "is Socialist but it is not International; Berne is an International but it is not Socialist."[106] In such a situation neither could be chosen. In the convention this position carried by a vote of 61 to 34. In a referendum of the membership, however, the minority report favoring affiliation with the Third International carried by a vote of 3,475 to 1,444.[107]

The Party then applied to the Third International for membership. In a long letter to Zinoviev, in which the Party's posi-

---

[105] *Proceedings*, pp. 725-728; *Revolutionary Radicalism*, pp. 624-626.
[106] *Proceedings*, pp. 716-717.
[107] *Shannon, op. cit.*, p. 153.

tion during the war was reviewed and defended, the Socialist Party leaders pointed out that the split in the United States had not occurred until a year after the armistice,[108] and implied that the issues raised then were false.

As Hillquit wrote in August 1920, the Socialists had "always supported the Soviet Government of Russia" because it was "the government of the working class of Russia," a government striving to "abolish every remnant of capitalism and for that reason" one which was "being persecuted by every imperialistic and reactionary power on the face of the globe." The reasons that impelled the United States government to "make war upon Russia," Hillquit continued, were "exactly the same reasons" that impelled American Socialists to "support Soviet Russia in all of its struggles."

"But that does not mean," Hillquit added, "that we abdicate our reason, forget the circumstances surrounding us, and blindly accept every formula, every dogma coming from Russia as holy, as a Papal decree." Nor did it mean that "we accept for this country . . . the special institutions and forms into which the struggles have been moulded by the historical conditions of Russia."[109]

That Hillquit had correctly stated the issue was confirmed by Zinoviev himself. In his reply, in 1921, to the request for affiliation which the Socialist Party had made in 1920, Zinoviev stated that the new International was "not a hotel" but "an

---

[108] Letter to Zinoviev [1919], in SPC, Duke.

[109] Hillquit, "Dictatorship and the International," *Socialist World*, August, 1920. Hillquit wrote to Debs along similar lines in June (Saranac Lake, June 30, 1920). "Like you," Hillquit wrote, "I believe our comrades in Russia are doing the most inspiring work ever attempted in the history of our race," and that they will "evolve a truly Socialistic order of society . . . which will serve in many ways" as a model to the entire civilized world.

"So long as they fight against the international forces of capitalism and reaction, I shall always support them with all the weapons at my command.

"This attitude on my part, however, does not imply that I am prepared to take every dictum that comes from Moscow . . . as gospel truth, or that I shall abdicate my own judgement as to the needs and chances of the Socialist and Labor movement in this country."

army in wartime." Volunteers who join the "Army of Revolution," he explained, "must adopt as their program the program of the Communist International—open and revolutionary mass struggle for Communism through the Dictatorship of the Proletariat, by means of the Workers' Soviets." Not only must they follow this formula, but they must also "create a strongly centralized form of organization, a military discipline"; and all Party members "must be absolutely subject to the full-powered Central Committee of the Party." In addition, "they must sever all connections with the petty bourgeoisie, and prepare for revolutionary action, for merciless civil war."[110] This, of course, the Socialists were not prepared to do.

X

By the end of 1919, then, there were three parties where there had been one. Even this, however, does not give a full picture of the splintering process that had taken place. In the Communist Party, for example, the Michigan organization had been out of place from the beginning. Indeed, if it had not been for the precipitous action of the NEC in expelling the state of Michigan, it probably would not have been part of the left wing. This group adhered to the left wing and joined in the first call for a Communist party because of its hostility to the Socialist Party leadership, but its analysis of the American scene was closer to the Socialists' than to the Communists'. The Michigan group ran into trouble with the Russian leadership at the founding convention of the Communist Party. Taking the position that American capitalism had emerged from the war stronger than before, the Michigan Socialists agreed with the Socialist Party that the system was likely to survive for an indefinite period. Also, like the Socialists, they favored political and educational means of preparing the workers for socialism, while unlike the Communists, they had little interest in unions,

[110] Quoted in *Socialist World*, May 15, 1921.

rating them low as a means for revolutionary preparation. Although their attacks on a program of immediate demands and their insistence on antireligious propaganda clearly violated the Socialist Party constitution, the position of the Michigan group on the other issues made it equally unpalatable to the Communists. A few weeks after the convention, the Communist Party expelled the Michigan group,[111] which then formed the Proletarian Party. It was but the first of many such splits to come.

XI

A fourth division in the ranks of the Socialist movement, though informal, had an even greater impact on the relationship between the Party and the trade union movement than did the splits to the left. This was the large-scale defection of Socialists, both "Left" and "Right" to the labor party movement and to the Committee of Forty-Eight, both organized in 1919.

Initiated on a significant scale by the Chicago Federation of Labor under the leadership of John Fitzpatrick and Edward N. Nockels on November 17, 1918, the Independent Labor Party of Illinois and the United States elicited a quick response. Two weeks after it was made, Fitzpatrick's proposal received the unanimous endorsement of the Illinois Federation of Labor, and by March 1919, the local unions in the state had concurred by a vote of better than ten to one.[112] Letters of support or interest, published in Fitzpatrick's *New Majority* in January 1919,

[111] *The Proletarian*, June-September 1919, summarized in Draper, *op. cit.*, p. 160; Shannon, *op. cit.*, p. 147.
[112] "The American Labor and Socialist Parties: Cooperation or Competition?" ed., Harry W. Laidler, *Intercollegiate Socialist*, April-May 1919, p. 8; E. N. Nockels to Frank P. Walsh, Bloomington, Illinois, December 3, 1918, Walsh papers; *Cleveland Citizen*, March 29, 1919. Actually, the Chicago group was not first to organize a labor party. One had appeared in Bridgeport and four other Connecticut cities in the election of November 1918. In Bridgeport, the Party polled 232 votes (about 2% of the total) compared to 468 for the Socialists.

came from all over Illinois and Michigan, and from such places as Barre, Vermont, Allentown, Pennsylvania, New Bedford, Massachusetts, and Miami, Florida. The Building Trades Council of Charleston, South Carolina, for example, wrote that they had "a similar organization in process, and that they planned to hold a "mass meeting shortly," for which they wanted copies of the Chicago platform.[113] The Central Unions of greater New York followed the lead of Fitzpatrick and organized the American Labor Party in New York City in January; and in the next four months central labor bodies had taken similar steps in over forty-five localities from coast to coast.[114]

In November 1919, a National Labor Party was organized at Chicago. This marked the high point of the movement. Delegates arrived from labor bodies in forty states; the heaviest representation was from Illinois, Indiana, and adjacent states. The leadership of the AFL, of course, strongly opposed this step toward independent political action on the part of labor, and this opposition reflected itself in the absence of international leaders from the convention. The overwhelming majority of delegates were from local unions, although many city central bodies and district councils also sent delegates. Despite the opposition of labor's top leadership, later to be more effective, over half the unions affiliated with the AFL were represented.[115]

Socialists did not participate in the initial stages of the labor party movement in Illinois or in New York, but the new experiment in political action intimately affected the Socialist Party and its internal development in 1918 and early 1919. Holding principles similar to those of the Socialists, many rad-

[113] "Like a Prairie Fire the Labor Party Spreads," *New Majority*, I, 1 (January 4, 1919).
[114] "The American Labor and Socialist Parties," *op. cit.*; "An American Labor Party," *Literary Digest*, CX (February 1, 1919), 14-15. On January 31, 1919, for example, a labor party was formed in Galesburg, Illinois; in early May, one was organized in Cleveland, Ohio. *Galesburg Labor News*, January 31, 1919; *Cleveland Citizen*, May 17, 1919.
[115] Nathan Fine, *Labor and Farmer Parties in the United States, 1828-1928* (New York, 1961), p. 383.

ical labor leaders had become convinced, especially after the low vote received by the Socialists in November 1918, that for one reason or another, the term "Socialist" had become an unnecessary handicap for working-class politicians.[116] In sharp contrast to Socialist Party fortunes, the striking success of the Nonpartisan League in North Dakota, under a leadership largely Socialist or ex-Socialist, encouraged a sanguine view of the Labor Party potential.[117] Thus, James G. Boyle, a founder of the American Labor Party, and a former president of the Brooklyn Central Labor Union, envisioned a coalition of Socialists, Laborites and Nonpartisan Leaguers in a new, strengthened radical movement. And John F. McNamee, editor of the *Brotherhood of Locomotive Firemen and Engineers Magazine,* urged coordination of "all movements that have for their purpose the emancipation of the working class from master exploitation." He believed that many working-class voters, to whom the Socialist label was obnoxious, would "eagerly accept public ownership . . . cooperative production, and practically all other economic reform principles advocated by the Socialist Party."[118]

In fact, the labor parties had a program and a perspective which was socialist in all but name. The Chicago Party had come into being because the leaders felt the major parties had "betrayed" the workers to the corporations; and when the National Labor Party formed, it declared that its purpose was "to assemble into a new majority the men and women who work, but who have been scattered as helpless minorities in the old parties." This step was taken as the result of an awareness that, "throughout the world," the workers had "reached the determination" to "take control of their own lives and their own

---

[116] The decline in the Socialist vote from 1917 to 1918 in Illinois was particularly sharp, but even in New York, the Socialist vote dropped from 145,000 for Hillquit in 1917 to 110,000 for the Socialist congressional candidates in New York City in 1918, although this was still much higher than the 53,000 votes polled by Benson in all of New York State in 1916.
[117] On Socialist leadership in the Nonpartisan League see Robert Morlan, *Political Prairie Fire* (Minneapolis, 1955), pp. 355 ff.
[118] "The American Labor and Socialist Parties," *loc. cit.*

government." The program called for socialization of railroads, mines, forests, water power, telegraphs, telephones, stock yards, grain elevators, natural gas and oil wells, cold storage and terminal warehouses, packing plants, flour mills, and of all basic industries which required large-scale production and were essentially noncompetitive. In addition, the National Labor Party demanded the federal government take over and operate all banks and banking facilities, and nationalize all unused land, which could then be rented only to actual users.[119]

Traditionally, of course, the Socialists had been hostile to labor party proposals, believing that radical workers should join the Socialist Party. This remained the official position in 1919 and 1920, supported by both left and right wingers. Thus, the left-wing L. E. Katterfeld opposed cooperation with a labor party, or any organization "that tolerates a continuation of capitalism"; this view was shared by John Work of Wisconsin. Others, however, took a position best expressed by Evans Clark. Regretting that these radicals in the labor parties were not Socialists, Clark nevertheless welcomed them to the ranks of independent working-class politics. Leaders such as Seymour Stedman of Chicago, James Oneal, and Scott Nearing were also cautiously cordial.[120] In California, the Oakland *World* best expressed the changing attitude of the Socialists in announcing its campaign for a West Coast daily newspaper. The *World* promised consistently to "fight the battles of labor, whether Socialist or non-Socialist, whether organized as craft unions or as industrial unions." It further pledged to "work for the solidarity of labor on both the political and industrial fields, with collectivism (Socialism under whatever name) as the chief objective." While it invited adherents of the AFL and members of the Farmer-Labor Party to cooperate, the paper "proposed no fusion." Its "objective is Socialism."[121] This dualism continued

[119] *New Majority,* January 4, 1919; Fine, *op. cit.,* p. 379.
[120] "The American Labor and Socialist Parties," *loc. cit.*
[121] "Socialists versus Farmer Laborites," Oakland *World,* January 14, 1920.

at the 1920 Socialist convention, where it took but one minute to vote down a resolution calling for electoral cooperation with other groups.[122]

For many Socialists this relatively cordial attitude was not enough. They preferred to drop their affiliation with the old Party and to join the new, and this tendency was accelerated by the Socialists' continuation of their official policy of non-cooperation. This movement away from the Socialist Party was not motivated by a repudiation of Socialist principles, but by a conviction that the factional disputes within the Party had so weakened and isolated it as to make it unsuitable as a vehicle of working-class politics.[123] As would be expected, this view was most common among prominent trade union Socialists, but many traditional "left wingers," especially on the West Coast, adopted an identical outlook and an identical course of action. *The New Justice,* edited in Los Angeles by Lena Morrow Lewis and others, regarded the splitting of the socialist movement into some "half dozen petty and impotent organizations" as "too deplorable to be amusing and too preposterous to be taken seriously."

"In sharp contrast to this disorganization," wrote Clarence Meily, "is the new Labor Party, which has behind it the most radical elements of the AFL, notably, the United Mine Workers." Meily asserted that this new movement would "profoundly interest every friend of working-class progress," and was of the "utmost import both for the radical theorist and the practical politician."[124]

In Seattle, too, the "Left" veered to the "Right." There, all but one of the branches of the Socialist Party had been left wing

---

[122] Fine, *op. cit.,* p. 424.
[123] The fact that a Socialist Party still capable of polling 900,000 votes was considered too weak and splintered to be taken seriously is a revealing indication of the scope of radical politics in 1919.
[124] "Proletarian Politics," *The New Justice,* October 1919. The November *New Justice* leaned toward an endorsement of the Socialists in the split and called for unity in the face of attacks by the capitalists.

before the split, but not one of the English-speaking branches went into the Communist or Communist Labor parties after September 1919. Convinced that the Socialist parties were too divided to be capable of further effective activity, most militant Socialists simply melted away and regrouped in the dynamic new Farmer-Labor Party. The situation in Seattle, however, was not typical. Under James Duncan's leadership, the Seattle Central Labor Council had relatively friendly relations with the Socialists and even with the IWW. Many of the CLC members were "two-card" men, active in both the union of their trade and in the One Big Union.[125]

Even such right-wing Labor Party supporters as Max Hayes took substantially the same position as the West Coast leftists. Hayes quit the Socialist Party in May 1919 and shortly thereafter joined the Labor Party, although unlike most of his comrades he took the occasion to restate his disagreement with the antiwar St. Louis Manifesto, as well as his opposition to the left wing (which had just captured the Cleveland local to which Hayes belonged). Calling the left wingers "anarchists at heart," Hayes regretted "the palpable fact that the line of cleavage between the Socialist party and the trade union movement" was "steadily widening when there ought to be greater unity and cooperation," and when "the future appeared most promising to make substantial headway."[126]

In Illinois, where the labor party movement began, defections of Socialist trade unionists were greatest. Duncan McDonald, veteran Socialist leader, who had still been an active Party member when he was elected president of the Illinois Federation of Labor in January 1919, was "driven" out of the Socialist

---

[125] Interview with Harvey O'Connor, Madison, November 6, 1961. There was, of course, no formal alliance between the Seattle CLC and the IWW, and, indeed, the Council leaders frequently made known their antagonism for the record. In the IWW-led lumber strike in 1917, however, the CLC gave support, and the IWW supported the CLC during the general strike.

[126] *Cleveland Citizen*, May 17, 24, 1919.

Party by the anti-trade union attitude of the dominant left-wing group in Chicago. At the first convention of the Illinois Labor Party in April 1919, McDonald was elected state chairman. Earlier such leading Socialists as Christian Madsen, former state legislator and a leader of the Chicago Painters Local; William E. Rodriguez, Chicago alderman and prominent trade unionist; and John C. Kennedy, former state chairman of the Party and Chicago alderman, had transferred their allegiance to the new movement.[127] Similarly in Pennsylvania, where a labor party was organized in May, R. J. Wheeler, Socialist councilman and Machinists leader in Allentown, joined the new movement. An exception to this trend, James H. Maurer remained loyal to his comrades, but even in Pennsylvania the State Federation of Labor which he led endorsed the Labor Party. The influence of the Labor Party among militant trade unionists in Pennsylvania was such that Maurer felt constrained not to run for the Vice Presidential nomination in early 1920.[128]

Although widespread, the labor party movement met with limited electoral success. Gompers opposed the movement bitterly, seeing in it only the possibility of strengthening his enemies in the Federation.[129] At the same time, the Socialists neither offered assistance nor stepped aside for the new movement in 1919 or 1920. At its strongest in Chicago in 1919, the Labor Party succeeded in polling only 54,467 votes in the spring mayoralty election, although there were an estimated 550,000 trade unionists and their wives in the city.[130] That the Labor Party had failed to attract any new forces to radical politics is

[127] *Cleveland Citizen*, May 17, March 29, 1919; *New Majority*, January 4, 25, April 19, 1919.
[128] *New Majority*, January 4, May 24, 1919; *Cleveland Citizen*, June 7, 1919; Maurer to Hillquit, Reading, April 16, 1920, Hillquit Papers, Wisconsin State Historical Society. At this time Hayes speculated on the possibility of Maurer's resigning from the Socialist Party, but Maurer remained a Socialist until his death.
[129] "An American Labor Party," *Literary Digest, loc. cit.; The Public,* XXII (January 25, 1919), 78.
[130] *New Majority*, April 5, 1919; *Cleveland Citizen,* April 5, 1919. The Socialists polled 23,105.

indicated by the fact that the combined labor and Socialist votes just about equalled the Socialist vote of 80,000 in 1917. In Chicago the Labor Party ran well ahead of the Socialists, but this was not universal. In Schenectady, for example, the Labor Party managed only to contribute to the defeat of the Socialist mayoralty candidate who lost the April election to the Republicans by 9,529 votes to 10,527, while the Laborite polled 1,523.[131] The Labor Party's greatest strength was in downstate Illinois and eastern Iowa. There the Laborites succeeded in electing several mayors and councilmen in the spring elections of 1919 and 1920.[132]

XII

Like the Laborites, the Committee of Forty-Eight came into being as a result of the feeling of many radicals that their convictions could not adequately be expressed through any of the old parties—Republican, Democratic, or Socialist.[133] Unlike the labor party movement, however, the Committee of Forty-Eight was composed of those "radical intellectual forces" disillusioned with the progressivism of Theodore Roosevelt and Woodrow Wilson. Called into being in late March 1919 by John A. H. Hopkins, Amos Pinchot, Allen McCurdy, George L. Record, Parley P. Christensen, and others, the Committee was formally organized at a convention in St. Louis on December 9, 1919. Present were some 300 delegates from diverse radical and liberal traditions. Supporters of La Follette, Debs, and the single tax all vied to have their views incorporated in the program; finally they agreed on three points not unlike the Labor Party's platform. The statement called for public ownership of the means of transportation—railroads, stockyards, grain elevators, warehouses—public utilities, and natural resources—coal, oil,

[131] *Ibid.* The Democrats polled 2,432 in this election.
[132] *New Majority*, April 5, 25, May 3, 1919; April 3, 17, 1920.
[133] Allen McCurdy, "The Forty-Eight's Position," *Nation*, CXI (July 31, 1920), 126.

natural gas, minerals, and lumber. In addition, it bowed in the direction of the Single Taxers by calling for a punitive tax on all unused private lands; and it demanded the restoration of full civil liberties, an end to antilabor injunctions, and full recognition of the right of collective bargaining. Further, the convention adopted resolutions opposing the Esch-Cummings Act, under which the railroads were returned to their private owners after the war, and called on the Administration to withdraw American troops from Russia and to lift the blockade of the Soviets.[134]

Composed as it was of intellectuals, most of whom had broken away from the left wing of insurgent progressivism, the Committee of Forty-Eight did not represent any large number of organized radicals. A few Socialists participated in Committee activity—notably Frank O'Hare in St. Louis—[135] but most of the leaders were disillusioned Bull Moosers or New Freedomites. Ideologically the Forty-Eighters had more in common with La Follette than with Hillquit or Debs. In the postwar period they might have given qualified support to a united and vital socialist movement, but with the Party breaking up they followed a course similar to that of the Labor Party. The existence of the Committee created a haven short of socialism for insurgent progressives moving left. A united socialist movement might have absorbed many of these radicals, just as the Farmer-Labor Party was to do in 1920.[136]

XIII

Before leaving this discussion of the split in the socialist movement, one last observation is in order. The growth in

[134] *Ibid.;* Lincoln Colcord, "The Committee of Forty-Eight," *Nation,* 109 (December 27, 1919), 821-822; "A New Political Alignment," *Nation,* 108 (March 29, 1919), 460.
[135] William A. Brandt to Otto Branstetter, St. Louis, March 2, 1920, SPC, Duke.
[136] From the beginning, the Labor Party had cordial relations with the Committee of Forty-Eight. Thus, Duncan McDonald attended the St. Louis convention, bringing greetings from his Party. Colcord, "The Committee of Forty-Eight."

socialist strength during the war, and the advent of the Russian Revolution were of serious concern to many leaders in the Wilson Administration. The subsequent events leading to the disruption and weakening of the socialist movement were of direct interest to Administration leaders such as Attorney General Palmer and Postmaster General Burleson. Many Socialists were convinced, as James H. Maurer put it, that the ranks of the Communists were "honeycombed with spies," and that many Communist leaders were "financed by the government and Big Business" to corrupt and destroy the Socialist Party.[137]

At the time of the Palmer raids, in January 1920, the *New York Times* shed some light on this question when it reported that "for months," that is, even before the split occurred, "Department of Justice men, dropping all other work, had concentrated on the Reds"; and that agents had "quietly infiltrated into the radical ranks," sometimes as cooks in remote mining colonies, sometimes as miners, again as steel workers, and, where the opportunity presented itself, as "agitators of the wildest type." Of course, the *Times* was quick to add, these agents did not "inspire" any "overt acts," but they did admit that several "under cover" men managed to "rise in the radical movement," becoming, at least in one instance, "the recognized leader of a district."[138]

The extent to which the representatives of the Department of Justice in the left wing encouraged the split in Socialist ranks cannot be determined; but agents of this type have traditionally played the role of provocateur. It must be assumed that in varying degrees these agents followed the custom of their profession. The Post Office Department, on the other hand, played a direct role in favoring the Left. In the spring of 1919 the Socialist Party *Bulletin,* its official organ, the *Eye Opener,* and the national office's first-class mail were all held up by Post Office officials. (The ban was partially overcome by taking letters and publications outside of Chicago to mail,

[137] James H. Maurer, *It Can Be Done* (New York, 1938), pp. 240-241.
[138] January 3, 1920.

although incoming Socialist mail was held up by postmasters
in some communities to which it was addressed.) At the same
time, *The Revolutionary Age*, and the *Proletarian*, organ of the
Michigan group, passed freely through the mails, unhindered
by patriotic postmasters.[139]

In 1922, at the time that the Workers' Party was formed,
the extent to which Department of Justice agents had infiltrated Communist ranks was given much publicity.[140] Even
in late 1919 and early 1920, however, there were occasional
indications that agents were exacerbating the differences between the Socialist Party and the left wing. In Michigan, for
example, John R. Ball, a former antiunion militia man, was
active in the left wing at its inception; while in Detroit the
reputed organizer of the first branch of the Russian Socialist
Federation, and a statewide organizer for the Federation, became the most prominent witness for the Department of Justice after the Palmer Raids. Similarly, in St. Louis, one of the
most active left wingers at the time of the split, Joseph Krieg,
was later exposed as an agent of the Industrial Service Corporation, a labor spy agency.[141] Of course the split would have
taken place even in the absence of these agents. It is significant,
however, that the role of the left wing and of the new Communist parties played so directly into the hands of the enemies
of the socialist movement.

At the end of 1919, then, the Socialist Party was fractured
in three directions and into many parts. In the early months
of 1919, the Socialist Party had 109,000 members, yet within
a year after the split the three parties would have only 36,000
members among them.[142] Socialist influence in the labor move-

---

[139] Adolph Germer to Morris Hillquit, Chicago, April 17, 1919, Hillquit
papers.
[140] On this see Draper, *op. cit.* Chapter 14, pp. 226 ff.
[141] Germer to Hillquit, Chicago, April 9, 1919, Hillquit papers; Henry W.
Glickman to Elizabeth Gurley Flynn, Detroit, February 3, 1920, Elizabeth G. Flynn papers WSHS; *Socialist World*, November 15, 1920.
[142] Draper, *op. cit.*, p. 207; Shannon, *op. cit.*, p. 158.

ment, except for pockets in the garment trades, was all but destroyed by the split, and the socialist press, struggling to make a comeback after wartime suppression, was permanently debilitated. In the decade that followed the split, the lines drawn in 1919 were erected into walls, and the movement became one of hostile and warring sects. In the following chapters we will trace this development, and attempt to show that by the mid-1920's the socialist movement in the United States had developed most of the characteristics possessed in the 1930's, 1940's, and 1950's.

5

DISINTEGRATION
1919-1921

In the first half of the 1920's, American radicals faced unprecedented difficulties, as well as unique opportunities. Socialist criticism of the United States' role in the war, and the Party's warnings that the wartime gains of worker and farmer would be fleeting, proved correct for all but the hard core of the AFL craft unions. As J. Louis Engdahl, then editor of the official Socialist organ, *The Eye Opener,* commented, the strength of the movement lay in the fact that the Socialists had "stood courageously by what they considered right," and in that their "predictions had come true."[1] Disillusionment was widespread among those who had supported the Wilson Administration in the belief that Government recognition of the right to organize into unions would be permanent, and that the war for world democracy would bring an increase in the social content of democracy at home. Union advances had been greatest in the war industries, and as these contracted, membership dropped rapidly. The railroad unions did not lose their wartime recruits, but after the roads were returned to their private owners, the newly created Railroad Labor Board assumed an increasingly antiunion attitude. Other gains made through trade union cooperation came under attack from corporate interests. The employers not only defeated attempts to extend organization, as in the steel and coal strikes in 1919, but initiated a counterattack in the open shop drive of the

[1] J. Louis Engdahl, "A Swing Around the Circle," *The Eye Opener,* April 15, 1920.

National Association of Manufacturers, launched under the euphemistic title of the American Plan in 1920. At the same time a steady decline in farm prices as the greatly expanded wartime markets in Europe began to contract led to a chronic agricultural depression. As a result, especially in the tier of states extending from Illinois to Washington, discontent and radical sentiment among workers and farmers smoldered and flared up continuously in the years from 1919 to 1925.

II

Had it not been for the split, many of these dissident political movements could have been expected to gravitate toward the Socialist Party. Certainly in the prewar years this would have been true. But the Socialists did not benefit from the new waves of radicalism. On the contrary, beset with both external and internal difficulties, the Party never did make a comeback. By 1925 it reached the lowest point in its two dozen years of existence. The National Civic Federation noted in 1921 that "Socialism in some form" was "everywhere," that "as a cult it has never been stronger." At the same time, the Federation admitted, the Socialist Party had "for the moment become a negligible force."[2]

In 1920 the Socialist Party came out of the split with some 40,000 members; but when J. Louis Engdahl toured the Midwest that April, he heard everywhere the same story: "We had a fine local, but the war came." A year and a half after the war had ended, chambers of commerce were continuing their fight for "Americanism"—breaking up radical meetings, terrorizing Party members and supporters.[3] When Debs ran for President from his cell in Atlanta, the Party had organizations in good working order in only seven states. In nineteen states there

[2] Confidential Memorandum marked "Exhibit F," Meeting of the Executive Council and Other Members, December 20, 1921, Box 188, NCF papers.
[3] Engdahl, "A Swing Around the Circle."

were only paper organizations, and in twenty-two none at all (in five of these the Socialists were not even on the ballot). Of course, where the Socialists were not organized to watch the counting of the vote, unknown thousands of Debs electors never had their choice recorded. But where the Party was able to maintain its machinery in good order, the Socialist vote substantially surpassed the 1912 totals.[4]

At the time, and since, Debs' vote of 915,000 was dismissed as a purely personal tribute. But this is true only in a very narrow sense. In several states Debs did not even run ahead of the ticket. In others, the combined vote of Debs and the Farmer-Labor Party's Presidential candidate just about equalled the combined Socialist and Farmer-Labor Party vote for state and local offices. In other words, where Debs ran ahead of his ticket, Parley Parker Christensen, Farmer-Labor Party candidate, ran behind his.[5]

In program and in general perspective, the Farmer-Laborites differed little from the Socialist Party. Christensen campaigned for nationalization of all major segments of the American economy, for amnesty of the wartime political prisoners, and for the restoration of full civil liberties. On the question of the Soviet Union, too, Christensen took a stand close to that of Debs and Stedman. As Christensen later informed President

---

[4] See the *World* (Oakland), January 7, 1921.
[5] In Oklahoma Debs ran only 4 percent ahead of the Socialist candidate for justice of the Supreme Court; in Pennsylvania he ran well behind the Socialist senatorial aspirant; in New York he ran 900 votes ahead of A. Phillip Randolph, in a total of over 200,000 votes. In Minnesota, on the other hand, Debs ran better than twice as well as the next highest candidate, but here the Farmer-Laborites had no Presidential line although they ran a full state ticket. The combined Party votes surpassed Debs' total by far. In Illinois, too, Debs ran 20 percent ahead of the ticket, but the state and local Farmer-Labor candidates ran well ahead of Christensen. *Directory of the State of Oklahoma State Election Board* (n.p., 1925), pp. 84-85; *Smull's Legislative Handbook and Manual of the State of Pennsylvania* (Harrisburg, 1922), pp. 731, 754; *New York Legislative Manual*, 1921 (Albany, 1921), pp. 761, 768, 776, 798; *Minnesota Legislative Manual*, 1921 (Minnesota, 1922), p. 525, facing p. 526; *Illinois Blue Book*, 1921-22 (Springfield, 1921), p. 765.

Wilson, he "spoke of Russia" at "every meeting" of his campaign, urging recognition of the Soviet Republic. The "mere mention" of Russia at these meetings "was electrifying," Christensen added; the demand for friendly relations invariably received a "tremendous" affirmative response. Similarly, in Montana, the Non-Partisan League endorsed Debs' wartime position.[6] Debs' vote does not seem to exaggerate the extent of radical sentiment in 1920, but to understate it by at least the extent of Christensen's poll—that is by at least 300,000 votes.

Even in the South, radicalism enjoyed a revival. In Georgia, Tom Watson had begun his amazing political comeback in 1918, when he narrowly missed defeating Carl Vinson for the Democratic nomination for Congress. Vinson, a "super-patriot," made the war the main issue, charging, among other things, that Watson had never bought a Liberty Bond. Watson admitted this and campaigned for "free speech; re-establishment of the press . . . and . . . stronger individual liberty." In the spring of 1920, Watson ran against A. Mitchell Palmer in the Georgia Presidential primaries. Basing his campaign on opposition to the Wilson Administration and to Palmer's famed raids, Watson proclaimed that "Woodrow Wilson should be in prison and Eugene Debs in the White House." Watson won in the popular vote, but because of the county unit system, Palmer got the delegates. That November, Watson won election to the United States Senate by a wide plurality.[7]

The election of 1920 did not record an ebb in popular Socialist consciousness, but marked both the disintegration of the Socialist Party as a truly national organization and the dispersal of organized radical forces. In 1912 and 1916, the

[6] "Christensen Protests Deportation of Russian Government Agent," *New Majority*, January 8, 1921; "Labor Swallows the Forty-Eighters," *The Survey*, 44 (August 2, 1920) 587-588; Shannon, *op. cit.*, p. 156.
[7] Woodward, *op. cit.*, pp. 462, 473; Stanley Coben, *A. Mitchell Palmer* (New York, 1963), pp. 257-258; *Minneapolis Labor Review*, April 30, 1920.

Socialist vote reflected the state of organized radicalism in
the United States (except for the small vote of the Socialist Labor Party, which remained static throughout this period). This
situation began to change with the organization of the Non-
Partisan League in North Dakota in 1916 and the emergence
of the Farmer-Labor Party of Minnesota in 1918. By 1920 it is
probable that only Debs' candidacy saved the Socialist Party
from the loss of its apparent position as popular leader of
American radicalism. Without Debs, the onslaught of both the
Communists and the Farmer-Laborites would have been much
more visible. Only in this sense was the vote essentially a
tribute to the aging leader.

In some few places the Socialists had maintained their
strength despite the collapse of the national organization. Before the split, in April 1919, Socialists in Sheboygan, Wisconsin,
elected 7 of 16 councilmen and the municipal judge, losing
the mayoralty by 2,062 votes to 2,347. And after the split, in
November 1919, the Party elected mayors in Byesville and
Massillon, Ohio, and in Lackawanna, New York, while in Buffalo, Frank C. Perkins led the Party to victory with 47,102
votes, placing first of three councilmen elected.[8] Even in 1920
and 1921, the Party ran well in New York City, Milwaukee,
Detroit, Minneapolis, Davenport, Iowa, and Livingston, Montana. Increasingly, however, these pockets of strength tended

---

[8] *Sheboygan Press,* April 2, 1919; *St. Louis Labor,* November 8, 1919;
Buffalo Express, November 5, 1919. In Lackawanna, the Socialist John H.
Gibbons defeated a Democrat 986 votes to 968. Perkins, a Socialist of
long standing, was put forward in July 1919 by the left wing, when it
controlled the Buffalo local. He was nominated again when the local was
reorganized. His program included demands that the street railway, the
Niagara Electric Company, and the natural gas company be munici-
palized. After the election he called for a policy of equal opportunity
regardless of race, color, or creed. The Socialist candidate for mayor of
Columbus, Ohio, polled 19,260 votes, or 25%. In Toledo, the Party
candidate received 15,212 votes, or 35% (*Columbus Labor News,* November 6, 1919; *Miami Valley Socialist,* November 7, 14, 21, 1919. In
Dayton, Ohio, Socialists carried 5. of 137 precincts and won 40% of
the vote.

to become isolated islands, rather than parts of a national movement.

After the 1920 election, the Party's national organization devoted its major efforts to a campaign for a general amnesty of the wartime political prisoners, and especially to its attempts to secure a pardon for Debs. To the end, President Wilson refused to free Debs, who was finally released by Harding, along with twenty-three other political prisoners, on Christmas Day, 1921. Even then, many hundreds of Socialists and other radicals remained in prison, and the Party continued its amnesty campaign in full swing for the next year or more.

By its very nature a defensive fight, the amnesty campaign could do little to help rebuild the Party organization. Its effectiveness depended on the extent to which non-Socialist support could be mustered, rather than on the development of Party program. Success in rallying many liberals, Farmer-Laborites, and trade unionists to the cause of amnesty did not reactivate thousands of dormant locals. From 1920 onward, Party membership dropped steadily. In January 1921, 24,661 Socialists remained within the fold, but the average membership for the year was only 11,223. This improved a bit in 1921—to 12,597—but thereafter Party membership gradually declined to only 8,477 by 1926.[9]

Most of the Party's losses were to the Left, but despite this many of the best-known left-wing victims of wartime suppression remained loyal Socialists. Not only Debs, but Kate O'Hare and lesser known leaders, such as Emil Herman of Washington, continued their association. When Herman emerged from the McNeil Island Penitentiary in February 1922, he rejoined the Party and became its organizer for the Central states.[10]

[9] Minutes of the NEC meeting, Cleveland, December 9 to 10, 1922; Agenda, NEC meeting, New York City, February 24 to 25, 1923; membership records, 1924, 1925, 1926, in SPC, Duke.
[10] Herman, "Where I Stand," *Socialist World,* March 1922; Herman had been a member of the left-wing group in Seattle led by Herman F. Titus, along with William Z. Foster and Alfred A. Wagenknecht, before the war. Titus published the *Seattle* and *Toledo Socialist* until his group quit

The continued allegiance to the Party of these left wingers did not square with the Communist characterization of the Socialists. Indeed, many Communists had believed that both Debs and O'Hare would join their ranks, and Communist Labor Party leaders even spoke at first of nominating Debs and O'Hare on their own ticket in 1920. Nor were some of these hopes totally without basis. There had been a good deal of hostility between Kate O'Hare and the Socialist Party national leadership, particularly Adolph Germer, during and after the war; O'Hare felt that she had "been most shamefully treated by the National Office," which, as we have seen, had voided her election as international representative while she was in prison.[11]

But when Kate O'Hare left prison in May 1920, she immediately plunged back into Party activity.[12] By late June she was on a speaking tour of the East, and the following summer was on another tour in the West (where she was kidnapped and prevented from speaking at Twin Falls, Idaho).[13] Four months after her pardon, she and her husband Frank resumed publication of their monthly paper, *The National Rip Saw,* and for two years she continued to support the Socialists.

Like Kate O'Hare, Eugene Debs did not waver in his loyalty to the Socialist Party after 1919. As we have seen, Debs was optimistic about the Party's prospects when he was in prison, and although he shared Hillquit's view of the issues involved in the split, he continued to believe that "all the differences

---

the Party in 1909. Unlike Titus and Foster, Herman remained a Socialist, and was state secretary of the Party in 1918 when he was convicted and given a ten-year sentence under the Espionage Act for possessing anti-militarist stickers and pamphlets. Throughout this period, he was "far to the Left." Hulet M. Wells to the author, Seattle, May 1, 1960; Kipnis, *op. cit.,* p. 291; Peterson and Fite, *op. cit.,* p. 185.

[11] Kate R. O'Hare to Otto Branstetter, Jefferson City, Missouri, February 8, 1920; Frank P. O'Hare to Branstetter, St. Louis, Friday [1920], SPC, Duke.

[12] Mrs. O'Hare was released by Presidential pardon at the end of May 1920 after a committee of St. Louis and other women intervened with President Wilson on her behalf. Otto Branstetter to O'Hare, Chicago, April 10, 1920; *New York Times,* May 30, 1920.

[13] *National Rip Saw,* August 1921.

are reconcilable."[14] Despite his almost instinctive understanding of the needs of American radicalism, Debs did not follow events in Europe closely and never gained full insight into the ideological disputes which led to the split. The hostility of those who became Communists toward their former comrades was viewed by Debs simply as an aberration, rather than as a concomitant of their acceptance of the program of the Third International and the concept of a Leninist party. In his inability to understand the relevance of the Third International to American politics, Debs remained true to the traditions of the prewar years; but while he entered prison very much a man of his world, he emerged a representative of a past era. His fidelity to the best of the prewar traditions contributed greatly to his immense personal popularity and to the almost mystical appeal he enjoyed in the early 1920's. But his failure to assimilate the wartime and postwar experience denied him the ability to contribute more solidly than he did to the rebuilding of the Party and movement after his release from prison.

Debs' biographer, and others, have imputed to him serious differences with Hillquit and Berger over the Russian Revolution,[15] but these in fact did not exist. When he was notified of his nomination in May 1920, Debs had expressed disappointment that the Socialist platform had not called for unconditional affiliation with the Third International. But by October 1920, after having seen Zinoviev's letter laying down eighteen conditions of affiliation (including the expulsion of Hillquit from the Party), Debs had changed his mind. "If you were," he said, "to commit the party in America to the International program laid down by Lenin, you would kill the party." The "angry wrangling over the Moscow program," he continued, was "disrupting parties everywhere . . . We must not enter a

[14] Samuel Castleton to Hillquit, Atlanta, Georgia, January 10, 1920; Hillquit to Castleton, The Santanoni, Saranac Lake, New York, January 30, 1920, Hillquit papers.
[15] Ginger, *Bending Cross*, p. 406. See also Herbert M. Morais and William Cahn, *Gene Debs: The Story of a Fighting American* (New York, 1948), p. 114.

policy that means disruption."[16] At the same time, however, along with most Socialists, Debs was still "heart and soul with our Russian comrades and the Soviet Republic." He viewed Lenin and Trotsky as "colossal figures" whose "marvelous achievements" had "struck terror to the ruling class and inspired the workers of all the world."[17]

After Debs recuperated from his imprisonment, he embarked upon a speaking tour for the Party. The meetings on this first tour stirred excitement, drew overflow crowds almost everywhere, and led to spurts of renewed Socialist organization. In Minneapolis, for example, Debs spoke to an overflow crowd of five thousand people and his appearance produced two new locals in the city.[18] For a few months in the late winter and early spring of 1923, Debs' tour stimulated activity in the Party, and a good deal of squabbling among the various state secretaries over the apportionment of his meetings.[19] Many young people who had never heard Debs in the old days went to hear the aging leader, along with old-timers who wished to pay homage or recall the happier times of prewar radicalism. But these meetings did not inspire the younger members to renewed activity. In 1924, Bertha Hale White, the Party's national secretary, admitted that since his release from prison, she had not been able to arrange a second meeting for Debs "that was not a bitter disappointment to him." He did not seem to realize, she wrote, that his imprisonment was "an old story," and that changes in his text were necessary. "The war is over

---

[16] William M. Feigenbaum, "Debs to the Socialist Party," *Socialist World,* October 15, 1920; Debs, "Why Are We Not Stronger?" Oakland *World,* December 31, 1920.
[17] *Ibid.*
[18] Emil Herman to Otto Branstetter, Minneapolis, March 1, 10, April 24, 1923, SPC, Duke. After Debs' meeting there were eight locals in Minneapolis, five English, one Finnish, one Jewish, and one YPSL.
[19] See, for example, Herbert Merrill to Otto Branstetter, Albany, New York, March 22, 1923, in which Merrill argues that Debs should appear both in Rochester and Buffalo, rather than twice in Massachusetts as scheduled.

long since. The old speeches will not do," she told Debs. But although audiences expected "a new theme," and the Party's own members were becoming dissatisfied, Debs had nothing new to say.[20] He never drew a large second crowd in any city, and soon after his tour ended the Party settled back to its previous condition.[21]

Debs' inability to stimulate independent initiative on the part of Party members was universal. The New England district secretary, William Boyd, complained of having to warm up each old member he visited, only to leave him to cool down again as soon as he left. Like the Party secretaries in Kansas and California, Boyd believed that the locals could be revived with some money for organization and a good weekly paper, but these were not available.[22] The real problem, however, was that the young blood was attracted more easily to the Communist parties than to the Socialist. Most of the English-speaking members who had left the Party had been young, and among those younger members who remained Socialists there was an increasing tendency to move toward the light of the Third International.

III

World politics in the 1920's presented a strange dilemma to the Socialists; the Party was friendly toward the Soviet

[20] Bertha Hale White to Hillquit, Chicago, June 8, 1924; George Kirkpatrick to Hillquit, Chicago, June 8, 1924, Hillquit papers. These letters relate a bitter argument with Debs over a poorly attended meeting in Cleveland in May 1924.

[21] See, for example, Wilbur Sheron to Indiana Locals and Members, n.p., December 6, 1923; also, similar letters from California and Idaho state secretaries in SPC, Duke.

[22] William Boyd to Otto Branstetter, Boston, January 29, 1923; Ross Magil to Branstetter, Garnett, Kansas, January 22, 1923; Isabel King to Branstetter, San Francisco, February 10, 1923. Where it was possible to reactivate an old comrade, organization took place. In Salt Lake City, for example, a reactivated Party member reorganized a local of 80 people, and in New Mexico another got the Party on the ballot in 1922, and it received 1,200 votes. G. A. Kennedy to Branstetter, Salt Lake City, December 21, 1922, all SPC, Duke.

Union, but it was under constant attack from the Third International. Under the impact of this hostility and the consequent stream of defections to the Left, the Socialist Party gravitated slowly toward anti-Sovietism. But in the early years after the split this tendency was not yet ascendant. Then the Socialists staunchly defended the Russian Revolution and the new Soviet state.

The dominant Socialist attitude toward the Soviet Union was enunciated by Hillquit in the years from 1920 to 1925. In his testimony at the Albany hearings in 1920—in which the Party attempted unsuccessfully to prevent the unseating of five Socialist assemblymen elected in New York City in November 1919—Hillquit described the Soviet government as "a great Socialist experiment," which was seeking a "change of the basis of human relations to a higher plane." Denouncing the Allied blockade of Russia, Hillquit asserted that "if left alone to work out their destinies," the people of Russia would reach "an ideal form of Socialist society." At the same time, of course, he pointed out that American Socialists did not "admit that the Soviet form of government would be good for other countries or for the United States," but simply that the Russians were "gradually evolving a form of government best suited to themselves."[23]

At the 1920 convention of the Party, the majority report of the Committee on International Relations again expressed the Party's ambivalence. Praising the Soviets, the delegates criticized the Third International as "inclined to impose upon all affiliated bodies the formula of the Russian Revolution."[24]

This was also Debs' view as we have seen, and Hillquit agreed. "Our comrades in Russia are doing the most inspiring work in the history of our race," he wrote Debs. "Sooner or

[23] Quoted and summarized in *The Appeal to Reason*, February 28, 1920.
[24] Quoted in Shannon, *op. cit.*, p. 153. See this and the following page for a good summary of the attitude of the Socialist Party to the Third International until its affiliation with the "two-and-a-half" International in 1922.

later," Hillquit added, the Russians would "evolve a truly Socialistic order of society in Russia," that in many ways would "serve as a model to the entire civilized world."[25]

Most of the Party's old "right wingers" took a similar stand. In 1920, for example, the Milwaukee Federated Trades Council, under Victor Berger's tight control, issued a report on the Soviet Union which was generous in its praise. A Special Committee of the Trades Council viewed the Soviets as the "first workingmen's Republic." Commenting that "from the enemies the Russian Soviet form of government has made, the workers may judge," the Committee declared that it saw in the Soviet Revolution the "beginning of the liberation of the toiling masses from the injustices of the capitalist system." It urged its members to study the Russian form of socialism so that the good features could "be fought for by legal means." Finally, the Committee suggested that affiliated unions purchase Soviet literature "in large lots" to distribute at cost, or free, among its members.[26]

While this view continued to be dominant in the Party,[27] a number of Socialists early developed anti-Soviet attitudes. When Max Hayes, then a Farmer-Laborite, introduced a resolution in support of recognition of the Soviet Union at the AFL convention of 1922, it was opposed by Benjamin Schlessinger, Socialist vice president of the ILGWU.[28]

[25] Hillquit to Debs, Saranac Lake, June 30, 1920, Hillquit papers.
[26] Report of Special Committee of the Council on the Question of the Soviet Form of Government [1920], Federated Trades Council of Milwaukee Papers, Wisconsin Historical Society.
[27] At the 1921 convention, for example, the delegates adopted a resolution which supported Soviet Russia without qualification. Denouncing the campaign of "slander and vilification" against her, the resolution declared that the "evils which exist in Russia" could be "wholly or largely brought home to the rulers of the United States. The enemies of Soviet Russia are everywhere the enemies of Socialism." *Socialist World*, July, 1921; see also "Two Important Dates," *loc. cit.*, October 1921. At the 1923 convention, the delegates passed another resolution favoring recognition, but also passed the first critical resolution on the question of Socialist political prisoners in Russia. *Socialist World*, June, 1923.
[28] *New Majority* (Chicago), October 26, 1922.

It was, of course, increasingly difficult to maintain a friendly attitude toward the Soviets while on the one hand criticizing the Third International, and on the other being attacked by it and by the American Communists. This difficulty was aggravated by the fact that Party members increasingly looked toward Britain and the British Labour Party, rather than to the Bolsheviks, for a strategic model. As early as 1918, Hillquit had pointed to the English Labour Party as being more relevant to American political development than the Bolshevik experience. By 1923, Hillquit was showing the strain of Bolshevik hostility. "To the sober observer of world politics," he remarked, "the development of the British Labour Party since the last election is a more thoroughgoing revolution than the Bolshevik coup d'etat in 1917. The latter was a dazzling historic adventure while the former is a great historic event."[29] This was meant as a defense of the Socialist policy of promoting a labor party, and in that sense was similar to Kate O'Hare's call for a coalition labor party in 1921, and to the views of many former and present Socialists who had gone into, or looked toward, a new farmer-labor party movement in the United States. But to many of the younger left wingers this sort of talk was understood as betrayal of the Russians. As the official Party moved away from the idea of affiliation with the Third International after 1920, large sections of the membership moved closer. To the younger American Socialists, it was not the American Communist parties that were attractive. Rather, it was a desire to defend and be a part of the revolutionary wave which had its source in the Bolshevik seizure of power in Russia. Thus, despite the fact that the overwhelming majority of Socialists remained friendly to the Soviet regime, there was an intermittent stream of defections of left wingers from the Party.

After the Socialist convention decided against affiliation with

[29] *Ladies Garment Worker,* June 1918; *Socialist World,* July 1923; *Cleveland Citizen,* July 14, 1923.

any international organization in May 1920, J. Louis Engdahl, Alexander Trachtenberg, William F. Kruse, J. B. Salutsky, M. J. Olgin, and others formed the Committee for the Third International of the Socialist Party. This group, subsequently known as the Workers' Council, functioned within the Party until September 1921, agitating for Socialist affiliation with the Comintern. Then it gave up and withdrew to take part in organizing the Workers' Party. The Finnish Federation had departed with essentially the same perspective in December 1920;[30] the Bohemian and Jewish Federations followed, after the Socialist convention in the spring of 1921.[31]

The dispute within the Socialist Party between the Hillquit-Debs-Berger group on the one hand, and the Committee for the Third International-Finnish-Bohemian and Jewish federations on the other, was essentially the same as that between the Third International and the "Two-and-a-half." A Manifesto of Independent Socialists, meeting in Berne in December 1920, expressed the view of the American majority group, as well as that of the Independent Socialist Party of Germany, the Independent Labour Party of Great Britain, and the Socialist parties of France and Austria. Criticizing the Moscow International for calling itself the Third International, "while in practice it was only a union of Communist parties," the manifesto accused the Communists of wanting to "apply the methods of the peasant and proletarian" revolution in Russia to the industrialized countries "without any modification." More important, the Berne conference condemned the Moscow International for desiring to "abolish the autonomy of the different socialistic parties," which alone were "capable of judging the actual conditions in their particular countries" and of determining "the means to be used for the purpose of the working class in these countries." To assure the imposition of its will on all parties, the Berne group added, the Third International "de-

[30] *Socialist World*, January 15, 1921.
[31] *Workers' Council*, September 15, 1921, p. 106.

liberately" set out to "shatter all socialist parties which do not unhesitatingly submit to its dictation," and to replace them with "a sectarian movement based upon the preconceived ideas" of the Russians.[32]

In answering for the Third International, Karl Radek made it clear that the relation of the Communist International and the Two-and-a-Half had to be "above all a relation of open hostility." He did not deny the charges of the Berne Conference, but merely characterized its ideas as a "poison" that had "eaten deeply into the body of the working class." The poison could be counteracted, Radek remarked, by filling the "masses with determination and conviction that hesitation at the decisive moment means death."[33]

Of course, the groups that had gone into the Two-and-a-Half International had, for the most part, never been guilty of "hesitation at the decisive moment." Most of them had opposed the war, and all supported the Soviets. Their "hesitation" consisted of their failure to call for open insurrection in their own countries at a time when such action had no chance of success. Significantly, at the time Radek wrote this attack, Lenin had already published his *Left Wing Communism,* which was an open admission that Western Europe had not been ready for the revolution which the Russians had originally demanded, and on which they had counted for survival.

By remaining in the Socialist Party in 1919, the Workers Council group had sided with the "Centrists" in this development. In 1921 they split with the Socialists because by then it was clear that the Third International would never have the Socialist Party, but also because the Russians had reversed themselves on the question of world revolution. In addition, the Workers Council group was alienated by Hillquit's attempts to "Americanize" the Party. Seeing a good issue in the

---

[32] Reprinted in the *Socialist World,* May 15, 1921.
[33] Karl Radek, "A Home for the Politically Homeless," *Workers Council,* I:1 (April 1, 1921), 9-10.

suppression of traditional American democratic rights during and after the war, Hillquit stressed the Socialist adherence to democracy and democratic procedures.[34] But in doing so, he incurred the wrath of the younger radicals. In the second issue of their new magazine, *The Workers' Council*, Benjamin Glassberg attacked the line pursued by the Socialists in the Albany hearings on the seating of New York City's five Socialist assemblymen. Hillquit's strategy of seeking "to capitalize on the existing American prejudices and illusions about Democracy and Republican Government and the sacredness of the ballot" was characterized as a "disgraceful surrender." Instead of "using the Albany ouster as a means of analyzing and exposing these notions," Glassberg commented sarcastically, "the party suddenly leaped forth as the defender of the Constitution, as the only party that stood for American liberties." Glassberg pointed in disgust to the subhead of the Party's official organ, *The Eye Opener*, "For a free press, free speech and free assemblage."[35]

IV

With the left wing of the Socialist party dropping off in large sections, one might expect that the Communist parties were gaining in membership and influence. But the Communists fared even worse than the Socialists in these early years. Only a few months after the Communist and Communist Labor parties were formed in September 1919, Attorney General A. Mitchell Palmer launched his unsuccessful Presidential campaign by initiating the raids that bear his name. The Palmer Raids, the most ambitious of which took place in January 1920, resulted in the arrest of 6,000 radicals (along with many total

[34] See Hillquit to Debs, Saranac Lake, New York, June 30, 1920, Hillquit papers; see also Hillquit speech at the 1920 convention quoted in *Eye Opener*, May 15, 1920.
[35] Benjamin Glassberg, "The Task Before Us," *Workers' Council*, 1:2 (April 15, 1921), 19.

innocents) and in the deportation of some 550 Communist aliens.[36] Confirming the Communists' view of the political situation in the United States, the raids drove the two parties firmly underground and left them with an enduring predisposition for conspiratorial modes of operation.

While they were underground, admitted Alexander Bittelman in October 1921, the Communist parties did "not exist as a factor in the class struggle." The "slogans, appeals and proclamations of the former two Communist parties," he confessed, had "never caused even a ripple on the surface" of American politics. The problem, as Bittelman saw it, was that "all along we have been working contentedly on the theory that by spreading general communist propaganda" (that is, by calling on the workers to rise and seize power), the desired end would be achieved. This had been "a very simple theory," and it resulted in "almost complete failure." Two years after the split with the old Socialist Party, the then united Communist Party of America claimed only ten thousand members.[37]

Bittelman's admission of failure occurred at a time when the Communist Party of America was about to change its basic attitude toward American politics and to adopt a program that in most respects would resemble that of the Socialists in 1919. Indeed, the history of the Communist Party from 1919 to 1922 is one of gradual abandonment of all the strategic and programmatic positions which distinguished it from the Socialist Party at the time of the split.

Only in their unwavering loyalty to the Third International and in their adherence to a semimilitary form of party organization did the Communists remain unique. This, however, was of major importance. In its early years, the Communist movement survived only because it was united in its dependence on

[36] Palmer's use of these anti-Communist raids to promote his Presidential ambitions may actually have cost him the Democratic nomination.
[37] A. Rafael (Bittelman), "The Task of the Hour," *The Communist*, Official Organ of the Communist Party of America, October 1921. Quoted in *Socialist World*, February 1922.

the International. Its adjustment to American realities developed primarily because of the insistent proddings of the Comintern leadership.[38]

This is not to say that no American Communists saw the shortcomings in the continued exclusive reliance on pure revolutionary appeals after 1919. Only months after the August split it was clear to Ruthenberg that the world, or at least the United States, was not on the brink of revolution. Just as Lenin was arguing with the Western European Communists, so Ruthenberg argued with the majority of the Communist Party the need to develop and extend contact with the masses. Ruthenberg fought for the development of a "party of action" that "participates in the everyday struggles of the workers and by such participation injects its principles into these struggles and gives them a wider meaning, thus developing the Communist movement."[39] Unlike Lenin, however, Ruthenberg did not have his way. The majority of the Communist Party opposed any "attempt to run after the masses, at a time when the masses are not ready." To do so would "reduce Communism" to the "politically immature" level of the masses, which would hold back the Party "when the time for real action arrives."[40] Thus Ruthenberg was forced to leave the original Communist Party. In a new alignment, the Ruthenberg forces joined with the Communist Labor Party, which, from the beginning, had a greater appreciation of the problems facing

[38] For the relationship of the American Communist parties to the Russians and to the Communist International see Theodore Draper, *American Communism and Soviet Russia* (New York; 1960), which gives a detailed account of the development of the Party, its intricate factionalism, and its relationship to the International. Draper's book suffers from being an attempt to prove the total dependence of American Communism on the Russians in the first ten years of its existence, and from a failure to place the Communists more firmly in the history of the period and to explore their relationship to other radical groups. As a source of information on the inner development of the Party, it is indispensable. My account is taken largely from Draper's two books.

[39] Damon (Ruthenberg), "Make the Party a 'Party of Action,' " *The Communist* (pro-Ruthenberg), April 25, 1920. Quoted in Draper, *Roots*, p. 216.

[40] *The Communist* (C.P.), May 1, 1920, pp. 2, 8. Quoted in *ibid.*

American radicals in search of political influence. The enlarged CLP became the United Communist Party, while the original Communist Party retained its name and its purity.[41]

Despite its coming into being as the result of an awareness of the fatal sectarian isolation of the Communist Party, the United Communist Party was still unable to break out of its IWW-oriented tradition. Criticizing the Socialist Party policy of "boring from within" the AFL as "only an indirect and hypocritical method of supporting an inherently reactionary labor organization," the UCP program called on Communists to "seize every opportunity," not to reform the AFL, "but to destroy it." At the same time, the IWW was to be "upheld as against the AFL," and industrial unionism was to be affirmed.[42]

As this program was being enunciated, the Third International held its Second Congress and Lenin published his *Left Wing Communism: An Infantile Disorder.* In a few months, after the texts of the Congress had been perused by the American comrades, a change in the UCP program was in order. Thus, in November, in answer to a letter from an Ohio coal miner, *The Toiler* admitted "the folly of voluntary withdrawal" from the trade unions. The letter asked whether or not a revolutionary should accept an executive post in a conservative trade union. *The Toiler* replied that he should, and that by viewing the situation in the AFL as "hopeless," Communists had effectively severed their connections not only with the reactionaries, but with the rank and file. "The thesis adopted at Moscow," *The Toiler* explained, had made clear the "necessity of revolutionists maintaining a direct contact with the masses of workers." Although this seemingly fundamental rule for revolutionaries had previously been overlooked by the

---

[41] The details of this development are in *ibid.* pp. 215 ff.
[42] United Communist Party program, adopted May, 1920, quoted in Draper, *Roots,* p. 220.

American comrades, *The Toiler* made it clear that it now understood that "unless they do this no progress can be made."[43]

This cursory admission, granted as if in revelation, that the Communists had been in error in their original estimate of the revolutionary potential in the United States was only the first among many to come. A source of ironic satisfaction to the Socialists, the admission served only to exacerbate the hostility between the parties; for while the Communists implicitly conceded their error, there was not the slightest hint that the Socialists had been correct in the debate over this issue. Indeed, there could not be such an admission without weakening the rationale for the existence of the new parties.

Far from growing more friendly toward the Socialists as the parties' estimates of the needs of the hour drew closer, the Communists continued to devote a good deal of their energies to attacks on the old Party. During Debs' campaign in 1920, for example, Communists attended meetings only to shower the audience with leaflets denouncing the Socialists and attacking Hillquit as a second Kerensky.[44] Debs strongly condemned this sort of activity. "I read this in a communist paper recently," he wrote: " 'The first thing we must do is smash the Socialist party.' " The writer of that sentiment, Debs commented, would "find ready allies in Wall Street" who would "pay a round price for the job." More in sadness than anger, Debs added that in all probability "this comrade who now calls himself a communist once belonged to the Socialist party."[45]

Unable, by the very process of its origin, fully to adjust to American reality or to develop a program flowing from political

[43] Quoted in full in *Truth* (Duluth, Minnesota), organ of the UCP, December 3, 1920, p. 1.
[44] Seymour Stedman to Hillquit, Chicago, January 13, 1921; Hillquit to Stedman, New York, January 17, 1921, Hillquit papers.
[45] Eugene V. Debs, "Why Are We Not Stronger?" *World* (Oakland), December 31, 1920.

developments in the United States, the Communist movement was pulled toward reality by external forces. The major force, of course, was the Communist International. But in 1921 a substantial influx of American radicals from older traditions also operated to rescue the Communists from the deep pit of sectarian isolation. From the spring of 1920, when Lenin wrote *Left Wing Communism,* until 1924, the policy of the International coincided with the general approach of the American radicals being newly drawn to the Communist movement in the United States. The result was a process at first fitful and reluctant and then headlong toward popular influence and support.

During the first year of their existence, the American Communists had received little attention from the International. Indeed, at a meeting of the Sub Bureau of the Third International in Amsterdam, Louis Fraina complained that the American Communists had been neglected by the Russians. Too much attention had been paid to Germany, Fraina charged, while what had been done in the United States had been done without the aid, tangible or moral, of Russia.[46] This shortcoming was corrected in July 1920, when the Second Congress of the International decided, against John Reed's opposition, that the American Communists should work in the AFL and gave the Communist Party and the United Communist Party two months to end their separate existences and form a single party.[47] It was no easy task to exert sufficient pressure on the reluctant Americans to effectuate unity. But in the spring of 1921 the Communist Party of America replaced the two earlier parties, even though the factional differences remained barely below the surface.

V

Meanwhile, the Workers' Council group and the Finnish

[46] *Bulletin of the Sub Bureau in Amsterdam of the Communist International,* Number 2 (March 1920), p. 4.
[47] Draper, *Roots,* pp. 256-271.

and Jewish federations, having left the Socialist Party, pushed
for the formation of a new, legal, popular Communist party.
These groups argued that although the original split had been
premature, a Communist party was necessary now because of
Socialist hostility to the Communist International. In writing
of the mistakes in 1919, Ludwig Lore referred to the "passion-
ate aggressiveness" of the American left wing which had "made
it impossible to withdraw from the Socialist party more than
a fraction of those who were at heart in accord with its position." Further, Lore asserted that the "opinion recently expressed by the leaders of the Third International concerning
the American 'split' " was "that the methods used by the American Communists to divide the Socialist Party were wrong."[48]

John Keracher, formerly of the Michigan Socialist Party,
and then (after an exceptionally brief stay in the Communist
Party) a leader of the Proletarian Party, agreed that the split
in the Socialist Party had come two years too soon. Keracher
reminded his readers of Dennis Batt's statement in the May
1919 issue of *The Proletarian,* to the effect that the left wing
was indulging in fantasy in seeing the revolution "just around
the corner." Keracher criticized the Communists for their refusal to participate in political activity, and asserted that most
of those who had originally gone into the Communist parties
were now either in jail, in Europe, or out of politics—a statement strongly supported by the membership figures of the
parties in question.

What the Workers' Council desired was not the secret, small
Communist Party that had existed since 1919, but an open one
that would function much as the old Socialist Party had done,
except that it would be an integral part of the Third International. In an ardent appeal for such a party, the *Workers' Council* in October 1921 reviewed the events which had led to the

[48] Ludwig Lore, "Communist Difficulties in Germany and Italy," *Workers' Council,* I:4, (May 15, 1921), 56.

present situation and called for the formation of another new party.

As a result of the war, the statement began, the working class had been "drifting and rudderless" all over the world in 1917. "Into this situation the November Revolution in Russia burst like a bombshell," carrying American Socialists off their feet by its daring and giving "back to us our lost ideals." The "powerful romantic appeal" of the revolution bore Socialists "away from a world of hopeless, cheerless realities in a flood of enthusiasm" the editors declared. *It was the one positive point in a world of negations, the one ray of light in all this hopeless demoralization.*" In such a situation it was only natural that in place of the German movement, which had failed to oppose, let alone prevent, the war, "Russia, its methods, its experiences, its theories" should stand "in the foreground of socialist thought."

By 1919, when the American Communist Party was formed, "this Russian influence had already been condensed into a concrete philosophy." The Communist Party "thought and acted as if the Russian Revolution had been bodily transplanted upon American soil." Thus, the editors charged, the "idea of a secret organization was not forced upon the communist movement by Palmer and his cohorts," but "had been lurking in the minds of most communist enthusiasts ever since the outbreak of the Russian Revolution." It was a "part of the atmosphere of revolution and romanticism that the Russian Revolution created."

"But even in Russia," the editors observed, "romance has had to give way to brutal realities. The world-revolution failed to materialize. Instead world imperialism emerged, for the moment, more powerful than ever before." In the face of this, "the fantastic dream that a small minority of determined revolutionaries may overturn capitalism and lead the proletariat into a communist state of society" had "vanished into thin air." Not only did the "bitter experiences of the German and the

Italian Communist uprisings" prove this, but in Russia, too, the "great mass of uneducated, indifferent and even counter-revolutionary workers and peasants" were "hanging like a millstone about" the Soviets' neck.

To supplement their own argument, the *Workers' Council* ended its plea for an open communist party with appeal to authority. *"The Third International,"* it commented, *"has learned. It no longer dreams of small minorities but demands mass movements.*

"It has deserted its policy of splendid isolation on the industrial field and demands that its adherents carry their agitation into the strongholds of conservative unionism.

"It openly condemns agitation for armed insurrection and open rebellion in countries where the revolution is still in the distant future, and insists that the communist movement, in every country, must proceed at once to the creation of an open, above board mass movement for the purpose of educating the proletariat and permeating it with communist ideals."[49]

At any earlier time a criticism of the international Communist movement as sharp as that of the *Workers' Council* would have elicited a vitriolic attack upon the authors. It did not in this case because the Third Congress of the International had adopted positions substantially similar to those expressed in the statement of the *Workers' Council.* Thus, under heavy pressure both from the International and from important new allies, the Communists agreed to the formation of a new and legal party.[50]

[49] "The Open Communist Party—The Task of the Hour," *Workers' Council,* I:8 (October 15, 1921), 120-121.
[50] Again, for those who are interested in the detailed process by which the Communist Party of America was led to form the Workers' Party, see Draper, *Roots,* Chapter XIX.

6 THE WORKERS' PARTY: PRESCRIPTIVE ANTIDOTE TO AN INFANTILE DISORDER 1921-1922

The Workers' Party came into being at a convention in New York City at Christmas time, 1921. Initially, the new Party did not entirely replace the Communist Party of America, but served only as a "legal extension of the illegal party."[1] The Communists kept their underground Party intact, but all members were supposed to become members of the Workers' Party as well. With the Communists, the Workers' Council group, a few recruits from the Socialist Labor Party, and the Jewish and Finnish federations, the Workers' Party numbered twelve thousand members in 1922.[2]

Almost inevitably, there was a split in the Communist Party of America over the advisability of forming the Workers' Party, and over its program. The opposition, which had a majority of the membership on its side, was brought back into line, however, by a decision of the International. By April of 1923, not only had the majority submitted to the policy of the minority but the underground Communist Party of America had been dissolved. The Workers' Party then emerged as the only American Communist party.[3]

Programmatically, the formation of the Workers' Party meant a full cycle return to the Socialist Party position of 1919. The new Party's program omitted all reference to the dictatorship

[1] Draper, *Roots*, p. 343.
[2] *The 4th National Convention* (Chicago, 1925), pp. 27-29, cited in Draper, *Roots*, p. 391.
[3] *Ibid.*, Chapters 21-23 for the details of this process.

of the proletariat, to workers' Soviets, to violent revolution; instead of calling on workers to seize power immediately, it included a set of limited immediate demands. This return to the Socialist position of an earlier day created an embarrassing situation, and the preface to the program indicated that the leadership of the new Party was aware of its embarrassment. The burden of attempting to distinguish the new from the old fell on Caleb Harrison, Workers' Party national secretary.

Characteristically, Harrison began with an attack, not on American capitalism, but on the two old Socialist parties. "The opportunistic leaders of the Socialist Party," he declared somewhat irrelevantly, "were not sincere supporters of the St. Louis Resolution." Later events had shown that many who had supported that resolution had been "merely playing for time." The Socialist Labor Party, on the other hand, while not opportunistic, had the "failing that is the twin brother of opportunism—doctrinairism."

The failings of the old Socialist parties having been taken care of, Harrison declined to discuss the nature of the Communist parties during their two years of underground existence. "The subsequent formation of the Communist parties," he wrote, "are matters too well known to repeat in detail here." He did, however, contrast a Communist to a Socialist (opportunist) and to a Socialist Laborite (doctrinaire). The Communist, Harrison revealed, was nothing other than a "practical man of action." For this man of action, no comments on the Workers' Party program were necessary, as "the documents speak for themselves." To "meet the objections of both the doctrinaire and the opportunist," however, a few comments were in order.

The doctrinaire, Harrison wrote, "believes that the sole duty of a revolutionary party is to preach the class struggle and outline the final aim—the workers' republic, the socialist commonwealth, or whatever name he chooses to call it." In so doing he hopes to win the masses "by preaching the new doctrine in its purity, and he will have nothing to do with immediate demands." The opportunist, on the other hand, "lays strong emphasis òn immediate demands," even though he might "not overlook the final aim." The opportunist failed in his insistence "that the masses are not intelligent enough to understand remote abstract theories such as socialism." His inclusion of immediate demands was not mistaken, but on the contrary, were practical and necessary. The real question was the nature of these demands. Harrison found Socialist Party demands to be such as would "dull the class struggle," as opposed to the Communist demands which were made to "sharpen it." Socialist demands such as cheap milk, cheap ice, municipal ownership, were "all demands that the capitalist state" could "meet with ease." They were not made with "the idea of destroying confidence in, and eventually disrupting, the capitalist state machine." On the contrary, Socialists made only "sentimental demands" in the interest of "suffering humanity."

Even so, Harrison lamented, the opportunist would probably say that the Workers' Party program was "the same as us," while the doctrinaire would probably concur and call the program opportunist because it included seven immediate demands. Presumably, a practical man of action would know that both erring politicos were mistaken. For whether the state attempted to meet the Workers' Party demands or not, the effect would "be the same." If the workers were "united by the Workers' Party to make them, a weakening and eventual disruption of the capitalist state machinery" would ensue.[4]

The Workers' Party then listed its seven demands uniquely designed "to sharpen" the class struggle. First was a demand for the protection of labor unions and of the right to strike and picket. A similar demand had appeared in both the Socialist Party congressional program of 1918 and in its platform of 1920. Second, the Party called for unemployed relief, to be ad-

[4] Caleb Harrison, National Secretary, Preface of the *Program and Constitution of the Workers' Party of America Adopted at the National Convention in New York City, December 24-25-26, 1921*, (New York: Workers' Party), pp. 1 ff.

ministered through the unions. This had not appeared in earlier Socialist programs, but the depression had not started until 1921. Third, these revolutionaries called on the capitalists, just as the Socialists had done in 1918 and 1920, to obey their own laws with respect to civil liberties. Fourth, the Party called for the protection of the civil rights of Negroes, again as the "opportunists" had done in both earlier years. Fifth, the program called for cessation of preparation for new wars, repeating, once more, the Socialists' earlier proposals. Sixth, finally breaking new ground, was a demand for withdrawal of United States military forces from Haiti, Santo Domingo, Puerto Rico, and for the independence of the Philippines. The seventh, and last point, called for recognition of the Soviet Union, which the Socialist Party had done consistently since 1918.[5]

All in all, Harrison's preface proved exactly the opposite of what he intended. Since the Workers' Party demands were the same as those of the Socialists, a "weakening and eventual disruption of the capitalist state machinery" might also have occurred if the Socialists had united the workers to make these demands. Even worse, Harrison's criticism of the opportunists' refusal to preach "abstract theories such as socialism" did not apply at all to the Socialists, but it did apply in general to the Workers' Party's new look and specifically to one of the Communists' latest recruits and by far its most important native radical, William Z. Foster.

At about the same time that Harrison's preface appeared, Foster was reported in *The Worker* to have said that Communists ought "not to use their radical philosophy to get control" of trade unions but should employ "day to day detail work" and "close association" with the rank and file, to convince the masses that they were "interested in their welfare."[6] Earlier, Foster had written that a Socialist perspective was not even necessary to bring on the revolution. In his book on the

---

[5] *Ibid.*, p. 12; *Eye Opener*, August 1918; May 15, 1920.
[6] April 22, 1922, p. 2. Cited in Draper, *Roots*, p. 350.

great steel strike, he wrote that the AFL was "making straight for the abolition of capitalism," and was "going incomparably faster toward this goal than any of the much advertised, so-called revolutionary unions, in spite of the latter's glittering preambles."[7]

The attack on the Socialist "opportunists" for their lack of faith in the intelligence of the masses and for their resulting unwillingness to talk socialism was particularly ironic. Exactly the opposite had always been true. The Socialist Party always advocated immediate demands, but it saw itself as fulfilling, primarily, an educational role—as having a responsibility to show the workers that only a reorganization of society along Socialist lines could lead to the good life for all. The Communists, on the other hand, had never conceived of themselves as having a major educational responsibility. They viewed a Leninist party as one that led the masses to the seizure of state power, not by convincing them of the superiority of socialism as a social system, but by rallying support behind slogans, such as the Bolsheviks had done when they called for "Peace, Land, Bread."[8] When the Communists reoriented themselves toward working within the AFL in 1920, they had done so only to place themselves "at strategic points so that in the time of revolutionary crisis we may seize control of the organization and turn the activities of the union into political channels."[9]

Socialists in the trade unions had traditionally worked openly as Socialists, had brought socialist propaganda into the unions. Moreover, they involved the unions in which their views prevailed in political activity in support of the Party. This the Communists were never to do. As Murray Kempton has pointed out, when the Communists controlled the National Maritime Union in the 1930's, they did not educate the membership along socialist lines, nor did they even have a substantial membership among the rank and file. Instead, Communist

[7] Quoted in *The Auto Worker,* August 1920, p. 7.
[8] Harrison, *loc. cit.*
[9] *The Toiler,* quoted in *Truth* (Duluth, Minnesota Communist weekly), December 3, 1920.

Party membership became little more than a prerequisite for holding leadership positions in the union. This failure to do what Harrison mistakenly accused the Socialists of failing to do paved the way for the easy removal from office of Communists in many CIO unions in later years.[10]

II

The formation of the Workers' Party was not well received by the existing radical organizations. The Socialist Party ignored or made light of the new development, and few outside Communist ranks gave much heed to the event. Max Hayes announced the arrival of the new Party in his *Cleveland Citizen* thus: "The so-called Workers' Party of America was launched in New York City last week, where about 100 delegates had assembled, mostly from the metropolitan district, and battled around several days to agree on a policy." The new Party's constitution and policies, Hayes went on, differ "very little from those of the Socialist Party, except that the new party will affiliate with the Third (Moscow) International." The tactics of "forming dual unions, sabotage, etc., were repudiated," he continued, "which resulted in IWW members expressing hostility" toward the new organization. "So far as can be learned there is little enthusiasm among Eastern workers for the new party."[11]

The IWW did indeed express hostility toward the Workers' Party, as it had done toward the Communists for several months before the formation of the new Party.[12] Communists had been close to the IWW in 1919; but after the policy of working within the AFL was adopted, the two groups drifted rapidly

[10] See Murray Kempton, *A Part of Our Time,* (New York, 1955) pp. 98-102.

[11] January 7, 1922.

[12] At the IWW convention in 1920, the delegates had voted unanimously to affiliate with the Third International, but this decision was defeated by a two-thirds majority in a referendum. The IWW did not affiliate in the end because of its traditional policy of remaining outside any political movement. Nevertheless, George Williams of the IWW was a delegate

apart. When the Workers' Party was organized, the IWW organ, *Industrial Solidarity*, attacked it and reviewed the vicissitudes of Communist development. Referring to John Reed, *Industrial Solidarity* recalled that the Communist Party had been "organized by a bunch of 'left wing' Socialists who in 1916 voted for Woodrow Wilson . . . because he kept us out of war." At that time, this crowd had "bewailed the fact that the IWW was too durned radical." But when the Communist Party was organized they changed their minds and "proclaimed far and wide," in a pamphlet entitled: "An appeal by the CEC of the CI to the IWW," that "owing to the high cost of revolutions or something, the IWW was too blamed conservative," and that it was up to the workers of America to "do as Russia did."

The "Wobs" were told to "unload their 'reactionary leaders,' join the Communist party, ditch their brains and do just what the 'CEC' told them to." As for the new party, it threw "the mantle of secrecy, and an air of mystery around it" in order to "inveigle the unorganized bank clerks and floor walkers" into its ranks. After making the Party a secret affair, the Communists allowed nobody but "lawyers, doctors, millionaires, petty larceny business men, secret agents and working stiffs to join." Then they introduced "mystic words and expressions" to "corral" all those who frequented Bohemian restaurants and sipped Russian tea. All of this might not have been so bad, however, had it not been accompanied by a repudiation of dual unionism.[13]

The United Automobile, Aircraft and Vehicle Workers was even more caustic in its comments. An industrial union which opposed the AFL, the Automobile Workers supported the Socialist Party despite the fact that most active Socialist trade

to the first congress of the Red International of Labor Unions (Profintern) in July 1921. When the congress opposed dual unionism and urged Communists to work within the AFL, Williams came home and opposed affiliation in a series of articles in the IWW press. *The Industrial Worker* (Seattle), September 25, October 30, 1920; *Industrial Solidarity* (Chicago), December-January, 1921; Draper, *Roots*, pp. 316-19.
[13] *Industrial Solidarity* (Chicago), December 31, 1921.

unionists were in AFL affiliates. *The Auto Worker,* organ of
the union, greeted the Workers' Party with an editorial entitled
"Saved Again." It read as follows:

A convention was held in New York City where gathered the
brains of the coming revolution. Resolutions were passed announcing the downfall of capitalism, the bankruptcy of business and the
end of the interests. All of the great working class organizations affiliated with the American Labor Alliance were represented, as was
also the Workers' Council and the Workers' Educational Association.

Thus representing nearly three hundred actual members this
mighty convention proceeded to solve the questions of the hour.
After disposing of a few minor matters such as the Dangers of Capitalistic Imperialism, Militarism, the Disarmament Conference, the
Indestructability of Matter, the Third International, the If-ness of the
What and the Consciousness of the Unconscious, the convention devoted several moments to the formation of a real revolutionary party
for the revolutionary revolutionists.

The chairman of the convention announced, "We offer to American labor a class conscious fighting organization, with a set of 'fighting leaders.'" Each and every one of the seventeen "fighting leaders"
guaranteed to be staggering around with a load of brains heavy
enough to cause flat feet.

These seventeen "fighting leaders" have fought their way to "leadership" despite the high cost of print paper and regardless of pied
type. They will now proceed to bore from within the unions, having
missed meals by being bores from without. So if you notice a new
"fighting leader" hanging around like a first mortgage on the old
homestead, take off your hat to one of the head ushers of the coming
revolution.

During election days watch for the Workers' Party to come leaping
to the surface like a ton of lead. The Workers' Party will be known
by its proclamations and communiques. They announce in advance
that they will arouse the millions by a cry of "hail, hail, hail." It will
be "Hail to the Workers' Republic of Russia," "Hail to the Workers'
Democracy of Japan," "Hail to the Workers' Party of America." So
take your hail insurance now while it is still cheap.

The Workers' Party will open all meetings with their membership
campaign song, "I'm Forever Blowing Bubbles." The official emblem
will be the sign of the cross (double) and the revolutionary augur
(signifying the bore). All local unions should be on the watch for the
messenger of revolutionary light assigned to bore from within their

organization. He should be welcomed as a "fighting leader" deserves to be welcomed. Remember these leaders are of the type who will take a foot if given an inch. Better give them the foot first.[14]

III

Despite the snide greetings accorded the Workers' Party by its radical compatriots, the new Party's formation placed the Communists in a position to exercise some influence on left-wing trade unionists for the first time. As has been noted, Foster joined the Communist Party in the summer of 1921 while attending the founding convention of the Red International of Labor Unions in Moscow (although his membership in the underground Party remained secret until 1923). He took this step only after the International had agreed that his Trade Union Educational League would assume responsibility for Communist work in the trade unions, with the Party retaining jurisdiction over strictly political matters.[15] The arrangement was mutually advantageous. In 1921 Foster's TUEL was an isolated and almost rootless organization, and Foster himself was cut off from the mainstream of the labor movement, as well as from the Socialists and the IWW. At the same time, the acquisition of Foster was a major aid in helping the Communists end their almost total isolation from labor and other left-wing groups.

Communists have tended to exaggerate Foster's stature somewhat (he was a national figure in the labor movement only briefly, during the steel strike of 1919), yet he was the first Party leader who was generally respected by radicals and Left trade unionists. Kate O'Hare, for example, often commented favorably on Foster in her *National Rip Saw*. In 1922, she reported a Foster meeting in St. Louis with the comment that Foster and she saw eye to eye, except that he tended to underrate the importance of the radical farmer. Two months

---

[14] "Saved Again," *The Auto Worker*, Detroit, February 1922, p. 4.
[15] Foster, *op. cit.*, p. 185; Draper, *Roots*, p. 321.

later the *Rip Saw* quoted the St. Louis *Post-Dispatch* as saying that Foster was "the greatest pamphleteer in the history of American labor." From his "indefatigable pen," the *Post-Dispatch* continued, "a veritable shower of books, pamphlets, leaflets, and all kinds of propaganda is running into the trade union locals throughout the length and breadth of this continent, irritating the great rank and file and giving thought to his ideas."[16]

Similarly, the organ of John Fitzpatrick's Farmer-Labor Party, *The New Majority*, often commented favorably on Foster, and gave his meetings good coverage. President of the Chicago Federation of Labor since 1904, Fitzpatrick had been the chairman, and Foster secretary, of the highly successful committee to organize the packinghouse workers in Chicago in 1917; in 1919, Fitzpatrick had served as organizer, when Foster was secretary, of the National Steel Committee during the unsuccessful steel strike. The close relationship between the two men later gave the Communists their first opportunity to make important allies in the labor movement.

Even among the old Socialist leadership Foster had respect not accorded his comrades. James H. Maurer, for example, believed that Communist ranks were "honeycombed with spies and stool pigeons," and that many of their leaders "were being financed by the government and Big Business" to corrupt and destroy legitimate trade unions and the Socialist Party. But Maurer did "not include in this category men like William Z. Foster." He had gotten to know Foster during the steel strike, when, as president of the Pennsylvania Federation of Labor, Maurer called an emergency convention of the Federation to organize support for the striking miners and steel workers.[17] Debs, too, respected Foster at this time, and when Foster was kidnapped by the Colorado state police to prevent him from

---

[16] *National Rip Saw*, August 1922, September 1922.
[17] Maurer, *It Can Be Done*, p. 240.

keeping a speaking engagement in Denver, Debs sent him a warm telegram of support.[18]

Of course, the respect that Foster had won from his fellow radicals flowed from activity prior to his conversion to communism, activity which had been directly opposed to the Communist policies of the day. During the war, Foster's success in the packinghouse organizing campaign was made possible only by his support of the Administration—including his efforts to sell Liberty bonds—at a time when Ruthenberg, Debs, Hillquit, and Berger were calling for an immediate end to hostilities and publicly refusing to buy bonds.[19] While Foster's wartime actions conflicted with the attitudes of both left and right wings of the Socialist Party, his leadership of the steel strike ran counter only to Communist policy. During the steel strike, Maurer and Foster worked together, while the Communists called on the workers to smash the AFL (which had sponsored Foster's organizing committee) and to join the IWW.

Only six months before Foster joined the Communist Party, he condemned the dogmatic sectarianism which had motivated the Communists in 1919. Speaking at an IWW meeting in Chicago, Foster charged, in the midst of great heated debate, that radicals had made four basic mistakes, one of which was the violation of "the first principle of working class solidarity." This mistake was forsaking the "real organizations of labor, based on the common economic interests," and forming instead "outside organizations, based upon revolutionary creed."[20] Thus it

---

[18] Ginger, *Bending Cross*, p. 433.

[19] *Investigation of Strike in Steel Industries;* Hearings before the Committee on Education and Labor, U.S. Senate, 66th Congress, 1st Session (Washington, D.C.: Government Printing Office, 1919), p. 423. Foster testified at this hearing that he bought $450 or $500 worth of bonds during the war, and that he made "dozens" of speeches urging workers to do likewise.

[20] "Fight it out Inside Your Unions—Foster," *New Majority*, January 15, 1921. Foster added, however, showing his affinity with one aspect of Communist perspective, that the radical should organize a militant minority within the unions to break the power of the conservatives. The radical could then "gain control of the rank and file" and carry them along to radical action.

became possible for Foster to affiliate with the Communists only after the Party had repudiated its earlier policies. Foster's affiliation and identification with the Party after its metamorphosis helped erase the memory of the earlier years, which further enhanced his value to the movement.

IV

The period from Foster's recruitment in the summer of 1921 until early 1923 was one of steady drift away from the idea of a purely illegal party and toward a fully legal one. When the Workers' Party was formed in 1921, all the factions in the Communist Party of America had agreed on the need to retain an underground Party as well as the legal one.[21] The Workers' Council group, it is true, opposed the continuation of the illegal Party, but it gave way on the issue.[22] Gradually, however, the logic of events overcame original Communist doctrine, both in Europe and in the United States. With considerable assistance from the Third International, the American Party not only established a fully legal Party but adopted a policy of seeking alliances with non-Communist, and even non-Socialist, organizations. This policy, first suggested by Lenin to the British Communists in 1920, became known as the united front.[23]

The united front, as originally conceived and applied in the early 1920's, was not essentially a policy of coalition around issues, designed to achieve unity at the top as was the popular front of the 1930's. Rather, it was a tacit admission of the bankruptcy of earlier policy and an attempt to secure contact with masses of workers or farmers in non-Communist organizations. Thus Lenin wrote in 1920 that the British Communists "very often find it hard to approach the masses and even to get

---

[21] Draper, *Roots,* pp. 335, 340-341.
[22] *Ibid.*
[23] V. I. Lenin, *"Left Wing" Communism: An Infantile Disorder* (New York, 1934), pp. 64-69. For the process by which the Communist Party abandoned its underground organization, see Draper, *Roots,* Chapter 23.

them to listen to them." However, he added, "If I as a Communist come out and call upon the workers to vote for the Hendersons against Lloyd George, they will certainly listen to me."[24] Lenin was not suggesting that the Communists work with the Labourites in order to reach a common goal. Instead, he made the suggestion that Communists support Labourites so they might be in a position to expose them as enemies of the workers. In urging the workers to vote for Henderson, Lenin made clear, he would at the same time "explain that I want to support Henderson with my vote in the same way that a rope supports one who is hanged."[25] Of course, under the circumstances outlined by Lenin, a Henderson might be inclined to reject Communist support. In such an event, Lenin argued, the Communists would "gain still more" than they would from a cordial welcome. Henderson's conjectured refusal would serve to expose him as preferring "closeness to the capitalists to the unity of all workers."[26]

Lenin's concept of the united front and its purpose became that of the Third International in this period. In response to pressure from European Socialists, the Third International agreed to a meeting with the Centrists and the Second International in Berlin, in April 1922. But at the executive committee meeting of the Communist International in December 1921, the Party defined the united front:

> Comrades of the Third International, there is a movement on foot in Europe for a united front. It does not matter whether we are in favor of it or not; our tactics compel us to *appear to be in favor of it;* but we ask the Communist sections all over Europe to take part in the creation of the united front, *not for the purpose of making it effective,* but for the purpose of *strengthening the Communists* through direct propaganda inside organizations taking part in this movement.[27]

[24] *Ibid.,* p. 68.
[25] *Ibid.*
[26] *Ibid.,* p. 67.
[27] Quoted in *The Socialist World,* June 1923.

In part, as Theodore Draper has pointed out, Lenin's united front policy was designed as an attempt to remove the onus from the Communists for having split the working-class movement, and to place it upon the Socialists. Nevertheless, there was more than political cynicism involved. Many Socialists in Europe did prefer "closeness with the capitalists" to support of the revolution in Russia and were accordingly viewed legitimately by the Bolsheviks as being outside any reasonable socialist consensus, and even as misleaders or enemies of the working class. But the Bolsheviks attacked the Centrists as strongly as they did the right-wing Socialists, although both in Europe and in the United States, these groups or parties supported the Russian Revolution, as they had opposed the war. It was the error (or the arrogance) of the Communists to view not only the right-wing Socialists but all those who declined to accept the leadership and guidance of the Comintern not only as non-Communists but as enemies of socialism. Communists firmly believed that there was only one path to socialism, and that that path led in whatever direction the International pointed at any particular moment. As late as 1950, the Italian Communist leader Palmiro Togliatti could proclaim that Leninism was "the sole correct path for mankind."[28]

Thus, it made little difference to the American Communists that their political perspective in 1922, insofar as it was oriented toward building an American Socialist movement, was virtually identical with that of the Socialists in 1919. The Workers' Party was embarrassed by what it viewed as the superficial similarities in the two programs, but their ideology made it impossible for them to perceive the disturbing implications in their return to the Socialist position. They reasoned that if the Hendersons were to be supported as a rope supports one who is hanged, then the Hillquits, the Fitzpatricks, and, certainly, the La Follettes deserved no better fate.

[28] Palmiro Togliatti, "The Sole Correct Path For Mankind," *Political Affairs*, XXXI, 1 (January 1952), p. 12.

7 SOCIALISTS, COMMUNISTS, AND FARMER-LABOR POLITICS 1922-1923

As the Socialist and Communist movements splintered apart in 1921 and 1922, the leadership of the Farmer-Labor party movement was doing its best to bring together all the radical forces in the United States committed to the development of an independent third party of workers and farmers. Situated outside the international political framework in which Communists and Socialists were enmeshed, the Farmer-Laborites were in a relatively good position to do so. As it turned out, they had little success.

In the 1920 Presidential election, the new Farmer-Labor Party had done poorly, even compared to the less vital Socialists; but in 1922 unity with the Socialists and Workers' Party appeared to be in sight. By early 1923, however, the Farmer-Labor Party had split with the Socialists over what policy to pursue in respect to the Conference for Progressive Political Action; and in July of that year, John Fitzpatrick and his Chicago Federation of Labor had their Party swept out from under them by their new-found ally, the Workers' Party. Ironically, Fitzpatrick's Farmer-Labor Party was to dissolve in disillusionment just at the time when major sections of the trade unions and almost all radicals were again moving toward third-party action. Nothing better illustrates the hopes and frustrations of radical politicians in the early 1920's than the experience of Chicago's Farmer-Laborites from 1920 to 1923.

When the National Labor Party met in convention to nominate a Presidential candidate in July 1920, it had already passed its peak. Under steady and heavy pressure from Samuel Gompers and the AFL officialdom, many locals of international unions and, especially, the central labor bodies (which, as organizations directly affiliated to the Federation, were particularly vulnerable), had been pressured into withdrawing support.[1] Even so, 200 to 300 union bodies, mostly from Illinois, Indiana, and Pennsylvania, were represented at the nominating convention in Chicago. In addition, delegates of the Committee of Forty-Eight, which met briefly in a separate convention, and representatives of many Nonpartisan Leagues joined the convention.

Allen McCurdy, J. A. H. Hopkins, and Amos Pinchot, of the Committee of Forty-Eight, attended the Labor convention in the hope of negotiating a platform on which Senator Robert M. La Follette would run. But the Laborites' perspective was more radical and more long range than the Forty-Eighters desired. Recognizing their limited potential in 1920, the Laborites looked as far ahead as 1940. Too radical for La Follette, they even talked of endorsing Debs; but the Socialists were not yet ready for such a step. Otto Branstetter, national secretary of the Party, took the floor expressly to withdraw Debs' name from consideration.[2] With La Follette and Debs eliminated, the delegates turned to a political unknown, Parley Parker Christensen, a Salt Lake City attorney who had been the chairman of the brief convention of the Committee of Forty-Eight. They then chose Max Hayes, ex-president of the National Labor Party, to run for Vice President.

Despite their reservations, most of the Forty-Eighters joined enthusiastically in the new Party convention. Hopkins, McCurdy, and Pinchot kept a skeleton organization in existence for possible future use, but the Committee of Forty-Eight ended its autonomous life in the merger of the two conventions.[3] Un-

[1] Fine, *Labor and Farmer Parties,* p. 390.
[2] Fine, *op. cit.,* p. 424; "Labor Swallows the Forty-Eighters," *The Survey,* 44 (August 2, 1920), p. 587.
[3] *Ibid.,* Arthur Warner, "Christensen's Convention," *Nation,* 111 (July 24,

like the Forty-Eighters, the national organization of the Non-partisan League did not endorse Christensen and Hayes, much less become a part of the new Party. Even so, the National Labor Party changed its name to the Farmer-Labor Party, and won the support of some state Leagues. The national League repudiated both Cox and Harding.[4]

Despite the relatively broad organizational support enjoyed by the new Farmer-Labor Party in 1920, Christensen polled a meagre 290,000 votes, compared to Debs' 915,000. Only in the state of Washington, where the Nonpartisan League and the State Grange had joined with the Seattle Central Labor Council to form a dynamic state Farmer-Labor Party—and in South Dakota and Montana—did Christensen run well. After the election, the National Farmer-Labor Party organization collapsed in almost every state but Illinois. In Washington, the Party continued to function under the leadership of John C. Kennedy, but without the support of the Seattle unionists or the Nonpartisan Leaguers. In Chicago, downstate Illinois, and Iowa, the Farmer-Laborites remained active, sponsored and supported by Fitzpatrick and his *New Majority*.

II

After 1920, the various radical parties moved closer together. When the Washington Farmer-Labor Party was reorganized in 1922, both Socialists and the Workers' Party withdrew their

---

1920), p. 93; Allen McCurdy, "The Forty-Eight's Position," *Nation*, 111 (July 31, 1920), p. 126; *New Majority*, July 1920; Fine, *op. cit.*, pp. 390-391.

[4] Morlan, *Political Prairie Fire*, pp. 295-296; from the inception of the Labor Party, the Nonpartisan League had been friendly and cooperative toward it. In January 1919, the National Committee of the League hailed the new Party. Lynn Frazier addressed several Labor Party meetings, commenting at one time that he felt "the only way that the workers of the country can accomplish anything politically is by the workers of the city and the workers of the farm uniting." Another time, Frazier observed that workers and farmers were "in the same boat." *New Majority*, January 18, February 1, 15, 1919.

candidates for state office.[5] Similarly, in November 1922, Max Hayes urged his readers to vote for the Socialist candidates whom he described as union men or supporters of union principles. And in 1923, the Chicago Farmer-Laborites supported William A. Cunnea, Socialist candidate for mayor in that city.[6]

This growing cooperation between Socialist and Farmer-Laborite reflected increasing awareness that neither party had proven a successful vehicle for working-class politics. Both groups looked toward the emergence of a major coalition third party which would be able to unite the various radical parties with major unions and the agrarian followers of the Nonpartisan League. Thus, when the railroad brotherhoods became increasingly restive and began to show serious interest in independent political activity at the end of 1921, neither the Socialists nor the Farmer-Laborites could refuse cooperation. While recognizing how remote the brotherhood leaders were from a genuine commitment to a working-class third party, the radicals joined in, hoping for the best.

Initiated by William Johnston, President of the International Association of Machinists, the call for the Conference of Progressive Political Action was issued over the names of the leaders of the sixteen standard railroad labor organizations. These unions had benefited immensely from the policies of the United States Railroad Administration during the war. The twelve unions which belonged to the AFL, for example, had increased their combined membership from 220,000 members before the war to 1,425,000 after. Together, the railroad affiliates made up 60 percent of over-all AFL gains in these years.[7] After the war, the railroad unions had favored the Plumb Plan for nationalization of the railroads, operated by the Government during the war. But in early 1920, Congress passed the Esch-Cummings Transportation Act, under which the roads

[5] Harvey O'Connor, "Farmer-Labor Grown Big in Washington," *New Majority*, June 10, 1922.
[6] *Cleveland Citizen*, November 4, 1922; *New Majority*, January 27, 1923.
[7] Fine, *op. cit.*, p. 398.

were returned to their respective private owners. Thereafter, the unions complained constantly about the administration of the Railroad Labor Board, which exercised broad powers over job classification and in the settlement of disputes between the workers and the roads. In itself, these irritations would not likely have moved the railroad unions to consider political action. The depression of 1921, however, greatly added to the railroadmen's woes, and the accompanying marked resurgence of agrarian unrest prompted them to act. As the call for the Conference of Progressives in Chicago noted, not only were farmers "unable profitably to market their crops," but "men and women who long to labor" were "denied that inherent right" even while factories lay idle with "millions demanding their products."[8]

In calling the February conference, the unions took pains to point out that they had no intention of forming a third party, but only desired to bring about the political unity of those "constructive forces already in existence." They proposed no more than a course of action directed against the depression and against the increasingly harsh attitude of the courts toward labor.[9]

At the organizing meeting of the CPPA in Chicago, many groups came together in political harmony for the first time. The core of the conference, of course, consisted of the sixteen raliroad unions, but they were joined by William Green of the United Mine Workers and by Sidney Hillman of the Amalgamated Clothing Workers. To carry on the activities of the conference between meetings, a Committee of Fifteen was chosen, with William Johnston as chairman. Others on the committee included Frederick C. Howe, secretary, Morris Hillquit, Jay G. Brown, of the Chicago Farmer-Labor Party, Green, Hillman, and Warren S. Stone, Edward J. Manion, and Martin

[8] "Call Issued for a Conference of Progressives at Chicago," *Brotherhood of Locomotive Firemen and Engineers' Magazine,* vol. 72, no. 4 (February 15, 1922), p. 8.
[9] *Ibid.*

F. Ryan of the brotherhoods. At the conference, a number of Socialists and former Socialists played leading roles. Hillquit and Johnston aside, these included James Maurer, Thomas Van Lear—no longer a Party member, but active in Farmer-Labor politics in Minneapolis—and the Reverend Herbert S. Bigelow of Cincinnati—who had joined the Party briefly in 1917 in support of its antiwar actions.[10]

As expected, the CPPA did not declare for a new party, nor even enunciate a coherent program. Nevertheless, it represented a definite break with the AFL policy, not only in that the gathering was called without consultation with Gompers or Federation leaders, but because it united the more militant unions with Socialists, Farmer-Laborites, and other groups. Within it, the CPPA had the unmistakable potential of a new mass coalition party of workers and farmers, the more so since a substantial minority of its supporters were already committed to that end. Fitzpatrick's *New Majority* greeted the conference as a big step in that direction, and Kate O'Hare saw it as the "first tentative move toward the creation of an American Labor Party."[11]

Unity and amity were under a greater strain at the second meeting of the CPPA. Well satisfied with the election of a large number of progressive congressmen in 1922, the leaders of the railroad unions were in no mood to extend their political venture into the untried field of third-party organization. The Chicago Farmer-Laborites, on the other hand, chafed impatiently for independent action. When the meeting gathered at Cleveland, the Chicago trade unionists introduced a resolution proposing the immediate formation of a new national party. The Missouri and Wisconsin Federations of Labor—both under

[10] "Political Movement Launched to Rescue Government from Control of Privileged Interests," *Brotherhood of Locomotive Firemen and Engineers' Magazine*, vol. 72, No. 6 (March 15, 1922), p. 1; George E. Hooker, "Conference," *The Survey*, vol. 47 (March 11, 1922), pp. 935-936.
[11] "Unified Political Action," *New Majority*, March 4, 1922; *National Rip Saw*, March 1922, p. 3.

strong Socialist influence—supported the resolution, as did the representatives of the Minnesota Farmer-Labor Party, a group not affiliated with the Chicagoans. Hillquit was ambivalent; he favored a third party, but was unwilling to push too hard for one, lest the unity of the conference be destroyed. In the vote, the Socialists supported the Farmer-Labor Party resolution.[12] By a show of hands, the vote stood 64 to 52 against an independent party; in fact, the power was overwhelmingly on the negative side since all the railroad unions stood with the majority. Recognizing this, the Socialists and the Minnesota Farmer-Laborites accepted the decision. The Chicago Farmer-Laborites, however, refused to go along. They bolted; J. G. Brown resigned from the Committee of Fifteen of the CPPA; the break was complete.[13]

III

Not long after their departure from the ranks of the CPPA, the Chicago group issued a call for a convention in Chicago on July 3, 1923, at which, according to Max Hayes, "a political federation of the minority parties similar to the plan that is in operation in Great Britain" would be brought about.[14]

Invitations went out to all groups on the left, as well as to many international unions and other labor bodies. Even the Workers' Party, which had been excluded from the Cleveland meeting of the CPPA, was invited.

For the Socialists, Fitzpatrick's invitation proved something of an embarrassment. Favoring independent labor-party action, they feared involvement in an isolated minority affair. They had agreed to compromise their long-standing opposition to cooperation with non-Socialist organizations, but only in exchange for being able to participate in a movement of consequence. Thus, after the Cleveland meeting of the CPPA, James Oneal had come out in favor of participation in a labor party

[12] Fine, pp. 403-404.
[13] *Ibid., New Majority,* February 24, 1923.
[14] *New Majority,* March 17, 1923; *Cleveland Citizen,* March 31, 1923.

as a means of giving Socialists the opportunity to strengthen their contacts with the masses of workers. Actually, Oneal wrote, the question was not whether or not there should be a labor party; such parties were already forming in three states, and the Socialists had to decide how to react.[15] Similarly, in April 1923, Hillquit took the affirmative on the question of an independent labor party in a debate with Edward Keating, editor of *Labor,* and a prominent Democrat.[16]

Nevertheless, when the Farmer-Labor Party invitation was received, the Socialists hesitated only momentarily before declining. Viewing Fitzpatrick's move as premature, the Socialists declared that they shared his goal, but that the "necessary condition to the establishment of a really powerful political party": —the "active support of at least a majority of the great unions"—had not been met. "Candor," the Socialist statement continued, "compels us to admit" that "comparatively few great unions are yet ready to take the decisive step of launching a working-class party on a national scale." This being so, the Socialists concluded, it was wiser to remain in the ranks of the CPPA.[17]

Like the Socialists, the Communists faced a difficult choice in the Farmer-Labor invitation. Only two months before the Chicago Farmer-Laborites bolted the CPPA meeting, John Pepper, Hungarian-born Comintern representative to the American party, had written in a Workers' Party pamphlet that a labor party "should be launched only if it is created by the trade unions." Anything less, he added, "would be a mere caricature, a political swindle, and a miscarriage."[18] Again, after

---

[15] "Why an Independent Labor Party," *Socialist World,* January 1923.

[16] See *Wyoming Labor Journal,* June 1, 1923.

[17] *Socialist World,* June 1923; *New Majority,* June 30, 1923. This statement of the Socialists was seized upon by the AFL news service as an admission by the *Party* that its tactics in the past twenty years had been incorrect, and that they were now finally forced to make an about face. See, for example, *Galesburg Labor News, Wyoming Labor Journal,* both June 20, 1923; *Duluth Labor World,* July 21, 1923.

[18] John Pepper, *For a Labor Party,* Third Edition (Workers' Party: Chicago, 1923), p. 19, cited in Howe and Coser, *op. cit.,* p. 117. Published originally in October 1922.

the Chicagoans had severed their affiliation with the railroad unions, and just a week before Fitzpatrick's initiative of calling the July convention, the *Worker* declared editorially that the FLP ambition to become the rallying center for a British-style labor party was a "lost hope." Even though the Workers' Party had been refused seats at the December CPPA meeting, the *Worker* shared the Socialists' view of the CPPA as the only possible basis for such a movement.[19]

Unlike the Socialists, however, the Communists could not resist the Chicago Laborites. Fitzpatrick was, after all, an old associate and admirer of Foster—and the Farmer-Labor Party had been the first recognized labor body to treat the Workers' Party as a legitimate part of a potential labor-radical coalition. Not only had the Chicago group invited Jack Carney to address its 1922 convention but in Cleveland the FLP delegates almost alone had voted to seat Ruthenberg and Foster when they appeared as delegates of the Workers' Party.[20] Furthermore, such open Communists as Arne Swabeck of the Painters' Local and Charles Krumbein of the Steamfitters were accepted by Fitzpatrick as delegates to the Chicago Central Labor Union. The Communists, in short, could not afford to oppose their only friends in the trade union movement to support a CPPA that would have nothing to do with them.

Actually, acceptance by the Farmer-Laborites was a big step forward for the Communists, even if the proposed FLP convention was much narrower than the Party had originally deemed necessary. Less than a year earlier, at the time of their secret convention in Bridgeman, Michigan, the American Communist Party was considered illegal, not only in its own eyes, but in the eyes of the public, and the federal and state governments. When Francis A. Morrow revealed the location of the

<hr>

[19] *The Worker*, March 10, 1923, cited in Howe and Coser, *op. cit.*, p. 119. The interpretation in this paragraph coincides closely to that of Howe and Coser on this point.

[20] *New Majority*, June 3, 1922; Fine, *op. cit.*, p. 405; Foster, *History of the Communist Party*, p. 214.

secret convention to his superiors in the Department of Justice and the gathering was raided, all those captured or identified were indicted under Michigan's criminal syndicalist law. Foster's acquittal (actually, he had a hung jury), after his attorney, Frank P. Walsh, had argued that the Party really had been forced underground against its will, was the first public acknowledgment that the Communists were a legitimate part of American politics and not merely agents of the Communist International. The trial not only made further illegality totally unjustifiable but, as Pepper commented, the "mere charge" that Foster was a Communist had "unintentionally presented full American citizenship to the hitherto foreign labelized communism."[21] Citizenship and leadership, however, were two different attributes. Until the Farmer-Laborites graciously extended their welcome, the Communists remained almost universally despised citizens. The invitation could not be turned down.

Once the Communists decided to go to the July convention, they labored energetically to bring a maximum number of delegates to Chicago. The Socialists, however, proved not to be alone in their reluctance to attend. As the date of the convention approached, it became clear to Fitzpatrick, J. G. Brown, and other leaders of the Farmer-Labor Party in Chicago that the gathering would include few, if any, new forces. Too late, the Farmer-Laborites realized the initial reactions of both the Socialists and Communists had been correct. Trying to draw back at the last minute, Fitzpatrick proposed to the Workers' Party that the convention be changed to a conference to explore the political basis for developing a broader unity and that, meanwhile, all bodies retain their existing identities.[22]

Unfortunately, by then the Communists had hypnotized themselves with the prospect of gaining, or sharing in, the lead-

[21] John Pepper, "William Z. Foster—Revolutionary Leader," *The Worker*, April 14, 1923.
[22] Draper, *American Communism and Soviet Russia*, pp. 42-43; "Report of J. G. Brown to the Convention," *New Majority*, July 7, 1923.

ership of a new mass party. They would have nothing to do
with delay. Before the convention assembled, it was clear that
a break between Fitzpatrick and the Workers' Party impended.
At the last minute, Ruthenberg and Foster, realizing that Fitzpatrick was an ally they could ill afford to lose, tried to accommodate him. But at Pepper's insistence, and with the overwhelming support of the Central Executive Committee of the
Workers' Party, the Communists pushed ahead for the immediate formation of a new federated farmer-labor party.[23]

At the convention, the Communists easily prevailed in their
intention to launch a new party on the spot. They were able to
do so, despite the vigorous opposition of their hosts, for two
reasons. First, the Workers' Party had maneuvered to have some
190 delegates present, of a total of 550 to 600—even though the
Party as such was entitled to only 10 representatives. William
Z. Foster came as a delegate of the Chicago local of the Brotherhood of Railway Carmen; Ludwig Lore represented the Workmen's Sick and Death Benefit Association of New York; and
Clarence Hathaway was sent by the Machinists' locals of St.
Paul. Furthermore, Communist numbers were swelled by the
presence of delegates from such questionable organizations as
the Joint Conference of Lithuanian Societies, the Workmen's
Gymnastic Association, the "Philadelphia United Workingmen
Singers and W. S. and D. B. S.," and the "P. D. and P. H. A.
of Bartlesville, Oklahoma."[24]

But even if the Workers' Party delegates comprised a full
third of the convention, they alone still constituted a distinct
minority. They were able to carry as much as 90 percent of
the convention for their major proposals, not because of their
numerical predominance, but because their position was in
line with the announced purpose of the convention. Since the
Chicago Farmer-Laborites had broken from the CPPA in the

[23] Draper, *American Communism*, p. 43.
[24] *New Majority*, July 14, 1923; John Pepper, "The First Mass Party of
American Workers and Farmers," *The Worker*, July 21, 1923; J. Louis
Engdahl, "He Sings His Hymn of Hate," *The Worker*, July 28, 1923;
Draper, *American Communism*, p. 450, n. 38.

belief that it was necessary to start a third party immediately, it was only natural that their call attracted those who shared a desire for an end to the political temporizing of the railroad unions. In other words, it was not the Workers' Party that reversed itself, but Fitzpatrick and his followers.[25] Called to Chicago to form a new party, the delegates did just that.

The decisive test of strength in the convention came early. In a move to exclude the Workers' Party, the Farmer-Laborites proposed that only their own delegates and those of trade union local and central labor bodies be given seats. The Communists, of course, moved to have all invited delegates seated. Their motion carried overwhelmingly, and from then on, they ran the show. In the end, the Communists, against the will of the Farmer-Laborites, used the convention to organize a new party —the Federated Farmer-Labor Party.

The Chicago group refused to go along. Accusing the Workers' Party of taking control "by ruthless force," Fitzpatrick and Brown withdrew from the convention they had called. Their original Farmer-Labor Party, they now asserted, offered a sufficient vehicle for united political action and any group subscribing to its principles should join that Party. It would, Fitzpatrick added, "be suicide" for the Laborites to bring into such affiliation "any organization which advocates other than lawful means to bring about political changes" or any party belonging to "international organizations . . . such as the Third International."[26] This belated discovery of the "red menace" made no impression. As Foster pointed out in reply, there was no one at the convention that had not been invited.[27]

On the last day of the convention, Fitzpatrick cried out that the Communists had "killed the Farmer-Labor Party."[28] But to the Workers' Party leadership, anaesthetized by their suc-

[25] *The Worker*, July 14, 1923; Draper, *ibid.*, pp. 44-45.
[26] "F. L. P. Disowns New Party: Workers' Party Takes Advantage of its Position as a Guest to Start a Dual Movement," *New Majority*, July 14, 1923.
[27] *The Worker*, July 14, 1923.
[28] Cited in Draper, *American Communism*, p. 45.

cess, this appeared ludicrous. After all, the delegates represented some 600,000 people, at least nominally. Four trade union
internationals, the largest of which was the Amalgamated Clothing Workers, sent delegates, as did such groups as the West
Virginia Federation of Labor and the central labor bodies of
Detroit, Buffalo, Minneapolis, and Butte, in addition to many
locals of the United Mine Workers, Machinists, and other
unions.[29] At the opening session of the convention—before the
split took place—Lieutenant Governor George F. Comings of
Wisconsin, former Populist Senator Robert F. Pettigrew of
South Dakota, Frederick A. Pike, chairman of the Minnesota
Farmer-Labor Party, and "Mother" Jones, then ninety years
old, addressed the delegates. Given the spirit which animated
the non-Communists present, and the Communists' own desire
for success, it is easy to understand how both groups were carried away. For a few days—maybe even weeks—the Communists were probably unable to see that their ability to win convention votes was far different from organizing a mass party.
Or, in their terms, that a "united front from below," if it can
be built, cannot be forged during a three-day convention of a
few hundred delegates.

Called, as the *New Majority* pointed out, "to make a sincere
effort to find a common meeting ground for Socialists and Communists," the convention had become a test of the "good faith"
of the Workers' Party once the Socialists decided not to attend.
In was the Communists' opportunity to demonstrate that they
were "folks other folks could work with." But they proved to
be "unruly guests." Sorrowfully, the *New Majority* observed
that confidence could not "be established with a sledge hammer,
a battering ram or a pile driver."[30]

Soon after the convention, the 600,000 members claimed by
the Federated Farmer-Labor Party began melting away. The

[29] *The American Labor Yearbook, 1923-24* (New York, 1924), p. 143;
New Majority, July 14, 1923; *The Worker,* July 14, 1923.
[30] "The F. L. P. Convention," *New Majority,* July 21, 1923.

St. Louis Labor commented that the "Workers' Party Captures Itself and Adopts a New Name,"[31] and this was almost literally true. The Washington Farmer-Labor Party, led by John C. Kennedy, did desert Fitzpatrick and cast its lot with the FF-LP. Kennedy had indicated his readiness to go "forward with the construction of a national labor party" the month before the Chicago convention. Having recognized then that "even under the most favorable conditions we will be a minority party for some time to come"—because of the opposition by the railroad and other unions—he could accept the narrow basis of organization presented by the new Party. According to Kennedy, the Farmer-Labor parties of California, Ohio and Kentucky also joined the FF-LP, but these organizations had little strength.[32] But in the following weeks, many more supporters of the immediate third-party action drew back and associated themselves with Fitzpatrick. The *Galesburg Labor News,* one of the Farmer-Labor Party's earliest supporters, lamented that the convention had been controlled by "those in a hurry," with the result "that now we have no party that is worth its name."[33] Similarly, the *Wyoming Labor Journal* regretted the split. Obviously favoring a third party, the paper, nevertheless, supported Brown and Fitzpatrick in their refusal to go along with the Workers' Party.[34]

The fate of the new Party was vividly reflected in its reception by the Detroit Federation of Labor. At the convention, George M. Tries, a member of the Board of Directors of the Detroit Federation, had been elected to the National Executive Council of the FF-LP. When he returned to Detroit, Tries reported that the convention was successful in that it had done what it had been called to do. Accordingly, he moved that the Detroit Federation affiliate with the new Party. But Dennis E.

[31] July 14, 1923.
[32] John C. Kennedy, "The Outlook for a Labor Party," *American Labor Monthly,* I, 3 (June 1923), 23; *Spokane Labor World,* July 6, 1923.
[33] July 13, 1923.
[34] July 13, 20, 1923.

Batt contended that the FF-LP as constituted was "not suffi-
ciently representative of American farmers and labor," and
should, therefore, not be supported. All the delegates to the
Detroit Federation favored a farmer-labor party, according to
the minutes of the group, and even Batt "made clear that opposition to affiliation" was "not based on objections to Communists being in the new organization." Without Fitzpatrick,
however, there was no basis for a meaningful party. The Detroit Federation voted not to affiliate. The central labor bodies
of Buffalo and of West Virginia similarly repudiated their delegates' action.[35]

Even as the Detroit unionists took this step, John Pepper
wrote that the Federated Farmer-Labor Party's 600,000 members made it the first "real mass party on the left" in American
history. He attacked Johnston, the railroad brotherhoods, and
the Socialists for desiring to "deliver the votes of the workers
and the exploited farmers" to La Follette and "the political representatives of the lower middle class and well-to-do farmers."
Then he attacked Fitzpatrick, Brown, Edward N. Nockels, and
Robert Buck of the Farmer-Labor Party for disrupting the Chicago convention. Of Fitzpatrick, Pepper wrote: "In Cleveland
he made the split for the Labor Party. In Chicago he made the
split against the Labor Party." As for the "600,000 workers and
farmers" who had "formed the Federated Farmer-Labor Party,"
they were admittedly "not as yet Communists," as the new
party's program indicated. But two points in the resolutions
adopted by the convention were "an absolute guarantee that
the new party" was "not a reformist party." First, that the masses
must "capture political power before they can have nationalization and public ownership." Second, that "the land shall belong
to its users."[36] Of course, less than two years earlier, these same

[35] *Detroit Labor News,* July 13, 27, 1923; Jay G. Brown, "The Farmer-
Labor Party Side," *The American Labor Monthly,* I, 4 (September 1923),
33.
[36] John Pepper, "The First Mass Party of American Workers and Farmers," *The Worker,* July 21, 1923.

two points in the programs of various groups on the left had been absolute proof of their petty-bourgeois and reformist character, and had led to Communist attacks on these groups for their betrayal of the working class.

Among the 600,000 members claimed by Pepper for the FF-LP were 87,000 members of the West Virginia Federation of Labor, 10,000 from the Philadelphia United Workingmen Singers and W.S. and D.B.A., and so on.[37] Some of these numbers, like the last, were grossly inflated, while others, like those given for the West Virginia Federation, would have been meaningless even had the delegates from West Virginia continued their affiliation. Since the Workers' Party admitted having 25 percent of the delegates at the convention,[38] and since the Party's membership was about 13,000 at the time, a more realistic total might have been 50,000 to 60,000.

In any case, it was only two weeks later that Moissaye J. Olgin had to remind his comrades that although "it may sound trite," the Federated Farmer-Labor Party was "not the Workers' Party." It was, he added for the information of his readers, "an independent political organization of workers and farmers where the Communists are in the minority both on the National Executive Committee and on the Executive Council."[39] But in this instance, the wish was not father to the deed. By the spring of 1924, when a new farmer-labor party was being organized in Minnesota, the Communists could comment officially that if the new party was formed, "*we* will merge the Federated Farmer-Labor Party in it, the Federated going out of existence as a separate organization."[40] As Joseph Manley, Communist and national secretary of the FF-LP later admitted, only the Workers' Party paid its per capita dues to the new party: most of the

[37] *Ibid.*
[38] Engdahl, "He Sings His Hymn of Hate."
[39] "Boost the Federated Farmer-Labor Party; But—Recruit Members for the Workers' Party," *The Worker*, July 28, 1923.
[40] "Decisions of the Central Executive Committee of the Workers Party of America Meeting May 2-3," *Daily Worker*, May 14, 1924. Emphasis added.

new party's members came from the Workers' Party; and those organizations affiliated with it had already been so close to the Workers' Party that they would just as soon have affiliated with the Communists.[41]

Actually, the enduring result of the capture of the Farmer-Labor Party convention was greatly to weaken the movement for a national third party, for not only did the Workers' Party's behavior at Chicago reinforce and justify the belief that the Communists could not be trusted but it also destroyed Fitzpatrick's party at the very time the national movement for a farmer-labor party was gaining momentum. After the Chicago convention, Fitzpatrick kept the Farmer-Labor Party of the United States in existence, but the previous enthusiasm was gone. In November 1923, William Mahoney of St. Paul initiated a new move for a farmer-labor party, along the lines originally desired by Fitzpatrick. Mahoney had a great deal more to work with than had Fitzpatrick. In many respects, the Minnesota movement of 1923 to 1924 fulfilled Fitzpatrick's dream, or showed signs of doing so until it was attacked by La Follette. Certainly, the Chicago Farmer-Laborites would have been an important part of the Minnesota movement, and a substantial ally, had it not been for their experience in July 1923. The disillusionment of the Chicago group was such that it never regained its original spirit. Instead of joining the new movement, Fitzpatrick, under heavy pressure from the leaders of both the Illinois and American Federations of Labor, steadily moved away from his independent position. In October 1923, Fitzpatrick remained silent while the Chicago Federation of Labor, in a complete reversal of its earlier stand, endorsed the position of the state leadership by opposing the formation of a labor party, the amalgamation of craft unions, and recognition of the Soviet Union.[42] Finally, in May 1924, Fitzpatrick pulled the Chi-

[41] Joseph Manley, "Goodbye 'Class' Farmer-Labor Party," *Daily Worker*, December 5, 1924.
[42] *Minnesota Union Advocate*, October 11, 1923.

cago Federation out of the Farmer-Labor Party of the United States, which, in effect, meant the collapse of the Party. At the same time, the Chicago trade unionists went back to the AFL policy of rewarding labor's friends and punishing its enemies.[43]

[43] *Galesburg Labor News*, April 18, May 23, 1924.

8 THE MINNESOTA FARMER-LABORITES AND THE 1924 ELECTION

While Fitzpatrick and his associates in the Chicago Federation of Labor tried prematurely to organize a national party, the Minnesota Farmer-Laborites busily attended to matters closer to hand. Organized in 1918, after Charles A. Lindbergh was defeated in the Republican gubernatorial primary, the Minnesota Farmer-Labor Party remained dormant until the spring of 1922.[1] That November, the revived Party demonstrated its strength by electing Henrik Shipstead to the United States Senate, and on July 6, 1923, only days after the abortive Chicago convention, it elected Magnus Johnson to the unexpired term of the state's other senate seat. The formal structure, required by statute, of the Minnesota Party was headed by Frederick A. Pike, but its real support came from the farmers' and trade unions' Nonpartisan Leagues, led by Henry G. Teigan and William Mahoney. Both Mahoney, editor of the *Minnesota Union Advocate*, official organ of the state Federation of Labor, and Teigan, secretary of the National Nonpartisan League, were deeply committed to an independent party of workers and farmers. They had, however, delayed their entry into national politics until the Minnesota organization was powerful enough to give such a movement "poise and prestige."[2]

---

[1] Morlan, *op. cit.*, p. 343.
[2] "Hopes of the National Farmer-Labor Convention Miscarry," *Minnesota Union Advocate*, July 12, 1923.

Mahoney had declined to participate in the Chicago convention and predicted its failure;[3] yet he took no pleasure in being proven correct, nor did he allow the Chicago events to disillusion him. Mahoney noted that the Minnesota Farmer-Labor movement had advanced beyond Fitzpatrick's; it would no longer be possible "for extremists of the right or the left to arrest or divert" it. In 1924 his Minnesota Farmer-Laborites planned to "form the nucleus of a national progressive party into which the producing classes and all progressives" might come.[4]

On July 16, 1923, only four days after Mahoney proclaimed the maturity of the Minnesota movement, the convention of the State Federation of Labor went on record as favoring the formation of a national farmer-labor party. A month later, Mahoney, as chairman of the Working People's Nonpartisan Political League, was joined by H. G. Teigan, secretary of the Farmer's Nonpartisan League, in a call for the formation of a new coordinating body for the Minnesota movement.[5] In September, the Farmer-Labor Federation, based upon individual membership, was organized to "weld the progressive forces of the state into a compact agency to promote the Farmer-Labor Party triumph."[6] The new federation then called a national conference in St. Paul on November 15, at which, according to Teigan, "a few live wires from different states of the Northwest," would make plans to "establish a united front for the presidential contest" in 1924.[7]

The November 15 conference was a success. Fitzpatrick and Brown came from Chicago, Joseph Manley and William Bouck (a Washington farmers' leader) represented the Federated

[3] "Farmer-Labor Convention and the Communists," *Minnesota Union Advocate*, June 21, 1923.
[4] "Hopes of the Farmer-Labor Convention Miscarry," *loc. cit.*
[5] *Minnesota Union Advocate*, July 19, August 16, 1923.
[6] *Minnesota Union Advocate*, September 13, 1923.
[7] Henry G. Teigan to Charles E. Taylor, Minneapolis, November 1, 1923; Teigan to Taylor, Minneapolis, November 6, 1923, Henry G. Teigan papers, Minnesota Historical Society.

Farmer-Labor Party, and J. A. H. Hopkins attended as spokesman for the Committee of Forty-Eight and the National Progressive Party. From South Dakota there was Alice Lorraine Daly, a former schoolteacher who had recently polled 50,000 votes in an almost successful race for governor, as well as Tom Ayres, an old-time Nonpartisan Leaguer. The Progressive Party of Idaho sent Ray McKaig, former master of the North Dakota Grange and one of the Nonpartisan League's earliest and best-known leaders. State Senator Charles E. Taylor, a farmer and leader of the Montana Farmer-Labor Party, attended, as did John C. Kennedy, secretary of the Washington Farmer-Labor Party (with Seattle labor leader James Duncan's blessings), and C. C. Platt, leader of the Wisconsin Nonpartisan League. Aside from Mahoney and Teigan, Minnesota delegates included E. G. Hall, president and organizer of the Minnesota Federation of Labor; Robert D. Cramer, editor of the *Minneapolis Labor Review;* E. A. Preuss; and Dr. William Schaper.[8]

The conference agreed unanimously on the need for a national convention to unite all existing groups for the 1924 elections and made plans for organizing such a nominating convention in St. Paul on May 30. Mahoney, Teigan, J. A. H. Hopkins, and Dr. William Schaper were put in charge of the arrangements. A tentative program called for public ownership of the railroads, control of money and credit through national and cooperative banks, nationalization of all natural resources, civil rights, and legislation to curb judicial abuses in respect to labor. Mahoney stressed that this was not an attempt at amalgamation, but merely a coalition for the coming election. Tom Ayres expressed the generally held conviction that La Follette would accept the nomination of this movement.[9]

[8] *Minnesota Union Advocate,* November 22, 1923. Lorraine Daly's vote on the Nonpartisan League line was 26.3% of the total. In Idaho, the Progressive Party's gubernatorial candidate polled 40,516 votes, or 31.2%. He ran ahead of the Democrat. In Washington, James Duncan received 35,326 votes (12%) as Farmer-Labor candidate for governor in 1922.

[9] *Ibid.* J. A. H. Hopkins to Hillquit, New York, February 20, 1924, Hill-

All present hoped for a genuine third party of workers and farmers in 1924; all but the Communists hoped to see La Follette as the new party's standard bearer. Yet most of these men were conscious of their ideological differences with the Wisconsin senator. John C. Kennedy told Teigan that, while personally he stood "for a more radical program than Bob La Follette has ever advocated," there was "no denying the fact that he would be a wonderfully strong candidate for President on a straight Farmer-Labor ticket." Teigan shared Kennedy's attitude "on the question of La Follette's radicalism, or rather, I should say: conservatism." La Follette did "not go far enough" to suit Teigan "by a long ways," but Teigan was "convinced that he does go as far as the people are prepared to go with him at the present time." Besides, Teigan noted, La Follette was "a fighter" and "the one man in the U. S. Senate for a considerable period of time" who had "actually grown more radical the longer he remains in that body."[10]

Tom Ayres of South Dakota was more explicit. He wanted La Follette on the ticket, but Ayres' first commitment was to "start a brand new clean party of farmers and workers." That was "the only thing that will do us any good," he told Senator Magnus Johnson. "We can pass piece-meal, patch-work legislation in Washington until the crack of doom, but so long as we have a Rockefeller, Morgan, Doheny, Sinclair dictatorship in possession of the political power, we shall get nowhere. This Wall Street dictatorship," he added, "has got to be substituted by a dictatorship of the farmers and workers. We are the majority—we do the work—we have the right to rule."[11]

---

quit papers. Mahoney's emphasis on coalition, as opposed to amalgamation, may have been prompted by Hathaway's attempt to have the delegates agree to affiliate with the FFLP, a move that never had the slightest chance of gaining serious consideration.

[10] John C. Kennedy to Teigan, Seattle, November 28, 1923; Teigan to Kennedy, Washington, D.C., December 6, 1923. Teigan papers.

[11] Tom Ayres to Magnus Johnson, Mitchell, South Dakota, March 20, 1924. Teigan papers.

Mahoney, too, had a generally Socialist outlook. Like Teigan, who was state chairman of the Socialist Campaign Committee when he was executive secretary of the North Dakota Nonpartisan League in 1916, Mahoney was an ex-Party member. He had —so he said in 1920—never viewed the old Socialist Party as of practical political significance, but as "an educational movement" that promoted "study and discussion of the great economic and social questions."[12] The Farmer-Labor movement, on the other hand, was to be "a coalition of progressive forces" designed to "break up the old party alignment" and supply radicals with personnel for a new major party. La Follette, Mahoney believed, "more than any other man," could "contribute in the largest measure to this end," and it would "well repay" the Farmer-Laborites "to cooperate with him" in 1924.[13] Mahoney argued for a new party to put through an "entire program of legislative action" along "fundamental lines." The times did not demand "occasional and fragmentary measures," entrusted to "the enemy to enforce," but "a definite campaign" by workers and farmers "for the conquest of all branches of government." Yet the Farmer-Labor Party was "not revolutionary in its methods, however much it may be in its ultimate implications and effects," Mahoney later wrote. It proposed "the gradual transformation of the industrial system from exploitation and oppression to one of cooperation and freedom." Mahoney knew that the Conference for Progressive Political Action opposed a radical third party. Seeing no possibility of converting the leaders of the CPPA to his point of view, he attacked both the Socialists and former Socialists in its leadership as backsliders who had once favored independent political action, but were now taking up "this nonpartisan hallucination as if it were an original idea." Only a third party could knit the

[12] William Mahoney to H. E. Soule, St. Paul, April 12, 1920. Mahoney papers, Minnesota Historical Society.
[13] Mahoney to Teigan, St. Paul, February 21, 1924, National Nonpartisan League papers, Minnesota Historical Society.

"forces for reform into a compact mass," Mahoney asserted; Minnesota was proof that such action could be effective.[14]

Mahoney, of course, recognized that a third party could not win in 1924. But powerful farmer-labor parties had developed in most of the states of the Northwest; a third ticket, capable of winning in several states, would help a new national party emerge. The unsatisfactory positions of old parties on the four most pressing issues—nationalization of the railroads, currency reform, taxation and the antilabor character and actions of the judiciary—made such a move imperative in 1924.[15] Every year since 1920, some group had tried to form a third party, the Committee of Forty-Eight, the Farmer-Labor Party of the United States, the American Labor Party. Until now the Minnesota movement had held aloof; 1924 was the year for action.[16]

II

Things did look promising in the closing months of 1923, especially since the CPPA seemed to be moving steadily toward support of William Gibbs McAdoo, at that time the leading contender for the Democratic nomination.[17] If the railroad unions supported McAdoo, the Minnesota Farmer-Laborites would be the unchallenged leaders of the third-party movement. When Mahoney sent out his call for the November 15 conference in St. Paul, only the Socialists declined, and their reaction was not entirely negative. Hillquit assured Mahoney that he had no illusions about the possibility of getting the

[14] "Nonpartisan vs. Independent Political Action of the Producers," *Minnesota Union Advocate,* October 11, 1923; see also, "What Magnus Johnson Represents," *ibid.,* October 18, 1923; "Communists and the Farmer-Labor Party of Minnesota," editorial in *Minnesota Union Advocate,* November 13, 1924.
[15] "The Problem of a Third Party," *Minnesota Union Advocate,* November 15, 1923.
[16] *Ibid.*
[17] On this point, see J. Leonard Bates, "The Teapot Dome Scandal and the Election of 1924," *American Historical Review,* LX, No. 2 (January 1955), 307-310.

CPPA to support third-party action. But more than anything, Hillquit feared a premature split with the major unions.[18] All Socialists did not agree. Kate O'Hare wrote that in declining to participate, the Socialists had failed to change with the times. Singing the Party's swan song, she observed that "all that can be done by political action" (the implication was that this was not much) now rested in a farmer-labor party.[19]

In Minnesota, some leaders of the Farmer-Labor movement opposed Mahoney and Teigan on the question of a grass-roots, radical third party. Senator Shipstead and F. A. Pike preferred a loose electoral machine that could be used to make deals with the Democrats, as the CPPA leaders hoped to do in support of McAdoo; the *Minnesota Daily Star*, an unofficial Nonpartisan League newspaper controlled by A. C. Townley and Thomas Van Lear, agreed.[20] Pike believed the decision to call a convention on May 30 was a mistake. Urging progressives to meet after the Democratic convention (in July), he argued that Farmer-Laborites should attempt to attract men "who have become acknowledged leaders in the old parties in the contest of the masses of people against special interest." Disagreeing with Pike, J. A. H. Hopkins strongly supported the May 30 date and insisted that the existing Farmer-Labor parties representing particular classes and economic interests must form the basis of the new party.[21]

In the *Star*, Van Lear attacked the Farmer-Labor Federation (which had called the November 15 meeting) as Communist inspired. But as Mahoney pointed out, the Federation began in St. Paul, where there was no Communist bloc. In fact, Mahoney had started to agitate for "closer and more effective"

[18] William Mahoney to Hillquit, St. Paul, November 3, 1923; Hillquit to Mahoney, New York, November 9, 1923. Hillquit papers.
[19] "Are We Headed Straight for Perdition?" *National Rip Saw*, November 1923.
[20] *Minnesota Union Advocate*, September 13, 20, 1923; February 7, 1924.
[21] F. A. Pike to J. A. H. Hopkins, St. Paul, January 21, 1924; Hopkins to Pike, New York, January 23, 1924. Copies in Teigan papers.

organization of the state Farmer-Labor Party in April 1923, before the Communists were interested in such politics.[22] Neither Mahoney nor Teigan needed to be lured into independent action. Indeed, there were few to lure them. English-speaking Communists were rare in Minnesota. Theodore Draper asserts that Clarence Hathaway, a Minneapolis Machinists leader and vice president of the state Federation of Labor at the time, was the only Communist connection with the Farmer-Labor movement in the state. He is mistaken, but Communist influence was limited to a small, active group in Minneapolis.[23]

Mahoney did welcome both the Workers' Party and the Federated Farmer-Labor Party into the movement on November 15. He did so although only a few months before, he had criticized Fitzpatrick for inviting the Communists to the Chicago convention and had expressed his strong disagreement with their basic approach to American politics.[24] Earlier, Mahoney had looked upon the Communists as "guerilla bands" that sought to divert and divide the practical progressives in the Farmer-Labor movement.[25] His reversal had several causes. Central was the belief that the Chicago convention was premature, and that unlike the Minnesota movement, Fitzpatrick's group did not have the organizational resources or political prestige to guarantee its ideological hegemony. Mahoney had never questioned the motives of the Workers' Party. He had always given Foster, Clarence Hathaway, and William F. Dunne

[22] *Minnesota Union Advocate*, September 13, 20; April 19, 1923.
[23] *American Communism*, p. 101. Draper ignores the implication in his own statement and assumes heavy Communist influence on Mahoney (Mahoney to Teigan, St. Paul, February 21, 1924, National Nonpartisan League papers). Mahoney wrote that "in Minneapolis the labor movement is largely dominated by this element."
[24] "The Farmer-Labor Convention and the Communists," *op. cit.* Here Mahoney argued that the Communists' "tactics and principles" placed them "wholly outside the pale of sympathy of the Farmer-Labor progressive movement," and that their presence "would be a source of perpetual irritation." Events in Europe, Mahoney added, showed the Communists had "wrecked every independent labor and political movement undertaken."
[25] *Ibid.*

a good press and had defended the right of the Workers' Party to exist as a legitimate political tendency. At the time of the Bridgeman trial, he wrote that the law under which Foster was being tried had been "inspired by war-mad fanatics," and that it was "only because these Communists are working people" that they were being "persecuted."[26]

At the same time, Mahoney was growing increasingly annoyed with the red-baiting in the AFL. In April 1923, the Federation leadership ordered the Seattle Central Labor Council to stop urging recognition of and trade with the Soviet Union. Mahoney condemned this, pointing out that the Minnesota movement had had the same program for four years. A few months later, Mahoney deplored the "martyrization of William Z. Foster." Trade union leadership automatically opposed everything Foster advocated, but Foster had not invented industrial unionism, or the other progressive measures he favored, all of which seemed sound to Mahoney. The AFL convention in October 1923, brought the issue to a head. Every progressive proposal had been defeated by raising the Communist bogey. Under the guise of anti-Communism, the AFL opposed independent political action, industrial unionism, and the recognition of Soviet Russia—and in addition had sanctioned the disciplining of the Seattle Central Labor Council for supporting these demands. These were simply progressive positions which the Communists had adopted after the failure of their earlier approach. By labeling them as Communist now, the leadership of the AFL was turning the clock back and putting themselves in opposition to the interests of the rank and file. "We hope," he concluded, that regardless of Communisty activity, "the rank and file are not going to be terrified by a foolish hysteria from adopting such methods and means as the conditions demand."[27]

By the time of the St. Paul conference in November, Ma-

[26] *Minnesota Union Advocate,* January 25, February 8, March 15, 29, 1923.
[27] *Minnesota Union Advocate,* October 11, 25, 1923.

honey openly described the Communists as a legitimate minority. Few would be won to their "extreme doctrines," but as long as their immediate proposals were in line with progressive demands, they should be included in a farmer-labor coalition. The best way to solve the problem of these "borers from within" was to "keep the movement clean and progressive" and to give them "plenty of work to do." The right of free speech, he concluded, "must not be abridged in the unions."[28] Mahoney could take this position because he realized that the Communists were a hopeless minority. Sentiment for La Follette was so strong in Minnesota and elsewere that he saw no danger of "any schemer subverting the Minnesota movement."[29] Furthermore, Mahoney had become convinced that the Farmer-Labor Party movement would be accused of being "red" in any case. In such a situation it might as well have the strongest possible organization.[30]

III

Thus, despite the Communists take-over of Fitzpatrick's Farmer-Labor Party in 1923, the Workers' Party participated successfully in the Minnesota movement in 1924. Mahoney's benevolence helped, but their participation was based on the clear recognition of their minority status, as well as on a policy of working openly as Communists.

At the third convention of the Workers' Party, in December 1923, the majority supported the concept of a party "which maneuvered in the political struggle" of the United States "for the purpose of securing the leadership over wide masses of workers." In contrast, the minority, led by Ludwig Lore, opposed the third-party alliance and advocated a "mere organization for propaganda and education and the organization of rev-

[28] "Communist Activity in the Trade Unions," *MUA*, November 29, 1923; Mahoney to Teigan, St. Paul, February 21, 1924, National Nonpartisan League papers.
[29] *Minnesota Union Advocate*, January 3, 1924.
[30] *Minnesota Union Advocate*, March 13, 1924.

olutionaries."[31] But in an unusual gesture to the minority, the majority did not force the issue. Instead, it agreed that "the question of the correctness of the policy . . . be referred to the Communist International for decision."[32]

This meant that in the interim between the convention in December and the time the International reached a decision, the third-party policy was carried out on the independent initiative of the American leadership, largely under Ruthenberg's direction.

With long experience in the prewar Socialist movement, Ruthenberg understood the necessity for both open educational efforts in behalf of socialist—or communist—principles, and maximum contact with workers and farmers. His interpretation of "maneuvering" in the political struggle, unique in Communist practice in the United States, was responsible for the acceptance of the Communists—as Communists—in the Farmer-Labor Party.

In a letter to the Executive Committee of District 9 of the Workers' Party, in Minneapolis, Ruthenberg explained the tactics to be followed. Members of the Workers' Party must seek nomination in the Farmer-Labor Party primaries in Minnesota, and during the primary campaign must "publicly announce themselves as Communists." In addition, they were openly to "support the full Communist program," stating "that they ask for support because they stand for a proletarian revolution, the establishment of the Soviet government, and the Dictatorship of the Proletariat." If, after campaigning for the full Communist program, Workers' Party members were defeated in the Farmer-Labor Party primaries, they would give "full support to the Farmer-Labor ticket" selected by the "masses of workers and farmers." Ruthenberg anticipated the objection that this policy might endanger the united front. "Let us say frankly,"

---

[31] C. E. Ruthenberg, "The American Revolutionary Movement Grows," *Daily Worker*, January 13, 1924, section II.
[32] *Ibid.*

he wrote, "that each time we show our Communist face and our Communist policy in a United Front, we endanger the United Front." To avoid jeopardizing the united front, it would be necessary "never [to] show our Communist face or advocate our Communist policies." But if Communists followed such a path, Ruthenberg concluded, there would be "no reason for joining in any United Front."[33]

Ruthenberg's tactics flowed from his belief that it was possible to win the majority of American workers and farmers to follow in Russia's footsteps and establish a Soviet America. He agreed with Mahoney that it would be "a great step forward" for the American labor movement if the workers and farmers formed a national party to "struggle against the capitalist parties." But Ruthenberg regarded Mahoney's perspective as insufficient. The Communist aim was "for the formation of such a Party, and then to work within that Party and force it forward, step by step, as the lessons of experience make possible, into more revolutionary action."[34]

Apparently, having learned from the disastrous split at Chicago the year before, the Communists were determined not to split with any of the progressive forces willing to work with them in 1924. Their strategy, as described by Alexander Bittelman, was to "drive with all your might for the formation of a class party of workers and exploited farmers. But at the same time make sure—doubly sure—that you get all the politically organized farmer-labor forces in it."[35] This independent "class" party would then join in an electoral alliance with the CPPA in support of La Follette and a "third party."[36] Although critical

[33] C. E. Ruthenberg to District Executive Committee, District 9, Minneapolis, Chicago, March 27, 1924. Printed in the *Daily Worker*, March 31, 1924.
[34] Letter from Ruthenberg to a group of Finnish comrades, reprinted in the *Daily Worker*, May 7, 1924.
[35] "The March Meeting of the Workers Party Central Executive Committee," *Worker Magazine Supplement*, March 22, 1924.
[36] C. E. Ruthenberg, "June 17th and July 4th," *Daily Worker*, April 12, 1924.

of La Follette, the Workers' Party was prepared to support him.[37]

The leadership of the Farmer-Labor movement accepted this policy, although not always with complete satisfaction. Publicly, Mahoney viewed Ruthenberg's approach as "a perfectly honest method of activity." It was "much better that they conduct their work openly, and when they fail, to join wholeheartedly back of the successful candidate than to have them secretly plot and intrigue and betray." Privately, Mahoney told Teigan that the Communists were "fanatical in their defense of their ideas" and did not "give a damn whether we win now or a century hence just so their principles are preserved. They are," he observed, "doubly afraid someone will steal their thunder" and "would rather get less in their own little party and feel it their own, than to risk any combination with the unknown elements in Washington." "You know," he reminded Teigan, "I haven't an overamount of confidence in the Communists, and while I am willing to give them a chance to work, I want to keep them in front of me all the time."[38]

Teigan also had "no particular objection" to the Communists, but he agreed with J. G. Brown that by demanding that La Follette endorse a class party in advance of the Republican convention in June, they were "not improving the outlook for harmony." To organize a "class Farmer-Labor Party" was "o.k." with him, "but at the same time," he noted, "we must use some common sense." "Surely, we want to avoid creating a political sect."[39]

Others in the leadership showed less concern. J. A. H. Hopkins worried about the effect a group of right-wing Farmer-Laborites in Denver might have on the May 30 convention, and

[37] "Decisions of the Central Executive Committee of the Workers Party of America Meeting, May 2-3," *Daily Worker*, May 14, 1924.
[38] *Minnesota Union Advocate*, April 10, 1924; Mahoney to Teigan, St. Paul, February 21, 1924, *loc. cit.*
[39] Teigan to W. G. Brown, n.p., February 13, 1924, Teigan papers.

told Teigan that the Denver group was the real source of worry, not the Workers' Party.[40] In Minnesota, Duluth's *Labor World* looked with increasing favor on the Workers' Party as the campaign progressed. Formerly strongly anti-Communist, the *Labor World* had applauded the decision of the United Mine Workers in June 1923 to expel all Communists from the union.[41] But by the time J. O. Bentall entered the Eighth District congressional primary in April 1924, the paper gave him prominent and friendly coverage. Bentall, a former Socialist gubernatorial candidate who had served eighteen months at Leavenworth for a conviction under the Espionage Act,[42] entered the primary several weeks after four other Farmer-Laborites had done so because the Workers' Party believed—so the Duluth *Labor World* reported—"that with the field divided against the four other candidates" Bentall could be elected. The editor of the *Labor World* was one of his opponents in the primary, but the paper described Bentall as "strong, forceful and effective," commented that he was "making an out and out fight for the things in which he believes," and reported that while he "boldly" announced "that he is for the overthrow of the capitalist system," he recognized "that there are certain remedial measures which must be enacted now."[43] The tone of the *Labor World's* reports, and the extent of its coverage, clearly indicated respect, even admiration, for Bentall and the Workers' Party.

Robert D. Cramer, a leading figure in the Farmer-Labor Party and the editor of the *Minneapolis Labor Review*, went further. Communists, he said, were "the dynamos of the move-

[40] J. A. H. Hopkins to Teigan, New York, January 22, 1924, Teigan papers.
[41] *Duluth Labor World*, July 7, 1923.
[42] *Minnesota Union Advocate*, September 13, 1923; *Daily Worker*, June 10, 1924.
[43] April 26, May 10, 31, 1924. On June 21, Bentall polled 25% and ran second in a field of five, losing by 5,306 votes to 6,438. *Leg. Manual of the State of Minnesota*, 1925, p. 307.

ment," without whom it could not "live and be successful."[44]

As Mahoney knew, the prestige of the Minnesota movement —after electing both United States senators, a congressman, twenty-four state senators, and forty-six representatives—was such that even the acceptance of Communists would not cause success-starved radicals to oppose it. Those who attacked Mahoney for working with the Communists had always opposed independent action on a national level and had red-baited him before he welcomed the Communists into the movement. In Minnesota, Mahoney's approach was sound, but he did not reckon with the CPPA and the railroad brotherhoods.

IV

From the beginning, Mahoney, Teigan, and virtually everyone else connected with the Farmer-Labor movement had not only favored La Follette as their Presidential candidate but had assumed that he would accept the honor.[45] Even the Communists had worked out a rationale to support him. Teigan, who, as Senator Magnus Johnson's secretary, spent a good deal of time in Washington, had seen La Follette occasionally and it was his impression that "the Senator will not object to becoming a candidate for President under Farmer-Labor auspices." It did seem likely, though, that "he would prefer waiting until after the Republican Convention before definitely severing his connection with the old party."[46] Mahoney, too, had been to

---

[44] *Daily Worker*, March 13, 1924. See also "Minutes of the St. Paul Conference, March 10-11, 1924," Mahoney papers, where Cramer defended the inclusion of the Workers' Party in the movement.

[45] *Minnesota Union Advocate*, January 31, 1924; J. A. H. Hopkins to Hillquit, New York, April 5, 1924, Hillquit papers; *Galesburg Labor News*, April 18, 1924; *Daily Worker*, March 17, 1924.

[46] Teigan to P. J. Wallace, n.p., February 13, 1924; see also Teigan to F. D. McMillen, Washington, D.C., February 7, 1924, in which Teigan writes as if there is no question but that La Follette will run. Teigan papers.

see the senator and believed he would accept the nomination of the Farmer-Labor Party.[47]

Until February 1924, furthermore, the Minnesota Farmer-Laborites had no competition. The CPPA did not desire to initiate a third party, despite their warning in December 1923 that if both old parties nominated reactionaries a "great new party will be organized overnight."[48] This threat was little more than a device to bring seemingly superfluous pressure on the Democrats to nominate William Gibbs McAdoo, already the leading candidate for the nomination and thoroughly acceptable to the brotherhood leaders. But as the Amalgamated Clothing Workers' journal commented, McAdoo was "drowned by the oil investigation flood"[49] which also engulfed so many of President Harding's close associates in the Teapot Dome Scandal. In February 1924, only days before the meeting of the CPPA in St. Louis, Edward L. Doheny testified that McAdoo had received retainers totaling $150,000 from his oil company. Almost overnight, the McAdoo bubble burst.[50]

The collapse of McAdoo's candidacy appeared to turn the CPPA threat into a prophecy. The brotherhoods could turn to no other Democrat and Coolidge was sure to be the Republican nominated. If the Farmer-Laborites nominated La Follette in St. Paul, the leaders of the CPPA would be forced to endorse their rival's action. To have their progressive ticket in 1924, and at the same time avoid a commitment to a genuine third party, and a "class" one at that, the brotherhoods had two tasks before them: to nominate La Follette themselves, and to destroy the Farmer-Labor Party movement.

[47] See, for example, Mahoney to Teigan, St. Paul, February 21, 1924, Teigan papers.

[48] *Labor*, December 1, 1923, cited in Howe and Coser, *op. cit.*, 132. In the same editorial, *Labor* had said: "Don't worry about new parties . . . concentrate on the task of naming true blue progressives in the approaching primaries."

[49] *Advance*, March 21, 1924.

[50] J. Leonard Bates, "The Teapot Dome Scandal . . . ," *loc. cit.*, pp. 305 ff.

That this was to be the strategy of the railroad brotherhoods was not immediately clear to Teigan or Mahoney. Both men attended the February meeting of the CPPA which called an endorsing convention for July 4 in Cleveland. Mahoney recognized that the CPPA intention to support La Follette added "complications" to his plans, but both he and Magnus Johnson hoped that on July 4 the brotherhoods would simply endorse the May 30 nomination of La Follette at St. Paul.[51] Others, notably F. A. Pike of the "legal" Farmer-Labor Party and a number of farmers' Nonpartisan League leaders differed. Understanding that the CPPA had no intention of endorsing a third party, Pike called for cancellation of the St. Paul convention. In Minnesota, no one listened.

By early March, things were happening so fast that even Mahoney was bewildered. The Farmer-Labor Federation call for the May 30 convention had not yet been officially endorsed by the farmers' Nonpartisan League, or by the Working People's Nonpartisan Political League or by Pike's Farmer-Labor Party. In March these three groups would decide their attitudes toward the coming Presidential election, but first, the Farmer-Labor Federation was faced with the problem of a change of date for the St. Paul convention.

Originally, supporters of McAdoo and of the CPPA had opposed May 30 and suggested a change to just after the Republican and Democratic conventions, so that the Farmer-Laborites could endorse La Follette or McAdoo if either should win his own party's nomination.[52] La Follette had told Teigan that he would prefer to have the Farmer-Laborites meet after the Republican convention. Mahoney, who had viewed McAdoo as a "bogus progressive" from the beginning, agreed with Teigan that they should accommodate La Follette, but not McAdoo, and change the St. Paul convention from May 30 to June 17,

[51] "Conference for Political Action Adds Complications," *MUA*, February 21, 1924; Teigan to Mahoney, n.p., February 29, 1924, National Nonpartisan League papers.
[52] *MUA*, February 7, 1924.

or after the Republican convention but before the Democratic
one. Within the Farmer-Labor Federation there was opposition
to the change, particularly from Hopkins and the Communists,
but when Teigan revealed that La Follette would announce his
candidacy only after the Republican convention and strongly
urged his colleagues to "defer to La Follette's wishes," only the
Communists remained in opposition. Mahoney and Teigan easily prevailed. The date was changed to June 17.[53]

Following the St. Paul conference on March 10 and 11, the
two Nonpartisan Leagues and the legal Farmer-Labor Party
met in three separate conventions between March 12 and March
14. To Mahoney's great surprise, all three endorsed the coming
convention in St. Paul. There had been no question how the
WPNPL would decide, but the farmers' Nonpartisan League
was another question. The *Minnesota Leader,* organ of the
FNPL, opposed Mahoney's convention plans, despite its support of La Follette, and even though Teigan was the secretary
of the Farmers' League. But in a close vote of 84 to 78, the
League followed the course of the WPNPL, dissolved, and
merged into the Farmer-Labor Federation. One "good Lu-
theran farmer" caught the spirit of the conventions when he
remarked that "next in importance to spreading the gospel is
the union of the farmers and the industrial workers."[54]

That the outcome of the Minneapolis conventions was not
simply the happy result of political manipulation by Mahoney
and Teigan was proven at St. Cloud. The "legal" party convention procedure, based on a system of county representation,
had been established by the anti-Farmer-Labor Party legisla-

[53] *Ibid.,* December 27, 1923; Teigan to Hopkins, n.p., Feb. 5, 1924;
Hopkins to Teigan, New York, Feb. 13, 1924; Teigan to Hopkins, n.p.,
Feb. 19, 1924, all Teigan papers; Mahoney to Teigan, St. Paul, Feb. 21,
1924, National Nonpartisan League papers; Minutes of the St. Paul Conference, March 10-11, Mahoney Papers.
[54] *St. Paul Pioneer Press,* March 14, 15, 1924; *Milwaukee Leader,* March
14, 1924; Murray E. King, "The Farmer-Labor Federation," *New Republic,* 38 (April 2, 1924), pp. 145-147. Even after March 12, the *Minnesota
Leader* remained cool to Mahoney. See the March 26, 1924 number.

ture, and Chairman Pike—in an obvious attempt to limit Mahoney's influence—had called the St. Cloud convention only two days after the Minneapolis gatherings.

Delegates to St. Cloud came from every county in the state, but they voted heavily against their state chairman and endorsed the St. Paul convention.[55]

Meanwhile, the CPPA, and especially Edward Keating, editor of *Labor* (official organ of sixteen railroad brotherhoods), were increasingly unhappy with the growth of the Minnesota movement. In December, *Labor* had commented mildly that a "great many well-meaning men and women are busily engaged formulating plans for new political parties."[56] But as the Farmer-Labor movement grew following the March 12 conventions, *Labor* became less benevolent. On March 29, the paper attacked the St. Paul convention as Communist, and again, on April 5, it claimed the Minnesota movement was under Communist control and urged the workers "to stay away from it."

These attacks were in line with the attitude assumed by John Fitzpatrick, J. G. Brown, and Robert M. Buck of the Chicago Farmer-Labor Party,[57] but they elicited little or no response from other early supporters of the Minnesota movement, or among a broad range of radicals. In March, the Amalgamated Clothing Workers called for a genuine labor party; and at the Union's convention in mid-May, the delegates instructed the General Executive Board to attend both the St. Paul and Cleveland conventions after hearing the Socialist Abraham Beckerman urge the inclusion of the Workers' Party in any new third party.[58] Victor Berger's *Milwaukee Leader* greeted the March 12 FLP endorsements with banner headlines, and conspicuously refrained from any red-baiting of the St. Paul convention

[55] *Minnesota Union Advocate*, March 20, 1924; *Daily Worker*, March 13, 1924; St. Paul *Pioneer Press*, March 14, 15, 1924.
[56] December 1, 1923.
[57] See open letter of Brown, Fitzpatrick and Buck, Chicago, February 6, 1924, Teigan papers.
[58] *Advance*, March 21, 28, May 23, 1924; *Daily Worker*, May 19, 1924; *Minnesota Union Advocate*, May 22, 1924.

in the weeks that followed.[59] In April, a survey of newspapers in Minnesota, North Dakota, South Dakota, and Wisconsin indicated to the *Literary Digest* that the wheat growers and industrial workers in those states were "disaffected," and that a third party headed by La Follette was "more than likely" in 1924.[60] In South Dakota, the *Sioux Falls Press* commented that if Coolidge were renominated, it was "reasonably certain that La Follette will head a third-party ticket." In such a case, fusion between the Farmer-Labor elements in the state and insurgent Republicans was a real possibility, and prospects for victory in the state were "not entirely remote."[61] In April, the convention of the West Virginia State Federation of Labor endorsed the St. Paul Farmer-Labor Party convention, although the State Executive Committee refused to follow the mandate of the convention.[62]

Throughout April and May, J. A. H. Hopkins carried on such an extensive correspondence in behalf of the St. Paul convention that Mahoney believed Hopkins had Presidential aspirations himself. Before the March 10 conference Mahoney wrote Teigan that "if we can get him out here . . . we will throw him up the river." But Hopkins' efforts were helpful and received widespread publicity in the labor press. In addition, he wrote to Socialist leaders, such as Hillquit, urging them to attend the June 17 convention.[63] By the end of April, even some groups opposed to Mahoney and Teigan urged attendance at St. Paul. The *Minnesota Leader*, for example, argued that farmers should

[59] March 13, 14, 1924, *passim*, March 15-April 30, 1924.
[60] *Literary Digest*, V. 81, No. 3 (April 19, 1924), pp. 14-16.
[61] *Sioux Falls Press*, March 27, 1924.
[62] Conference held in Samuel Gompers' office, April 21, 1924, Files, Office of the President, Samuel L. Gompers, Conferences 1919-1930, Box 58, Wisconsin State Historical Society. Hereafter referred to as Gompers papers.
[63] Mahoney to Teigan, St. Paul, February 21, 1924, *loc. cit.; Galesburg Labor News*, April 18, 1924, for a Hopkins statement urging attendance at St. Paul and support of La Follette; Hopkins to Hillquit, New York, May 14, 1924, Hillquit papers.

attend, reasoning that if the anti-Communists stayed away, "the Communists will most certainly rule the roost."[64]

As June approached, it appeared that Mahoney's prediction of over two thousand delegates in St. Paul might be low. Several straws in the wind indicated the direction events were going. Among them were letters from Senator Magnus Johnson to Ray McKaig of the Progressive Party of Idaho and to Tom Ayres of South Dakota, assuring them that the senator supported a third party, and that he had placed no obstacle in the path of June 17 (although he specifically declined to express a preference for June 17 over July 4). In addition, railroad union leaders in Minnesota approached Mahoney, admitted that *Labor* had been wrong and asked the *Minnesota Union Advocate* to cease its counterattack against the brotherhood organ.[65]

Mahoney, of course, was eager to do so, but the Minnesota railroad men did not speak for the national leadership of the brotherhoods. Except for the Socialists, the CPPA leadership was dead set against the formation of a genuine third party, the more so because such a step would entirely alienate Gompers and the AFL. Johnston viewed the situation in Minnesota with apprehension, and had warned Mahoney about the inclusion of the Workers' Party.[66]

AFL officials, particularly Gompers, anxiously watched the developments in Minnesota. At a conference on April 21, Gompers told his fellow unionists Frank Morrison, W. C. Roberts, and Paul J. Smith that the new party would "play into the hands of Moscow." Its continuation, Gompers added, could only injure the nonpartisan political campaigns of the AFL. In order to prevent this, and put a stop to the further develop-

[64] April 28, 1924.
[65] Magnus Johnson to Tom Ayres, n.p., May 2, 1924, Teigan papers. *MUA*, May 8, 15, 1924; see also, *Detroit Labor News*, May 23, 1924, for editorial statement similar to Johnson's.
[66] Minutes of Conference to discuss the "St. Paul Communist Convention," April 28, 1924, Gompers papers.

ment of the movement, Gompers called a large group of trade unionists and progressive congressmen to a meeting the next week.[67]

The meeting of April 28 was attended by Senators Magnus Johnson and Henrik Shipstead of Minnesota; the Minnesota representatives Oscar E. Keller, Ole J. Kvale, and Knud Wefald; Wisconsin congressman Joseph D. Beck, John M. Nelson, Hubert H. Peavey, and George J. Schneider; and several trade unionists, including Gompers, Morrison, Smith, William H. Johnston, James Duncan, and Edward Keating. "Speaking freely" of the "substantial success" of the Farmer-Labor Party in a few states, Gompers warned that the Communists controlled the Farmer-Labor movement, and that "unless something is done to expose this convention, your senatorial togas will go and we will be set back a decade." William Johnston and some of the congressmen present supported Gompers, but others resisted direct opposition to Mahoney. Representative Keller remarked that Mahoney "had given good service," and Senator Johnson said he hoped these suspicions were not well founded. Teigan was his secretary. Johnson would "go into no convention that will have anything to do with Ruthenberg and Foster," yet he observed that men like R. D. Cramer had been "very active" in his recent campaign. Johnson did not wish to offend Gompers, but he knew that La Follette would in all likelihood be nominated by the FLP, since Coolidge's nomination was certain. All in all, Johnson appeared reluctant to accept Gompers' view but was not inclined to offend the aged leader.

Paul Smith, speaking for the AFL, admitted that Mahoney and Teigan were honest and able, but said they had poor judgment and had "been trapped" by Foster and Ruthenberg. To this, Senator Shipstead replied that Mahoney "was always for labor." Gompers conceded this, and said that he allowed for "a certain percent of mistakes," but, he added, "when mistakes

[67] Minutes of conference on third-party politics, April 21, 1924, Gompers papers.

have been made and repeated, no defense can be made." The rest of the conference led no place. Obviously reluctant to break with Mahoney and his movement, the congressmen were also respectful of Gompers and wary about his charges of communism. Representative Wefald remarked that Farmer-Laborites should not "waver because we are called Communists," and when Representative Beck asked him what he would do if the Communists got behind him, he replied that "it can have no effect." This led to the following exchange:

Beck: We will say you are opposed to the dictation of the proletariat?
Wefald: Yes.
Johnson: We cannot afford to get into any groups with which Foster and Manley are connected.
Wefald: We do not want the reds.
Duncan: Are you prepared to repudiate the dictation of the proletariat?
Nelson: I wish to thank those present for the information I have received. I did not know what was going on. . . . We have to do everything to purge ourselves, to disavow any connection with Communists.

But some of the congressmen were unconvinced. Keller concluded that he would "not recognize the statements made about Russia and the Communists as facts." Kvale and Nelson, along with Edward Keating, on the other hand, were concerned about rescuing La Follette from Mahoney and his associates. No one had a proposal to put forward.[68]

There was, of course, only one way to destroy the Farmer-Labor movement and that was to deprive it of its candidate. It is not possible to say how much pressure the CPPA and the AFL leaders exerted on La Follette to induce him to attack Mahoney's efforts in his behalf, but it seems certain that the urging must have been insistent. For over eight months, La Follette had allowed dozens of respected labor leaders, farmers, politicians, and liberals publicly to advocate his nomination

[68] Minutes of the Conference of April 28, 1924, *loc. cit.*

on an independent ticket in 1924. He could not openly acknowledge or welcome these overtures, but he could easily have denounced or discouraged them. Instead, according to Mahoney, he gave assurances "that the third party movement could depend on [him] to lead it this fall," and added that "there must be a third party."[69] Throughout this period, La Follette gave no indication, public or private, that he would repudiate the Farmer-Laborites but had encouraged Teigan and Mahoney to believe he would accept their nomination. Until late in May, both friend and foe of the Farmer-Labor Party movement assumed not only that La Follette would be nominated in St. Paul but that he would accept the nomination.

V

On May 29, 1924, La Follette released a letter to Herman L. Ekern, attorney general of Wisconsin. In it, the senator publicly took cognizance of the St. Paul convention for the first time. He wrote that he would not declare himself were it not for the fact that followers in many different parts of the country planned to attend, and that his name was being used in such a manner as to convey the impression that the convention had his approval. Expressing "no doubt that very many of those" involved in bringing about the St. Paul meeting were "actuated by the purest desire to promote genuine political and economic progress," La Follette declared that the June 17 convention would "not command the support of the farmers, the workers, or other progressives," because of the "fatal error" of admitting the Communists into the coalition. Quoting from the *Daily Worker*, he charged that their ultimate aim was not democracy, but "a soviet form of government and the dictatorship of the proletariat." The Communists were acting under "orders from the Communist International in Moscow." To prove this, he quoted from a Central Executive Committee

[69] St. Paul *Pioneer Press*, March 15, 1924.

statement that had appeared in the *Daily Worker* on May 16. Signed by both Foster and Ruthenberg, the statement recalled that "in order to settle the question of whether the Farmer-Labor united front was a policy that a communist party" should follow, it had been submitted to the Communist International for decision. Foster and Ruthenberg went on to quote a cable-gram from the Executive Committee of the Communist International which said, in part, that the Comintern "urges C.E.C. not to slacken activities preparation June 17. Utilize every available force to make St. Paul convention great representative gathering labor and left wing."

La Follette also charged that the Communists had already "secured a strategic position" in the direction of the convention. C. A. Hathaway, an avowed Communist, was secretary-treasurer of the Committee on Arrangements for St. Paul, and Joseph Manley, Foster's son-in-law, was also on the Committee of Arrangements (as head of the Federated Farmer-Labor Party). Without questioning "the right of the Communists, under the Constitution," to submit their issues to the people, La Follette concluded that they were "antagonistic to the progressive cause and their only purpose in joining such a movement is to disrupt it." Under such circumstances, to "pretend that the Communists can work with the progressives is deliberately to deceive the public."[70]

La Follette's letter threw the supporters of the St. Paul convention into complete confusion. The day it appeared Hopkins wrote Johnston of the CPPA that he now planned to support the CPPA and send his delegates to Cleveland. He had, he added, always been wary of Communist control.[71] In the next week, many others who had either supported Mahoney or remained neutral between Cleveland and St. Paul, joined in the exodus. The *Detroit Labor News*, which had earlier stood firmly between the two conventions, now supported La Follette and

[70] Text in *The Herald Tribune*, May 29, 1924.
[71] Hopkins to Johnston, New York, May 29, 1924, copy in Hillquit papers.

the CPPA.[72] The *Wyoming Labor Journal* followed suit.[73] In Minnesota, too, there was a deep split over the role of the Communists. Those forces, such as the *Minnesota Leader,* that had opposed Mahoney used the La Follette letter as the basis for sharp attacks.[74]

Charles E. Taylor wrote Teigan from Montana that he could not understand how a man of La Follette's obvious personal courage and integrity could "lie about those who have stood so loyally by him, in order to . . . win the support of the luke-warm respectable good for nothing middle class liberals." Why he would destroy the hopes of the workers and farmers "God only can answer," Taylor complained. But Taylor understood that "the capitalist press are shouting for glee—for good reason." They knew, he added, "that Bob and his advisors have lost their political sense," for "Wall Street fears not Cleveland, it fears St. Paul."[75]

Others also recognized that La Follette's move had been directed against the formation of a third party, rather than against the Communists. In Milwaukee, where Socialists had recaptured the mayoralty by a record majority of 18,000 votes only a few weeks before, Victor Berger's *Milwaukee Leader* condemned La Follette's action. Since 1920, Berger had favored a national labor party and had moved toward cooperation with the Progressives. In 1922, the Socialists in Wisconsin had supported La Follette in order to help him vindicate his wartime acts. Later, the Wisconsin delegates to the CPPA meeting voted with Fitzpatrick for the immediate formation of a Farmer-Labor Party. This stand the Wisconsin group reaffirmed in May 1924, despite the walkout of five railroad unions from the state CPPA convention.[76] Only the day before La Follette re-

---

[72] June 6, 1924.
[73] June 6, 1924.
[74] June 11, 1924.
[75] Charles E. Taylor to Teigan, Plentywood, Montana, June 8, 1924, Teigan papers.
[76] *St. Louis Labor,* May 31, 1924.

leased his letter to the press, Berger had said in a speech before
the House of Representatives "that now is the psychological
moment for the creation of a new party."[77] The *Leader* agreed
that the inclusion of Communists was an error, but whether or
not it was a fatal error (as La Follette charged), remained to
be seen. "Had La Follette wanted the convention to be a success," the *Leader* observed, "had he wanted to overwhelm the
Communists and make them look like a frog in the ocean—
had he wanted a strong and virile new party formed, all he
had to do was urge his supporters to go to the convention in
large numbers."[78]

Despite La Follette's attack on the June 17 convention, the
Leader urged unions and others to send a big delegation to
St. Paul and prevent Communist control. Taking a similar position, the *Duluth Labor World* argued that "if the Communists
now get control of the June 17 convention, it will be because
of the advice to union labor and progressives recently given
by Senator La Follette and the National Non-Partisan Political
Campaign Committee of the AFL."[79] This point of view found
some support in the remaining two weeks before the scheduled
opening of the St. Paul convention. In Milwaukee, a meeting
of District 73 of the International Association of Machinists
endorsed the convention; State Senator Charles E. Taylor of
Montana wired that his Party remained firm; Duncan Mc-
Donald, head of the newly formed Illinois Farmer-Labor Party,
commented that La Follette was "not needed"; and the *Baltimore Afro-American* reiterated its support of the Farmer-Labor
Party.[80]

---

[77] Quoted in the *Daily Worker*, June 3, 1924.
[78] *Milwaukee Leader*, May 30, 1924. See also *St. Louis Labor*, which,
though more firmly committed to the CPPA than Berger, had also been
friendly to Mahoney. It did not report or comment on La Follette's
attack, March 22, April 12, 26, May 3, 10, 31, June 7, 1924.
[79] "Fear Not the Reds, But the Crooks," *Duluth Labor World*, June 7,
1924.
[80] *Daily Worker*, June 4, 19, 12, 1924.

To Teigan, Mahoney admitted that La Follette's statement had had a "very disconcerting effect." He realized that he and Teigan had "been undermined by the Washington group of labor leaders," whom he suspected of having written La Follette's letter. "We had things pretty well arranged so that the Communists would be unobtrusive in the convention," he reminded Teigan; "everything would have been put through without a disturbance," but now, "everybody is ready to throw a brick at the Communists or anybody who is in any way associated with them." As to the future, Mahoney said he would get out of the national convention if the state movement wanted him to; his first loyalty was to the state Party.[81] A few days later, however, Mahoney announced that there was much sentiment for a third party, even without La Follette, and that the Executive Committee of the FLP had decided that the convention would be held as planned. The Communists, Mahoney said, had not sneaked into the FLP, but had worked openly. The CPPA opposed the Minnesota movement not because of the Workers' Party role in it but because the brotherhoods saw the FLP as a threat to their power.[82] But even Minnesota was deeply split over the issue of the Communists and La Follette.

On June 17, only 542 delegates assembled in St. Paul. La Follette's attack had cut the expected size of the convention by 80 percent.[83] The delegates who came were strongly committed to the formation of a third party on the spot, but there was a great deal of sentiment for the nomination of La Follette. The Reverend James L. Beebe of Nebraska expressed the widely held view of the need for a third party: "If I wasn't a preacher," he proclaimed, "I would say to hell with the capitalist system right now."[84] Above all was the feeling that unity must be pre-

[81] Mahoney to Teigan, St. Paul, May 29, 1924, National Nonpartisan League papers.
[82] *Daily Worker*, June 3, 1924; *MUA*, June 5, 1924.
[83] Report of the Nation Farmer-Labor Convention, St. Paul, June 17, 1924, Mahoney papers; *MUA*, June 19, 26, 1924.
[84] Report of the National Farmer-Labor Convention, St. Paul, June 17,

served in the convention, so La Follette was neither nominated nor repudiated. Mahoney argued strongly against the immediate formation of an independent party, as the Communists and others desired. He considered the gathering a success in that it nominated Duncan McDonald for President with the specific understanding that he would withdraw when the CPPA nominated La Follette at Cleveland on July 4. Frank T. Starkey, president of the St. Paul Trades and Labor Assembly (and others), argued that the Communists and their allies controlled the convention with ease, and the dominant sentiment did favor the formation of a third party. The decisive test of strength came on this issue early when Mahoney, who advocated delay, was overwhelmingly defeated for permanent chairman by Charles E. Taylor, who advocated a new party even without La Follette. But while Mahoney could not win for delay, the Communists could not force through a repudiation of La Follette without disastrously splitting the convention, and so they agreed to the compromise on McDonald.[85]

Many of those who had supported the June 17 convention even after La Follette had attacked it shared Kate O'Hare's "sick and disappointed feeling about it all." Especially outside Minnesota, there were many who felt that "a great movement had been sacrificed to the rule or ruin policy of a very small group who know little, and seem to care less, of the psychology of the American people."[86] Mahoney disagreed. The weaknesses of the convention, he wrote, were the result of "the machinations of those who are opposed to a great national political movement of the farmers and workers."[87]

1924, Mahoney papers; *MUA*, June 19, 26, 1924. In 1922, Beebe had been the Progressive Party candidate for United States senator in Nebraska. He received 19,076 votes, or about 5%.

[85] On this, see Draper, *American Communism*, pp. 115-116; *MUA*, July 3, 1924; *Duluth Labor World*, June 28, 1924.

[86] "Choosing the Loser," *National Rip Saw*, July 1924.

[87] *MUA*, July 3, 1924; Foster admitted that La Follette could have controlled St. Paul "for the mere asking." He, too, accused La Follette of acting not out of fear of Communist control but out of fear of the formation of a genuine class party (*Daily Worker*, June 27, 1924).

In Cleveland, on July 4, the CPPA met. La Follette was nominated, as planned; Mahoney was denied a seat as a delegate because of his role in the June 17 convention. No third party was formed.

Those Socialists who had seen "The Socialist Party's Opportunity" in working with the CPPA were sorely disappointed.[88] They had hoped to see a labor party emerge in which they could participate, just as the Independent Labour Party worked within the British Labour Party. But except in those states, such as California and Nevada, in which the La Follette people were dependent on the Socialists for a place on the ballot, the CPPA leaders would not even cooperate with them during the campaign.[89] Indeed, even in Minnesota, where there was a powerful Farmer-Labor Party in existence, La Follette's managers, in order to broaden his appeal, insisted on an independent line. This strategy may have worked well in other states, but in Minnesota, La Follette ran 40,000 votes behind Floyd Olson, FLP candidate for governor.[90]

As for the Communists, despite La Follette's letter and the subsequent collapse of the St. Paul convention, they came out of the June 17 convention with substantial gains. Mahoney's attitude after the convention contrasted sharply to that of Fitzpatrick in 1923, largely because the Communists had appeared to compromise with Mahoney. Following the nomination of La Follette in Cleveland, however, it became clear that the difference was only in appearance. Ironically, La Follette's letter had served only to save face for the Communists. On June 1, two days after La Follette's attack was published, Foster had returned home from Moscow with the long-awaited decision on the relationship of the Workers' Party to the CPPA and a third ticket. The news was not good.

[88] Alfred Baker Lewis, "The Socialist Party's Opportunity," *St. Louis Labor,* March 15, 1924.
[89] Bertha Hale White to the National Executive Committee, Chicago, August 18, 1924, Hillquit papers.
[90] *Minnesota Union Advocate,* November 13, 1924. *Legislative Manual of the State of Minnesota, 1925* (Minneapolis 1925), facing p. 319. La Follette polled 339,000 votes to Olson's 380,000.

Foster had gone to Moscow for a meeting of the Executive Committee of the Communist International, held during April and May 1924. There he hoped to win endorsement for the Workers' Party "third-party alliance" policy. But as he later admitted, "No sooner did I hit Europe and explain it to the first revolutionist I met, than I encountered a drastic condemnation of it as a most dangerous opportunism." So it continued all the time Foster was on the Continent. "Never on my whole trip, in Russia and elsewhere," Foster added, "did I meet a single Communist who did not wholeheartedly repudiate this proposition. The action of the Comintern presidium was unanimous in rejecting it as a maneuver unfit for the Workers' Party to make." In the light of this, Foster added, "there is no need here to make further argument."[91]

The impact of this sudden decision left Alexander Bittelman somewhat dazed even a year later. "From January until May, until the Communist International decision became known to us," he wrote, "our party was basing its policy on the third party alliance." It was true, Bittelman added, that the last Party convention had referred the matter to the C.I., "but that did not help matters much from January until May for the reason that the Central Executive Committee and the party as a whole had to function." Observing that "political life does not stop for a Communist Party to make up its mind," Bittelman noted that during these months the Party had acted on the basis of "a policy in which it believed," that it "was nearly unanimous in believing that the policy of the third-party alliance was the policy to apply under these conditions." All its tactics, all its literature, all the slogans formulated during months from January to May "were based on this general idea of the third party alliance and then at a certain moment, the Communist International said to the party, you cannot do it." The Communists, Bittelman continued, were "confronted with the necessity of completely reorienting [themselves] practically within twenty-four hours, and comrades, a reorientation which was to take place . . . on the open political arena, under the very fire of the enemy" (since at about the same time, La Follette and Gompers had opened their attack on the June 17 convention). "We maintain," Bittelman concluded, that the "ability of our party to . . . have changed within one day, almost, fundamentally, our main political line" was "proof not only of the political flexibility of the Central Executive Committee, but also of the discipline and Communist quality of the party as a whole."[92]

La Follette's attack made the job of a complete reversal of policy in twenty-four hours easier for the Communists. If La Follette had allowed the Farmer-Labor convention in St. Paul to go ahead as planned, it would have been many times larger than it was, and it would overwhelmingly have endorsed him and repudiated Communist attempts to denounce an alliance with him and the CPPA. As it was, many who attended on June 17 had a greater devotion to a genuine Farmer-Labor Party than to La Follette personally. The majority were willing to go along without La Follette, as the lopsided vote for Taylor against Mahoney indicated. But a substantial minority in St. Paul still favored La Follette, and this included Mahoney, Teigan, R. D. Cramer, and most of the other leading trade unionists in Minnesota. Since the Communists hesitated to repeat the mistake of 1923, a compromise was arranged at the convention. After La Follette was nominated in Cleveland, however, the Communists were forced into a split anyway. On July 8, the Communist-controlled National Executive Commit-

[92] "The Report of the Party's Executive," *Daily Worker*, August 29, 1925. The International had declared against the third-party alliance because it was "a united front at the top," as contrasted to a united front from below. The former was not permissible, according to early Communist dogma, because it was reminiscent of Socialist participation in the war-time governments and in anti-Soviet machinations of the western European states. Only a united front from below, in which the Communists attemted to win over the rank and file of other organizations, thereby separating them from their (seemingly inevitably) "corrupt" leaders, was good Communist practice. For an admission that "all factions alike were responsible," see Joseph Manley, "Minority Mumbo-Jumbo—The Farmer-Labor Party," *Daily Worker*, January 7, 1925.

tee of the new Party, organized at St. Paul, met and issued a statement withdrawing McDonald, and nominating Foster for President and Benjamin Gitlow for Vice President.[93]

During the campaign the Communists finished the job of alienating those who had recently been closest to them. The Communists, Mahoney wrote, devoted their "entire campaign" in Minnesota to "villification of La Follette and leaders of the Farmer-Labor Party." Their tactics, he concluded, "were apparently well calculated to destroy the progressive movement of the state and nation."[94]

This appeared to be true. Prepared to support La Follette only four months before, the *Daily Worker* in August observed that "American Fascism" was "strongly represented" in his ranks. Again, in October, the paper called La Follette's supporters "the American expression of reformist national socialism" who "when a real crisis comes for capitalism" would "become fascist openly as in Italy or mask their terrorist activities behind a thin veil of parliamentarism as in Germany."[95] Not content to attack Mahoney, Foster maligned Debs for his "capitulation to this petty-bourgeois reformer." The "petty-bourgeois united front," Foster wrote, "is now complete from Hearst to Debs." In reply Debs noted: "You may be right in your criticism of my position and I may be wrong, as I have often been before. Having no Vatican in Moscow to guide me I must follow the light I have."[96]

For the Communists these tactics won only a new level of isolation from American radicalism. Thus, despite the fact that Bentall, running as a Communist, received 5,306 votes in the Eighth Congressional District primary in June, Foster received only 4,400 votes in all of Minnesota in November.[97] In Decem-

---

[93] See Draper, *American Communism*, pp. 117-118.
[94] *Minnesota Union Advocate*, November 13, 1924.
[95] *Daily Worker*, August 30, October 19, 1924.
[96] *American Appeal*, August, 1924. Also cited in Shannon, *op. cit.*, p. 178.
[97] *Legislative Manual of the State of Minnesota, 1925* (Minneapolis 1925), facing p. 319, p. 307.

ber, R. D. Cramer, who the previous March had said that "no movement" could "live and be successful" without the Communists, initiated the expulsion of C. A. Hathaway as a delegate to the Minneapolis Trades and Labor Assembly. The following September, with Mahoney's approval, the convention of the Minnesota Federation of Labor adopted an amendment to its constitution, barring Communists from sitting as delegates to its meetings.[98] The process of isolation was complete. Once again, the Communists had managed to turn their closest allies into staunch anti-Communists.

However, the Socialists did not gain much from supporting La Follette. Of La Follette's 4,826,471 votes, 858,264 were recorded on the Socialist line. But this total is somewhat misleading, since in some states, notably California, La Follette did not have an independent line and all his votes were recorded as Socialist. What really mattered was that the Socialists had sacrificed much of their remaining organizational and political resources in a campaign that did not lead to the results they desired. Soon after the end of the campaign, the AFL announced that the election had proven, once again, the fallacy of independent action, and that the trade unions were returning to their old nonpartisan policies. The Socialists were left high and dry. Victor Berger had been returned to Congress, but other than in Milwaukee and one or two other cities, the Party had no organization. It was thoroughly demoralized. "The hope for an American labor party," wrote Debs, "lies not in the official labor leaders, but in the rank and file." As Debs realized, however, the rank and file were in no position to launch a new party upon "the foul and stagnant waters of American politics."[99]

[98] *Daily Worker,* March 13, December 20, 1924; *MUA,* September 24, 1924.
[99] Eugene V. Debs, "The American Labor Party," *Socialist World,* January 1925; Shannon, *op. cit.,* pp. 179-180.

9 · CONCLUSION

The events surrounding La Follette's candidacy were filled with irony. Having gained AFL support by his attack on the Minnesota Farmer-Laborites and the Workers' Party, he was condemned by the Republicans throughout the campaign as a front for the Third International. For its part, the AFL, having broken its self-imposed rule and embarked on its first independent presidential endorsement, contributed almost no money to the Progressives, and gradually withdrew its support so that by the end of October it was almost openly apologizing for its association with La Follette.[1] For the radicals, the greatest irony lay in the fact that although La Follette polled almost five million votes—far more than any previous candidate of labor and the Socialists—the events preceding the election had almost completely disrupted, and all but obliterated, the Socialist, Communist, and Farmer-Labor party movements.

The 1924 elections marked the end of the Farmer-Laborites' dream of organizing a national third party of radicals and progressives. Since the inception of the National Labor Party in early 1919, the movement had been attacked from two directions. Initially, it suffered from the hostility of the AFL leadership, whose pressure forced many central labor bodies to withdraw their support. The implacable opposition of the labor

---

[1] The action of the AFL in dissociating itself, as much as possible, from La Follette even during the campaign, suggests that the Federation's support was given not as a change in policy, but as an inducement for the senator to repudiate Mahoney and to destroy the Farmer-Labor Party movement.

bureaucracy was predictable. The perspective of the Farmer-Labor movement was essentially Socialist from the inception of the movement to its demise in 1924. A major section of the Farmer-Labor leadership came from the Socialist Party when it split in 1919: Max Hayes; Christian Madsen and William Rodriguez of Chicago; Duncan McDonald of the Illinois Miners; Robert J. Wheeler of Allentown, Pennsylvania; Thomas Van Lear of Minneapolis; John C. Kennedy and Hulet M. Wells of the state of Washington; and William Mahoney and H. G. Teigan. Max Hayes explained in 1919 that his participation in the Labor Party did not mean a renunciation of his Socialist principles, and William Mahoney made it clear in 1923 that he aimed at the "ultimate transformation of an industrial system that causes strife and suffering."[2] Even the non-Socialists in the Farmer-Labor leadership, men like Fitzpatrick, and John F. McNamee of the Brotherhood of Locomotive Firemen and Engineers, shared this outlook and sought cooperation with the Socialists.

For their part, the Socialists could never quite bring themselves to work with the Farmer-Laborites. In 1920, as we have seen, the Party was not ready to relinquish its claim as the only legitimate center of working-class politics in the United States, and thus withdrew Debs' name from consideration at the Farmer-Labor Party convention. By 1923, after a brief period of cooperation, the two movements again had drawn apart when the Chicago Farmer-Laborites prematurely attempted to organize a national party. And finally in 1924, the Socialists decided not to join Mahoney, both because of their own close but tenuous association with the CPPA, whose leaders they feared to antagonize, and because of Mahoney's association with the Workers' Party.

Whether or not Socialist cooperation with the Minnesota Farmer-Laborites would have made any difference by 1924 is a moot point. What is significant is that the Farmer-Laborites

[2] "The Ultimate Aim of Organized Labor," *MUA*, March 22, 1923.

desired such cooperation with the Socialists from 1919 forward, as well as with the Communists after the formation of the Workers' Party in 1922. Failure to bring about unity on the left, in other words, did not arise from the policies or ideology of the Farmer-Labor party movement. Caught between the warring Socialist sects on the Left and the trade union bureaucracy on the Right, the Farmer-Labor movement was severely limited in its potential. The extent of its popular appeal in Minnesota, Washington, South Dakota, Southern Illinois, and Eastern Iowa indicates that popular radicalism was widespread in the first half of the 1920's. Before 1919 the Socialist Party had united within its folds almost all the forces attracted to the three movements—Socialist, Farmer-Labor, and Workers' Party—in the early 1920's. No organization was able to do this from 1919 forward, but that was not because radical anti-capitalism was on the wane.

II

For the Socialist Party, 1924 ended all hope either of becoming a major national movement in its own right or of being an essential participant in a coalition on the left. After two dozen years of activity, the Socialist Party had returned to the beginning, except that its initiative, youth, and identification with the international revolutionary movement had passed to the Communists. Debs' death in 1926 symbolized the fate of the Party. For another two decades the Socialists would continue to go through the motions, but they would never regain their position as the political center of American radicalism.

The Party had reached the peak of its strength just halfway to 1924. As we have seen, its decline was not a simple or steady process of disintegration. From 1912 until the United States entered the war, the Socialist Party remained a vital radical force in America, despite the widespread disillusionment with the world Socialist movement that followed the failure of the European Socialists to prevent, or even to oppose, the war in

1914. While it lost support and strength in some areas in these years, it gained adherents and influence in others. During the war the Party sustained serious losses. Many of its best-known intellectuals and trade unionists quit it to support the war. Socialist newspapers and magazines were banned from the mails and hundreds of locals were disrupted or destroyed. In addition, the federal government prosecuted hundreds of Socialists under the Espionage Acts of 1917 and 1918, while local and state vigilante groups denied halls to Socialists and broke up their meetings in thousands of small towns and cities throughout the country. To make the world safe for democracy, the Wilson Administration sponsored a reign of terror far worse than any conducted in Europe, either among the Allied Powers or within the German Empire.

Nevertheless, despite these unprecedented denials of even the most elementary democratic rights, the Party grew in size and prestige during the war. As the only national political organization in opposition to the Administration's war policies, the Socialists won support from substantial numbers of Americans. In addition, after the Russian Revolution in November 1917, thousands of immigrants flocked into the Party. By 1919, Party membership had climbed back to 109,000, only a few thousand below its 1912 total. There were, however, many differences between the postwar and prewar parties. First, the geographical distribution of Party membership and strength had shifted heavily eastward and into the large cities. States like Oklahoma, Texas, Nevada, Montana, Idaho, and Minnesota no longer led in relative numbers of Socialists, whereas New York City, Milwaukee, Buffalo, Cleveland, and Chicago did. New York, for example, had contributed only 7.6 percent to the total Socialist vote in 1916, but it accounted for 22 percent of Debs' vote in 1920.[3]

---

[3] Since the 1916 national total was only 590,000, against 915,000 in 1920, the absolute increase in New York was even greater—from 45,000 to 203,000.

Second, as a concomitant of the first, the percentage of foreign born in the Party increased sharply during the war years, from 20 percent before the war to 53 percent just before the split.

Third, under the impact of the Russian Revolution and the expulsion of pro-war Socialists, the Party as a whole had shifted decisively to the left. This movement was accelerated by a conviction, even among such "right-wingers" as the Milwaukee Socialists, that the AFL had proven to be hopelessly corrupt, and that it had acted as the "tail of capitalism."[4] All factions in the Party actively supported the Russian Revolution, fought for recognition and trade, and opposed the American invasion of Siberia.

When the war ended, Socialists of every tendency looked to the future with optimism. They did so not only because of the revolutionary wave that seemed to be sweeping Europe but because their criticisms of the war were daily being vindicated. As the details of the postwar settlement became public, it was clear to all that the war had not been one for democracy, that it had not ended colonialism, that secret diplomacy had not been repudiated, that the people of the world had not won the right of self-determination. In other words, Wilson's Fourteen Points had been proven a sham. Furthermore, within the United States, workers and farmers were finding that their wartime gains had been only temporary, and that those who pressed for fulfillment of wartime promises were branded as Bolsheviks. Given a period in which it could rebuild its organization and press, prospects looked bright to the Socialists in 1919.

The Party was, of course, not to have that opportunity. Instead, it faced further organizational disintegration as a result of the Bolshevik insistence that the Russian Revolution was only the first step in the imminent overthrow of world capitalism. The Russians, as we have seen, not only desired revolution in the West but believed their own survival was

[4] Victor Berger, above, p. 178.

impossible without it. For three years following their revolution, they called on all Socialists to rise and seize power without delay and looked upon those who refused to do so as traitors to the working class. This policy led to a series of splits in the European Socialist parties, although in countries such as Germany, Britain, and France it was partly obscured by the earlier splits which had resulted from the support given the war by the Socialist leaders. In Germany, the Socialists had not only joined the wartime government but had also participated in the attacks on the Bolsheviks after the revolution. In Europe, in other words, the basis for splitting with the pro-war Socialists was real, even though the Bolshevik demands for immediate revolution had been inappropriate in some countries.

Whatever political justification existed for the splits in Europe, there was none in the United States. The so-called right wing of the American Socialist Party had opposed the war with at least as much vigor as the left. But immediate revolution was out of the question in the United States, and those Socialists who recognized this pushed for unity and reorganization, rather than for splits and insurrectionary tactics. Only a small group of English-speaking Socialists took up the cry for revolution in 1919, supported—or rather pushed—by the vast majority of newly recruited Eastern Europeans in the Party foreign language federations. One of the reasons the Left moved so easily toward its mistaken position was that many of its most effective and respected leaders were revolutionaries from Europe or Asia who had sought sanctuary in the United States during the war. In the early organizational activity of the new left wing, Trotsky, Bukharin, V. Volodorsky, Grigorii Chudnovsky, and Mme. Kollantai were both active and prominent. So was Sen Katayama, who returned to the United States from his native Japan in 1916, and followed the Russians to Moscow after the split. Even among the English-speaking Socialists who organized the Communist Labor Party, foreigners were prominent. The Irish Socialists, James Larkin, Eadmonn MacAlpine, one of the original editors of *The Revolutionary Age* in 1918, and Jack Carney, editor of the Duluth left-wing paper *Truth*, were heavily influenced by European syndicalism. Larkin came to the United States when war broke out in 1914 and recognized his limited understanding of conditions in the United States, but still helped lead the movement toward a Communist party.[5]

Most of the Americans who joined the left wing and helped form the Communist Labor Party (the majority of the Party in such states as California and Washington) had no concept of what later came to be called the Leninist party. Quite the contrary, they had traditionally opposed Hillquit and Berger as bureaucrats, and had advocated greater decentralization and autonomy. In 1914, Robert F. Hoxie, a political economist at the University of Chicago, confided to Ralph Easley that "the chief trouble with the Socialist party is lack of discipline. When a majority decision is reached (especially if the minority is ultra-radical, red, IWW-ish) the minority gets up on its hind legs and yells 'boss rule,' 'steam roller.'" Hoxie's conclusion was that the Socialist situation indicated "the impossibility of attempting to combine democracy and efficiency";[6] but we know now that this seemingly inefficient, yet open and diverse Party, was much more viable than the highly centralized and disciplined Communist parties of the 1920's and 1930's. The native left-wingers who went Communist did so out of romantic identification with the Russian Revolution, and because of the panicked, bureaucratic action of the Old Guard in expelling the foreign-language federations in the spring of 1919. But few of them could remain for long in a Party that boasted, as Alexander Bittelman did in 1924, of its ability to change its line in twenty-four hours at the behest of the International, despite

[5] Draper, *Roots*, pp. 81, 132; Hyman Kublin, *Asian Revolutionary, The Life of Sen. Katayama* (Princeton, 1964), pp. 251-252; Emmet Larkin, *James Larkin, 1876-1947* (Cambridge, 1965), Chapter X, p. 236.
[6] Robert F. Hoxie to Easley, Chicago, March 11, 1914, NCF papers.

the fact that the policy changed was that of an overwhelming majority and had been followed successfully for six months.

Had the Party still been 70 percent native born, substantial unity might have been preserved. But almost to a man the Eastern European federations sided with the position of the Third International. Together with some 15 percent of the English-speaking Socialists—whose ranks were increased by the unprincipled maneuvers of the Old Guard—they split off to form the several new Communist parties.

After the split the Socialist Party was in an anomalous position. Friendly to Soviet Russia, it was unceasingly and bitterly attacked by the Third International and the American Communist parties. Actually, by expelling seven language federations and the state organizations of Michigan and Massachusetts, the Right had effectuated the split. But it was the Left that had pursued the policies that made the split inevitable. Under the impact of these attacks, and with a growing belief that the example of the British Labour Party was more relevant to American conditions than the Russian experience, the Socialists moved gradually away from close identification with the Bolsheviks. By 1925, the Party convention was openly and sharply critical of the Russians.[7] Increasingly, the Party leadership took this position, although for the next decade many leaders—James H. Maurer and Norman Thomas, for example —remained defenders of the Soviets.

But the Socialist position, theoretically sound, was politically untenable. As the Party moved away from identification with the world revolutionary movement it suffered a steady stream of defections to the Workers' Party. At the same time, as it espoused a British-style labor party it experienced continuous losses to the various Farmer-Labor party movements. At first the Socialists reacted to the Labor Party by jealously guarding their own leadership. Later, when it had become clear that their Party was disintegrating, they tied their hopes so closely

[7] *Socialist World*, April 1925.

to the CPPA that they were unwilling to cooperate with the
Chicago or Minnesota Farmer-Laborites. In 1924 they finally
won admission to a major coalition of labor and the left, but
when the trade unions abandoned independent political action
after the La Follette campaign, the Socialists were stranded
and isolated. From then on the Party declined steadily until
the crash of 1929 revived it and gave it brief renewed growth
in the 1930's.

III

Unlike the Socialists, the Communists were not to have their
major impact on American political life until the middle 1930's.
Even so, the events of 1924 established the pattern of their
work and revealed their insurmountable weaknesses, marking
them as essentially irrelevant and as a divisive political force
among radicals. Ironically, the Communists' primary source of
strength and appeal also made success as a mass political movement impossible. Their relationship with the Third International attracted radicals and others who sought identification
with the world revolutionary movement, but their attempts to
duplicate the Russian experience and form of party organization alienated the Communists from American radicals, from
labor, and from the farmers. The very formation of the Communist parties had been a mistake, both from the point of view
of the best interests of the Socialist movement in the United
States and the national interests of Soviet Russia. At a time
when the Soviets desperately needed support, the Communists
had split the pro-Soviet radicals in the United States into a
myriad of warring sects. Nor had they merely debilitated the
Socialists. So far out of touch with American life were they
that in less than two years their original combined membership
of almost 70,000 had faded away to less than 10,000.

At the end of these two years, after it had become clear that
the revolutionary wave in Europe had receded, the American
Communists were rescued from permanent obscurity by the

insistence of the Third International that they give up their illegal status, begin to work in the trade unions, and adopt a program of immediate demands so as to appeal to the masses of American workers and farmers. In effect, the Communists had returned to the policies and assumptions of the Socialists in 1919, even though they still harbored illusions about securing positions of influence so that when the right moment came their small, tightly disciplined Party would be ready to seize power.

From 1922 to 1924 the Workers' Party developed a strategy of working within the Farmer-Labor movement in the same manner in which the Socialists hoped to work in a British-style labor party. Despite a theory of the united front that always implicitly (and often explicitly) viewed the leadership of organizations other than their own as traitors to or misleaders of labor, the Communists met with considerable success. True, in 1923 their sense of destiny led them to maneuver Fitzpatrick out of his own convention; but in 1924 the party demonstrated that it had learned from its mistake. Until Foster returned from Moscow with the disheartening news that their carefully worked out policy of third-party alliance was an impermissable "united front from above," the Communists had accomplished the considerable, and admirable, feat of working openly as Communists and still being accepted as an integral part of the Minnesota movement. Only as a result of the sudden Communist repudiation of La Follette, the unexpected nomination of Foster and Gitlow, and the subsequent Workers' Party campaign of vilification of its recent allies, were Mahoney, R. D. Cramer, and other Minnesota leaders converted to bitter anti-Communists, just as Fitzpatrick had been a year before. Stripped of their political prestige and made vulnerable to the pressures of the trade union bureaucracy, both the Chicago and Minnesota trade unionists had been made to look like political simpletons. But the Communists, constitutionally unable to admit responsibility for the political regressions forced upon

Fitzpatrick and Mahoney, added insult to injury by pointing to their retreat as proof of their innate corruption.

Of course, in later years the Communists would publicly admit that they had been mistaken, and that they should have supported La Follette,[8] but at the time even those who knew better were unable to oppose the abandonment of the third-party alliance. The reason for this had been made clear by H. M. Wicks, in an editorial in *The Worker*, on March 31, 1923. Writing at a time when there were still splinter groups outside the Workers' Party, Wicks warned that once these dissidents understood "our relation to the Communist International," they would see that the Workers' Party program was "the best Communist program ever issued in this country," and that "no Marxist can possibly criticize one line of it." He went on to prove this by pointing out that the Party's union work was "in complete harmony with the principles of the Red Trade Union International." Wick's final argument, however, was the decisive one. It was quite simple: Those who wished to avoid stigmatizing themselves as sectarians must join "the recognized Party." Otherwise, they would be forced to "remain outside the world movement."[9]

Wicks, of course, was correct. No matter how inappropriate a policy of the Third International might be, a Communist leader must espouse it. Even worse, since his position depended, more than anything else, on his loyalty to the International (or, in later years, to the Soviet Union), a leader of the Communist Party had to fight for the militant application of such a policy, despite his better knowledge or judgment. Failure to do so could not lead to a change in policy. Opposition could only lead to the isolation of the dissenter.

The Communists were proud of this. They counterposed the tight discipline of the Third International to the situation in

---

[8] Foster, *History of the Communist Party of the United States*, pp. 219-220.
[9] Sentence sequence altered.

the Second International which had allowed most of the European Socialist parties to betray their prewar pledges and to support the war. In compensating for the weaknesses of the Second International, however, the Communists did not attempt to develop a firmer adherence to socialist principles among the masses. Instead, they relied upon organizational means to guarantee ideological hegemony. It did not work; the establishment of a highly centralized "Leninist" party in the United States led to a procession of crises and splits and contributed to a continuous process of fragmentation of the broader radical movements. The Communists were not entirely to blame for the latter. As we have seen, their presence in the Minnesota movement was used as a pretext to attack the Farmer-Laborites by those opposed to a third party.

But the Communists certainly helped the enemies of radicalism, both by their concept of organization and their strategy. In the 1920's they openly proclaimed their intention to isolate the leaders of any organization with which they worked from the membership. In the 1930's and 40's, they acted in a similar manner, even though denying an intention to do so. At least until 1956, the Communists saw themselves as the only true socialists, and the Russian example as a model for American Socialism. Thus, in Foster's campaign speeches in 1932 he would devote a sentence or two to attacking Roosevelt and Hoover, and spend the bulk of his energies fulminating against the Socialists—as if the Socialist Party were the main barrier to revolution in the United States. Similarly, in reporting the vote in 1930, the *Daily Worker* listed the Socialists along with the Democrats and Republicans as a "capitalist" party.[10]

By the 1930's the Communists, not without a degree of Socialist acquiescence, had erected an entire mythology about the origins of their movement. In 1936, for example, Joseph Freeman described a meeting that had taken place in 1925 sponsored by the International Political Prisoners Committee.

[10] *Daily Worker*, November 5, 1930.

Among the scheduled speakers was Charney Vladeck, business manager of the anti-Soviet *Jewish Daily Forward,* by then a right-wing Socialist paper. Vladeck was to speak on political prisoners in Russia, following Carleton Beal's address on political prisoners in Latin America. When he began to speak the entire gallery "lumbered to its feet" and commenced to sing the "International," breaking up the meeting. This disturbed Freeman, and the next day he commented to a Communist organizer that it was too bad Communists and Socialists had to fight each other. "It's too bad," the organizer replied, "but whose fault is it? They split the labor movement when they supported the war, when they threw the left out of the Socialist party. They're splitting it now by kicking us out of the unions, by attacking the Soviet Union. We are with the socialist workers, and if they have anything against us it's because of the lies they are told by their misleaders."[11]

Similarly, John Gates, in a passage describing his conversion to communism while attending City College, reveals the manner in which this myth complemented the Communists' basic appeal. "Had not the Communists," Gates asks, "brought into being the first successful socialist country, the Soviet Union? And wasn't this accomplished over the opposition of the Socialists? Was not the Soviet Union moving forward with its Five Year plans, was it not planning production and abolishing unemployment when the richest country in the world, the United States, was in the throes of terrible depression?"[12]

IV

By the late 1920's both Socialist and Communist ideological positions concerning the Soviet Union had hardened and were central to the development of their political movements. Neither was able to view Russian Communism essentially within the

[11] Freeman, *American Testament,* pp. 349-351.
[12] John Gates, *The Story of an American Communist* (New York, 1958), p. 17.

context of Russian history. The Communists were committed to the view that the Soviets represented utopia, and that all of Russia's internal problems and experience had universal application. For their part, the Socialists tended to accept the Communist view that every policy forced upon the Soviets had general relevance and to see this as proof that the Russian experience was not a specific combination of Marxism and Russian history, but a new form of political theory. Insisting on evaluating the Soviets in terms of conditions in the United States, even those Socialists most friendly to the Russians adopted the position expressed by James H. Maurer in 1927. If, Maurer wrote, the Soviets were really anxious for the workers of the world to throw off the yoke of capitalism, they should "turn the old Russia of poverty, suffering, despair, and official corruption into a workers' paradise and then invite suffering humanity to look them over—in other words, demonstrate to the world their fitness as a proletarian government and the crumbling system of capitalism would pass into history."[13]

To the extent that Maurer and his comrades followed through on the implications of this statement, they were abdicating their responsibility as American Socialists. But this was not the main weakness of the multiform socialist parties in the 1920's and 1930's. Rather, it was the extent to which Soviet developments, for the most part irrelevant in so far as American workers and farmers were concerned, was so close to the center of Communist and Socialist attention. The major events in the United States did not shape basic Communist and Socialist attitudes in this period. The crash of 1929, the New Deal of the NRA and AAA, the policy of "neutrality" during the Spanish Civil War, the organizing drives of the CIO, and the process by which the United States became involved in the Second World War, loom large in Socialist and Communist histories of the late 1920's and 1930's; but the expulsion of Trotsky from the Russian Party in 1929, the adoption of the popular front policy

[13] *It Can Be Done*, p. 241.

in 1934, the Soviet treason trials in 1936, and the Nazi-Soviet pact in 1939 emerge as equally important milestones.

From 1929 to 1934 the Socialist Party did experience a resurgence under the leadership of Norman Thomas. Party membership increased and the number of locals multiplied to 1,600 (compared to 5,000 in 1917). In 1932, Thomas received 885,000 votes, and many leading intellectuals endorsed him. But the membership had a different character from that of the old Socialist Party. Farmers were virtually absent, strength among industrial workers and in the trade unions (except for the needle trades) was slight. The difference was symbolized by the contrast between Debs and Thomas. Debs came to socialism through his experience as a trade unionist and as a railroad worker; Thomas was converted during the World War as a pacifist Presbyterian minister. A Princeton graduate, he appealed to and brought into the Party many intellectuals and urban middle-class voters, but he did this more on the basis of a thoroughgoing program of reform than on the basis of an ideological commitment to social transformation. And, within the Socialist Party, those who fought to re-establish a revolutionary strategy were attacked by the Old Guard as Communist.[14] By 1934, a statement of the militant majority within the Socialist Party on war and on social transformation, although more mild than Hillquit's own writing before and during the World War, was condemned by the Old Guard as "anarchist, illegal and communist."[15] Two years later, when the Old Guard was gone, the debate was over the individual's relationship to the Party, with the newly allied Trotskyists insisting on the "Leninist" concept of total discipline. The merits of either debate are not of concern here. The point is that both the Communists and the Socialists had been hopelessly caught up in conflict over forms of organization, attitudes toward fellow So-

[14] Shannon, *op. cit.*, Chapters VII, IX, X and especially pp. 210-216, 224, 243.
[15] *Ibid.*, p. 240.

cialists, and concepts of strategy and tactics that did not grow out of American experience or the problems of transforming American society. The legacy of 1919 was the alienation of American socialism.

BIBLIOGRAPHY

Manuscript Collections

Socialist Party Collection, Duke University.
American Federation of Labor Papers, Files, Office of the President, Wisconsin State Historical Society.
Elizabeth Gurley Flynn Papers, Wisconsin State Historical Society.
Morris Hillquit Papers, Wisconsin State Historical Society.
Milwaukee Federated Trades Council Papers, Wisconsin State Historical Society.
William B. Rubin Papers, Wisconsin State Historical Society.
Robert Schilling Papers, Wisconsin State Historical Society.
David J. Saposs Papers, Wisconsin State Historical Society.
Algie M. Simons Papers, Wisconsin State Historical Society.
National Civic Federation Papers, New York Public Library.
Frank P. Walsh Papers, New York Public Library. ·
Randolph Bourne Papers, Special Collections, Columbia University.
Seth Low Papers, Special Collections, Columbia University.
George W. Perkins Papers, Special Collections, Columbia University.
J. G. Phelps Stokes Papers, Special Collections, Columbia University.
National Nonpartisan League Papers, Minnesota Historical Society.
Henry G. Teigan Papers, Minnesota Historical Society.
William Mahoney Papers, Minnesota Historical Society.
Minute Books of the New York Local of the Socialist Party, Tamiment Institute.
Minute Books of the American Labor Party, Tamiment Institute.

Federal Government Publications

Congressional Record, 65th Congress, Special Session, 1917.
————, 65th Congress, 2nd Session, 1918.
Hearings Before the Special Committee Concerning the Right of Victor L. Berger to be Sworn in as a Member of the Sixty-Sixth Congress, II Volumes, Washington, D.C., Government Printing Office, 1919.
Investigation of Strike in Steel Industry; Hearings before the Committee on Education and Labor, U.S. Senate, 66th Congress, 1st Session (Washington, D.C.: Government Printing Office, 1919).

341

United States Bureau of the Census, 14th Census, 1920, Volume III,
Washington, D.C., Government Printing Office, 1920.

State Government Publications

Alabama Official and Statistical Register, 1915.
Arizona Blue Book, 1915; 1917.
Annual Register of the State of Maine, 1918-19.
*A Manual for the Use of the General Court of the State of Massachu-
setts,* 1913; 1915; 1917; 1919.
Annual Report of the Board of Elections of the City of New York,
1913; 1914; 1915; 1916; 1917; 1918; 1919; 1920.
Annual Report of the Secretary of State of Ohio, 1916-17.
Biennial Report of the Secretary of State of Nevada, 1911-12; 1913-
14; 1915-16; 1917-18.
California Blue Book, 1913-1915; 1924.
Connecticut Register and Manual, 1916; 1917.
Directory of the State of Kentucky, 1916; 1920.
Directory of the State of Oklahoma, State Election Board, 1914, 1915,
1916, 1920, 1925.
Directory of the State of Tennessee, 1916.
*Eighteenth, Nineteenth, Twentieth Biennial Reports of the Secretary
of State of the State of Kansas,* 1911-12, 1913-14, 1915-16.
Illinois Blue Book, 1913-14; 1915-1916; 1917-1918; 1919-1920; 1921-
1922; 1923-1924.
Legislative Directory of the State of Vermont, 1917.
Legislative Manual of the State of Washington, 1913.
Manual of the Legislature of the State of New Jersey, 1916; 1917;
1920.
Manual for the Use of the Legislature of the State of New York,
1913; 1914; 1915; 1916; 1917; 1918; 1919; 1920.
Manual of the State of Rhode Island, 1912; 1917.
Manual of the State of South Dakota, 1917; 1919.
Maryland Manual, 1915-16; 1917-18.
Michigan Manual, 1917.
Minnesota Legislative Manual, 1913; 1915; 1917; 1919; 1921; 1923;
1925.
Mississippi Register, 1917.
Montana Federal, State and County Officials, 1919.
Nebraska Blue Book, 1918.
New York Red Book, 1918.
North Dakota Blue Book, 1916.

Official Register of the State of Iowa, 1913; 1917; 1919; 1921.

Official Manual of the State of Missouri, 1913-14; 1915-16; 1917-18; 1919-20.

Official Canvass of the Result of the Election in the Borough of Naugatuck (Connecticut), May 5, 1913.

Oregon Blue Book, 1917-1918.

Report of the Secretary of State of the State of Utah, 1911-12; 1915-16.

Result of the General Elections, 1916-1917 (New Jersey State Department).

Revolutionary Radicalism, Its History, Purpose and Tactics: Report of the Joint Legislative Committee Investigating Seditious Activities, Filed April 24, 1920 in the Senate of the State of New York, IV Volumes, 1920.

Roster of State, County, City, and Township Officials of the State of California, 1913.

Smull's Legislative Handbook of the State of Pennsylvania, 1913-14; 1915-16; 1917-18; 1919-20; 1921-1922.

Twelfth, Fourteenth Biennial Reports of the Secretary of State of the State of Washington, 1913; 1917.

West Virginia Legislative Handbook, 1917.

Wisconsin Blue Book, 1913; 1915; 1917; 1919; 1921; 1923; 1925.

Yearbook of the State of Indiana, 1917.

Convention, Conference and Meeting Minutes, Proceedings, and Reports

American Federation of Labor, *Report of the Proceedings of the Forty-Third Annual Convention,* 1923.

Brotherhood of Railway Carmen, *Proceedings of the Thirteenth Convention,* 1917.

Illinois State Federation of Labor, *Proceedings of the Thirty-Seventh Annual Convention,* 1919.

Minnesota State Federation of Labor, *Proceedings of the Thirty-Fifth Convention,* 1917.

———, *Proceedings of the Thirty-Sixth Convention,* 1918.

National American Women Suffrage Association, *Handbook and Proceedings of the Forty-Ninth Annual Convention,* 1918.

Socialist Party, Minutes of the National Convention, 1912.

———, *Minutes of the Emergency Convention, St. Louis,* 1917.

———, Proceedings of the Joint Conference of National Executive Committee and State Secretaries, 1918.

————, Proceedings of the National Convention, 1919.
United Brewery and Soft Drink Workers of America, *Proceedings of the Twenty-First Convention*, 1917.
United Mine Workers of America, *Proceedings of the Twenty-Fifth Convention*, 1916.
Western Federation of Miners, *Official Proceedings of the Twenty-Second Annual and Second Biennial Convention*, 1916.
Wisconsin State Federation of Labor, *Report on Proceedings of the Twenty-Fifth Annual Convention*, 1917.

Newspapers and Other Periodicals

Advance (New York), 1917-1924.
Akron (Ohio) *Beacon-Journal*, 1917 (July-November).
Albany (New York) *Times-Union*, 1917 (September-November).
Allentown (Pennsylvania) *Democrat*, 1917 (September-November).
American Labor Monthly, 1923-24.
American Socialist (Chicago), 1915-1917 (May).
Appeal to Reason (New Appeal) (Girard, Kansas), 1912-1920.
Bakersfield (California) *Labor Journal*, 1916-1920.
Baltimore Labor Leader, 1917-1919.
Baltimore *News*, 1917 (August-November).
Birmingham (Alabama) *Age-Herald*, 1915, 1917.
Birmingham Labor Advocate, 1917.
Blairsville (Pennsylvania) *Courier*, 1917.
Brockton (Massachusetts) *Searchlight*, 1916-1921.
Brookneal (Virginia) *Union Star*, 1914-1918.
Brotherhood of Locomotive Firemen and Engineers' Magazine, 1922-24.
Buffalo *New Age*, 1918.
Buffalo *Express*, 1919 (October-November).
Buffalo Socialist, 1912.
Carmen's Journal (St. Louis?), 1917-1918.
Charleroi (Pennsylvania) *Union Worker*, 1915-16.
Chicago Socialist, 1912.
Chicago Tribune, 1917-1918.
Christian Socialist (Chicago), 1910-1917.
The Class Struggle (New York), 1917-1919.
Cleveland Citizen, 1914-1924.
Cleveland *News*, 1917 (August-November).
Cleveland *Plain Dealer*, 1917 (August-November).

Cleveland *Socialist News,* 1915-1916.

Columbus (Ohio) *Dispatch,* 1917 (October-November).

The Communist (Chicago), 1919 (May).

The Communist International (Petrograd), 1919.

Communist Labor Party News (New York), 1919.

Crisis (New York), 1912-1920.

Davenport (Iowa) *Democrat,* 1918, 1920.

Dayton (Ohio) *News,* 1917 (August-December).

Dayton (Ohio) *Journal,* 1917 (July-November).

Detroit Labor News, 1922-24.

Duluth Labor World, 1916-1924.

Duluth *Truth,* 1920-1922.

Erie (Pennsylvania) *Dispatch,* 1917 (August-November).

Eureka (Utah) *Reporter,* 1917 (April-November).

Eye Opener (Chicago), 1917-1920.

Galesburg (Illinois) *Labor News,* 1915-1924.

Gloversville (New York) *Herald,* 1917 (October-November).

Hagerstown (Maryland) *Globe,* 1917 (October-November).

Hamilton (Ohio) *Evening Journal,* 1917 (September-November).

Hammond (Indiana) *Times,* 1917 (November).

Indianapolis, *The Union,* 1912-1916.

Industrial Solidarity (Chicago), 1921.

Industrial Worker (Seattle), 1920.

Intercollegiate Socialist (Socialist Review), 1913-1920.

International Socialist Review, 1912-1918 (January).

Jamestown, New York, *Union Advocate,* 1917-1918.

Labor, 1923-1924.

Ladies Garment Worker, 1916-1919.

Liberator, 1919.

Lima, Ohio, *News,* 1917 (October-November).

Machinists Monthly Journal, 1912, 1916-1918, 1923-1924.

Madison, Wisconsin, *Capital Times,* 1917-1924.

Masses, 1912-1917.

Massillon, Ohio, *Evening Independent,* 1917 (October-November).

Messenger (New York), 1917-1924.

Miami Valley Socialist (Dayton, Ohio), 1914-1916, 1922-1923.

Milwaukee Journal, 1917-1918, 1924.

Milwaukee Leader, 1917-1920, 1924.

Miners' Magazine, 1912, 1916-1918.

Minneapolis Journal, 1917-1918.

Minneapolis Labor Review, 1917-1920.

Minnesota Leader, 1924.
Minnesota Union Advocate, 1923-1924.
Missoula, Montana, *New Northwest*, 1917-1923.
Muscatine, Iowa, *Journal*, 1918 (April-June).
Nation, 1917-1920, 1923-1924.
National Civic Federation Monthly Review, 1903-1912, 1920-21.
National Labor Journal (Pittsburgh), 1917.
National Rip Saw (American Guardian), 1916-1918, 1922-1924.
New Castle (Pennsylvania) *Herald*, 1917 (August-November).
New Justice (Los Angeles), 1919-1920.
New Majority (Chicago), 1919-1924.
New Review, 1913-1916.
New York *American*, 1917 (August-November).
New York *Call, passim*, 1912-1921.
New York *Evening Post*, 1917 (August-November).
New York *Herald*, 1917 (August-September).
New York *Herald-Tribune*, 1924 (April-May).
New York Times, 1917-1918, *passim*.
New York *Tribune*, 1917 (August-November).
New York *World*, 1917 (August-November).
Oakland (California) *World*, 1914-1922.
Ohio Socialist (Cleveland), 1919.
Oklahoma Federationist, 1924.
Philadelphia Public Ledger, 1917 (August-November).
Piqua, Ohio, *Leader-Dispatch*, 1917 (October-November).
Plymouth (Wisconsin) *Review*, 1917 (April-November).
Proportional Representation Review, 1914-1922.
Quarry Workers Journal (Barre, Vermont), 1916-1920.
Quincy (Illinois) *Labor News*, 1913-1915.
Rebel, Hallettsville, Texas, 1914-1917.
Reading, Pennsylvania, *News-Times*, 1917 (July-November).
Revolutionary Age (New York), 1918-1919.
Rochester, New York, *Democrat and Chronicle*, 1917 (October-November).
Rockford, Illinois, *Register-Gazette*, 1917 (March-April).
St. Louis Labor, 1911-1924.
St. Paul, *Pioneer Press*, 1924 (January-June).
Sandusky, Ohio, *Register*, 1917 (August-November).
Seattle, Washington, *Post-Intelligencer*, 1917-1918.
Seattle Union Record, 1919-20.
Sheboygan, Wisconsin, *Press*, 1917, 1919.
Sioux Falls, South Dakota, *Press*, 1924 (March-May).

Socialist Woman (Progressive Woman), 1908-1914.
Socialist World (American Appeal), 1920-1925.
The Spark Plug (Auto Worker), Buffalo, Chicago, 1917-1922.
Spokane (Washington) *Labor World*, 1923.
Syracuse, New York, *Herald*, 1917 (October-November).
Syracuse *Industrial Weekly*, 1917-1918.
The Tailor (Chicago), 1917-1920.
Toledo *Blade*, 1917 (August-November).
Toledo *News-Bee*, 1917 (July-November).
Toledo *Union Leader*, 1917-1920.
United Mine Workers Journal, 1914, 1924.
Western Worker (San Francisco), 1920.
Wisconsin Comrade (Milwaukee), 1914-1917.
Woman's Protest Against Woman Suffrage, 1914-1915.
Worker (Daily Worker), Chicago, 1922-1924.
Workers' Council (New York), 1921.
Wyoming Labor Journal (Cheyenne), 1923-1924.
Youngstown (Ohio) *Vindicator*, 1917 (August-November).

Unpublished Dissertations and Theses

Bush, Charles C., "The Green Corn Rebellion," Master's Thesis, University of Oklahoma, 1932.

Forcey, Charles B., "Intellectuals in Crisis: Croly, Weyl, Lippmann and the New Republic," Ph.D. dissertation, University of Wisconsin, 1954.

Iverson, Robert W., "Morris Hillquit, American Social Democrat," Ph.D. dissertation, University of Iowa, 1951.

Jensen, Maurice G., "The National Civic Federation: American Business in an Age of Social Reform, 1900-1910," Ph.D. dissertation, Princeton University, 1956.

McWhiney, Grady, "The Socialist Vote in Louisiana, 1912," Master's Thesis, Louisiana State University, 1951.

Seyler, William C., "The Rise and Decline of the Socialist Party in the United States," Ph.D. dissertation, Duke University, 1952.

Articles

(Articles appearing in periodicals listed in the Newspapers and Periodicals section are not cited here.)

"Americanism and Socialism," *The Outlook*, CXVI (June 13, 1917), 245.

"An American Labor Party," *Literary Digest*, LX (February 1, 1919), 14-15.

"A Presidential Straw Vote of Union Labor," *Literary Digest*, LII (October 7, 1916), 871-872.

Bates, Leonard J., "The Teapot Dome Scandal and the Election of 1924," *American Historical Review*, LX (January 1955), 303-322.

Benson, Allan L., "Socialism *vs.* Militarism," *The Independent* (October 30, 1916), 88.

————, "What War Has Done to Socialism," *Current Opinion.*

Best, Harry, "The Melting Pot in the United States," *Social Forces* (May 1936), 591-607.

Blumberg, Dorothy Rose, "Florence Kelly: Revolutionary Reformer," *Monthly Review*, XI (November 1959), 234-242.

Collegiate League for Hillquit, *Letter to New Republic* (October 27, 1917), pp. 356-357.

"Conference for Progressive Political Action," *Literary Digest*, CXXV (December 30, 1922), 11.

"Deporting a Political Party," *New Republic*, XXI (January 14, 1920), 186.

Dewhurst, Mary, "The Food Demonstrations in New York," *Current Opinion* (March 7, 1917), p. 405.

"Divergent Effects of the War on the Socialist Movement," *Current Opinion* (August 1917), pp. 73-75.

Dorr, Rheta Childe, "Breaking Into the Human Race," *Hampton's Broadway Magazine* (September 1911), pp. 317-327.

————, "The Twentieth Child," *Hampton's Broadway Magazine* (January 1912), pp. 793-796.

Douglas, Paul H., "The Socialist Vote in the Municipal Elections of 1917," *National Municipal Review*, VI (March 1918), 131-138.

Dubovsky, Melvin, "Organized Labor in New York City and the First World War," *New York History*, XLII (October 1961), 380-397.

"Efforts of American Pacifists to Avert War," *The Literary Digest* (February 24, 1917), p. 533.

Ferguson, Charles, "Business *vs.* Socialism," *Forum*, LV (May 1916), 614-624.

Gilbertson, H. S., "Municipal Revolution under Mayor Mitchel," *American Review of Reviews* (September 1917), pp. 300-303.

Goldman, Lawrence, "W. J. Ghent and the Left," *Studies on the Left*, III, 3 (Summer 1963), 21-40.

Hard, William, "John Mitchel," *Everybody's Magazine* (October 1917), pp. 465-478.

————, "Making Steel and Killing Men," *Everybody's Magazine*, XVII (November 1907), 579-592.

Hayes, Max S., "Socialists in the Unions," *Socialism and Organized Labor* (Girard, Kansas: Appeal to Reason, 1916).

Hooker, George E., "Conference," *Survey*, XLVII (March 11, 1922), 935-936.

Hoxie, R. F., "The Rising Tide of Socialism," *Journal of Political Economy*, XIX (October 1911), 609-631.

Hunter, Robert, "The Drift Toward Unity," *Socialism and Organized Labor* (Girard, Appeal to Reason, 1916).

"Intercollegiate Socialist Society Convention," *Survey*, XXXVIII (September 29, 1917), 578-579.

King, Murray E., "The Farmer-Labor Federation," *New Republic*, XXXVIII (April 2, 1924), 145-147.

"Labor Swallows the Forty-Eighters," *Survey*, XLIV (August 2, 1920), 587-588.

Leuchtenberg, William E., "Progressivism and Imperialism: The Progressive Movement and American Foreign Policy, 1896-1916," *Mississippi Valley Historical Review*, XXXIX (December 1952), 483-501.

Lovett, Robert Morss, "The Farmer-Labor-Communist Party," *New Republic*, XXXIX (July 2, 1924), 153-154.

"Mayor Mitchel's Record," *New Republic* (October 13, 1917), pp. 291-293.

Merz, Charles, "Enter: The Labor Party," *New Republic*, XXI (December 10, 1919), 53-55.

"National Aspects of the Mayoralty Contest in New York City," *Current Opinion* (November 1917), pp. 292-294.

"New York Labor's First Campaign," *New Republic*, XX (September 3, 1919), 138-139.

"New York's Return to Tammany," *Literary Digest* (November 7, 1917), p. 12.

"Not a Local Issue," *The Bellman* (October 20, 1917), p. 426.

"Our Bolsheviks Show Their Colors," *Literary Digest*, LXII (September 20, 1919), 7.

"Political Reports from 3,000 Communities," *Literary Digest*, LIII (October 28, 1916), 1087-1091.

Rogers, Lindsay, "Freedom of the Press in the United States," *Living Age* (September 28, 1918), pp. 769-774.

Russell, C. E., "Socialism, Just Where it Stands Today," *Hampton's Broadway Magazine* (January 1912), pp. 752-762.

Russell, C. E., "The Growing Menace of Socialism, *Hampton's Broadway Magazine* (July 1911), pp. 119-126.

Scudder, Vida D., "Woman and Socialism," *Yale Review*, III (April 1914), pp. 459-464.

Shannon, David A., "The Socialist Party Before the First World War," *Mississippi Valley Historical Review*, XXXVIII (September 1951), 279-301.

Sinclair, Upton, "What Life Means to Me," *Cosmopolitan*, XLI (October 1906), 591-595.

"The New Labor Party," *Literary Digest*, LXIII (December 13, 1919), 19-20.

"The New York Mayoralty Campaign," *New Republic* (October 6, 1917), p. 270.

"The Socialist as Patriot," *Literary Digest* (June 16, 1917), pp. 1836-1837.

Togliatti, Palmiro, "Leninism: The Sole Correct Path for Mankind," *Political Affairs*, XXXI (January 1952), 12-29.

Tyler, Robert L., "The United States Government as Union Organizer: The Loyal Legion of Loggers and Lumbermen," *Mississippi Valley Historical Review*, XLVII (December 1960), 434-449.

Walling, William E., "The Race War in the North," *The Independent*, LXV (September 3, 1908), 529-534.

——, "Socialists: The Kaiser Party," *The Independent* (November 10, 1917), p. 303.

Watkins, Gordon S., "The Present Status of Socialism in the United States," *Atlantic Monthly*, CXXIV (December 30, 1919), 821-830.

"Why Mr. Benson Has Resigned from the Socialist Party," *Current Opinion* (August 1918), p. 82.

Books and Pamphlets

Too numerous to list; those cited in text are most important.

INDEX

Dunne, William F., 205, 212, 297
Dunning, William A., 64
Dutton, E. M., 171

Easley, Ralph, 31, 46, 104, 109, 131, 330
Eastman, Max, 1, 164
Ebert, 119, 215n
Einstein, Reuben, 155n
Ekern, Herman L., 313
Engdahl, J. Louis, 171, 235
  and *Daily Worker*, 217
  and Third International, 218, 219, 247
  and *Eye Opener*, 234
Engels, 75
Erie (Pa.), *Dispatch*, 136
Esch-Cummings Transportation Act, 230, 275
Espionage Act of 1917, 90-91, 143, 144n, 160-162, 168, 186, 240n
Everybody's, 79
Eye Opener, The, 231, 234, 249

Farmer-Labor Federation, 296
Farmer-Labor Party, 230
  and American Federation of Labor, 324n
  election results, 292n
  and Fitzpatrick, 267
  and Hayes, 245
  in 1920 Presidential election, 272, 274, 336
  and Oakland *World,* 225
  and Socialists, 227, 274-275
  and Workers' Party, 280
Farmer-Labor Party of Minnesota. *See* Minnesota Farmer-Labor Party.
Farmers Educational and Cooperative Union, 138
Farmer's Nonpartisan League, 291
Federal Farm Loan Act, 105
Federal Trade Commission Act, 105
Federated Farmer-Labor Party, 283-289, 291-292, 297
Federated Trades Council of Milwaukee, 5
Ferguson, I. E., 210
Filler, Louis, 77, 78
Finnish Federation, 247, 258

Fitzpatrick, John, 271, 277, 279, 286, 291
  and American Labor Party, 223
  and Communists, 299, 308, 333, 334
  and Farmer-Labor Party, 272, 274, 281, 283, 288-289, 319
  and Federated Farmer-Labor Party, 286
  and Foster, 267, 280
  and Independent Labor Party of Illinois, 222
  and Mahoney, 297
  and Washington Farmer-Labor Party, 285
  and Workers' Party, 281-282
Florida Colored Baptist Convention, 71
Flynn, Elizabeth Gurley, 58, 58n
Foreign language federations, 194, 196, 197, 201, 209. *See also* under individual names of.
Foster, William Z., 280, 311
  acquitted, 281
  on American Federation of Labor, 261-262
  at Farmer-Labor Party convention, 282-283
  and Fitzpatrick, 282
  on La Follette, 318n
  and Liberty Bonds, 268n
  Maurer and Debs on, 267-268
  and 1932 Presidential election, 335
  reputation of, 267, 268, 297, 298
  in Seattle left-wing group, 239n, 240n
  and Third International, 314, 319-320, 333
  on trade unions, 268-269
  and Workers' Party, 266-269
Fourteen Points, 48, 162-164, 173
Fraina, Louis, 86, 86n, 87n, 201
  and *Class Struggle,* 188, 189
  and formation of Communist Party, 184, 194, 196, 210
  as International delegate, 197n, 254
  on Lenin, 209n
Frazier, Lynn, 274n
Freeman, Joseph, 163, 355
Frey, John P., 52